The UCSF AIDS Health Project
Guide to Counseling

Published in association with the AIDS Health Project
of the University of California, San Francisco

The UCSF AIDS Health Project Guide to Counseling

Perspectives on Psychotherapy, Prevention, and Therapeutic Practice

James W. Dilley

Robert Marks

Editors

Jossey-Bass Publishers • San Francisco

Jossey-Bass books and products are available through most bookstores. To contact Jossey-Bass directly, call (888) 378–2537, fax to (800) 605–2665, or visit our website at www.josseybass.com.

Substantial discounts on bulk quantities of Jossey-Bass books are available to corporations, professional associations, and other organizations. For details and discount information, contact the special sales department at Jossey-Bass.

For sales outside the United States, please contact your local Simon & Schuster International Office.

 Manufactured in the United States of America on Lyons Falls Turin Book. This paper is acid-free and 100 percent totally chlorine-free.

Library of Congress Cataloging-in-Publication Data

The UCSF AIDS Health Project guide to counseling : perspectives on psychotherapy, prevention, and therapeutic practice / James W. Dilley, Robert Marks, editors.
    p. cm.
  Includes bibliographical references and index.
  ISBN 0-7879-4194-8 (pbk. : alk. paper). — ISBN 0-7879-4194-8
(pbk. : alk. paper)
    1. AIDS (Disease)—Psychological aspects. 2. AIDS (Disease)—
Patients—Counseling of. 3. Psychotherapy. I. Dilley, James W.,
1951–   . II. Marks, Robert, 1958–   . III. AIDS Health Project.
  [DNLM: 1. Acquired Immunodeficiency Syndrome—prevention &
control. 2. Acquired Immunodeficiency Syndrome—therapy.
3. Psychotherapy—methods. 4. Counseling—methods. WC 503 U17
1998]
RC607.A26U27 1998
616.97'92'0019—dc21
DNLM/DLC
for Library of Congress   98-18757

FIRST EDITION
PB Printing 10 9 8 7 6 5 4 3 2 1

Contents

The UCSF AIDS Health Project gratefully acknowledges the Eli Lilly Foundation, the Pacific Telesis Foundation, and Steven Sams for funding this book.

Introduction

Robert Marks

Today there are stacks of books about AIDS and a surprising number about the "psychosocial issues associated with AIDS." HIV professionals have been well occupied for fifteen years, not only as providers but also as authors, and the result of their efforts has been not just quantity of information and research but also quality. The UCSF AIDS Health Project (AHP) has been fortunate to be able to make useful additions to this library. But before undertaking each project, we have asked ourselves, "Does the world need yet another publication about HIV? What can our work contribute to this literature?"

The answer is experience. Founded in 1984, AHP is one of the world's oldest HIV-related mental health programs and has pioneered some of the most successful mental health responses to the epidemic. AHP is fortunate to be a part of an internationally renowned medical school, and as such has had the opportunity to work with others to develop and staff the number-one ranked AIDS clinical care program in the country at San Francisco General Hospital. AHP also works with a leading prevention research center, the Center for AIDS Prevention Studies.

Channeling Experience

Since 1984, AHP has provided a large proportion of the HIV-related mental health services in San Francisco. In almost fifteen years, we've helped more than one hundred thousand clients.

The AIDS Health Project formulated the first HIV antibody test counseling protocol and went on to develop one of the first counseling and testing programs, a service that counsels and tests more than ten thousand people a year. We created HIV-specific psychiatric and social work services at the first outpatient and in-patient hospital AIDS wards at San Francisco General Hospital. We pioneered support-group programs for seropositive people and were among the first to recognize the need to offer emotional support to seronegative clients struggling with multiple loss and the challenge of sustaining safer behaviors over time.

We established the first hospital-based AIDS and substance abuse program, targeted toward providing risk-reduction counseling to those with primary substance abuse disorder, and piloted and refined an innovative substance abuse case management program. We developed a mental health crisis team and a mobile psychiatric consultation team that works with community hospice and home health care programs to keep people with HIV disease in their homes for as long as possible. Finally, we led the way in applying a brief psychotherapy model to counseling people with HIV disease.

AHP has also made publications and training a priority. We published the first books on HIV and mental health: *Working with AIDS* and *Face to Face: A Guide to AIDS Counseling*. Since 1985, we have published what is probably the longest-running AIDS newsletter in the country (and perhaps the world)—*FOCUS: A Guide to AIDS Research and Counseling*—certainly the grandfather of all HIV-related mental health publications.

We developed one of the first curricula for training antibody test counselors and have conducted training for both counselors and trainers of counselors throughout the state of California; as part of this effort, we pioneered what may be the only newsletter in the country that targets HIV test counselors, *HIV Counselor PERSPECTIVES*. We wrote the first book on AIDS and substance abuse and followed this up with a book on HIV and alcohol, and have developed a wide range of training for substance abuse providers. More recently, with the UCSF AIDS Health Project Monograph Series, we are publishing brief, pointed, and practical books on key topics, such as cognitive impairment and triple diagnosis.

Mountain Climbing

In geological time, the AIDS epidemic is barely noticeable, a blip of fifteen years. But in AIDS time, even six months can be an eon of revolutionary change, during which fundamental principles may be reconceived and a new vocabulary invented. Things move too quickly for us to stop innovating; it's stasis, not silence, that equals death. And we have felt compelled to share our insights with others, as they have shared theirs with us.

AHP's experience is the foundation on which this book rests, but we have not been content to limit its reach to what we know. When we started developing an outline for the book, we began by searching for authors who we knew could bring expertise, insight, creativity, and clarity to the process of writing about issues that we believed were the most salient—and that we predicted would remain central over time. The result is a faculty of contributors from throughout the country as well as from our own backyard, from such research institutions as Columbia, Cornell, and Stanford universities as well as from frontline organizations in such places as Austin, Texas; Fremont, California; and New York City.

There are plenty of good books about HIV and mental health; our hope is that this book is different. It is not a primer, but it does embody the fundamental principles and central elements of HIV-related counseling. It is not a survey of the field, but it covers the key issues facing counselors working in the full range of settings that compose the front lines of the epidemic. It is not a handbook, but it abounds with case studies and practical applications of theory. It is not a research report, but it has made a concerted effort to offer a review of the relevant recent literature.

What this book is, then, is a compilation of perspectives that depicts the mountain range of HIV-related counseling and psychotherapy by mapping its highest peaks—its most prominent and difficult issues—a portrait of those viewpoints, themes, and topics that in some way define the current landscape of HIV-related care. It is conceived as a guide, a complement to the existing literature, a companion not merely to its AHP sibling *Face to Face* but also to the bulk of the counseling and mental health volumes in the AIDS archive.

Four Realms of Discourse

We have organized this book to focus on four realms that define the role of counselors working in the epidemic: risk and behavior, psychotherapy and transformation, distress and disorder, and countertransference and therapeutic practice. Another way of thinking about these realms is in terms of the goal of the provider at each juncture: to prevent transmission, to help clients adjust to HIV, to manage psychiatric complications, and to sustain a practice in light of the unusual conditions HIV imposes. All clients and therapists are called by fictitious names.

Risk and Behavior

Prevention is most often discussed in terms of large-scale interventions focusing on providing information or changing community norms. But what has become increasingly clear over the past decade is not simply that information is not enough for everyone to make and maintain behavior changes—we learned that lesson very early in the epidemic—but also that the greatest barriers to risk reduction are individual psychological ones. Each of the chapters in the prevention section is ultimately about perspectives that can help counselors define the unique obstacles each individual faces and the ways in which the therapeutic relationship can be a tool to help clients identify and implement achievable risk-reduction goals.

Psychotherapy and Transformation

Adjusting to HIV is like aiming at a moving target. At each point in the epidemic, as more information refined definitions of the virus, the syndrome, the conditions, the treatments, and the prognoses, the task of adjustment has been closely related to the current state and limitations of our knowledge. When HIV was an emergency, it was about adjusting to terror, stigma, shock, fear, and not knowing—but this adjustment occurred in the context of medicine's history of triumph, a history that engendered a belief that despite governmental inaction, the baffling array of symptoms, and the horror of young people dying, this was a crisis that would pass.

When it became clear that the crisis was here to stay, each bit of knowledge was met with enthusiasm, and each contradiction to that knowledge with despair; as we learned more and more, we realized that we knew less and less and, worse, that no amount of knowledge seemed to have meaningful practical applications. During this long period of time, adjusting to HIV was about adjusting to disability and death. There were many ups and downs during this period: highs when AZT appeared to work, when vaccine studies suggested achievable cures, when combination therapy extended life; lows when the limitations of each advance were understood and when it seemed that progress was only about adding a year or two or three—precious time nonetheless—to what would still end as truncated lives.

Today, with the success of triple and quadruple combination therapy, more effective treatment and prophylaxis for opportunistic conditions, the identification of new surrogate markers such as viral load, and the compelling reality of people rising from near-death, adjusting to HIV for many has become about adhering to complex drug regimens, managing a chronic condition, and dealing with a newly extended future, interpersonal relationships, and life goals. There remains uncertainty, an ingredient that has always been part of the adjustment process. And for many, the failure or inaccessibility of these miracle treatments has made adjusting to disability and waning health all the more difficult as there arise feelings of inadequacy, isolation, abandonment, and deepening despair.

Whatever one's perspective, HIV has always been about change. It could be no other way. And HIV-related psychotherapy has been about achieving a positive transformation no matter what the content of the adjustment. This is not a Pollyannaish response; it is the reality of human psychology. The chapters in the psychotherapy and transformation section offer a variety of perspectives on the wide range of approaches therapists have at their disposal. The section also includes chapters on two particularly difficult challenges that arise in psychotherapy: the psychosocial concerns that are arising in the context of the new treatment successes, and the effect of stereotypes and assumptions on the psychotherapeutic process.

Distress and Disorder

As overwhelming as HIV is, it is not the only influence on a person's life. Each client brings to the experience a set of preexisting strengths and weaknesses. The third section of the book focuses on distress and disorder and, to a large extent, on the role of a person's preexisting psychology in complicating the adjustment to HIV. The chapters in this section catalogue the range of disorders that may arise in this context. They also discuss the extent to which HIV disease itself may lead to or create psychiatric disorders where none had existed before.

Therapeutic Practice and Countertransference

Surprisingly little has been written about the challenges therapists face as they work with HIV, both in terms of countertransference—the reflections of their own lives in the lives of their clients—and their experience of the epidemic as participants rather than providers. The section on therapeutic practice surveys the literature and looks at the ways in which HIV alters the therapeutic frame, the ways in which therapists undertake and respond to the process of practicing psychotherapy, the difficult decisions HIV requires therapists to make, and the monumental effect of grief and loss on burnout and care.

∞

The goal of any book about HIV must be to help us all transcend the struggle. Most of the time, work in the field sweeps you along; there is a lot to do, and pausing appears to be a luxury that few can afford (even though, in reality, it is a necessity that few can afford to deny). But reading can be a reminder that there are others out there also struggling and sometimes even transcending the struggle in creative ways.

This book represents an opportunity for you not only to learn from the unique experiences of others but also to reflect on those experiences. If this book does nothing more than validate what you have learned over the years, it will have made a contribution. But we also hope it introduces you to ideas and approaches that foster new ways of thinking and doing, proving to be more than just a contribution and revealing itself instead as a gift and an inspiration to continue this important work.

Prologue: Living with Therapy

Michael Helquist

Nothing from my experience of ten years of working with AIDS prepared me for the shock, confusion, and depression that came with my diagnosis of *Pneumocystis carinii* pneumonia (PCP) in 1992. It wasn't for lack of familiarity that I felt so ill equipped. I had lost a lover to AIDS in 1983—he was one of the first hundred people with AIDS in San Francisco. There have been far too many other losses since: best friends, colleagues, roommates. For many of them I had been a primary caregiver. I knew about the devastation HIV disease brings upon others. I didn't have a clue about the devastation it would bring upon me.

I had joined the "AIDS industry" in the early 1980s as a journalist and eventually took on assignments as a columnist, consultant, and editor of five books. I had interviewed researchers, medical doctors, and people with HIV disease and their families, lovers, and friends. For five years, I researched and modified international HIV prevention programs for use in developing countries and traveled extensively to help implement them. I was fully immersed in all facets of the epidemic. I had become an AIDS professional.

Yet AIDS, in the form of PCP, came at me like a hard, cold slap in the face. The shock I might have expected, but I could not have anticipated the confusing and threatening mix of new emotions. During the following four years, I continued to be jolted by the onset of new infections and disabilities. Now, however, I am less

An earlier version of this prologue appeared in *FOCUS: A Guide to AIDS Research and Counseling*, May 1996, *11*(6).

surprised about what I do not understand. I know that I have to work very hard to grasp what is happening to someone else with AIDS, someone who is ostensibly in the same predicament but is, in reality, facing a condition different from mine. I recognize that my knowledge of the emotional and psychic effects of HIV infection is limited mostly to my own experience with the disease.

I believe that other AIDS professionals, including mental health practitioners, even those with many years of experience, may very well be in the same position. Just because we provide counseling to people with HIV disease, or lead group discussions, or write papers for publication, or generally "talk AIDS" does not mean we understand the experience. In the end, I have found that familiarity with AIDS is not enough. I fear that as providers immersed in the epidemic, we may develop an overblown sense of our own knowledge, and that many of us have come to think we understand more than we can.

Knowledge, Empathy, and Flexibility

Several months into my own therapy, I realized that I wanted to achieve a sense of being heard, of being understood in a way that is different, perhaps more profound, than a friend or lover might understand. As part of my own seeking, I came to identify what I consider some of the basic skills and knowledge that would facilitate this goal, that I would want and expect a therapist to possess.

Knowledge

The key medical facts about HIV disease are prerequisites. Familiarity with the primary treatments for HIV disease and its associated infections is essential, and this familiarity must be more than knowing about the primary antivirals and protease inhibitors. I would want a therapist to know of the dozen or so prophylactic drugs prescribed for various infections, their possible side effects, alternatives to these drugs, and the general track record of their effectiveness. I do not believe that it is sufficient for practitioners simply to refer clients to AIDS hotlines, health care providers, or treatment advocacy groups. Such referrals can be invaluable, but I think they should supplement the information therapists can give directly.

For example, I have been greatly aided when my therapist has been able to explain some of the possible manifestations of different infections, especially when he has given me some perspective on the degree of discomfort or pain that might be involved. I have not looked to my therapist for medical advice; I have an excellent physician to turn to for that assistance. But my therapist has helped me manage my anxiety around certain medical procedures, and he has guided me in dealing with my fears about, for example, loss of vision, disfigurement, and dementia.

Empathic Surrender

Time and schedule demands for therapists can be restrictive and unrelenting, possibly interfering with their ability to learn about the HIV experience. A convenient and likely source of HIV-related information, especially the more subtle manifestations and implications, can be the client. If I had CMV retinitis, I would welcome a therapist acknowledging, for example, that he or she could not fully comprehend the reality of losing one's vision but was interested in knowing more about what I was experiencing. The therapist could follow this acknowledgment of limits and of being uninformed with questions to the client about the physical and psychological impact of vision loss.

I think practitioners may need to surrender themselves to particular experiences of their clients. In addition to listening, analyzing, and being supportive, therapists need to be willing, in a sense, to enter the world of their clients. For instance, three years ago I was diagnosed with an uncommon HIV-related blood circulation problem that resulted in bone cell death in my hip joints. Walking became difficult and often required my using a cane. Although I could identify for my therapist some of my feelings about these circumstances, his extra effort to enter my world allowed both of us to confront and feel my panic, fear, shame, and despair over my disability. During this time, each of us expressed, through silence and conversation, the pain of so many losses and the courage it required to surmount the embarrassment and shame of living with an AIDS disability in public. This experience emphasized for me that my therapist was truly present with me. I felt that I could trust him even more to accompany me on the journey I face with AIDS.

Flexibility

I have felt profoundly humbled by the challenges of living with AIDS. I never imagined that I would have such difficulty expressing my feelings. In therapy, sometimes I do not want to have to struggle to verbalize what I am experiencing on the deepest levels. I don't want to be cognitive and rational and explanatory—a process that seems to glide over my feelings. In these instances, I do not want my therapist to exhort me to express myself simply. I want a therapist who understands the limits of language, who understands that there are no words to describe the profound nature of many feelings.

What I have found helpful is to define with my therapist ahead of time a way of conducting a session or part of a session in nonverbal ways, to explore my most profound feelings. For example, during one session, I acknowledged my belief in a Divine Spirit and talked with my therapist about my desire to find a way of more emphatically experiencing spirituality in my life. My therapist suggested that throughout my day I might invoke the Spirit and request help and guidance from it. We decided that I would also pursue this engagement with the Spirit in my next session.

I arrived the following week to find the lights dimmed and candles lit in my therapist's office. I was quite moved by his willingness to alter the therapeutic environment and process. I sat this time on the couch closer to his chair. I asked that we hold hands to help me focus as we recognized the Divine Spirit among us. I asked the Spirit for help with specific personal struggles and for guidance in general. In the ensuing silence, I felt calm and grounded in my own reality.

During other sessions with my therapist, I found it helpful when he disclosed something of his own life that was relevant to the feelings I presented. For example, when I was talking about my fear of losing my mental abilities, my therapist mentioned that one of his close friends had experienced such a loss. We did not dwell on his friend's fate, but the disclosure reduced my sense of isolation. I felt that he knew firsthand some of what I feared. Although some might fear that such a flexible and creative response would transform the therapeutic relationship into a "friendship," I have found that my therapist's actions have strengthened the therapeutic bond. When further physical decline seemed imminent, I often felt separated and isolated, and I cherished any demonstration of understanding and empathy with heartfelt gratitude.

Treatment, Health, and Self-Esteem

With the increasing availability of protease inhibitors and other new medications, many people with HIV disease have watched their CD4+ cell counts climb and their viral loads plummet. The number of HIV-related deaths has dropped dramatically across the nation. Now that I have experienced the benefits of combination therapy and the protease inhibitors, my own self-definition as it relates to AIDS has changed. I have come to think of my HIV status not as positive or negative but as one of "extension": my life has been extended as a result of my treatment.

I have been immensely thankful, and a little stunned, by my shift to relatively good health. I know there are many others who have not received the same benefit from the new medications or who haven't had the chance to try out the treatments. Again, I realize that I cannot fully understand their experience, but I imagine many feel greater isolation from the "world of the well" and experience a sense of general abandonment. These clients especially will need reassurance that their therapists will remain focused on their difficulties.

Although the media has presented the phenomenon of renewed health in simplistic terms, the individual experience can be quite complex. I have faced a general disorientation about my new health status: having self-identified with my "end-stage" condition for so long, I have been unsure what meaning my new healthier life might hold. My everyday world of social contacts and experiences had shrunk so much during the years of illness that I have struggled—and stumbled—in my attempts to re-create a larger family of diverse relationships.

The opportunity to become more productive and creative also stymied me: What was meaningful to me now? I can laugh sometimes at the unexpected arrival of a human passage I thought AIDS had helped me avoid: a full-blown midlife crisis!

No matter how much my health has improved, I still feel like an outsider. The experience of declining toward death, and then of an uncertain recovery, has changed me; I do not feel the same as those whose lives were not similarly disrupted. Therapists may need to try even more to understand these disparities once their clients with AIDS outwardly appear more similar to their general patient population.

⁓

During the course of the last fifteen years, mental health practitioners have provided invaluable assistance to thousands of people with AIDS. Working with AIDS may be professionally challenging and rewarding, but the generosity and compassion of the therapeutic spirit must get battered and worn down by these struggles with roller-coaster crises, dying, and death. I believe the best therapists are those who recognize their own limits of understanding and who commit themselves to greater learning and experience to bridge such gaps with their clients. In seeking therapy, I would make a commitment to a practitioner who was willing to alter standard practice to deal effectively with my unique issues and needs. Finally, I would question any practitioner who does not feel humbled by the invasive power of this disease and who does not feel awed by the endurance and courage of those who live with it daily.

Acknowledgments

Like many of the authors and editors of AIDS books who we know, we've fit the enterprise of creating this book into lives filled with clinical work on the front lines, research, program planning and management, and, of course, grant applications and fundraising. We could not have made this book come together without the help of many. Our most heartfelt thanks must then go to the contributors to this volume, also working on the front lines yet maintaining their composure and cooperation as we journeyed from revision to revision, deadline to deadline. Thank you for your patience, certainly; but more, thank you for your commitment, your knowledge, your openness, your insights, your help, your generosity.

The only way to undertake a project of such magnitude is to carve out time, and the only way to do this is with the support and commitment of allies. At the UCSF AIDS Health Project (AHP), three allies have been particularly important. Joanna Rinaldi, deputy director, played the delicate role of taskmaster, facilitator, sounding board, and cheerleader; more than any other, she was the person who helped us move forward with gentle prodding and a constant eye toward the task of managing multiple tasks. We offer her our heartfelt thanks. Shauna O'Donnell, publications assistant, must have bitten her tongue many times as she put up with the craziness that occurs over the final year of a process like this one. Her good sense, organization, ingenuity and creativity, and editorial expertise were invaluable. John Tighe, senior editor at AHP, was at our right hand, able to handle other publication projects and offer support to allow us, at times, to focus on this project to the exclusion of others.

There are many other people at AHP who were involved in the conceptualization, the production, or the support necessary to the successful completion of this journey. A while ago, we sat around a table with JD Benson, Jackie Brookman, Paul Causey, Marcia Quackenbush, and John Tighe to plan the book, and their ideas form the backbone of what has evolved over time. JD, in particular, was very involved and was crucial to our efforts, not only in terms of developing the concepts for the chapters but also in seeking out authors who would ensure the quality and integrity of the book.

Michael Helquist and Steven Follansbee—each an outside volunteer adviser to AHP's publications program—are ubiquitous in our publications process. Their beneficent influence and clinical insight are everywhere.

Julie Balovich, Meredith Faggen, Miriam Garfinkel, Israel Katz, Susan LaCroix, and Emily Leavitt, among others, helped us help authors of specific chapters, offering both clinical and editorial insights. Patricia Sullivan deserves special thanks for reviewing the whole book and offering many important comments. These individuals provided authors the feedback crucial to honing their work.

During the editing process, several AHP staff, volunteers, and interns provided proofreading and copyediting services. Among these were Kathy Barr, who donated her services, Jennifer Cohen, Elisa Flynn, Tania Lihatsch, Erin Merritt, Shauna O'Donnell, Dorothy Stinnett, and George Velasquez. Interns and volunteers Julie Balovich, Meredith Faggen, Shirley Gibson, Cathy Hultin, Sari Kasper, and David King researched particular issues. Over the past nine months Jesse Ritvo and especially Gloria Chung and Tania Lihatsch performed countless on-line literature searches to confirm references and to help authors identify material to review.

During the production process, Kelly Costa, Leslie Samuels, and Andrew Tavoni provided desktop support. Shauna O'Donnell organized the production prior to sending the final manuscript to the publisher.

The infrastructure of AHP delivered a great deal of invisible support. Among those whose administrative, fiscal, personnel, and technological efforts contributed to the book were Sandra Kriletich, Francisco Molieri, Roxanne Romero, Joel Shapiro, Susan Sunshine, Joseph Wilson, and Helen Prince, director of operations—plus several other people already mentioned.

We have also relied on AHP's management team, the composition of which has changed over time, for support and feedback:

Barbara Adler, Dymond Austin, John Grima, Jeffrey Leiphart, Helen Prince, Joanna Rinaldi, and Patricia Sullivan.

Two groups of people from the "outside" were critical to our process. First, our editors at Jossey-Bass—Alan Rinzler and Katie Levine, and Jossey-Bass president Lynn Luckow—were supportive and patient through missed deadlines and territorial posturing, and wise in their suggestions. Second, three funders contributed much-needed financial support: Steven Sams, a Pacific Bell employee and a member of AHP's Community Advisory Board; the Pacific Telesis Foundation; and the Eli Lilly Foundation (through the work of local supporter Lou Smaldino).

Finally, we have been blessed in our personal lives with people of unfathomable patience, good cheer, and great wisdom. A special thanks to Jorge Morales and Saul Rosenfield, who offered not only their love and respect but also their advice, guidance, and good humor.

The Editors

James W. Dilley, M.D., is clinical professor of psychiatry at UCSF and executive director of the UCSF AIDS Health Project (AHP). He has published widely on the psychiatric and neuropsychological aspects of HIV disease. He is the executive editor of *FOCUS: A Guide to AIDS Research and Counseling,* AHP's monthly professional newsletter; coeditor of *Face to Face: A Guide to AIDS Counseling;* coeditor of the UCSF AIDS Health Project Monograph Series, and coauthor of *AIDS Law for Mental Health Professionals: A Guide to Judicious Practice.* Dilley received his B.A. and M.D. from the University of Missouri and completed his residency in psychiatry at the University of California, San Francisco.

Robert Marks is publications and training director of the UCSF AIDS Health Project and the editor of *FOCUS: A Guide to AIDS Research and Counseling,* AHP's monthly professional newsletter. He is the coeditor of the UCSF AIDS Health Project Monograph Series and coauthor of *AIDS Law for Mental Health Professionals: A Guide to Judicious Practice.* Marks received his B.A. from the University of Pennsylvania and his M.J. in journalism from the University of California, Berkeley. He has been writing about AIDS since 1985.

The *UCSF AIDS Health Project* (AHP) is affiliated with the Langley Porter Psychiatric Institute of the world-renowned medical school at the University of California, San Francisco, and has been a leader in developing clinical services and professional education to meet the mental health needs of people living with HIV disease. Since 1984, AHP has been nationally recognized for pioneering programs in a variety of areas: HIV-related counseling and support, HIV prevention services including antibody testing and counseling, and HIV and substance abuse services. AHP publishes *FOCUS: A Guide to AIDS Research and Counseling,* one of the longest-running

HIV-related newsletters in the country; books, including *Face to Face: A Guide to AIDS Counseling;* and newsletters. It also publishes the UCSF AIDS Health Project Monograph Series, including short volumes on topics such as HIV-associated cognitive impairment; the triple diagnosis of HIV, addiction, and psychiatric disorder; bereavement; and the psychosocial implications of successful antiviral treatment.

The Contributors

Sharone Abramowitz, M.D., is the director of behavioral health training at Highland Hospital Primary Care Medicine, Alameda County Medical Center. She is a member of the Northern California Society for Psychoanalytic Psychology and is in private psychotherapy practice in Oakland and San Francisco.

Thomas A. Beaumont, M.S.W., is an assistant professor and psychiatric social worker at the Boynton (Student) Health Service at the University of Minnesota in Minneapolis.

JD Benson, M.F.C.C., is a Unitarian Universalist seminarian at the Pacific School of Religion in Berkeley, California; senior trainer with the UCSF AIDS Health Project; and a consultant in private practice.

Jaklyn Brookman, M.F.C.C., is a therapist and a trainer and organizational development consultant to organizations in the United States and Africa. She is based in the San Francisco Bay Area.

Steve L. Buckingham, A.C.S.W., is a psychotherapist who has worked with people with HIV disease from the outset of the epidemic. In 1984, with Michael Gottlieb he helped establish the first psychosocial services program for people with HIV disease at the UCLA Medical Center, and for several years he served as director of psychosocial services for Pacific Oaks Medical Group, a large medical group serving primarily people with HIV disease in Los Angeles.

Kathleen F. Clougherty, A.C.S.W., is a psychotherapist in private practice in New York City and a research associate in psychiatry at Cornell University Medical College. Trained in interpersonal psychotherapy

(IPT) by the late Gerald L. Klerman, she treated patients in the Cornell psychotherapy study of depressed HIV-positive patients.

David W. Cramer, Ph.D., has been helping people cope with HIV-related issues since 1984, counseling individuals, couples, and families, and facilitating groups. He is the past president of the Austin Group Psychotherapy Society and the Capitol Area Psychological Association. He has published several articles and chapters on HIV and gay and lesbian issues.

Barbara E. Davis, M.S.S.W., draws on thirty years of clinical experience. Because of her interest in extending psychodynamic thinking into the realm of the body, she has worked extensively with people with cancer and HIV disease. She is the founder of Project Transitions, Inc., a residential AIDS hospice; has been leading therapy groups for men and women with HIV disease since 1985; and has supervised a large number of therapists who are working with HIV-related issues. She is past president of the Austin Group Psychotherapy Society and is on the teaching faculty of the Austin Society for Bioenergetic Analysis.

Until his death in 1995, *Noel A. Day* was chief executive officer of the URSA Group and president of Polaris Research and Development, a policy and applied social science research group in San Francisco and Washington, D.C. Day had been a senior consultant and university instructor for more than twenty-five years in the fields of education, mental health, organizational development, and social services. He developed the Center for AIDS Prevention at Polaris in 1986 to focus on research and training to reach underserved populations.

John Devine, M.D., is an assistant clinical professor of psychiatry at the University of California, San Francisco, and director of the Mental Health Outpatient Services HIV Program at the San Francisco Veterans Administration (SFVA) Medical Center. He is also the associate director of the residency training program in psychiatry at the SFVA.

Sarah Erickson, Ph.D., is the co-investigator of the Stanford Caregiving and Bereavement Study. She is a postdoctoral fellow in child psychiatry at the Stanford University Medical School and the coordinator of the Stanford Mental Health Project for Children and Adolescents.

Mindy Thompson Fullilove, M.D., is an associate professor of clinical psychiatry and public health at Columbia University and the New York State Psychiatric Institute. She has been involved in AIDS research since 1986 and has published widely. She has a particular interest in understanding HIV risk among African Americans and Hispanics in the United States.

Miriam Garfinkel, M.F.C.C., is training coordinator at the UCSF AIDS Health Project, and she formerly managed AHP's mental health and substance abuse services at San Francisco General Hospital, including the AIDS and Substance Abuse Case Management Program. She also maintains a private practice in San Francisco.

Eric Glassgold, M.D., is assistant clinical professor of psychiatry at the University of California, San Francisco, where he supervises advanced trainees in psychotherapy and teaches courses on human development and the interface between primary care medicine, psychology, and psychiatry. He is the staff psychiatrist with the multidiagnosis project at the Castro-Mission Health Center, a primary care clinic in San Francisco, where he works with an interdisciplinary team of primary care and mental health professionals providing care to people living with HIV. He also conducts dynamic psychotherapy in private practice.

Peter B. Goldblum, Ph.D., M.P.H., is the director of the Stanford Caregiving and Bereavement Study. A founder and former deputy director of the UCSF AIDS Health Project, he is currently an associate professor of psychology at the Pacific Graduate School of Psychology and a practicing psychologist in San Francisco.

Michael Helquist was one of the first journalists in the world to cover the AIDS epidemic, publishing some of the earliest interviews with people with AIDS and their lovers, friends, and families. In 1985, Mr. Helquist became the founding editor of *FOCUS: A Guide to AIDS Research and Counseling.*

Since then, Mr. Helquist has written a column, "The Helquist Report," for the *Advocate* and coedited two books for the AIDS Health Project: *Working with AIDS* and *Face to Face: A Guide to AIDS Counseling.* He also directed AIDSCOM, a federally funded and internationally focused HIV prevention project located in Washington, D.C. He now lives in San Francisco, retired on disability, and is building a new life under changed circumstances.

Mark Hochhauser, Ph.D., is a faculty member at the Graduate School of America in Minneapolis and has worked on AIDS education and prevention issues since 1985.

Amanda Houston-Hamilton, D.M.H., is a psychotherapist with clinical, teaching, and research experience focusing in particular on the needs of underserved populations. For the past fifteen years, she has worked on HIV-related mental health and minority group issues at the community, state, and national levels. Houston-Hamilton has served as chair of the San Francisco Black Coalition on AIDS and has been a member of numerous panels, boards, and commissions concerned with the health of minorities and women. She has had considerable research experience in program evaluation and in documenting the African American experience and has managed a range of training and technical assistance efforts.

Dan H. Karasic, M.D., is assistant clinical professor of psychiatry at the University of California, San Francisco, attending psychiatrist with the UCSF AIDS Health Project in the AIDS outpatient medical clinic at San Francisco General Hospital, and a member of the Consultation-Liaison Service of the SFGH Department of Psychiatry. He is also a consultant to the CARE Unit at St. Mary's Medical Center.

Israel Katz, M.D., is the attending psychiatrist for the Adelante Case Management Program at the UCSF Department of Psychiatry at San Francisco General Hospital. He specializes in bilingual and bicultural services, working with Latino and Asian/Pacific Islander populations, HIV-positive clients, and the chronically mentally ill.

Rochelle L. Klinger, M.D., is a psychiatrist and an associate professor of psychiatry at the Medical College of Virginia–Virginia Commonwealth University.

John C. Markowitz, M.D., is an associate professor of psychiatry at Cornell University Medical College and director of the outpatient psychotherapy clinic at the Payne Whitney Clinic, New York Hospital–Cornell Medical Center. He worked with the late Samuel Perry and succeeded him after his death as principal investigator of the first study of individual psychotherapy for depressed HIV-positive patients, which was funded by the National Institute of Mental Health (MH-46250).

Susanne B. Montgomery, Ph.D., is a social and behavioral epidemiologist and associate professor in public health and preventive medicine at Loma Linda University in California. Since 1987, she has worked predominantly on HIV disease and alcohol and drug-related high-risk behaviors in adolescents, including gay and bisexual and homeless and runaway youth. She serves as a reviewer for the National Institutes of Health and a number of peer-reviewed journals, and has published widely.

Michele Killough Nelson, Ph.D., is a clinical psychologist in private practice and a clinical faculty member in the Department of Psychiatry at the Medical College of Virginia–Virginia Commonwealth University.

Walt Odets, Ph.D., is a clinical psychologist in private practice in Berkeley, California. He has lectured widely on HIV prevention for gay men and is the author of *In the Shadow of the Epidemic: Being HIV-Negative in the Age of AIDS* (Duke University Press, 1995) and coeditor of *The Second Decade of AIDS: A Mental Health Practice Handbook* (Hatherly Press, 1995).

David G. Ostrow, M.D., Ph.D., is director of research at the Howard Brown Health Center of Chicago, which he cofounded in 1973. He is the principal investigator of a study funded by the National Institute of Drug Abuse to develop interventions for gay men who combine substance use with unprotected intercourse. He has published more than one hundred articles and seven books on mental health issues and various aspects of gay health and AIDS prevention.

Avi Rose, L.C.S.W., is executive director of Tri-City Health Center in Fremont, California. He has worked with HIV-related issues since 1985.

David Silven, Ph.D., is a clinical psychologist in private practice in San Francisco and regional director for a national mental health management care company. He coordinated mental health and prevention programs at the UCSF AIDS Health Project between 1989 and 1997.

Wilfred G. Van Gorp, Ph.D., is an associate professor of psychology in psychiatry at Cornell University Medical College and an associate attending psychologist at New York Hospital. He is director of the neuropsychology program for New York Hospital–Cornell Medical Center Mental Health System.

Joan E. Zweben, Ph.D., is the founder and executive director of the 14th Street Clinic and Medical Group and the East Bay Community Recovery Project, both in Oakland, California, which provide medical and psychosocial services to alcohol- and other drug-dependent patients and their families and serve as training sites for graduate students and interns. Dr. Zweben is a clinical professor of psychiatry at the University of California, San Francisco, and has written more than forty articles and book chapters and edited numerous monographs on treating addiction. She is active in training professionals from a variety of disciplines who work in mental health or addiction treatment settings.

The UCSF AIDS Health Project
Guide to Counseling

Part One

Risk and Behavior
Helping Clients Remain Uninfected

At first glance, preventing AIDS appears straightforward, even simple: HIV infection is a sexually transmitted disease, and as with any STD, protection from it requires that transmission be interrupted. Yet from the first moments of the epidemic, confusion has reigned about what was "safe," "possibly safe," and "unsafe." It has also been clear that for many, changing behavior was going to be difficult and that maintaining these changes over time was bound to be an even greater challenge.

What may have seemed so simple in the context of an emergency became more complex as prevention practices became more normal. This might appear paradoxical, but of course it is not; having protected sex, even being abstinent, seemed an attainable goal when it was the prescription for only six months, or two years, or perhaps even a decade. But to accept as normal—forever normal—the loss of sexual practices that for many are fundamental to intimacy and pleasure stretches beyond the limits of imagination.

Gay and bisexual men responded heroically when HIV prevention was urgent; but grief, bewilderment, anger, and time have worn that resolution thin. Gonorrhea rates—one sign of the efficacy of HIV prevention efforts—are rising, even as the rate of death from AIDS is falling, a tribute to new HIV treatments and a sad commentary on the long-term efficacy of the HIV prevention interventions that have redefined sex for a generation of people. And despite significant decreases in seroprevalence among injection drug users, it also remains true that for drug users, as for people who don't use drugs, changing sexual behavior and maintaining those changes remain difficult.

These conclusions do not negate the fact that huge numbers of people have adopted safer sex practices and will continue to protect themselves. Nor do they overlook the fact that it has been and continues to be the failure of governments to support needle exchange, and not primarily the failure of drug users to change their behaviors, that has cost thousands of lives. Instead, these conclusions act only as reminders that the task of HIV prevention remains critical as the risk of HIV transmission endures.

In this part of the book, a number of authors discuss the need for mental health approaches to HIV prevention. They go on to suggest new perspectives and strategies for functioning in the complex and ongoing struggle to stop the epidemic.

Chapter One

HIV Test Site Counseling for Gay Men

Harm Reduction and a Client-Centered Approach

Walt Odets

Born in the emergency of the early and mid-1980s, HIV prevention for gay men has drawn intuitively on traditional public health approaches, which relied primarily on the provision of information. Since then, this approach has changed little, although it has been augmented with aspects of cognitive-behavioral learning theory (the Stages of Behavior Change,[1] the theory of reasoned action,[2] and the health belief model[3]) and "social marketing" concepts, particularly the work of Jeffrey Kelly.[4] (For more information on these models, see Chapter Three.) These approaches to AIDS prevention have borrowed largely from work on "addictive" behaviors (substance use, overeating, and "addictive" sexual behavior), criminal behavior, and other nonsexual public health issues. Cognitive-behavioral learning theory and social marketing have been applied through media and clinically based prevention interventions, including the counseling opportunity provided by HIV antibody testing. All forms of intervention have almost invariably assumed the *elimination* of risk. We believed that we would stop the epidemic by preventing any new infections in informed—and properly "educated"—populations. Today, many still believe that we will stop the epidemic by applying these same approaches even more vigorously.

In the context of the emergency of the early years of the epidemic—which we hoped, if not fully believed, would be quickly limited by a medical solution to HIV infection and AIDS—the idea of risk elimination made sense. In fact, during these early years, many gay men heeded the message by adopting significant changes in sexual practices, including what was, for many, the radical solution of temporary abstinence. Many decided to avoid any possibility of exposure to a potentially fatal infection until there was treatment, and even the most conservative and emotionally costly measures against infection often felt appropriate and achievable in the short term.

The Unavoidable Truth of Continuing Transmission

For the first decade of the epidemic, newly discovered infections could be attributed to behavior that had occurred before we had knowledge of HIV and its transmission. Although the general public constructed its own definition of the "innocent victim of AIDS"—these were almost invariably nonsexual transmissions—in gay communities, innocent victims were those infected "before we knew." As the epidemic matured, unabated and medically uncontrolled, through the remainder of the 1980s and into the 1990s, and as those who had once tested seronegative suddenly tested seropositive, it became increasingly apparent that short-term, risk-elimination approaches to prevention were falling far short of the relatively complete results we had earlier expected. At first, both educators and gay men themselves denied that informed gay men were continuing to allow themselves to be exposed to HIV or were exposing others. But there was substantial evidence as early as 1988—at the very time prevention programs for gay men were widely being abandoned because their "success" rendered them unnecessary—that as many as one-third of San Francisco's gay men were willing to *self-report* that they were engaging in the most stigmatized of behaviors, unprotected anal sex.[5]

From the perspective of public health traditions, which equated information with the elimination of risk, such behavior could be understood only as a result of continued ignorance, substance-induced impairment, sociopathy, or psychopathology. "There is," a San Francisco educator said in 1990, "a lunatic fringe we will never reach." But as HIV providers finally began to acknowledge the inescapable fact that there were new infections among a broad cross section of "informed" gay men, we also came very slowly to acknowledge—but only sometimes understand—the relative complexity of the issues.

Certainly, a significant portion of new infections among gay men could no longer be attributed to ignorance of the transmission risks, and only a small percentage seemed *causally* attributable to substance-related impairment, sociopathy, or psychopathology. The message from gay men should have been clear. Social and psychological identifications with particular sexual behaviors, HIV, and AIDS were unexpectedly complex in a stigmatized minority community with seroprevalence rates as high as 50 percent in urban, gay male populations. Despite widely held assumptions that gay sex was substantially "recreational" and thus dispensable, sex and sexual intimacy between gay men came to be understood to have many of the same important meanings for gay men that it did for heterosexuals. The forbidden "exchange of body fluids" was not only a medical issue but one connected to fundamental feelings about intimacy.

Other feelings—about trust, relationships, and sexual communication—were affecting what gay men actually did in the privacy of the sexual encounter. Men were attaching importance to unprotected sex within relationships (and sometimes outside them) as evidenced by the practice of "negotiating" safety with partners of like serostatus.[6] They were almost universally rejecting the use of condoms for oral sex,[7] despite inconsistent but continuing suggestions by some prevention educators in the United States that it "might be risky." In other words, even as it was becoming widely accepted that prevention, rather than the treatment of HIV infection, offered the only hope for controlling the epidemic, many compelling issues were motivating gay men to practice de facto harm-reduction approaches rather than the risk elimination assumed and expected by public health.

By definition, harm reduction is not intended to completely eliminate behavioral risk; instead, it aims to help minimize possibly adverse consequences of the behavior. Harm reduction assumes that some risks are not entirely avoidable and that others are risks that an individual does not wish to avoid because of the value he or she places on the activity. But even by the standards of harm reduction, gay men's attempts at minimizing HIV-related sexual risk during the first decade of the epidemic resulted in a high, probably unnecessary level of seroconversion. Unfortunately, this attempt was almost completely unsupported in public health messages, and gay men were thus left in ignorance of facts and approaches that might have facilitated their effort. Furthermore, many educators have used the results of this flawed effort to justify the retrenchment and redoubling of risk-elimination approaches, with little or no effort to understand why gay men had rejected risk elimination in the first place. Public health, in assumptively positing risk elimination, has insisted on values that many gay men do not share, and has thus withheld support that might save many lives.

Balancing Risk Against Value

In our daily lives, we attempt to completely eliminate risk only for those activities on which we place little or no value. For activities we do value, we routinely exercise harm-reduction approaches by weighing the relative value of the activity in our lives—the costs of *not* taking the risk—against the costs of the potential risk. A vast majority of Americans drive or ride in automobiles despite the knowledge that approximately forty-five thousand people—roughly the entire American death toll of the Vietnam War—are killed on the road annually. Because we value mobility, the costs of not taking the risk of *reasonably conducted* automobile travel are considered too high. We achieve a level of reasonableness through the safety engineering of automobiles, careful road design, and the exercise of personal responsibility in when and how we drive.

But we do not fully exercise known technology to manufacture automobiles that might nearly eliminate risk, because the price to the consumer, increased fuel consumption, and relatively poor drivability would be too costly. We do not require occupants to wear helmets because of cost, personal inconvenience, and vanity. We do not insist that drivers be alcohol free because of the personal and social costs of abstinence. In others words, we establish an expected way of going about automobile travel that allows a balance between the value we derive from it—and from related activities that increase its risk—and the potential costs of taking the risk.

This harm-reduction approach is expressed every time we enter an automobile.

Our behavior, if not always our public assertions, suggests that the majority of people value sexual expression at least as much as mobility. But most AIDS prevention work to date, rooted in the assumptions of risk elimination, has defined "safe" sexual expression in ways that large numbers of gay men are demonstrably finding unreasonable because it impinges too severely on the aspects of sexuality that gay men value. Contrary to a relatively broad acceptance of the necessity of vaginal sex for heterosexuals—and uncounted millions spent on contraceptive methods to allow it without pregnancy or condoms—we have consistently told gay men to use condoms or abstain from anal sex. Despite a paucity of evidence for HIV transmission through oral sex—and a huge body of data suggesting it is an extremely low risk activity on a par with many other daily activities—prevention organizations have persisted in instructing gay men to routinely "suck latex."[8] Many of the same educators who promote mutually monogamous relationships—which include ordinary, unprotected sex—as a "most effective" prevention approach for heterosexuals[9] have insisted that, for gay men, such negotiated safety may simply be "negotiated danger."[10,11]

These unreasonable attitudes and prescriptions are rooted in many feelings. They often reflect authentic concern for the welfare of gay men and, thus, a belief that prevention should "err on the safe side." Unfortunately, these cautious prescriptions also often express the public health official's, educator's, or counselor's anxieties and unclarified feelings about both sexuality and risk. Too much of our educational approach for gay men reflects an erotophobic and homophobic dismissal of the importance of human sexuality and a deeply held American belief that longevity is more important than quality of life. "What I think about when I read the New York Times obituaries," an official of the British National Health Service said to me, "is how long Americans live—and why they would want to."

American society, which is now almost alone among Western countries in pursuing a risk-elimination approach to HIV prevention, has traditionally been reluctant to accept any costs for "socially unproductive" activity, particularly if it is experienced as sexual, sensual, or "indulgent."[12] This is an attitude that many gay men, internalizing societal erotophobia and homophobia, are inclined to collude with, at least publicly. Thus it is the rare gay man in the United States who would not feel more comfortable about dying in an automobile accident—preferably while commuting to a respectable job—than by contracting HIV through sexual intimacy. It would also be the rare HIV counselor who would not feel similarly about those whom they have counseled. Unfortunately, such values fail to consider the serious costs in lives constrained by fear of censure and impoverished by excessive compliance with social expectations. For all the American dialogue about "individualism," we have much less tolerance for certain kinds of differences among individuals than many, more apparently conformist, Western societies.

By its very nature, a risk-elimination approach to HIV prevention must provide minimum-risk behavioral guidelines and information and advice on how to adhere to those guidelines. In contrast, harm reduction assists people in the clarification of personal values and their expression in a life balanced between the costs of taking risk and not taking risk. In asserting that *no* risk is or ought to be acceptable, risk elimination assumes values for the individual: that the activity is never worth the risk. If the risk is connected to activity about which people are already acculturated to feel ambivalence, shame, or guilt—as many gay men are about their sexuality—many will publicly voice compliance with risk elimination, even as they retreat, sometimes unconsciously, into harm-reduction alternatives. Although unprotected anal sex has become the single most stigmatized behavior in the public rhetoric of gay communities, it is widely practiced, a fact evidenced by rates of new infection. This unfortunate consequence is not a result of inadequately asserted risk-elimination approaches. It is instead a result of dismissing the real values and needs of gay men and thus denying gay men the information, education, and counseling necessary for authentic, lifelong adjustments that reduce harm.

Without such assistance—and with the insistence that many obvious and widely practiced harm-reduction approaches may be "negotiated danger"—many gay men have been unable to make informed, conscious decisions about the balance between benefit and risk. Currently, gay men are in the same predicament in which we would all find ourselves if health and safety authorities decided that any automobile travel over thirty miles per hour was unacceptably risky and prohibited it rather than educating the driving population about reducing risk while exercising the obvious, often desirable possibility of highway travel at higher speeds. The results of the restrictive approach—an unnecessarily large highway death toll as uneducated drivers flaunted the unreasonably low speed limit—would indicate not a need for more vigorous enforcement of the thirty-mile-per-hour limit but rather the need to examine the conflict between personal and publicly dictated values. As with gay men and sexual risk, to say that "speeders" acted solely out of incompetence or noncompliance—that they were, in the words of some AIDS educators, merely "unable or unwilling to immediately cease all risky behaviors"[13]—would miss an important point about useful approaches for health and safety promotion and about human life and its potential enrichment through mobility and interpersonal intercourse.

Client-Centered Counseling: A New Mandate

In May 1994, the Centers for Disease Control and Prevention (CDC) released new guidelines describing "client-centered" counseling for clients at HIV antibody test sites. Aware that information-based prevention—even with the addition of behavior change models and social marketing techniques—was falling short of expectations, the CDC hoped that client-centered counseling would be helpful in addressing some of the more complex individual issues, including so-called psychosocial issues.

Long before the new guidelines were released, many HIV test site counselors had gained substantial experience with the limitations of the traditional public health approaches they had been practicing.[14] Historically having achieved poor results with sexual issues, public health was doing particularly badly with the AIDS epidemic in gay communities. "Risk assessment" and information and counseling derived from a structured behavior change model were producing startlingly poor results. By 1996, two in every three gay men who tested positive at a San Francisco alternative test site (ATS) had previously tested negative and received counseling at a California ATS.[15] In gay communities, with seroprevalence rates as high as 50 percent, the social and psychological issues were deeply rooted, complex, and unlike anything public health had ever been called on to address. Gay men were deeply identified with HIV and AIDS, and many seemed to experience HIV infection as inevitable, plausible, or even desirable. Many HIV-negative test results were producing bewilderment or overt distress, while some HIV-positive tests were appearing to provide resolution and relief. Such complex, ambivalent feelings about HIV were clearly unaddressed by simply counseling men about how to avoid HIV.

Many test site counselors, as well as others working with gay men, thus welcomed the CDC's mandate for a client-centered approach that might help address psychosocial issues. But the relatively broad guidelines issued in support of the mandate left many counselors in a quandary about what exactly client-centered counseling was and how it might be implemented in the context of what had been a traditional public health risk assessment directed toward structured behavior change. There are, in fact, many assumptions intrinsic to a traditional public health approach and to cognitive-behavioral learning theory models that cannot be part of a truly client-centered approach. The CDC mandate may have thus implied more—and introduced more complexity and contradiction—than was appreciated or intended by its authors.

Client-centered counseling is, by definition, concerned with a *process* intended to help a client make personal clarifications (which may lead to individually desired changes and results), rather than with directing the client toward an assumed set of results.[16] Although the process of client-centered counseling may help a client reframe his initial presentation of his experience, client-centered counseling always begins with acknowledgment of and unconditional respect for the client's framing of his values, needs, and purposes. Client-centered counseling is thus largely incompatible with the intent to assess risk, provide information, and lead the client through a structured progression of expected behavior change.[17]

In contradiction to the assumptions and expectations of risk-elimination counseling, many clients do not experience themselves at risk, even when they clearly are; some unrealistically experience themselves at risk when, in fact, they are not, and some experience no desire or intent to change behaviors even when they perceive the risk. Some gay men may not even believe it desirable to avoid HIV infection. To simply describe such clients as arrested in one of a progressive series of stages of behavior change posits assumptions and values many clients would not accept and ignores the complexity and variety of individual experience. A client-centered approach could only help such individuals clarify the reasons they framed their experience as they did, which might or might not result in the clients themselves beginning to reframe their values and purposes. Risk assessment, the provision of information, and a structured approach to behavior change could thus qualify as a client-centered approach only for those clients who clearly—and credibly—expressed their purpose as the change of any behaviors that entailed any risk, regardless of the value of that behavior.

In the context of HIV test site counseling for gay men, client-centered approaches will usually dictate a harm-reduction approach because HIV is usually contracted by gay men, as it is by heterosexuals, through behaviors that many value, sometimes considerably. The client-centered approach will help the client clarify his values and his feelings about risk and thus ultimately arrive at a personal balance between the value derived from the behavior—value suggested by the costs of modifying or abstaining from the behavior—and the potential risk entailed in the behavior. Most people will accept risk in some proportion to the value they place on the activity.

Helping an individual clarify his values about behavior and its potential risk is not always a straightforward process, and the process may be limited by the duration or setting of the counseling opportunity. Gay men seeking HIV testing and counseling very often experience a complex mix of conscious and unconscious feelings and desires, an anticipation of what is expected of them by public health personnel, and an awareness of social values and expectations that may be partially or wholly inconsistent with their own. The client's initial presentation of this complex mix of needs, desires, and internal and external expectations often obscures the real issues with which the client is grappling. Contradictions—for example, between a client's stated values and his actual behavior—often provide the clues that allow a counselor to begin to help the client clarify his situation.

More often than not, the strictly time-limited opportunity of HIV antibody test counseling will allow a client-centered approach to do little more than introduce the client to the process of clarification and, when appropriate, refer the client to additional services. This effort may produce a wide range of results, including unexpected or even undesired ones. Time-limited counseling will only very rarely lead to a resolution of any issue, will often produce no behavior change whatsoever, and will usually not even result in an authentic decision to change behavior. Many clients will refuse referrals or not follow them through. The entire process of client-centered counseling is predicated on the counselor's willingness to relinquish control of the outcome and place trust in the client's own motivations and ultimate ability to live his own life as constructively and richly as he might. A client cannot be made to change—and can only rarely even be motivated to change—complex private behaviors by means of instruction or coercion.

Nevertheless, the time-limited client-centered approach will often initiate a process that may help the client ultimately generate his own clarifications about the desirability, possibility, and implementation of behavior change. The process can provide authentic, long-term changes in behavior that exposes the individual to unknown, unnecessary, or unintended risk.

Case Studies: Client-Centered Counseling in Context

The following case studies demonstrate a client-centered approach in time-limited HIV antibody test counseling. In addition, the vignettes illustrate some common issues encountered during HIV counseling for gay men.

John: The Risk of Oral Transmission

John is a twenty-four-year-old Latino man who has lived in San Francisco for one year and is not currently involved in a long-term relationship. On receiving his HIV-negative test results from a counselor, Ross, at an anonymous test site, he shows considerable relief. In response to his counselor's question about why he came in for this test, John says, "I know all about safe sex, and I know that AIDS is not going to be part of *my* life." He also reports that he has tested for HIV "maybe six or eight times" and that he came in for this test because, "I guess I have a lot of oral sex and I just wanted to be sure I was OK."

Ross: And do you feel that oral sex might put you at risk for contracting HIV?

John: Well, I don't think so, but you never know. I mean some people say it's possible, but I don't think so myself. I'm not really sure.

Ross: It sounds to me like you might be worrying about it. You've had quite a few tests. Are there other things that you feel you might have gotten HIV from?

John: No, all I ever do now is oral sex. I mean I had anal sex with my boyfriend but we always used condoms for that. But since we split up I haven't done anal sex. I don't have anal sex with guys I'm not in a relationship with because for me it's too personal. I know you can get HIV a lot easier from that. And I'm not worrying about sucking guys off, which I do when I go out, but I'm not sure. I mean, have you ever had anyone who got it from oral sex?

Ross: The California Office of AIDS, which has collected data on about fifty thousand gay and bisexual men, tells us that oral sex is an extremely low risk activity. But that doesn't mean it's 100 percent safe or that it's impossible to get HIV through oral sex. But I feel like maybe you're uncomfortable with the idea that there's any risk at all.

John: Well, getting AIDS would be a big deal. I know there are a lot of treatments now, but . . . I also know that some people say you should use condoms for oral sex, but I've never met anyone who wants to do that. I mean, it's pretty bad, and I don't want to do it either. Even if I did, I'd have trouble asking another guy to do it anyway.

Ross: Well, I'm wondering now if oral sex with other guys—without condoms—is important to you. Or how important it is.

John: Well, like I said, it's the only kind of sex I have. . . .

Ross: And is sex important for you?

John: I feel like you're saying it shouldn't be important. Well, I don't know if you're saying that, but I know that a lot of people would say it's a lot more important not to get AIDS. That's your job, isn't it? To tell me to not get AIDS, which I already know? I mean, most of society doesn't even think I should be doing it at all.

Ross: I didn't mean to suggest that sex shouldn't be important to you or that it should be important. I'm trying to understand how you feel. You say that you do oral sex fairly often, that it's the only kind of sex you have, but you also seem afraid of getting HIV from it. I feel like you want me to assure you that it's completely OK, and if I could only tell you it was completely safe, you could feel better about it.

John: Well, it's important to me. And I don't think I deserve AIDS for it. But if I had to tell my family I was positive, I know they'd just kill me. I would never want to have to tell them that, especially my mother, because I know it would just be too much for her. I could never tell her.

Ross: Tell me if I'm wrong. If it were just you, I feel like you're telling me that you'd take a very small risk for the oral sex you're having, that it's important enough to you that you'd do that. Normally, we do take some risk for things we value. For the moment, I'm just thinking about how you feel.

John: Yeah, when you put it that way, then I'd say that I know I'm not going to stop having sex, that I don't want to do that. If there's a little bit of a risk, well, I'd say that I just have to take that chance, because I know you can't be completely safe and still have a life. I'm not having sex all the time, but having sex with guys is important to me.

Ross: I believe that a lot of people would support your sexual feelings—and that they would want no harm to come to you for expressing them. I also know that you have some other feelings here too, especially about your family and maybe about what society—at least some of it—think about gay sex. I know that those feelings may be important to you too and that they can affect how you feel about sex—that you worry some about it—even though sex is important to you and even though you seem to be having sex in a very reasonable way.

John, we have to stop in a few minutes, and I have a couple of ideas. One is that I can tell you about a few commonsense things that we think may lower the very low risk of getting HIV through oral sex. And the other thing I thought of is that we have groups of gay men about your age in San Francisco who get together to talk about all kinds of things—including sex and their families! I thought that you might find one of these groups fun and that it could help you think through some of your feelings that we haven't had time to talk about today. I can tell you who to call about a group if you think you might like to do that, even if you just want to see what it's like.

In this vignette, the counselor believes that John is well educated about the facts of HIV transmission, that his behavior probably falls in a very low range of risk, and that, with assistance, John is capable of clarifying his feelings and values. John is probably not engaging in activities that pose an unknown, unnecessary, or unintended risk. He does not seem to be using sex in unconscious, compulsive, or destructive ways, and Ross feels that John needs some reassurance about his sexual feelings and behavior.

It is also apparent that John feels some conflict between his own sexual feelings and needs and his sense of others' expectations of him: "Well, it's important to me. And I don't think I deserve AIDS for it." The latter assertion, a feeling introduced by John himself, suggests that John might actually have some unstated or unconscious feeling that he does deserve AIDS for gay sex, that others are expecting him to get AIDS, or that gay sex might somehow inevitably lead to contracting HIV. Ross believes that such unstated or unconscious feelings might contribute to John taking more risk than he would otherwise take. Thus, more comfort with his sexuality (as well as insight about the prohibitive or punitive feelings and expectations of other people) might lower John's risk of contracting HIV.

Although this issue seems too complex to address in the session, a peer group of gay men might help John clarify some of his feelings. Because John has been living in San Francisco such a short time, the counselor also believes that John may lack nonsexual connections with other gay men and adequate social support. John's comment that he would "have trouble asking another guy to do it anyway" suggests that he might also benefit from talking about sex with other gay men in a nonsexual setting.

Roger: Taking Risks for Unsatisfying Sex

Roger is a thirty-nine-year-old gay man who has been living in San Francisco for eleven years and is not currently in a relationship. Roger tells his counselor, Ann, that he "probably does some things I shouldn't do" and that he has not tested for HIV in four years. His response to his negative result is flat—"Well, that's good"—and he seems anxious to leave the counseling session.

Ann: I'm wondering what we could talk about that would be useful for you.

Roger: Well, this was more your idea than mine. Apparently I'm negative, and I don't know what else there is to say about it.

Ann: It was sort of my idea—the state of California is paying for me to spend some time with you. But maybe we could do something with the time that would be useful to you anyway. One thing I'm wondering about is why you tested at this particular time. You haven't tested in several years.

Roger: No particular reason. Like I said, I've probably done a couple of things I shouldn't have.

Ann: When you say you "shouldn't have," I'm not sure what you mean. Do you mean things you didn't want to do but did anyway?

Roger: Yeah, things I could've gotten HIV from. I know all about safe sex, but I've had some unsafe sex. I've had anal sex without a condom—twice with a guy I know was positive. I don't usually do that. And I've had anal sex with guys whose status I didn't know, once or twice.

Ann: I'm wondering about the possibility that you wanted to do this, but that it also posed an HIV risk, which you didn't want. I know you know that receptive anal sex without a condom is one of the easiest ways to get HIV. And I guess what I'm wondering about is whether you did what you did because it was important enough to you that you felt like it was worth the risk.

Roger: It seemed like it at the time.

Ann: But not later? Not now?

Roger: No, I don't think so. I mean, it depends. I have a lot of sex when I have nothing else to do. I get restless. I usually go out on the weekend for sex, and, you know, it's very easy to find. And mostly it's—well you don't get much from it. I usually feel worse afterwards.

Ann: Could it help you feel better?

Roger: It could help me feel better, I guess, but it usually doesn't. I guess if I'm down or feeling bad about myself, I have the idea that it will help me feel better.

Ann: And do you feel down a lot?

Roger: Yeah. I mean, I have this incredibly boring job, and I feel like I should be going somewhere with my life. And I don't have that many friends anymore. Some of them have died and a lot of them have moved away.

Ann: So it sounds to me as if you are feeling pretty bad a lot of the time. And also that you've been using sex to try to feel better.

Roger: Yeah, that sounds right. Mostly I don't go out anymore, but when I do, it seems to be for sex. The part I'm leaving out is—well, last year I was dating a guy for a while, and that really made a difference. It didn't work out, but it made a big difference anyway.

Ann: Sex with different people can be very different. Some of it can be very important and some of it you can take it or leave it. But I have the idea that it's been the sex that isn't important to you that you've been taking the HIV risk for. Does that seem right to you?

Roger: Yeah, I'd say that's right. It's the anonymous sex. With Tim—the guy
I was dating—I didn't know my status, so we always used condoms.
With guys I meet when I'm just out having sex, that's when I've had
unsafe sex.

Ann: Well, normally we take some risk for things we value. But it sounds
like at least some of the risk you've been taking—that it wasn't that
you valued it but that you were feeling down and were trying to feel
better. And we don't take as good care of ourselves when we're down,
and it makes sense that this is when you would have unprotected sex
and put yourself at the most risk. That's the part that bothers me in
what you're telling me: that you take risk for sex that doesn't mean
much to you, and it's not making you feel better anyway.

Roger: That's right.

Ann: Roger, we're going to have to stop in few minutes, but I want to make
a suggestion that might be helpful. Even if your feeling down were
not motivating you to have unprotected sex that you might get HIV
from, I'd be concerned about it just because it makes you feel bad.

Ann closed the session by briefly mentioning that many HIV-negative
men are experiencing some feelings about loss and isolation because of the
epidemic and that sometimes such feelings can lead to sexual behavior that
they later regret. She also gave Roger information about available groups for
HIV-negative men.

Clearly Roger is well educated about HIV transmission, but he
is taking considerable risks and is disturbed by that behavior, even
if he does not conceptualize his situation as being primarily about
HIV risk. Ann begins to help Roger understand that there may be
some connection between his "down" feelings and the unsatisfying
behaviors that are also potentially exposing him to HIV. Because
of Roger's lack of satisfaction with much of his sexual activity, Ann
feels that Roger may be using sex compulsively, perhaps in response to anxiety (his feeling "restless"), loneliness (friends have
"died or moved away"), or depression (feeling "down").

Ann uses information Roger provides to discuss this connection between his feelings and his experience of unsatisfying sex,
but she does this while remaining within Roger's framing of the
problem, that he has done "a couple of things I shouldn't have"
and is not happy with his life. She helps Roger clarify the meanings

of that experience without affirming or denying Roger's self-judgment that he has done something "wrong." She suggests that Roger may, in part, be having unprotected sex for understandable reasons—wondering if Roger "felt like it was worth the risk."

Because of the complexity of the issue, Ann does not address the possibility that Roger may actually be ambivalent about getting HIV. But she is aware that Roger might have some feelings that being HIV-positive connects him to other gay men and gives his life focus and purpose. Ann does help Roger notice that he values different sex differently but that he is not expressing these values in the way he takes risk. By reflecting back Roger's own description of his experience, she is able to point out that Roger is taking the most risk for the sex he values least.

⊂◊⊃

Although they present different issues, both of these counseling vignettes demonstrate a client-centered approach intended to help the client clarify his experience related to HIV risk. In both instances, the counselors work from within the client's own description of his experience. They help their clients clarify both the feelings as well as the implications of sexual behavior. Because each counselor recognizes the complexity of the client's experience and the need for the client to develop his own motivations for any desired change, both sessions are concerned with clarification rather than resolution.

The focus is not on risk assessment per se, and the counselor does not suggest specific behavior changes. The counselor recognizes and accepts that there are reasons each client behaves as he does. These reasons are often different from the rationale the client initially presented, but they are usually discoverable in the client's explication of his own experience. For example, although Roger says he has sex when he has "nothing else to do," he discovers later in the session that it may have more to do with "feeling down." The counselors in these vignettes also recognize that the client must clarify and mobilize his own motivations in order to remain free of HIV and that neither the counselor's desire that he do so nor the assertion of expected standards of behavior will be useful in accomplishing this. In fact, to ensure that the counselor-client interaction is not prejudiced by the expectations implied by a checklist of "bad," "unsafe," or disapproved behaviors, any formal collection of risk-assessment data is conducted at the end of the session.

Impediments to Client-Centered Counseling

A client-centered approach to HIV counseling offers the possibility of helping clients initiate a process that can help motivate substantial, enduring changes in behavior. But the public health context of most HIV test site counseling and the counselor's own experience, values, and feelings may hamper or obstruct a truly client-centered approach. For purposes of discussion, two kinds of potential impediments might be described as "organizational" and "transferential," respectively.

Organizational Impediments

The potential organizational impediments to client-centered HIV counseling flow largely from the purposes of traditional public health and the institutions that represent it. Public health is dedicated to the greater public good and has, traditionally, not substantially concerned itself with the issues and needs of individuals—particularly "carriers"—unless addressing those issues can be shown to most effectively protect the larger public. Thus HIV counseling and testing for gay men has appeared to concern itself largely with collecting epidemiological data, influencing risk behavior in the short term, and, for HIV-positive results, providing referral for medical and psychological treatment. Other elements of traditional public health—including mandatory reporting of infection and partner notification—might also have been implemented had it not been for political pressures from AIDS advocates concerned with the potential stigmatization of people with HIV disease. Partly because of the traditional assumptions of public health, it has generally been assumed that knowledge of HIV status would change individual behavior and reduce transmission. In fact, research on gay men living in a community-wide epidemic is far from providing conclusive support for this assumption. The equation between knowledge of infection and behavior change is probably less supportable in communities with 50 percent rates of infection and the complex identifications with HIV that many gay men experience.[18]

Although many of the traditional elements of public health are probably incompatible with client-centered counseling, the collection of epidemiological data per se is not. The way data collection is performed, however, can easily impede a client-centered approach. The very idea of "risk behaviors" suggests that these behaviors are without other purpose or meaning in the individual's life, and it is thus contrary to a client-centered approach. People engage in very little behavior that is, subjectively, about nothing more than undesired risk. If the counseling session begins with an inventory of risk behaviors around which the rest of the session is structured, a client-centered approach is not possible. The risk assessment will have already established the meanings—which is to say, the undesirability and meaninglessness—of the behaviors. The client-centered approach is about helping the individual clarify precisely those subjective meanings, meanings that motivate the client to engage in the behaviors *despite* the risk or *because* of the risk. This problem can be substantially eliminated by collecting epidemiological data unobtrusively in the course of the session and supplementing that data with other, still-needed information on completion of the session. Data collection can be nothing more than a perfunctory addendum to the client-centered session.

More serious organizational impediments to client-centered HIV counseling arise from the cognitive-behavioral assumptions of traditional public health and its apparently limited confidence in more psychological, less structured, and less directive approaches. It is little exaggeration to say that cognitive-behavioral models of human experience, as well as the structured behavior change models that have grown from them, assume that individuals lack conscious or unconscious motivations for seemingly "irrational" behaviors, are generally conscious of any motivations they do have, and will wish to change any behavior that is demonstrably irrational. Through such "behavioral reductionism," cognitive-behavioral models dismiss important unconscious feelings or motivations, thereby defining many important human behaviors as dispensable. This dismissal is particularly noteworthy in the psychologically complex, almost entirely irrational realm of human sexuality.

In contrast, a client-centered approach assumes that a client who engages in complex, fundamentally irrational—and, perhaps, potentially self-injurious—behaviors may have motivations that are partly or wholly unconscious. Further, the approach recognizes that an individual's feelings about the risk-benefit balance of any behavior may contradict the rationalistic assumption of risk elimination. A measure of the substantial, fundamental difference between cognitive-behavioral models and client-centered counseling is suggested by public health's common adaptation of behavior change models for substance addiction to the "problem" of normal human sexual behavior. While addictive, long-term cocaine use may not be a natural human condition, the practice of penetrative sex without condoms most certainly is.

Transferential Impediments

Transferential impediments to client-centered counseling arise from any of the counselor's beliefs, values, or feelings that interfere with his or her ability to work from within the client's frame of experience. Transferential impediments may also be supported by organizational ones. Broadly speaking, public health does not pay for the subjective well-being of the individual. The public health context of most HIV counseling places the counselor in the position of "representing" the state, which is primarily concerned with protecting the health and welfare of the greater public, reducing the public expense for HIV infection, and helping stop individual behaviors that contradict those ends. Although a counselor's personal motivations might partly or wholly include such public purposes, they are purposes that cannot be pursued in client-centered counseling. Thus the counselor may experience his or her responsibilities as divided between the state and the individual client and hence conflicted.

Whether or not this conflict exists, the counselor's transference feelings may inhibit the neutrality basic to client-centered counseling. For example, HIV test site counseling for gay men must *assume* the acceptability—and human importance—of sexuality in general and homosexuality in particular, and must affirm the client's values by assuming a harm-reduction, rather than a risk-elimination, approach. Client-centered counseling must constantly affirm respect for the individual in acknowledging that only the client himself can take responsibility for his life. Counselors with strong feelings about the importance or unimportance of their own sexuality, and counselors who are anxious about or adverse to any risk must examine the ways in which such feelings can easily impede a truly client-centered approach. Likewise, counselors who wish to help gay men by "saving them from themselves" must remind themselves that client-centered approaches can be grounded only in authentic respect for the client, his values, and his efforts to create for himself a life that is rich and satisfying enough to be worth protecting from unknown, unnecessary, or unintended risk.

Notes

1. Prochaska, J. O., Velicer, W. F., DiClemente, C. C., and others. "Measuring Processes of Change: Applications to the Cessation of Smoking." *Journal of Consulting and Clinical Psychology,* 1988, *56*(4), 520–528. Prochaska and associates have also discussed stages of behavioral change in the context of other behaviors, including weight loss, HIV prevention, and drug addiction. Prochaska's work is among the most frequently cited in describing structured behavioral change. His Stages of Behavior Change model is rooted in cognitive and behavioral psychological models and describes individuals as falling into one of five categories leading to change: precontemplative, contemplative, ready for action, action, and maintenance.

2. Fishbein, M., and Middlestadt, S. "Using the Theory of Reasoned Action as a Framework for Understanding and Changing AIDS-Related Behaviors." In V. M. Mays, G. W. Albee, and S. F. Schneider (eds.), *Primary Prevention of AIDS.* Vol. 13. Thousand Oaks, Calif.: Sage, 1989.

3. Kirscht, J. P., and Joseph, J. G. "The Health Belief Model: Some Implications for Behavior Change, with Reference to Homosexual Males." In V. M. Mays, G. W. Albee, and S. F. Schneider (eds.), *Primary Prevention of AIDS.* Vol. 13. Thousand Oaks, Calif.: Sage, 1989.

4. Kelly, J. A. *Changing HIV Risk Behaviors: Practical Strategies.* New York: Guilford Press, 1995.

5. Ekstrand, M. "Risky Sex Relapse, the Next Challenge for AIDS Prevention Programs: The AIDS Behavioral Research Project." Presented at the Fifth International Conference on AIDS, Montreal, June 1989. (Abstract no. T.D.O. 8)

6. The term *negotiated safety* was first suggested by S. Kippax, J. Crawford, M. Davis, and others in "Sustaining Safe Sex: A Longitudinal Study of a Sample of Homosexual Men." *AIDS,* 1993, *7*(2), 257–263. Negoti-

ated safety is essentially the practice of preventing HIV transmission through seroconcordant partner selection rather than by preventing HIV transmission between serodiscordant partners by behavioral means. Although some American educators argue against negotiated safety because gay men are thought to be less monogamous than heterosexuals, the real issue is whether sex outside the relationship, if any, is conducted "safely" to prevent HIV from being introduced into the relationship.

7. Virtually all the epidemiological literature on gay men that has tabulated data about condom use for oral sex has shown very low levels of use, typically less that 3 percent. For example, see Ostrow, D. G., Di Francisco, W. J., Chmiel, J. S., and others, "A Case-Control Study of HIV Type I Seroconversion and Risk-Related Behaviors in the Chicago MACS/CCS Cohort, 1984–1992." *American Journal of Epidemiology*, 1995, *142*(8), 875–883.

8. A 1995 campaign of the STOP AIDS Project of San Francisco.

9. DeCarlo, P. "Do Condoms Work?" *HIV Prevention: Looking Back, Looking Ahead.* San Francisco: Center for AIDS Prevention Studies, University of California, San Francisco, and the Harvard AIDS Institute, 1995.

10. Ekstrand, M., Stall, R., Kegeles, S. M., and others. "Safer Sex Among Gay Men: What Is the Ultimate Goal?" *AIDS,* 1993, *7*(2), 281–282.

11. Although educators usually argue against "negotiated safety" (unprotected sex between partners of mutually known antibody status) because gay men are thought to be less monogamous than heterosexuals, the critical issue would be whether or not protected sex was practiced outside the relationship to prevent HIV from being introduced into the relationship. If protected sex would not serve this purpose, it would not prevent HIV from being transmitted within the relationship. Thus, the monogamy of a couple ought not to be the issue in discussing negotiated safety.

12. King, E. *Safety in Numbers: Safer Sex and Gay Men.* New York: Routledge, 1993. This book is a comprehensive, intelligent, eloquent discussion of harm-reduction approaches applied specifically to gay men and HIV. It reflects a much more widely used approach to the issue than the risk-elimination practiced in the United States.

13. Ekstrand, Stall, Kegeles, and others, "Safer Sex Among Gay Men."

14. I am grateful to Susan Thompson and Edward Wolf, both working in counseling and testing for the UCSF AIDS Health Project, for their insights on the problems confronting counselors.

15. Personal communication with Bob Poindexter, California Department of Health Services Office of AIDS, Oct. 3, 1996.

16. The term *client-centered* was first introduced in Rogers, C. R., *Client-Centered Therapy, Its Current Practice, Implications, and Theory.* Boston and Cambridge: Houghton Mifflin and the Riverside Press, 1951.

17. For a very useful and thorough discussion of various counseling approaches and their utility for HIV prevention, see Sikkema, K. J., and Bissett, R. T., "Concepts, Goals, and Techniques of Counseling: Review and Implications for HIV Counseling and Testing." *AIDS Education and Prevention,* 1997, *9*(Suppl. B), 14–26.

18. Sikkema and Bissett, "Concepts."

Chapter Two

HIV Test Counseling

Does It Change Behavior?

Susanne B. Montgomery
David G. Ostrow

HIV antibody counseling and testing has been one of the corner-stones of the national AIDS prevention strategy since testing first became available in 1985.[1] It seems a reasonable assumption that knowledge of HIV serostatus in conjunction with individualized prevention counseling will lead to behavior change. For this reason, counseling and testing has been promoted as a simple solution to a difficult problem, and most experts agree that this seeming simplicity has led to unrealistic expectations about the powers of counseling and testing.[2,3] But others see counseling and testing as an important and rare opportunity to reach people at high risk of HIV infection in the context of a personal interaction.[4,5]

Counseling and testing has also been promoted as a means of guiding newly identified HIV-infected people who may be candidates for early medical intervention toward treatment. Medical intervention has become an increasingly significant option in light of new treatment regimens using protease inhibitors and combination antiviral therapy. Counseling and testing has also become a venue for secondary prevention, a forum for educating people with HIV disease about protecting their partners.

At a time when local governments are seeking to reduce spending on counseling and testing and some public health experts are advocating home testing with only rudimentary counseling, it is useful to consider the efficacy of current counseling and testing approaches. Taking into account more than a decade of experience, this chapter describes the counseling and testing process and reviews the evidence concerning the efficacy of counseling and testing in terms of both behavioral and mental health consequences. It also discusses the role of private practice therapists in the counseling and testing process.

The Counseling and Testing Paradigm

The Centers for Disease Control and Prevention (CDC) now mandates that publicly funded antibody test sites provide client-centered counseling according to specific guidelines.[6] In this context, the term *counseling and testing* refers to a three-part process: pre-test counseling (known in California as the risk assessment session), the blood draw procedure, and post-test counseling (known in California as the disclosure session), at which time the counselor discloses the test results. This process combines informed consent for testing and information about the medical aspects of the testing procedure with risk-reduction education, emotional support, and referral for follow-up regarding any problems that might be identified through counseling, such as substance abuse, spousal abuse, or psychiatric disorders.

Pre-Test Counseling

During pre-test counseling, providers lead clients through the decision-making process of the testing experience, ensuring that clients understand the physical process of the test and the emotional implications of testing and of the information they will learn from testing. Pre-test counseling offers a unique opportunity to provide focused education to people who identify themselves as being at risk for infection. The pre-test session is an ideal time to help clients assess personal risk, develop an individualized plan for behavior modification, address barriers to this plan, and develop responses to these barriers. Practitioners generally agree that behavior change messages are more likely to be effective during pre-test counseling than during post-test counseling, when clients are likely to be preoccupied with the imminence of their results or the results themselves.

Pre-test counseling also addresses the emotional charge related to the decision to test, including fears about being seropositive, potentially having to disclose that fact to friends and family, getting sick, and having to come out as gay or bisexual, as a drug user, or as someone who has had sex outside a primary relationship. Finally, during pre-test counseling, providers explain the testing procedure, the meaning and limitations of laboratory findings, and conditions under which primary care follow-up or retesting is recommended. The testing procedure itself is usually carried out by a nurse or phlebotomist, who draws the blood on the same day as the pre-test counseling. The sample is then sent to a diagnostic laboratory for analysis. See Exhibit 2.1 for an outline of the pre-test process.

Post-Test Counseling

Post-test counseling, which follows pre-test counseling any time from a few days to two weeks later (depending on the program structure, the volume of testing, and the process of confirmation of test results), focuses on disclosing test results, dealing with clients' emotional response to the results, and helping clients plan next steps to deal with the implications of the results. Much of this task depends on whether the client expected the result that he or she received, on the adequacy of his or her social support system, and on the strength of his or her personal coping mechanisms. In all cases, providers must be gentle and compassionate, allow clients sufficient time and opportunity to express their feelings, be open to the ambiguity and uncertainty that arise during the window period before which antibodies develop, and emphasize the behavioral consequences of both seropositive and seronegative results.

The greatest challenge for the counselor in the pre- and post-testing situation is to be empathic and supportive while at the same time confronting misinformation and denial. A counselor's ability to create an atmosphere that encourages communication and understanding may determine the adherence of the client to post-test recommendations, particularly the referral of the client for medical and mental health follow-up in the case of a positive test result. Exhibit 2.2 outlines the post-test session process.

Exhibit 2.1. Elements of Pre-Test Counseling.

Assessment of Client

Behavioral risk
Psychological needs
Adequacy of social support
Intentions to share results with others
Coping style
Clarification of values and health belief systems related to self and partners

Discussion of Reasons Individuals Fail to Return for Results

Procrastination
Denial/fatalism
Fear of inability to cope with positive test results
Fear of lack of confidentiality
Concern about laws regarding "knowing exposure" of others

Discussion of Behavior Modification

Development of a realistic personal plan for behavior modification
    based on risk behaviors
Agreement about feasibility of the behavior modification plan
Identification of anticipated reactions and possible barriers to
    suggested changes

Supportive Interventions for Waiting Period

Availability of counselor for questions and supportive counseling by
    telephone if needed to help client deal with, among other concerns,
    prenotification anxiety and suicidal ideation

The Demographics of Testing

Counseling and testing is carried out in a number of venues ranging from publicly funded anonymous and confidential test sites
to doctor's offices, hospitals, and blood banks. The most complete
data regarding the demographics of testing come from public test
sites, which are monitored by the CDC. The use of these sites increased markedly between 1989 and 1992 and then decreased
slightly after that: from 1,014,973 tests in 1989 to 2,689,056 tests
in 1992 and 2,399,529 tests in 1994.[7] As of the end of 1995, the

Exhibit 2.2. Elements of Post-Test Counseling.

Assessment of Client

Behavioral risk
Psychological needs
Adequacy of social support
Coping style
Discussion of test results
Meaning and limitations of laboratory findings
Assurances that results are certain
Recommended follow-up procedures, including whether or not client
  should retest

Behavioral Assessment and Counseling

Emphasis of behavioral consequences: infection (for seronegatives)
  and reinfection (for seropositives)
Denial/fatalism
Importance of protecting others and notifying partners (for
  seropositives)
Introduction to behavior modification interventions as needed

Psychological Reactions to a Positive Result

Expression of feelings and reactions to result
Assessment of immediate reaction to test results, including possible
  psychogenic shock
Counseling or referral regarding potential adverse mental health or
  behavioral outcomes
Acknowledgment of legitimate fears and concerns, including past
  behavioral decisions, anger toward individuals who might have
  transmitted HIV, possibility of having infected loved ones, disclosure of results, fears of abandonment, employment and insurance
  coverage issues
Assessment of potential psychological or behavioral decompensation if
  denial mechanisms are disrupted
Referral to community supports and primary medical and psychosocial
  care

number started to rise again, to 2,491,434. Among these sites are dedicated HIV counseling and testing centers, which in 1995 accounted for 29.8 percent of all tests and 34.9 percent of all seropositive test results in 1995, and sexually transmitted disease (STD) clinics, which in the same year accounted for 26.7 percent of reported tests and 25.1 percent of all seropositive results. In 1995, family planning and prenatal-obstetric clinics accounted for 12.6 percent of tests (2.3 percent of seropositive results) and drug abuse treatment centers and prisons accounted for another 8.2 percent of tests (14.3 percent of seropositive results).

Among clients at publicly funded sites, both African American and Hispanic clients were overrepresented compared to their proportion in the national population: 48.7 percent of clients were White; 32.6 percent were African American; and 14.9 percent were Hispanic.[8] Similarly, the proportion of seropositive tests in these populations was high: 20.7 percent of the seropositive tests were among Hispanics and 49.0 percent were among African Americans, compared to 27.7 percent among Whites. More than half of the tests at publicly funded sites in 1995 were of women, although more than two-thirds of seropositive tests were among men. Among both men and women, the twenty to twenty-nine age group accounted for the largest proportion of all antibody tests; the thirty to thirty-nine age group accounted for the largest proportion of seropositive tests. Also, although people with a history of male-to-male sex or injection drug use accounted for only 12.7 percent of all tests, they made up 48.6 percent of all seropositive tests. Finally, the proportion of tests reported that included post-test counseling rose from 38.9 percent in 1989 to 59.6 percent in 1995, with HIV counseling and testing centers reporting the highest rate of post-test counseling (82.7 percent).

Home Testing

It is important to acknowledge the potential movement away from formal testing, either at anonymous or confidential test sites, at STD or public health clinics, or in private medical offices. In May 1996, the U.S. Food and Drug Administration approved the HIV antibody home test, the first HIV testing system that is not entirely linked to the medical setting.[9] The introduction of this technology has been touted by some prevention advocates as a way to dramatically improve access to antibody testing[10,11] and by others as a potentially dangerous undertaking. Detractors argue that home testing will lead to "missed opportunities" for behavioral counseling and leave individuals open to potential abuse by institutions—employers, insurance, border patrols—as well as by sexual partners.[12]

Home testing kits are available through pharmacies or through mail order. (Johnson and Johnson, one of the home test manufacturers, discontinued its product after losing the rights to market it. The remaining manufacturer is Home Access.) To conduct the test, the individual pricks his or her finger to obtain a blood sample, which is placed on the designated areas of the test card and mailed to the manufacturer for analysis. Seven days later, the individual can call for the results. For seropositive individuals, testing company representatives give results over the telephone, providing counseling that consists of a review of treatment and prevention information and referrals to local medical practitioners and AIDS agencies. For seronegative individuals, counseling consists of information regarding prevention. However, seronegative clients have the choice of a tape-recorded message or a live counselor, and the majority choose the recording.[13]

The important issues raised by home test kits include whether or not adequate pre- and post-test counseling can be provided; whether the kits are used by people who currently do not get tested at counseling and testing sites; whether the psychological and behavioral impact of receiving HIV antibody test results at home differs from the impact of receiving results face-to-face at testing sites; and whether linkage to early medical care and prevention interventions is adequate. Home testing advocates hold that the most crucial prevention tool in the counseling and testing process is the testing—that is, once a person knows his or her serostatus, he or she is more likely to implement prevention strategies. They also assert that the home testing population is different from the population of people who receive counseling and testing at established sites, and that those who would access home testing compose a large population of at-risk individuals who are failing to be tested because they are unwilling to use public and even private test sites.

Opponents of home testing counter that without face-to-face counseling and referral, individuals conducting their own HIV test will experience adverse psychological reactions (such as depression and anxiety) to the testing process. In addition, opponents contend that the automated disclosure or brief counseling that accompanies seronegative results fails to take advantage of prevention counseling opportunities.

Rates of use of the home test kits are lower than were expected by manufacturers and prevention planners, mediating both beneficial or problematic consequences and, for the moment, making arguments about the pros and cons moot. However, new technologies that would permit home testing with *immediate* results are on the horizon and will undoubtedly raise similar and additional concerns. It will not be long before such instant tests will be available for testing of potential sexual and drug use partners in the moment. These will raise a variety of ethical and public policy issues, not the least of which will be whether consumers will have the right to interpret their own HIV antibody test results.

Viral Load Testing

Given recent advances in viral load testing and antiviral prophylaxis at very early stages of infection,[14] many clinicians and public health officials suggest there is an even stronger need for HIV testing for those who have reason to worry about the possibility of infection. This potential influx of individuals requesting testing will likely also affect the counseling and testing paradigm.

As viral load testing of seropositive people becomes more widely available, it is likely to have profound prevention implications.[15] Viral load testing and antibody testing will likely be used extensively by people who have a slip in protected behavior significant enough to frighten them into action (even despite the fact that the antibody window period is as long as twelve weeks following exposure). Such individuals may be the ripest for prevention counseling: they are likely to have had a recent and what they define as a clear instance of risky behavior and to have a clear memory of the situational and emotional factors related to the slip. This may be the best time to counsel about behavior change among people who are most likely to take sexual or drug use risks.

The Motivation to Test

The decision to get tested is a complex and difficult one composed of several stages. Testing requires confronting a multitude of difficult emotions: fear, anger, and guilt about past behavioral decisions; fear about the possibility of having infected loved ones; and concerns about potential loss of family and livelihood. For these reasons, understanding why people choose to get tested and the decision-making process that surrounds HIV antibody testing is important.

Although reasons for taking the test are varied,[16] refusal tends to be higher among men than women, and higher among African Americans than among Whites. Several studies suggest that specific psychological and situational motivators drive the testing decision.[17] For instance, individuals choosing not to be tested said that being afraid of the heightened anxiety and depression following a seropositive test result dissuaded them, whereas those who did test said that the belief that their results would help them cope with and reduce high-risk behaviors was a significant motivator. Additional potential barriers to testing include the misperception of risk of HIV infection, confidentiality and anonymity concerns, fear of stigmatization, and fear of rejection if seropositive.[18,19] Among other reasons for electing to test was to be reassured that safer sex was working, that unsafe sex had not led to transmission, and that earlier test results were accurate.[20]

Although some studies found seroprevalence among those who took the test to be twice as high as it was among those who did not,[21] other studies found the opposite: people who refused antibody testing were approximately twice as likely to be seropositive as people who tested.[22] Despite the methodological and substantive differences among these studies, they did uncover one consistent finding: there were significant discrepancies between subjective perceptions of risk and actual seroprevalence. The basis for misperception and the psychological reasons for refusing testing, however, may differ among subgroups. For example, an Australian study of 545 sexually active men who refused testing found that bisexual men acknowledged risk but procrastinated before being tested; heterosexual men denied risk; and gay men feared antibody-positive results and distrusted confidentiality practices.[23]

It is important to understand not only why people get tested but also what motivates them to return for results once they have been tested. CDC data indicate that failing to return for results is not a rare event: only 74 percent of seropositive and 63 percent of seronegative individuals return; and freestanding HIV antibody counseling and test sites were more successful than STD clinics in getting individuals to do so.[24] These data provoke us to ask what the mental health and behavioral consequences are of going through pre-test counseling and antibody testing without the closure provided by post-test counseling. Might behavior modification plans made during pre-test counseling be negated by the same psychological response—perhaps denial—that impels the clients to avoid post-test counseling? In order to increase a client's likelihood of returning, it is of the utmost importance that pre-test counseling address unresolved fear and guilt, and provide help with the psychological implications of both seropositive and seronegative test results. This can only be done by assessing a person's reasons for seeking testing and his or her emotional state, coping strategies, and social supports—including whether he or she intends to share test results with partners, family, or friends. This approach is likely not only to communicate concern about a client's well-being but also to increase the chances that the client will return for test results.

Testing and Behavior Change

The efficacy of counseling and testing in bringing about behavior change has been the focus of controversy since the HIV antibody test was developed in 1985. This debate became especially vigorous when home-based testing was approved. Today, despite the market failure of home-based testing, the essential question remains: Does knowledge of serostatus bring about behavior change, and if so, is counseling a necessary component of any risk reduction that is associated with the testing process?

Overall, the evidence for the behavioral impact of HIV testing remains mixed at best.[25] Although it has been shown that voluntary counseling and testing can enhance safer sexual behavior in couples in which each partner has a different serostatus and each partner receives counseling,[26] there is little evidence for behavior change after counseling for heterosexuals if only one partner is tested,[27] and some studies have even documented an increase in risky behavior in people who receive a seronegative result.[28]

It is important to note, however, that few studies control for the quality of the counseling process—a troubling fact, considering the findings of an external review of the CDC's counseling, testing, referral, and partner notification program.[29] This review found that pre-test counseling typically lasted between two and ten minutes and post-test counseling between ten and thirty minutes. It also revealed that counselors tended to deemphasize the prevention message in favor of more technical jargon about the test. The review also found considerable variation in the content of the counseling, the intensity of sessions, and the training of counselors. Such variations in the extent and quality of HIV antibody test counseling may well taint any summary results about the efficacy of prevention counseling in the testing setting; we must remember this as we review the following summary of the data for particular subgroups—including gay and bisexual men, injection drug users, and women.

Behavior Change Among Gay and Bisexual Men

In 1987, the U.S. assistant secretary of health mandated that everyone undergoing HIV antibody testing be informed of their test results. Since that time, only a few controlled studies have been able to compare the behavior change of gay and bisexual men who were aware of their HIV antibody status to those who were unaware. Overall, according to a 1997 analysis of published longitudinal studies and cross-sectional studies, much of the observed risk reduction was independent of HIV counseling and testing and was consistent with overall behavior change in this population.[30] The magnitude of behavior change in three of these studies was independent of knowledge of serostatus—hence counseling and testing—and also of actual serostatus.[31,32,33] Furthermore, several of the studies present data suggesting that even if counseling and testing may have led to the observed behavior change, the magnitude of change was greater among seropositive men than among seronegative men.[34,35,36]

A few studies identified particular patterns of unsafe behavior following testing. A New York City study found increased receptive anal intercourse among HIV-infected men.[37] Several other studies found that some seronegative individuals infer from their test results that they are in some way naturally immune to HIV whether or not they reduce risk.[38,39,40] Finally, a Chicago study found that men who were depressed, had weaker social supports, felt greater isolation, and had engaged in higher levels of denial and fatalistic coping were more likely to lapse from safer sex to unsafe sex after testing.[41]

All of this evidence indicates that although much behavior change was observed, it is difficult to clearly link this change to counseling and testing. For those studies that attempted to isolate the effects of knowledge of serostatus itself, the evidence that successful behavior change is based merely on antibody counseling and testing is negative or weak at best.

Behavior Change Among Injection Drug Users

Overall, HIV risk reduction—that is, sexual and needle-sharing behavior change—has been less substantial among injection drug users than among gay and bisexual men. However, what little has been published on the relationship between counseling and testing and behavior change in this population suggests that the counseling and testing process motivates risk-reducing behavior,[42] specifically safer needle-use behaviors,[43,44] and smaller reductions in sexual risk behaviors, especially among injection drug users receiving drug treatment. Two small longitudinal studies comparing seronegative to seropositive injection drug users report both drug-related and sexual behavior changes among subjects who knew their serostatus, with more significant changes occurring in HIV-infected individuals.[45,46] The single most important change was the reduced frequency and regularity of equipment sharing.

However, most published studies draw participants from methadone maintenance treatment programs; the results therefore have limited generalizability to injection drug users who are not in treatment. For example, although one study found that "in clinic" testing was widely accepted by injection drug users and that most clients in treatment (63 percent) elected to learn their serostatus,[47] this number is bound to be lower among drug users not in treatment. Furthermore, in the only random prospective study—

comparing HIV education alone to HIV education plus counseling and testing—researchers found increases in condom use and needle hygiene among all participants, with no significant differences between groups.[48]

Behavior Change Among Women

Although women use publicly funded counseling and testing sites slightly more than men,[49] there has been little research on women and their behavioral responses to antibody testing.[50] What has been published focuses mainly on serostatus and reproductive decision making. Given the high probability of perinatal transmission in the absence of any prophylactic antiviral treatment, additional counseling is recommended for high-risk or seropositive pregnant women. This counseling should include, among other topics, discussing rates of transmission, the option of terminating the pregnancy, and treatment with zidovudine (ZDV), which has been shown to reduce perinatal transmission.[51] There is considerable and ongoing research to determine both the optimal and least costly forms of antiviral treatment to prevent perinatal HIV transmission.

A recent review article suggests that findings with respect to counseling and testing of women are inconsistent.[52] Half of the studies found serostatus to be unrelated to pregnancy decisions, whereas the other half found that seropositive women were significantly less likely than seronegative women to become pregnant. There were similarly inconsistent findings regarding birth control, condom use, and pregnancy termination (although overall, seropositive women were slightly more likely than seronegative women to terminate pregnancy). In summary, the majority of the data show that knowledge of serostatus does not have an important influence on pregnancy decisions among seropositive women, although increasing publicity about the efficacy of perinatal prophylaxis will undoubtedly motivate increasing numbers of pregnant women to seek testing. Whatever decision a seropositive woman makes regarding pregnancy, she will have an increased need for ongoing support and follow-up to help her navigate a medical care system that is not well informed about the HIV-related issues women face.

Studies of women who are not pregnant but who are at high risk of HIV infection demonstrate a clearer relationship between risk, serostatus, and counseling and testing. A longitudinal study of a representative sample of women of childbearing age who received counseling and testing in Africa found that seropositive women were more likely to negotiate their partner's use of condoms than were seronegative women.[53] Moreover, seropositive women whose partners were also tested were more likely to negotiate their partner's use of condoms than those whose partners were not tested, yielding a lower rate of new infections.

A study of sex workers found that women who underwent both counseling and testing and a skills-based intervention reported a significant increase in condom use during vaginal intercourse with their customers.[54] Although women who received counseling and testing alone changed their condom use behaviors during vaginal sex, they reported a significant decrease in condom use during oral sex with their customers, indicating the need for both clarification of oral sex guidelines for counselors and skills-building regarding the process of negotiating condom use for oral sex. This and other studies with similar findings suggest that more intensive counseling and testing interventions may be necessary to lead to behavior change.

Behavior Change in Other Subpopulations

Although research has found higher HIV seroprevalence rates among clients at STD clinics than in the general population,[55,56] there has been little formal research into the issue of counseling and testing in these settings. It appears, however, that heterosexuals who are at high risk of infection but who do not fall into other risk categories have not been accessing HIV antibody counseling and testing. For example, half of the respondents of an STD clinic population who identified themselves at very high risk for HIV infection said that they had never been referred for counseling and testing.[57] Similarly, one U.S. study found that 36 percent of individuals newly diagnosed with AIDS were first tested for HIV antibody only two months prior to their diagnosis, and 51 percent only within one year of diagnosis. Testing so late in the course of HIV disease represents a missed opportunity for early intervention;

58 percent of those studied had finally tested because of symptomatic illness.[58]

Most research shows that knowledge of serostatus in STD clinic populations is effective in reducing risk among at least the infected subpopulation.[59] Studies comparing seropositive to seronegative individuals found that counseling and testing for seropositive individuals was associated with reductions in sexual risk behaviors. However, there was no such effect for seronegative individuals; in some cases, knowing their serostatus led to increases in unprotected behaviors. For example a study of people who underwent counseling and testing at a large, urban STD clinic found at one-year follow-up that there was a 29 percent decrease in gonorrhea rates among people who tested seropositive, but a 106 percent increase in gonorrhea rates among those who tested seronegative.[60] These startling results suggest a disinhibiting effect or false belief in immunity, which seems to be validated by a general population study in which a significant number of seronegative people knowingly engaged in unsafe sex after receiving their test results.[61]

The body of research on heterosexual couples in which partners have different serostatuses (serodiscordant couples) has provided the strongest support for the effects of counseling and testing. Several longitudinal studies have found high levels of consistent condom use and abstinence among serodiscordant couples when compared to concordant couples.[62,63]

Adolescents are another important group to consider, as many currently infected individuals were infected during late adolescence—a time for experimentation. However, there is little published research because of the special legal issues regarding research with minors. One of the few published studies looked at college students.[64] The study found that students who received education plus counseling and testing increased their communication with sexual partners about HIV infection as compared to students who received either the educational intervention alone or no intervention at all. However, the study showed no reduction in risk behaviors.

Another study, conducted on seropositive youth in an urban clinic, found that the majority of males—but none of the females— said that they had increased safer sex behaviors, that they had been consistent in using safer sex only in ongoing relationships, and that the ceasing of drug use increased safer sex behaviors more than knowledge of serostatus did.[65] Finally, in a study exploring HIV risk in homeless youth, counseling and testing was, in fact, associated with higher levels of behavioral risk. For the most part, it seemed that youth used serial testing as a tool for monitoring their serostatus.[66] In sum, the evidence for a risk-reducing effect of counseling and testing for adolescents is not encouraging. It may well be that the perceived need to experiment at this point of development supersedes rational decisions about HIV risk and protective behaviors (see Chapter Four).

Resolving Ambiguous Research Literature

In agreement with the key literature review on the subject,[67] it is clear that although there is a mixed pattern of counseling and testing efficacy, the process nevertheless seems to motivate behavior change (including seeking early or prophylactic treatment) across a variety of different populations. The most unequivocal evidence for this comes from studies of heterosexual serodiscordant couples. The evidence in other populations, such as men who have sex with men, is harder to link to the counseling and testing process because of the tremendous overall risk reduction that has occurred in these populations during the past fifteen years. This does not mean that counseling and testing is not effective in this or the other populations, nor can the widespread availability of counseling and testing be dismissed as a contributing factor in these behavior change trends. It is notable that seropositive individuals are clearly more likely than their seronegative counterparts to have reduced their risk behavior practices as a result of counseling and testing. Furthermore, the literature on injection drug users indicates a pattern of successful behavior modification, although because most of the data were obtained from treatment populations, the generalizability of these findings is limited.

There are many possible reasons for the lack of consistency in the data. Primary among these is the unrealistic assumption that any short-term, brief intervention such as counseling and testing will bring about sustained behavior change in sexuality. As important, the counseling and testing protocols studied in the literature vary tremendously in both quality and quantity, a fact confirmed by the external review of the CDC's counseling and testing programs. Among the variations in protocol were factors as fundamental as counselor training, the use of lay people as counselors (some of whom were poorly trained), and the time spent on each of the many tasks of the counseling session.

Responding to Programmatic Weaknesses

Rather than conclude that counseling and testing is in and of itself ineffective, it would seem wise to develop approaches that respond to the limitations identified in the literature. For instance, there seems to be a "dose-response" relationship between HIV antibody counseling and testing and behavior change.[68] The combination of testing plus single sessions of pre- and post-test counseling alone is unlikely to help an individual sustain behavior change. However, several sessions of individual, couples, or group counseling, ideally in conjunction with a variety of skills-based interventions, may reduce risk. Unfortunately, although an intensive counseling and testing process promises to be the most successful approach, scarce resources make it difficult to implement.

Given this scarcity, it is useful to identify those who are most likely to benefit from or need intensive counseling and intervention—for example, individuals who participate in activities that put them at risk of infection but who have not yet thought about testing. The studies reviewed in this chapter show that many of those who defer testing are indeed more likely to be HIV-infected. The reasons for deciding not to get tested may include individuals' failure to recognize risk, their fears of the results coupled with the sense of being unable to respond, and their concerns about breaches in confidentiality and the resulting stigmatization. Improved outreach can identify and attract those clients at highest risk. Protection and promotion of test site confidentiality can allay fears of discrimination. Client-friendly sites, as defined by the particular community a site serves, can enable counselors to capitalize on the teachable moments provided by the counseling and testing experience.

Another population that might be targeted is of those at highest risk for adverse mental health outcomes in the usual counseling and testing process. In addition to its prevention role, counseling and testing may provide support to people facing the testing process.[69-75] To aid in the identification of such clients, pre-test counseling should include mental health screening in addition to a multidimensional assessment for both sexual and drug-related risk behaviors. This is especially important considering that a significant proportion of clients do not return for their results. In this area, a psychotherapist can play a role in the counseling and testing process. Most lay counselors are not well trained in the assessment of an individual's coping and social support resources, nor do they have the time to adequately undertake such an assessment in most counseling and testing settings. By adopting a supporting and consultative role to the counseling and testing staff, psychotherapists can help counselors develop the skills they will need to assess a client's need for further counseling either on-site or through referral to an outside resource. Such assessment and referral is cost-effective and can be accomplished easily using a few short, standard questions.[76]

Recommendations

Given that a significant number of people at high risk of being HIV-infected are likely to continue to resist antibody counseling and testing, what practical recommendations emerge from this review? In the first place, all health care providers need to be well informed regarding the basic implications of HIV antibody testing and test results. This includes being knowledgeable about reporting and contact-tracing requirements, local laws regarding confidentiality of test results, and the basics of early intervention with potent antiviral combinations. Furthermore, health care providers need to be versed in the essentials of post-test counseling, as they may well be put into a situation where they have to provide counseling services and, at the least, be knowledgeable about appropriate HIV-related referrals for their clients.

Test program planners and antibody test counselors need to understand the psychological and behavioral implications of both positive and negative test results and ensure there are appropriate resources at hand during the counseling of clients with a variety of backgrounds. Primary health care providers need to recognize that they may be the most influential in helping their clients decide to take the antibody test and that they must be able to perform adequate HIV risk assessment and discuss the importance of the testing option. Because it is likely that testing will increasingly take place in medical offices, primary health care providers and office staff must be able to perform pre- and post-test counseling, which requires among other things a familiarity with behavior change approaches.

Finally, in light of at-home and rapid testing procedures, greater numbers of clients will be turning to primary medical and mental health caregivers for assistance in coping with the psychological, behavioral, and medical results of antibody testing. And once clients have been motivated to seek testing, they must be able to access not only high-quality counseling and testing but also the most up-to-date counseling, treatment, and support services for both seropositive and seronegative people. In following these recommendations, HIV counseling and testing can achieve its intended goals and be a crucial entry point for everyone in need of HIV prevention and support.

Improvements in five areas can facilitate prevention goals in the HIV counseling and testing setting:

- Using the test as an entry to longer-term and more intensive interventions rather than as an end in itself
- Actively linking clients to other HIV-related prevention resources
- Developing and enforcing minimal standards for the quantity and quality of a counseling interaction
- Ensuring that counselors are well trained in terms of behavior change approaches, resource development and referral, the whole range of HIV-related issues, and most important, counseling skills
- Targeting future research on defining ways to counsel people with negative test results who have participated in risky behaviors, so that these results do not reinforce risky behaviors

Test counseling remains for many people the only, and sometimes the most comprehensive, HIV-related prevention intervention to which they will be exposed. To the extent that awareness and education are crucial precursors to action, it would seem that simply talking about risk and risk reduction becomes an important preventive step. But the counseling and testing encounter is an opportunity to go even further, perhaps the only one for most of us: a chance to go beyond education, to help people think through the issues involved in instituting and maintaining safer behaviors. If we are serious about HIV prevention, how can we pass up this opportunity?

Notes

1. Centers for Disease Control. "Additional Recommendations to Reduce Sexual and Drug Abuse–Related Transmission of the Human T-Lymphotrophic Virus Type III/Lymphadenopathy-Associated Virus." *Morbidity and Mortality Weekly Report,* 1986, *35*(10), 152–155.
2. Goldblum, P., and Marks, R. "The HIV Testing Debate." *FOCUS: A Guide to AIDS Research and Counseling,* 1988, *3*(12), 1–3.
3. Coates, T. J., Stall, R., Kegeles, S. M., and others. "AIDS Antibody Testing: Will It Stop the AIDS Epidemic? Will It Help People Infected with HIV?" *American Psychologist,* 1988, *43*(11, special issue), 859–864.
4. Rhame, F., and Maki, D. "The Case for Wider Use of Testing for HIV Infection." *New England Journal of Medicine,* 1989, *320*(19), 1248–1254.
5. Cates, W., Jr., and Handsfield, H. H. "HIV Counseling and Testing: Does It Work?" *American Journal of Public Health,* 1988, *78*(12), 533–534.
6. Centers for Disease Control. "Technical Guidance on HIV Counseling." *Morbidity and Mortality Weekly Report,* 1993, *42*(RR-2), 11–17.
7. Centers for Disease Control and Prevention. *HIV Counseling and Testing in Publicly Funded Sites. 1995 Summary Report.* Atlanta: Centers for Disease Control and Prevention, U.S. Department of Health and Human Services, Sept. 1997.
8. Ibid.
9. U.S. Department of Health and Human Services. "FDA Approves First HIV Home Test System." Press release, May 14, 1996.
10. Bayer, R., Stryker, J., and Smith, M. D. "Testing for HIV Infection at Home." *New England Journal of Medicine,* 1995, *332*(19), 1296–1299.
11. Frerichs, R. R. "Personal Screening for HIV in Developing Countries." *Lancet,* 1994, *343*(8903), 960–962.
12. Salbu, S. R. "HIV Home Testing and the FDA: The Case for Regulatory Constraint." *Hastings Law Journal,* 1995, *46*, 403–547.
13. Personal communication between Frank Allen, chief executive officer of Home Access, and James W. Dilley, Jan. 1998.

14. Feder, H. M., and Milch, L. M. "Viral Load and Combination Therapy for Human Immunodeficiency Virus." *New England Journal of Medicine,* 1997, *336*(13), 959–960.

15. Ostrow, D. G., and Kalichman, S. C. (eds.). *Psychosocial and Public Health Implications of New HIV Therapies.* New York: Plenum, 1998.

16. Simon, P., Weber, M., Ford, W., and others. "Reasons for HIV Antibody Test Refusal in a Heterosexual Sexually Transmitted Disease Clinic Population." *AIDS,* 1996, *10*(13), 1549–1553.

17. Valdiserri, R., Lyter, D., Leviton, L., and others. "Variables Influencing Condom Use in a Cohort of Homosexual and Bisexual Men." *American Journal of Public Health,* 1988, *78*(7), 801–805.

18. Simon, Weber, Ford, and others, "Reasons for HIV Antibody Test Refusal."

19. Myers, T., Orr, K., Locker, D., and others. "Factors Affecting Gay and Bisexual Men's Decisions and Intentions to Seek HIV Testing." *American Journal of Public Health,* 1993, *83*(5), 701–704.

20. Simon, Weber, Ford, and others, "Reasons for HIV Antibody Test Refusal."

21. Hart, G. "Factors Associated with Requesting and Refusing Human Immunodeficiency Virus Antibody Testing." *Medical Journal of Australia,* 1991, *155*(4), 586–589.

22. Jones, J., Hutto, P., Mayer, P., and others. "HIV Seroprevalence and Reasons for Refusing and Accepting HIV Testing." *Sexually Transmitted Diseases,* 1993, *20*(6), 334–337.

23. Waddell, C. "Testing for HIV Infection Among Heterosexual, Bisexual and Gay Men." *Australian Journal of Public Health,* 1993, *17*(1), 27–31.

24. Centers for Disease Control. *CTS Clients Record Data Base: U.S. Total, 1991 Annual Report.* Atlanta: Public Health Service, U.S. Department of Health and Human Services, 1992.

25. Wolitski, R. J., MacGowan, R. J., Higgins, D. L., and Jorgensen, C. M. "The Effects of HIV Counseling and Testing on Risk-Related Practices and Help Seeking Behavior." *AIDS Education and Prevention,* 1997, *9*(3 Suppl.), 52–67.

26. Allen, S., Tice, J., Van de Perre, P., and others. "Effect of Serotesting with Counselling on Condom Use and Seroconversion Among HIV Discordant Couples in Africa." *British Medical Journal* (Clinical Research Edition), 1992, *304*(6842), 1605–1609.

27. Wolitski, MacGowan, Higgins, and Jorgensen, "Effects of HIV Counseling and Testing on Risk-Related Practices."

28. Otten, M. W., Zaidi, A. A., Wroten, J. E., and others. "Changes in Sexually Transmitted Disease Rates After HIV Testing and Post-Test

Counseling, Miami, 1988–1989." *American Journal of Public Health,* 1993, *83*(4), 529–633.

29. Walsh, C., Campbell, C., and Willingham, M. "HIV/STD Prevention Program Assessment, United States, 1992." Abstract presented at the Ninth International Conference on AIDS, Berlin, June 1993.

30. Wolitski, MacGowan, Higgins, and Jorgensen, "Effects of HIV Counseling and Testing on Risk-Related Practices."

31. Ostrow, D. G., Joseph, J. G., Beltran, E., and others. "Characteristics and Responses of Men Seeking HIV Antibody Test Results." Presented at the Fifth International Conference on AIDS, Montreal, June 1989.

32. Doll, L., O'Malley, P., Pershing, A., and others. "High-Risk Sexual Behavior and Knowledge of HIV Antibody Status in the San Francisco City Clinic Cohort." *Health Psychology,* 1990, *9*(3), 253–256.

33. Schechter, M., Craib, K., Willoughby, B., and others. "Patterns of Sexual Behavior and Condom Use in a Cohort of Homosexual Men." *American Journal of Public Health,* 1988, *78*(12), 1535–1538.

34. Phair, J., Jacobsen, L., Detels, R., and others. "Acquired Immune Deficiency Syndrome Occurring Within 5 Years of Infections with Human Immunodeficiency Virus Type 1: The Multi-Center AIDS Cohort Study." *Journal of Acquired Immune Deficiency Syndromes,* 1992, *5*(5), 490–496.

35. Coates, T. J., Morin, S., and McKusick, L. "Behavioral Consequences of AIDS Antibody Testing Among Gay Men." *Journal of the American Medical Association,* 1987, *258*(14), 1989.

36. Van Griensven, G., de Vroome, E., Tielman, R., and others. "Effect of Human Immunodeficiency Virus (HIV) Antibody Knowledge on High-Risk Sexual Behavior with Steady and Nonsteady Partners Among Homosexual Men." *American Journal of Epidemiology,* 1989, *129*(3), 596–603.

37. Martin, J. L. "Psychological Consequences of AIDS-Related Bereavement Among Gay Men." *Journal of Consulting and Clinical Psychology,* 1988, *56*(6), 856–862.

38. Schechter, Craib, Willoughby, and others, "Patterns of Sexual Behavior and Condom Use."

39. McCusker, J., Stoddard, A., Mayer, K., and others. "Effects of HIV Antibody Test Knowledge on Subsequent Sexual Behaviors in a Cohort of Homosexually Active Men." *American Journal of Public Health,* 1988, *78*(4), 462–467. Published erratum appears in *American Journal of Public Health,* 1988, *78*(12), 1530.

40. Beltran, E., Ostrow, D. G., and Joseph, J. G. "Predictors of Sexual Behavior Among Men Requesting Their HIV-1 Antibody Status: The

Chicago MACS/CCS Cohort of Homosexual/Bisexual Men, 1985–1986." *AIDS Education and Prevention*, 1993, *5*(3), 185–195.

41. Ostrow, D. G., Di Francisco, W. J., and Beltran, E. "Performance of Pre-Screening for Adverse Behavioral Outcomes Among Homosexual Men Undergoing HIV Antibody Test Disclosure." Presented at the Ninth International Conference on AIDS, Berlin, June 1993.

42. Wolitski, MacGowan, Higgins, and Jorgensen, "Effects of HIV Counseling and Testing on Risk-Related Practices."

43. Descenclos, J. C., Papaevangelou, G., and Ancelle-Park, R. "Knowledge of HIV Serostatus and Preventive Behaviour Among European Injecting Drug Users." *AIDS*, 1993, *7*(10), 1371–1377.

44. Magura, S., Siddiqi, Q., Shapiro, J., and others. "Outcomes of an AIDS Prevention Program for Methadone Patients." *International Journal of the Addictions*, 1991, *26*(6), 629–655.

45. Skidmore, C., Robertson, J., and Roberts, J. "Changes in HIV Risk-Taking Behavior in Intravenous Drug Users: A Second Follow-Up." *British Journal of Addiction*, 1989, *84*(6), 695–696.

46. Van den Hoek, A., van Haastrecht, H., and Coutinho, R. "Heterosexual Behavior of Intravenous Drug Users in Amsterdam: Implications for the AIDS Epidemic." *AIDS*, 1990, *4*(5), 449–453.

47. Reardon, J., Warren, N., Keilch, R., and others. "Are HIV-Infected Injection Drug Users Taking HIV Tests?" *American Journal of Public Health*, 1993, *85*(10), 1414–1417.

48. Calsyn, D., Saxon, A., Freeman, G., Jr., and others. "Ineffectiveness of AIDS Education in Reducing HIV High-Risk Behaviors Among Injection Drug Users." *American Journal of Public Health*, 1992, *82*(4), 573–575.

49. Centers for Disease Control and Prevention, *HIV Counseling and Testing in Publicly Funded Sites.*

50. Ickovics, J., and Rodin, J. "Women and AIDS in the United States: Epidemiology, Natural History and Mediating Mechanisms." *Health Psychology*, 1992, *11*(1), 1–16.

51. Conner, E. M., Sperling, R. S., Gelber, R., and others. "Reduction of Maternal-Infant Transmission of Human Immunodeficiency Virus Type 1 with Zidovudine Treatment." *New England Journal of Medicine*, 1994, *331*(18), 1173–1180.

52. Wolitski, MacGowan, Higgins, and Jorgensen, "Effects of HIV Counseling and Testing on Risk-Related Practices."

53. Allen, S., Serufilira, A., Bogaerts, J., and others. "Confidential HIV Testing and Condom Promotion in Africa: Impact on HIV and Gonorrhea Rates." *Journal of the American Medical Association*, 1992, *268*(23), 3338.

54. Corby, N., Barchi, P., Wolitski, R. J., and others. "Effects of Condom Skills Training and HIV Testing on AIDS Prevention Behaviors Among Sex Workers." Presented at the Sixth International Conference on AIDS, San Francisco, June 1990.

55. Centers for Disease Control and Prevention. *HIV Counseling and Testing in Publicly Funded Sites.*

56. Onorato, I., McCray, E., Pappaioanou, M., and others. "HIV Seroprevalence Surveys in Sexually Transmitted Disease Clinics." *Public Health Reports,* 1990, *105*(2), 119–124.

57. Pope, S., Koopman, J., Ostrow, D. G., and others. "The Link Between Sexually Transmitted Disease Clinics and HIV Counseling and Testing Centers: Who Is Getting Referred?" *AIDS Education and Prevention,* 1992, *43*(3), 219–226.

58. Wortley, P. M., Chu, S. Y., Diaz, T., and others. "HIV Testing Patterns: Where, Why, and When Were Persons with AIDS Tested for HIV?" *AIDS,* 1995, *9*(5), 487–492.

59. Wolitski, MacGowan, Higgins, and Jorgensen, "Effects of HIV Counseling and Testing on Risk-Related Practices."

60. Otten, Zaidi, Wroten, and others, "Changes in Sexually Transmitted Disease Rates."

61. Mayer, K., Zierler, S., Feingold, L., and others. "Heterosexual Behavior and HIV Status in a Cohort of Persons at Increased Risk for HIV Infection." Presented at the Fifth International Conference on AIDS, Montreal, June 1989.

62. Wolitski, MacGowan, Higgins, and Jorgensen, "Effects of HIV Counseling and Testing on Risk-Related Practices."

63. Allen, Tice, Van de Perre, and others, "Effect of Serotesting with Counselling."

64. Wenger, N., Greenberg, J., Hilborne, L., and others. "Effect of HIV Antibody Testing and AIDS Education on Communication About HIV Risk and Sexual Behavior: A Randomized, Controlled Trial in College Students." *Annals of Internal Medicine,* 1992, *117*(11), 905–911.

65. Futterman, D., Hein, K., Kipke, M. D., and others. "HIV Adolescents: HIV Testing Experiences and Changes in Risk-Related Sexual and Drug Use Behavior." Presented at the Sixth International Conference on AIDS, San Francisco, June 1990.

66. Johnston, C., Montgomery, S. B., and Kipke, M. D. "Self-Reported HIV Testing Among Homeless and Runaway Youth in San Diego: Prevalence Rates and Associated Factors." Presented at the 18th annual scientific sessions, Society for Behavioral Medicine, San Francisco, Apr. 1997.

67. Wolitski, MacGowan, Higgins, and Jorgensen, "Effects of HIV Counseling and Testing on Risk-Related Practices."

68. Corby, Barchi, Wolitski, and others, "Effects of Condom Skills Training."

69. Marzuk, P. M., Tierney, H., Tardiff, K., and others. "Increased Risk of Suicide in Persons with AIDS." *Journal of the American Medical Association,* 1988, *259*(9), 1333–1337.

70. Faulstich, M. E. "Psychiatric Aspects of AIDS." *American Journal of Psychiatry,* 1987, *144*(5), 551–556.

71. Kelly, J. A., and Murphy, D. "Psychological Interventions with AIDS and HIV: Prevention and Treatment." *Journal of Consulting and Clinical Psychology,* 1992, *60*(4), 576–585.

72. Perry, S. W., Jacobsberg, L., Fishman, B., and others. "Psychological Responses to Serological Testing for HIV." *AIDS,* 1990, *4*(2), 145–152.

73. Casadonte, P., Des Jarlais, D., Friedman, S., and Rotrosen, J. "Psychological and Behavioral Impact Among Intravenous Drug Users of Learning HIV Test Results." *International Journal of Addictions,* 1990, *25*(4), 409–426.

74. Beevor, A., and Catalana, J. "Women's Experience of HIV Testing: The Views of HIV-Positive and HIV-Negative Women." *AIDS Care,* 1993, *5*(2), 177–186.

75. Cleary, P., Van Devanter, N., Rogers, T., and others. "Depressive Symptoms in Blood Donors Notified of HIV Infection." *American Journal of Public Health,* 1993, *83*(4), 534–539.

76. Ostrow, Di Francisco, and Beltran, "Performance of Pre-Screening."

Chapter Three

Behavior Change Theory and HIV Prevention

David Silven

A few years ago, at a conference for health educators on the topic of preventing continued unsafe sex among gay and bisexual men, a participant suggested that theory-based principles of behavior change be used as guides for developing interventions. Other participants responded with skepticism: they believed instead that focusing on theory might impede tangible progress and that theory should remain in academic settings.

What use, if any, does theory have in this critical area? To address this question, this chapter summarizes the research on high-risk sexual behavior change and presents an overview of four basic behavior change theories—the Health Belief Model, Social Cognitive Theory, Stages of Behavior Change, and Marlatt's Relapse Prevention Model. To help us appreciate the utility of these theories in understanding and responding to risk behaviors, I propose to integrate the theories and apply the resulting model to the prevention challenge faced by gay and bisexual men. My primary emphasis, particularly in the case examples in the final section, is on interventions provided to individuals or small groups rather than on mass media strategies aimed at large audiences.

An earlier version of this chapter appeared in *FOCUS: A Guide to AIDS Research and Counseling,* January 1993, 8(2).

Behavior Change Theories

A number of research studies have attempted to identify factors associated with sexual risk reduction among gay men. The findings are not always consistent across studies, a result that we can at least partially attribute to variations in the research methods used. The studies identify a variety of factors, including the level of substance use preceding sex;[1-6] degree of social isolation;[7] existence of peer norms supportive of risk-reduction changes;[8-11] perceptions of personal susceptibility to HIV infection;[12,13,14] level of reinforcement value, or gratification, associated with high-risk behaviors;[15-18] attribution of probability of becoming infected to external factors such as chance or luck versus internal factors such as effort and ability;[19] and self-efficacy, that is, the belief in one's own ability to reduce risk.[20,21,22]

A separate body of research has examined small-group, primarily single-session, interventions to reduce high-risk sexual behavior among gay and bisexual men and other target populations. Some of the single-session interventions involve lecture and discussion of sexual risks and preventive behaviors, with limited modeling of condom use or negotiating safer sex, but these interventions include no guided practice of risk-reduction skills.[23,24,25] Others combine lecture and discussion with skills training, including role-playing, for handling high-risk situations.[26,27,28] One describes the use of a self-instructional guide and introduces a problem-solving strategy for coping with high-risk situations.[29]

Multiple-session interventions reported in the literature range from four to twelve sessions.[30-33] Most of these interventions combine lecture, discussion, guidance in identifying barriers to risk reduction and methods for dealing with those barriers, and modeling and role-playing of risk-reduction behaviors. Modeling is usually accompanied by reinforcement of successes and help in thinking about and resolving difficulties.

One or more of the four behavior change theories discussed in the sections that follow address each of the factors that the research literature associates with sexual risk reduction among gay men. The interventions reported in the literature also encompass many of the recommendations derived from these theories.

The Health Belief Model

The Health Belief Model grew out of research in the 1950s and 1960s by a group of social psychologists at the U.S. Public Health Service—Godfrey Hochbaum, Stephen Kegeles, Howard Leventhal, and Irwin Rosenstock—examining the widespread failure of people to take preventive measures against health threats.[34,35,36] Such measures included annual physical checkups and screening tests for tuberculosis and dental disease. The model postulates that individuals will take preventive health-related actions when they

- Perceive that they are personally susceptible to a disease that would have at least moderately severe negative consequences
- Perceive that taking a preventive action would be beneficial in reducing the threat of the disease and that the benefits of that action sufficiently outweigh costs such as the inconvenience and effort required, embarrassment, and financial expense
- Perceive a stimulus or "cue to action," either internal, such as perception of an uncomfortable bodily state, or external, such as mass media campaigns, newspaper articles, or personal knowledge of someone affected by the disease

The perception of threat and the occurrence of a cue to action that raises the individual's awareness of feelings of threat are what lead to the decision to act. The direction that the action takes is influenced by the individual's beliefs regarding the relative availability and effectiveness of alternatives for reducing the threat. These factors, in turn, are influenced by social norms. Demographic variables, such as age, ethnicity, and social class, influence an individual's beliefs regarding the seriousness of the disease, his or her perceived susceptibility to it, and the benefits and costs of preventive action.

Social Cognitive Theory

Albert Bandura's Social Cognitive Theory—formerly called Social Learning Theory—holds that in order to take a particular course of action, individuals must not only possess the required skills to execute the action but also believe that the action will lead to a desired outcome and that they are personally capable of performing the action.[37-40] This belief in personal capability, known as self-efficacy, is a pivotal concept.

Given that an individual possesses adequate skills and incentives to execute the desired behavior, the theory considers self-efficacy to be the primary determinant of the extent to which individuals will initiate and maintain desired behavior changes. The degree of self-efficacy influences how much effort a person will invest when taking an action, and how long he or she will persevere in the face of difficulties or disappointing results. Unlike more generalized concepts such as self-esteem or self-confidence, self-efficacy refers to the individual's beliefs about his or her ability to perform a specific desired behavior.

A person develops self-efficacy with respect to a particular behavior or action by accumulating feedback from four primary sources: personal experiences of successfully performing the behavior, vicarious experience through observing and imitating others perform the behavior ("modeling"), verbal persuasion by others who convey to the individual that he or she is capable of performing the behavior, and the individual's own physiological states.

Of these four sources, successful performance, also referred to as "mastery" experiences, is considered the most potent in raising the level of self-efficacy. Proficiency with new behaviors requires extensive practice. Ideally, practice occurs with the help of considerable external guidance, encouragement, and feedback. In order for the individual to attain a maximum level of self-efficacy, practice is structured so that he or she approaches progressively more challenging situations, followed by the gradual removal of external aids and increased opportunities for self-guided practice. Repeated failures, particularly if they occur early in the course of trying out the new behavior, can have devastating effects on self-efficacy. This problem can be minimized by starting with realistic, achievable subgoals and working gradually toward the ultimate behavioral goal. Failures and difficulties are not to be completely avoided, however; they constitute an important ingredient in the learning process. People build a strong and resilient sense of self-efficacy by overcoming setbacks through perseverance.

The second source of self-efficacy feedback—learning by modeling—is the most common way by which humans acquire new behaviors. People judge their capabilities in comparison to others whom they regard as similar to themselves. Greater degrees of similarity increase the model's personal relevance for the observer and the model's impact on the observer's judgment of his or her own self-efficacy. For example, a person who is afraid of a particular situation benefits more from seeing models overcome their own fears and the difficulties associated with the process in that situation than from observing fearless models who overcome obstacles seemingly without effort. Using multiple models with diverse characteristics increases the probability of identification with one or more models.

The third source—verbal persuasion—provides suggestions and encouragement that can lead an individual to believe that he or she is capable of performing a desired behavior. Self-efficacy expectations induced this way, however, are likely to be substantially weaker than those arising from personal mastery experiences, because persuasion does not provide a direct experience of capability. The impact of verbal persuasion on self-efficacy varies according to the perceived credibility of the persuaders.

Finally, individuals rely partly on their state of physiological arousal as the fourth source of information for judging their ability to perform desired behaviors. Because high arousal usually interferes with performance, individuals are more likely to expect success when they feel relatively free of internal agitation or tension. People can strengthen their self-efficacy by acquiring skills for reducing uncomfortable physiological reactions, such as tension and agitation, and by learning to interpret these reactions as normal rather than as signs of inefficacy.

Stages of Behavior Change Theory

In the early 1980s, James Prochaska and Carlo DiClemente outlined several fundamental stages through which individuals typically progress when making behavior changes: precontemplation, contemplation, action, and maintenance of change.[41,42,43] More recently, Prochaska and DiClemente have added a fifth stage, between contemplation and action, called preparation.[44]

Precontemplators are unaware of having a particular problem in need of change, even though others may recognize them as having a problem. They are either naively uninformed about the consequences of their behaviors, or they actively resist being informed about their problems. Precontemplators avoid changing their thinking and behavior and tend to be defensive.

Contemplators are seriously thinking about changing their behavior. They tend to be highly responsive to feedback and education as sources of information. Along with this increased openness to information about their problem behaviors, contemplators report feeling and thinking more about themselves in relationship to their problem behaviors. This increased self-evaluation can lead contemplators to become upset enough with themselves and their behaviors to make commitments to change. The contemplation stage ends at the point that a person makes a commitment to change.

In the preparation stage, individuals intend to take action in the very near future to change their behaviors. Typically, they have taken action in the recent past that has fallen short of the level of change they desired, and they are deciding how and when to proceed more effectively. The action stage involves carrying out the decision to change. Finally, the maintenance stage has to do with the stability of changes over time. People in this stage work to prevent relapse and to build on the achievements made during the action stage.

Progression through the stages is cyclical rather than linear. That is, people do not generally progress from one stage to the next; rather, they often revert to an earlier stage, which is then repeated.

Different processes of change tend to be associated with the different stages of change. For example, in the preparation stage, people tend to use counterconditioning, substituting alternatives such as relaxation or positive self-statements for the problem behaviors, and stimulus control, avoiding situations or stimuli that evoke the problem behaviors. In the action stage, individuals add three other goals: self-liberation, which focuses on their beliefs in their own capacity to change; relationship building, which garners support from others; and reinforcement management, which incorporates rewards for behavior changes. In the maintenance stage—still an active rather than a static process—people continue to rely on counterconditioning and stimulus control.

Marlatt's Relapse Prevention Model

In the mid-1980s, Alan Marlatt and his colleagues developed a cognitive-behavioral model for understanding relapse based on Social Learning (Social Cognitive) Theory.[45,46] Because it specifically addresses relapse rather than behavior change in general, the model focuses on coping responses in "high-risk situations." These are situations that pose a threat to the individual's sense of control and that increase the risk of relapse. Marlatt identifies three types of high-risk situations associated with the majority of relapse episodes: negative emotional states such as frustration, anger, anxiety, depression, or boredom; interpersonal conflict that is ongoing or relatively recent; and social pressure to engage in the taboo behavior, including the indirect pressure resulting from being in the presence of others engaging in the behavior.

If the individual effectively copes with a high-risk situation, his or her self-efficacy in dealing with such situations increases. This, in turn, increases the likelihood of effective coping in the future. If the person does not carry out a successful coping response—either because he or she lacked the required coping skills, was inhibited by fear or anxiety, or failed to recognize the risk in time to respond effectively—his or her sense of self-efficacy will be diminished. This will often be accompanied by feelings of helplessness and a tendency to passively give in to the situation. In order to cope with uncomfortable feelings associated with decreased self-efficacy, the individual may be tempted to engage in the avoided behavior, leading to an initial "lapse" or "slip." This risk is increased by the lure of the immediate gratification anticipated from engaging in the prohibited behavior.

In Marlatt's model, lapses are considered important and expected components of the behavior change process. The model views the maintenance stage, which follows the implementation of the changed behavior, as a period of "unlearning" old habits and learning new ones through a process of trial and error. Lapses in high-risk situations are beneficial to the extent that they provide corrective information about coping.

Whether a single lapse is followed by a total relapse—that is, a complete return to baseline levels of the former habit or behavior—is largely determined by how the individual reacts to the lapse.

Marlatt calls this the "abstinence violation effect." If the individual attributes the slip to the fact that the situation was a particularly difficult one or regards it as a sign that he or she needs more practice, the lapse is unlikely to lead to a relapse. On the other hand, if the person attributes it to personal weakness or failure, there is an increased risk of relapse.

Another aspect of the abstinence violation effect is the experience of cognitive dissonance resulting from the disparity between the individual's self-perception as an abstainer and the occurrence of the prohibited behavior. The dissonance creates conflict or guilt and motivates efforts to eliminate these unpleasant feelings. In an attempt to produce positive feelings to replace the unpleasant ones, the individual may engage further in the prohibited behavior. Alternately, the individual may change his or her self-image and begin thinking of himself or herself as a nonabstainer. In either of these cases, the stage is set for relapse.

Several additional cognitive factors may increase the probability of relapse. Denial allows an individual to remain ostensibly unaware of potential negative consequences of lapses. Through the "reactance effect," some individuals may perceive a commitment to abstinence as a threat to their personal freedom and choice, leading them to relapse in an attempt to free themselves from this oppression. In addition, many individuals who relapse can be seen as making a series of decisions or choices that place them in a chain of events eventually leading to an extremely tempting high-risk situation. Once in that situation, they may regard themselves as overwhelmed by the external circumstances and therefore unable to avoid a relapse.

Finally, rationalization acts to justify prohibited behavior. A common rationalization is that indulging in the behavior provides balance for the demands of everyday life. Recent research has explored rationalization in the context of self-justification. Australian psychologist Ron Gold interviewed 296 gay men who have had unprotected anal intercourse and found that 20 percent of them used self-justifications—for example, believing that unprotected anal intercourse is "OK" as long as the insertive partner withdraws before ejaculation; fearing that the use of condoms will "spoil" the sexual encounter; feeling "fed up" with having to worry about AIDS; refusing to think about AIDS; and adopting the nihilistic notion embodied in such statements as "After all the risks I've taken, I'm probably already infected, so I've got nothing to lose." Additional rationalizations included a sense of boredom, the desire for excitement, and the desire to replace feelings of sadness with "something to make me feel good."[47]

The success of new combination antiviral treatments for people with HIV disease has begun to influence the justifications some people use for engaging in unsafe behaviors. A San Francisco study of fifty-five high-risk, seronegative gay men (men who had tested HIV antibody negative at least once before and who admitted to unprotected anal insertive or receptive intercourse in the previous twelve months) included questions regarding the effects of the new treatment success on decision making.[48] Of twenty-two men responding to a separate questionnaire, 18 percent reported that at the time of a recent high-risk sexual encounter, they had the thought, "If I am exposed to HIV, I can take the new drugs (protease inhibitors, the "cocktail") that will prevent me from becoming infected."

The study also included general data on how the new treatment success affected attitudes toward prevention (although it was not explicit that these were justifications considered in the moment of relapse). Of the 55 men, 26 percent said that they were "less concerned about becoming HIV infected" because of the new treatments; 13 percent said they were more willing to take a chance of getting infected when having sex, and 15 percent stated they had already done so.

An Integrated Model

This section integrates concepts from the four behavior change theories previously discussed into a model specific to high-risk sexual behavior. The model draws from the four behavior change theories to address a wide range of reasons why gay and bisexual men might continue to have unsafe sex and to suggest strategies for how to intervene. Among these reasons are the lack of accurate information, inadequate skills, insufficient belief in the capacity to change behavior, the absence of external "cues to action" and perceived social norms, and the lack of internal readiness to change. It may be useful to compare this integrated model to other models that have been proposed to explain HIV-related changes in sexual risk behavior.[49-53]

Lack of Accurate Information

Some individuals may lack information regarding the degree of risk of their behaviors, the efficacy of preventive measures, the degree of sacrifice and the actual steps involved in carrying out preventive measures, the process of behavior change, or any combination of these factors.

Degree of Risk

Many situations demonstrate a person's lack of information about the degree to which behaviors constitute real risks to well-being. Young seronegative men may think that only older men get AIDS and that the risk is somehow significantly less or negligible for them. Men who have remained uninfected despite repeated incidents of unsafe sex may also believe that the risk is low or negligible for them. People who have not been subjected to media or personal discussions about AIDS and unsafe sex may not recognize their susceptibility to, or the gravity of, HIV infection.

Some men with HIV disease may continue to have unsafe sex with other seropositive men because they question the legitimacy of warnings against the dangers of "reinfection" by HIV. Many seropositive men may be unaware of the serious risk to their immune systems of other diseases that can be contracted through unsafe sex. Some men are unaware that some behaviors—for example, being the insertive partner during anal intercourse—involve potentially serious risks of being infected.

According to the Health Belief Model, all of these individuals may lack the perception of personal susceptibility needed to motivate effective preventive action. Social Cognitive Theory suggests that they may also lack adequate incentives for engaging in preventive behaviors.

Efficacy

A person's lack of information about the degree to which available preventive measures actually succeed in reducing the risk can lead to high-risk behavior. Many men doubt the effectiveness of condoms in preventing HIV transmission. They may have heard stories about condoms breaking or about men becoming infected presumably without having engaged in unsafe sex or other high-risk activities. As the Health Belief Model and Social Cognitive Theory assert, the belief in the efficacy of particular actions in achieving desired outcomes is a key motivating factor underlying effective implementation of those actions.

Sacrifice

For men who have had limited enjoyable experiences with condoms or with safer sex activities that do not require condoms—for example, frottage and mutual masturbation—the notion of safer sex may connote extreme sacrifice and loss of a key source of pleasure in life. According to the Health Belief Model, these men may perceive that the costs of preventive action outweigh the benefits, thus reducing the likelihood of their taking such action. This may be particularly true if they have doubts about the efficacy of safer sex behaviors or if they do not recognize their degree of susceptibility to HIV infection.

The Process of Behavior Change

Men who make attempts to use condoms or to focus on safer sex activities other than anal intercourse may prematurely stop trying if they do not understand that acquiring new behaviors normally requires practice and learning from mistakes, which entails making slips. Without this understanding, they are more likely to give up when they encounter difficulties or when they fail to perform according to their own expectations. Social Cognitive Theory and Marlatt's model both address the role of trial and error in learning and sustaining new behaviors.

Inadequate Skills

People may lack skills in using condoms, negotiating safer sex, engaging in safer sex, managing distress, dealing with high-risk situations and with slips, and disengaging from risk-associated chains of events. As Social Cognitive Theory asserts, inadequate skills will sabotage the development of self-efficacy even among those who are motivated to change their behavior and who are reasonably confident about being able to do so.

Using Condoms

Many men may be unaware of important details of condom use. These include the correct way to unroll, apply, or remove the condom, the importance of water-based versus oil-based lubricants, and the differences among brands of condoms in terms of size, texture, and taste. Others may have adequate information about use and type, but may lack sufficient practice in a variety of situations for building solid and effective skills. For example, attending one or two "safer sex" workshops where the presenter demonstrates condom use on models, even if accompanied by guided practice, is likely to be insufficient unless there is follow-up practice.

Negotiating Safer Sex

Many men lack experience talking frankly with partners about what they will and will not do during sex. As with other skills, developing comfort and efficacy in negotiating safer sex requires guided practice through trial-and-error learning.

Engaging in Safer Sex

Even though they may be aware of the range of safer sex activities that exist, many men have not had sufficient opportunities to develop their abilities and the comfort to engage in these activities in ways that are truly pleasurable to them. This lack of opportunities may strengthen any doubts they may have about the benefits versus the costs of safer sex. According to the Health Belief Model precept that action is related to a perceived cost-benefit ratio, such doubts may predict a decreased likelihood of sexual behavior change.

Managing Distress

Some people experience high levels of anxiety or tension when they contemplate or attempt using condoms, experimenting with new types of safer sex, or negotiating safer sex with a partner, and they react by feeling overwhelmed or defeated. If they lack skills in managing their distress, they may tend at least temporarily to forego further efforts to change.

Dealing with High-Risk Situations

For some men, high-risk situations may include being intoxicated while having sex or while attempting to negotiate safer sex; having sex following a period of prolonged sexual abstinence; having sex in settings they associate with high-risk sex, such as parks or sex clubs; or having sex with a partner who is exceptionally attractive to them. Because these men lack experience effectively responding to such high-risk situations, these circumstances continue to trigger unsafe sex. Marlatt's model points out that failure to respond effectively in high-risk situations reduces self-efficacy, resulting in increased distress, which in turn increases the potential for a lapse in behavior to occur.

Dealing with Slips

Even if men have heard that slips are a natural part of the behavior change process, the perceived societal pressure to avoid unsafe sex 100 percent of the time may make a single slip feel like a terrible failure. This can lead some men to give up trying. In accordance with Marlatt's model, men who have had insufficient experience "recovering" from unsafe sex slips are at increased risk of repeating their slips.

Disengaging from Risky Chains of Events

As Marlatt's model points out, we can view high-risk situations as the final link on a chain of events—a chain that can be broken. For example, an individual may typically end up going to bars to drink and look for sex on weekend evenings when he has nothing to do and is sitting at home feeling bored or frustrated about his work. Alternatives would require interrupting the pattern by identifying enjoyable interests or activities that do not involve drinking, seeking help for a possible drinking problem, or making weekend plans in advance with friends.

Insufficient Belief in Capability to Change

Whether or not they possess necessary information and skills, individuals may lack a sense of self-efficacy: they may question their ability to carry out changes in behavior. For instance, an individual may feel that he cannot effectively use condoms, especially when his partner seems to want to avoid using them. Or, fearing that his partner will lose interest in him, he may feel incapable of saying that he wants to limit the couple's sexual activities to safer sex. According to Social Cognitive Theory, low self-efficacy can arise from insufficient experience with mastering a behavior, inadequate exposure to credible models, or agitation that gets interpreted as inadequacy.

Absence of External "Cues" and Perceived Social Norms

The Health Belief Model emphasizes the importance of "cues to action" in motivating prevention behaviors. In the absence of sufficient environmental cues, a person may not develop an awareness of the need to act without delay. Many men in large urban areas may have stopped attending to the safer sex media messages that captured their attention during the early years of the epidemic. In some cases, long-standing media messages may no longer be compelling; new messages as well as new methods of disseminating the messages may be required.

The Stages of Behavioral Change Theory recognizes the importance of being able to rely on the support of helping relationships in order to sustain momentum after making a commitment to action. Relatively isolated gay and bisexual men without supportive peer networks to reinforce positive behavior changes are therefore likely to have difficulty maintaining changes over time.

For gay and bisexual men living in places without a strong and visible gay community, safer sex messages in the media may be scarce or weak, and peer norms reinforcing the need for safer sex may be rare or absent. For gay and bisexual youth, peer norms may not consistently and strongly reinforce safer sex and may, in some cases, convey approval of continued unsafe sex.

Furthermore, some individuals may perceive strong safer sex social norms in one context (for example, at home with a new sex partner) but not in another context (for example, in a public sex environment such as a sex club). Gold cites recent research suggesting that for a number of gay men, the stronger their link to the gay community—and, presumably, the greater their exposure to peer norms promoting safer sex—the more likely they are to engage in unsafe sex.[54] The reasons for this unexpected finding are unclear, but it suggests that in addition to peer norms, one's degree of motivation to comply with peer norms influences behavior.

Lack of Internal Readiness to Change

The Stages of Behavior Change Theory implies that many people, at various times in their lives, may be psychologically unready to commit to change. This may be true even for those who have been exposed to considerable information about risk and who recognize the consequences of postponing change. For this reason, attempts to even enter into a dialogue about changing behavior are likely to fail.

Others may be contemplating changing their behaviors but may be resistant to pressure to act immediately. They may need more time to accumulate information and fully evaluate risks and alternative courses of action. Many who are feeling the effects of loss and grief may lack the motivation to invest effort in changing behavior for the sake of long-term goals. As psychologist Walt Odets has described, people who have experienced multiple losses and grief may come to feel hopeless about the future.[55,56] As a consequence, they may regard the idea of surviving the AIDS epidemic as neither favorable or desirable and may view becoming infected as a way to avoid such a fate. Another possible explanation for such a lack of motivation to change is Marlatt's notion that people may rationalize their continuing engagement in high-risk behaviors as a way of balancing the burdens and demands of everyday life.

Guidelines for Intervention

A central implication of this overview of behavior change theories is the need to identify the obstacles to unsafe sex before implementing prevention interventions. Providing a homogeneous intervention to a heterogeneous target population will likely help some, alienate others, and discourage the many who fail to respond because their particular needs are not addressed.

Among any particular pool of gay and bisexual men recruited to participate in a risk-reduction intervention—for example, counseling, a safer sex workshop, or a support group—there will be a broad mix of types. Some men will be motivated to change but lack essential information about risks or about alternative behaviors. Others will have adequate information but lack skills or confidence to implement low-risk behaviors. Still others may be well informed and have the necessary skills and confidence but lack the internal motivation to commit to change or a supportive peer network that provides models and norms reinforcing sustained behavior changes. Each of these subgroups requires specific types of help. By carefully screening clients prior to implementing interventions, counselors can ensure that individuals receive appropriate support.

For those who lack basic information, interventions should include the necessary education in areas where participants are deficient. Ideally, this education will be provided by credible presenters with whom the participants can easily identify. Those with information deficits are also likely to be deficient in one or more skills related to risk reduction. Modeling of risk-reduction behaviors, again preferably by people who share many characteristics with the participants—including some degree of anxiety—will enhance skill acquisition. Structured practice over time, which incorporates opportunities for coping with failures, will build resiliency. Counselors can enhance such an intervention by providing or promoting a peer support network that encourages and reinforces low-risk behaviors.

Individuals lacking the internal motivation to change their sexual behavior require different approaches. Those who are not even considering change are unlikely to have sustained interest in interventions clearly designed to promote sexual behavior change. They may be more amenable to participating in less specific interventions, such as counseling aimed at dealing with painful emotions or other areas of personal concern, or social activities that will put them into contact with peers who may eventually influence them to consider changes. Those who are contemplating or preparing for change would likely benefit from opportunities to talk about their decision-making process and considerations and to observe others at the same stage, opportunities that would promote modeling of decision making and exchange of information about how best to proceed. For those who lack a supportive peer network that establishes and reinforces norms encouraging low-risk sexual behavior, interventions should mobilize the formation of such a network rather than simply transmit information or teach skills.

Theory is often easier said than done, and applying several theories at once can daunt the most committed counselor. Case examples offer the opportunity to test out and practice theoretical approaches. The following two cases deal with two central aspects of HIV prevention: acknowledging risk and interrupting a pattern of unsafe behavior.

Jimmy: Acknowledging Risk

Jimmy is a twenty-two-year-old seronegative man who finally agrees to join an eight-session HIV-related support group after having been urged to do so for several months by a close friend, Tom. Most of Jimmy's friends are sexually active with multiple partners, and using condoms with anal sex is the exception rather than the rule. Jimmy, like his friends, finds anal sex without condoms to be much easier and more pleasurable, and he frequently has unprotected anal intercourse. He does not seem to be particularly worried about this behavior and feels that Tom's concerns are overblown.

Jimmy is understandably resistant to participating in the group but, encouraged upon learning that others in the group also have unsafe sex and question the need to change behavior, he decides to continue coming to the meetings. Jimmy reaches a turning point in the second session of the group, when one of the other group members discloses that he became infected with HIV at age nineteen, having had unprotected anal intercourse only a few times. Others in the group report knowing men around Jimmy's same age who have become infected. Jimmy is motivated by these incidents to ask a few HIV-knowledgeable acquaintances about the frequency of young men becoming infected, and the information he gathers is consistent with the reports of the members of the group.

By the fifth session of the group, Jimmy still expresses skepticism about changing his behavior but has actively begun to solicit information about HIV infection and unsafe sex from other group members. Although he has always disliked condoms, after the group spends almost an entire session practicing placing condoms on dildos and giving each other encouragement, Jimmy feels confident enough to commit to using condoms with a supportive sexual partner who understands that he is "learning."

When he returns to the group the following week, Jimmy reports that he still needs practice with condoms and intends to continue experimenting with them. Group members laugh as they share stories about the mishaps and embarrassments they experienced when trying out condoms. Jimmy also reports that despite feeling more comfortable using condoms, he is having trouble insisting on condoms with partners who want to have unprotected anal sex.

Other group members give understanding nods. The facilitator guides the group through a number of role-plays. In each role-play, group members set up the scene to depict a situation in which it would be especially difficult for them to negotiate safer sex. Whenever a participant in a role-play feels "stuck," the action is temporarily stopped, and other group members are invited to give suggestions or to enter the role-play and try out their approach.

At the final session of the group, Jimmy reports that he failed to insist on safer sex during his most recent sexual encounter. He notes, however, that he realizes how he could have handled the situation differently and intends to use this information to help him in such situations in the future. The group members exchange phone numbers, and Jimmy looks forward to keeping in touch with those in the group whom he regards as new friends.

The group was helpful to Jimmy in a number of ways. It provided him with needed information about risk and personal susceptibility, as prescribed by the Health Belief Model, and about how to carry out lower-risk behaviors. In witnessing other group members in similar circumstances trying to change, he came to appreciate that developing new behaviors takes time and practice (an important component of Social Cognitive Theory) and that setbacks can be opportunities for learning rather than signs of failure (a crucial understanding in terms of Social Cognitive Theory and Marlatt's model). Jimmy received guided practice in new behaviors during the group meetings, and encouragement from the group members to continue practicing outside the meetings. As he began taking action to change, he used the support of his peers in the group and the reinforcement provided by their encouragement to persist in his efforts to change, conforming to the Stages of Behavior Change Theory. Finally, by allowing him the time he needed to accumulate information, evaluate his risks and alternative courses of action, and arrive at a commitment to change on his own, the group respected the Stages of Behavior Change—that change is a process rather than an instantaneous event.

Michael: Interrupting the Pattern of Unsafe Sex

Michael is a forty-year-old seronegative man who seeks safer sex counseling at a local AIDS organization because he has concerns about occasional slips into unsafe sex. He has often felt emotionally drained and depressed since his lover's death eighteen months ago. Michael says he generally feels optimistic about being able to go on with his life, but sometimes he gets the urge to escape, and he lets go of his inhibitions and has anal sex without protection.

Michael weeps during his first counseling session as he describes missing his lover and the other friends who have died. He explains that he has rarely used condoms and that he never used them with his lover. Two things are readily apparent to the counselor: Michael is suffering grief and perhaps depression associated with the death of his lover and friends, and he has not had much experience using condoms.

Michael accepts the counselor's referral to a therapist with expertise in the area of grief and loss, and he later joins a ten-week grief support group facilitated by the therapist. He agrees with the safer sex counselor that he may need more practice using condoms, and they use time in one of the early sessions practicing putting condoms on a dildo.

During the following month, Michael hesitatingly admits to the counselor that he slipped the week before and had unprotected anal intercourse. He feels devastated by the slip, expressing doubts that he can ever change. When Michael mentions that he has several friends who have stopped having unprotected anal intercourse, the counselor suggests that he ask a few of them about the process they went through trying to change. Michael discovers that a good friend had several slips during the first months of his efforts to change.

Michael subsequently reveals that, despite earlier denials, he does have concerns about the amount of alcohol he drinks. He admits that when he has unsafe sex, it is usually when he is intoxicated. In response to the gentle but persistent efforts of both his therapist and the counselor, Michael eventually makes a commitment to stop drinking. Over the course of the following month, he slips twice, and both times counseling helps Michael identify what led to the slip and how he might handle things differently in the future.

During this period, his counselor also realizes that Michael is afraid to initiate safer sex with the men he typically meets in bars. He and his counselor discuss alternative ways to meet men, and Michael decides to consider joining a gay club as a way to meet friends and potential sexual partners.

Individual counseling provided Michael with an opportunity to begin to release painful feelings of grief in a setting where he

felt heard and respected. The resulting rapport is likely what motivated him in large part to accept the counselor's suggestions to seek therapy and to acknowledge his alcohol problem. By refraining from pressuring Michael to commit to complete abstinence from unsafe sex, the counselor allowed Michael to proceed at his own pace through the Stages of Behavior Change: contemplation, preparation, and action.

Similarly, support and encouragement to get help for his alcohol problem allowed Michael to interrupt one chain of events—drinking followed by sex—that repeatedly led to unsafe behavior. Guided practice in using condoms, along with encouragement to explore additional avenues of sexual activity, helped increase his sense of self-efficacy to avoid unsafe sex and to enjoy alternatives. Support in viewing his slips as natural elements of the behavior change process decreased his self-criticism and pessimism and increased his confidence in his ability to keep trying, a result predicted by both Social Cognitive Theory and Marlatt's model. Perhaps equally important, counseling enabled Michael to expand his social contacts, reducing his isolation and increasing his exposure to new peer norms that could reinforce his behavior changes.

∽

Behavior theory points to the wide variety of reasons that can account for a person's failure to avoid high-risk sexual behavior. Before intervening, counselors should first attempt to identify the obstacles to change that are specific to each individual. Simply providing general information, persuasion, and a limited amount of practice with generic behaviors (such as using condoms) may fail to address these specific obstacles.

Behavior change theories emphasize several factors in motivating behavior change. These include awareness of the need for and the benefits of change, practice in the skills for implementing new behaviors in a variety of settings, and confidence in the capacity to engage in and maintain new behaviors in light of changing circumstances and setbacks or failures. Being aware of this complexity of factors should help practitioners more precisely identify problems and select suitable interventions.

Notes

1. Ekstrand, M. L., and Coates, T. J. "Maintenance of Safer Sexual Behaviors and Predictors of Risky Sex: The San Francisco Men's Health Study." *American Journal of Public Health*, 1990, *80*(8), 973–977.

2. Kelly, J. A., Kalichman, S. C., Kauth, M. R., and others. "Situational Factors Associated with AIDS Risk Behavior Lapses and Coping Strategies Used by Gay Men Who Successfully Avoid Lapses." *American Journal of Public Health*, 1991, *81*(10), 1335–1338.

3. Kelly, J. A., St. Lawrence, J. S., and Brasfield, T. L. "Predictors of Vulnerability to AIDS Risk Behavior Relapse." *Journal of Consulting and Clinical Psychology*, 1991, *59*(1), 163–166.

4. McCusker, J., Westenhouse, J., Stoddard, A. M., and others. "Use of Drugs and Alcohol by Homosexually Active Men in Relation to Sexual Practices." *Journal of Acquired Immune Deficiency Syndromes*, 1990, *3*(7), 729–736.

5. McCusker, J., Stoddard, A. M., McDonald, M., and others. "Maintenance of Behavior Change in a Cohort of Homosexually Active Men." *AIDS*, 1992, *6*(8), 861–868.

6. Stall, R., McKusick, L., Wiley, J., and others. "Alcohol and Drug Use During Sexual Activity and Compliance with Safe Sex Guidelines for AIDS: The AIDS Behavioral Research Project." *Health Education Quarterly*, 1986, *13*(4), 359–371.

7. Prieur, A. "Norwegian Gay Men: Reasons for Continued Practice of Unsafe Sex." *AIDS Education and Prevention*, 1990, *2*(2), 109–115.

8. Joseph, J. G., Montgomery, S. B., Emmons, C., and others. "Magnitude and Determinants of Behavioral Risk Reduction: Longitudinal Analysis of a Cohort at Risk for AIDS." *Psychology and Health*, 1987, *1*(1), 73–96.

9. McKusick, L., Coates, T. J., Morin, S. F., and others. "Longitudinal Predictors of Reductions in Unprotected Anal Intercourse Among Gay Men in San Francisco: The AIDS Behavioral Research Project." *American Journal of Public Health*, 1990, *80*(8), 978–983.

10. Stall, R., Ekstrand, M., Pollack, L., and others. "Relapse from Safer Sex: The Next Challenge for AIDS Prevention Efforts." *Journal of Acquired Immune Deficiency Syndromes*, 1990, *3*(12), 1181–1187.

11. Centers for Disease Control. "Patterns of Sexual Behavior Change Among Homosexual/Bisexual Men: Selected U.S. Sites, 1987–1990." *Morbidity and Mortality Weekly Report*, 1991, *40*(46), 792–794.

12. Aspinwall, L. G., Kemeny, M. E., Taylor, S. E., and others. "Psychosocial Predictors of Gay Men's AIDS Risk-Reduction Behavior." *Health Psychology*, 1991, *10*(6), 432–444.

13. Emmons, C., Joseph, J. G., Kessler, R. C., and others. "Psychosocial Predictors of Reported Behavior Change in Homosexual Men at Risk for AIDS." *Health Education Quarterly,* 1986, *13*(4), 331–345.

14. McCusker, J., Stoddard, A. M., Zapka, J. G., and others. "Predictors of AIDS-Preventive Behavior Among Homosexually Active Men: A Longitudinal Study." *AIDS,* 1989, *3*(7), 443–448.

15. Kelly, Kalichman, Kauth, and others, "Situational Factors."

16. Kelly, St. Lawrence, and Brasfield, "Predictors of Vulnerability."

17. McKusick, Coates, Morin, and others, "Longitudinal Predictors of Reductions."

18. Stall, Ekstrand, Pollack, and others, "Relapse from Safer Sex."

19. Kelly, St. Lawrence, and Brasfield, "Predictors of Vulnerability."

20. McKusick, Coates, Morin, and others, "Longitudinal Predictors of Reductions."

21. Centers for Disease Control, "Patterns of Sexual Behavior Change."

22. Aspinwall, Kemeny, Taylor, and others, "Psychosocial Predictors."

23. Flowers, J. V., Booraem, C., Miller, T. E., and others. "Comparison of the Results of a Standardized AIDS Prevention Program in Three Geographic Locations." *AIDS Education and Prevention,* 1991, *3*(3), 189–196.

24. Shulkin, J. J., Mayer, J. A., Wessel, L. G., and others. "Effects of a Peer-Led AIDS Intervention with University Students." *Journal of American College Health,* 1991, *40*(2), 75–79.

25. Valdiserri, R. O., Lyter, D. W., Kingsley, L. A., and others. "The Effect of Group Education on Improving Attitudes About AIDS Risk Reduction." *New York State Journal of Medicine,* 1987, *87*(5), 272–278.

26. Jemmott, J. B., Jemmott, L. S., and Fong, G. T. "Reductions in HIV Risk-Associated Sexual Behaviors Among Black Male Adolescents: Effects of an AIDS Prevention Intervention." *American Journal of Public Health,* 1992, *82*(3), 372–377.

27. Leviton, L. C., Valdiserri, R. O., Lyter, D. W., and others. "Preventing HIV Infection in Gay and Bisexual Men: Experimental Evaluation of Attitude Change from Two Risk Reduction Interventions." *AIDS Education and Prevention,* 1990, *2*(2), 95–108.

28. Valdiserri, R. O., Lyter, D. W., Leviton, L. C., and others. "AIDS Prevention in Homosexual and Bisexual Men: Results of a Randomized Trial Evaluating Two Risk Reduction Interventions." *AIDS,* 1989, *3*(1), 21–26.

29. Schinke, S. P., Gordon, A. N., and Weston, R. E. "Self-Instruction to Prevent HIV Infection Among African-American and Hispanic-American Adolescents." *Journal of Consulting and Clinical Psychology,* 1990, *58*(4), 432–436.

30. Kelly, J. A., St. Lawrence, J. S., Betts, R., and others. "A Skills-Training Group Intervention Model to Assist Persons in Reducing Risk Behaviors for HIV Infection." *AIDS Education and Prevention*, 1990, *2*(1), 24–35.

31. Kelly, J. A., St. Lawrence, J. S., Hood, H. V., and others. "Behavioral Intervention to Reduce AIDS Risk Activities." *Journal of Consulting and Clinical Psychology*, 1989, *57*(1), 60–67.

32. Rhodes, F., Wolitski, R. J., and Thornton-Johnson, S. "An Experiential Program to Reduce AIDS Risk Among Female Partners of Injection-Drug Users." *Health and Social Work*, 1992, *17*(4), 261–272.

33. Schilling, R. F., El Bassel, N., Schinke, S. P., and others. "Building Skills of Recovering Women Drug Users to Reduce Heterosexual AIDS Transmission." *Public Health Reports*, 1991, *106*(3), 297–303.

34. Becker, M. H. (ed.). "The Health Belief Model and Personal Health Behavior." *Health Education Monographs*, 1974, *2*(4), 324–473.

35. Becker, M. H., Drachman, R. H., and Kirscht, J. P. "A New Approach to Explaining Sick-Role Behavior in Low-Income Populations." *American Journal of Public Health*, 1974, *64*(3), 205–216.

36. Janz, N. K., and Becker, M. H. "The Health Belief Model: A Decade Later." *Health Education Quarterly*, 1984, *11*(1), 1–47.

37. Bandura, A. "Self-Efficacy: Toward a Unifying Theory of Behavior Change." *Psychological Review*, 1977, *84*(2), 191–215.

38. Bandura, A. *Social Learning Theory*. Upper Saddle River, N.J.: Prentice Hall, 1977.

39. Bandura, A. *Social Foundations of Thought and Action: A Social Cognitive Theory*. Upper Saddle River, N.J.: Prentice Hall, 1986.

40. Bandura, A. "Perceived Self-Efficacy in the Exercise of Control over AIDS Infection." In V. M. Mays, G. W. Albee, and S. F. Schneider (eds.), *The Primary Prevention of AIDS: Psychological Approaches*. Thousand Oaks, Calif.: Sage, 1989.

41. Prochaska, J. O., and DiClemente, C. C. "Transtheoretical Therapy: Toward a More Integrated Model of Change." *Psychotherapy Theory, Research, and Practice*, 1982, *19*(3), 276–288.

42. Prochaska, J. O., and DiClemente, C. C. "Stages and Processes of Self-Change of Smoking: Toward an Integrative Model of Change." *Journal of Consulting and Clinical Psychology*, 1983, *51*(3), 390–395.

43. Prochaska, J. O., and DiClemente, C. C. *The Transtheoretical Approach: Crossing Traditional Boundaries of Therapy*. Howewood, Ill.: Dow Jones/Irwin, 1984.

44. Prochaska, J. O., DiClemente, C. C., and Norcross, J. C. "In Search of How People Change." *American Psychologist*, 1992, *47*(9), 1102–1114.

45. Marlatt, A., and George, W. "Relapse Prevention: Introduction and Overview of the Model." *British Journal of Addiction*, 1984, *79*(3), 261–273.
46. Marlatt, A., and Gordon, J. R. (eds.). *Relapse Prevention: Maintenance Strategies in Addictive Behavior Change*. New York: Guilford Press, 1985.
47. Gold, R. S., Skinner, M. J., and Ross, M. W. "Unprotected Anal Intercourse in HIV-Infected and Non-HIV Infected Gay Men." *Journal of Sex Research*, 1994, *31*(1), 59–77.
48. Dilley, J. W., Woods, W., and McFarland, W. "Advances in HIV Medical Treatment and High Risk Sexual Behavior." Letter. *New England Journal of Medicine*, 1997, *337*(7), 501–502.
49. Catania, J. A., Kegeles, S. M., and Coates, T. J. "Towards an Understanding of Risk Behavior: An AIDS Risk Reduction Model (ARRM)." *Health Education Quarterly*, 1990, *17*(1), 53–72.
50. Catania, J. A., Coates, T. J., and Kegeles, S. M. "A Test of the AIDS Risk Reduction Model: Psychosocial Correlates of Condom Use in the AMEN Cohort Survey." *Health Psychology*, 1994, *13*(6), 1–8.
51. Fisher, J. D., and Fisher, W. A. "Changing AIDS-Risk Behavior." *Psychological Bulletin*, 1992, *111*(3), 455–474.
52. Fisher, J. D., Fisher, W. A., Williams, S. S., and others. "Empirical Tests of an Information-Motivation-Behavioral Skills Model of AIDS-Preventive Behavior with Gay Men and Heterosexual University Students." *Health Psychology*, 1994, *13*(3), 238–250.
53. Fisher, W. A., Fisher, J. D., Williams, S. S., and others. "Testing the Information-Motivation-Behavioral Skills Model with Minority High School Students." Unpublished manuscript, University of Western Ontario, 1993.
54. Gold, R. S. "Gay Community Links and Safety." *Focus: A Guide to AIDS Research and Counseling*, 1995, *10*(3), 5–6.
55. Odets, W. "Seronegative Gay Men and Considerations of Unsafe and Unsafe Sex." In S. A. Caldwell, R. A. Burnham, and M. Forstein (eds.), *Therapists on the Front Line: Psychotherapy with Gay Men in the Age of AIDS*. Washington, D.C.: American Psychiatric Press, 1994.
56. Odets, W. "Why We Stopped Doing Primary Prevention for Gay Men in 1985." *AIDS and Public Policy Journal*, forthcoming.

Chapter Four

A Developmental Perspective on Behavior Change

Mark Hochhauser
Thomas A. Beaumont

Why do people behave the way they do? One way to answer this question is to study the continuing process of human development: of how a person changes and how he or she stays the same over time.[1] Behavior change must include a developmental component, because the ability to understand HIV risk-reduction messages and to change sexual and drug-using behaviors is determined by levels of cognitive, psychological, and moral development.

Development is a lifelong process, and a developmental perspective can be useful in designing HIV prevention approaches for people in all age groups. However, development is most apparent during adolescence and youth, and understanding development is particularly important for educators and counselors seeking to understand the motivations of younger people. Too often, HIV-related behavior change approaches are based more on what is known about AIDS than on what is known about a target population. Communicating with adolescents and young adults involves more than just simplifying a message that seems to work for adults: it requires an understanding of development.

This chapter, which focuses on younger people but is applicable to all age groups, defines theories of cognitive, psychological, and moral development, identifies the major proponents of these theories, and discusses how these theories relate to HIV prevention and prevention counseling. Psychological development addresses how issues such as personal identity and intimacy develop over time. In particular, two of Erik Erikson's eight developmental "crises" are central to behavior change. A cognitive developmental approach, exemplified by the works of Jean Piaget and of Roger Bibace and Mary Walsh, "focuses not on what people know, but rather on how they understand."[2] Finally, theories of moral development, as reflected in the work of Lawrence Kohlberg and Carol Gilligan, describe how a person's perspectives on what is "right" and "wrong" change on the basis of age, experience, and perhaps even gender, and how these changes affect behavior.

Although these developmental perspectives are central to understanding behavior change, individual, group, and cultural differences make it difficult to define absolute developmental stages and draw firm conclusions about behavior. Even a basic concept such as *adolescence* is defined variously by different cultures, and this is reflected in research. For example, Laurence Steinberg defines adolescence in terms of three subperiods ranging from ages ten to nineteen.[3] Other researchers consider adolescence as one homogeneous period running from age eleven to eighteen.[4] There are many pieces to the developmental puzzle, which in the solving turns out to be a Rubik's cube, with an almost infinite number of combinations. Nonetheless, because a person's understanding of HIV disease is based on his or her development, an awareness of developmental tendencies is critical to effective HIV prevention.

Psychological Development: Identity and Intimacy

Although there are several perspectives on adolescent and young adult development, Erik Erikson's theory (one of the earliest) serves as a good introduction to the basic issues of psychological development. Erikson identified eight "crises" that an individual may confront throughout life and concluded that healthy development is achieved if a person successfully resolves these crises; unsuccessful resolution produces psychological distress. This section will focus on the two crises that Erikson identified as being relevant to adolescence and young adulthood.

Identity Versus Role Confusion: Who Am I?

For Erikson, a major aspect of adolescent development is the resolution of a crisis he defines as "identity versus role confusion."[5] During this time, a typical adolescent works to answer the question, Who am I? He or she develops a sense of self by testing a variety of roles—including sexual ones—and integrating these different roles to form a single identity. If HIV prevention programs try to discourage role testing because, for example, such testing is considered "risky," will adolescents be able to develop coherent identities? Identity is not achieved by having people tell you who you are; it is discovered by finding out who you are.

As identity develops, so do the elements of trust and self-understanding, creating the potential for relationships that are based on mutual caring and need fulfillment. If these two elements do not develop, relationships may involve "using" others and not "caring" about them. In particular, trust, identity, and self-understanding have powerful implications for the counseling experience, insofar as the client can understand his or her relationship with the counselor as well as with others in his or her life.

Erikson's perspective was exclusively heterosexual, hence his belief that identity formation was primarily an activity of adolescence and early adulthood. For gay men and lesbians, however, identity formation is likely to be achieved somewhat later, perhaps in the mid- to late twenties or even later.[6] Prevention messages targeted specifically toward gay men and lesbians will be effective only for those who have achieved a gay or lesbian identity; such messages are likely to be virtually irrelevant to those who are still struggling to define sexual identity. This insight has two important implications for efforts at prevention: messages aimed at "gay teens" may not reach many young men who are having sex with men but who do not perceive themselves as "gay"; and gay adults may continue in "adolescent" identity development beyond adolescence.

In response, in the same way that mass marketing targets specific messages to specific segments of a consumer audience, client-centered counseling approaches, which already acknowledge the individuality of each client, are best served by a deeper understanding of a client's psychological development. This understanding enables the counselor to respond in ways that are not only consistent with a client's values and beliefs but also developmentally comprehensible to that client. Further, client-centered counseling approaches must acknowledge and address issues of social class and educational level, as differences in these areas may affect the expression of sexual identity.[7]

Likewise, substance use during adolescence may complicate and delay psychological development. For example, in a longitudinal study of adolescent drug use from the mid-1970s to the present, Peter Bentler found that "heavy drug use as a teenager, in turn, further interferes with the mastery of critical developmental tasks, such as formation of a prosocial behavior identity [behavior based on helping and sharing done to benefit other people without an expected reward], gaining interpersonal and educational skills, and learning to take on family and work role responsibilities. Thus, drug users may develop a pseudomaturity that does not adequately prepare them for the real difficulties of adult life."[8]

Intimacy Versus Isolation: How Close Can I Get?

The word *intimacy* is often used as a euphemism for sexual intercourse. Psychologically, intimacy relates to personal disclosure: the ability to reveal parts of the self that are normally hidden from others. Although sexual intimacy and psychological intimacy often go together, the distinction between the two is important, and confusing sexual intimacy with psychological intimacy has important implications for prevention.

Erikson defined the crisis of intimacy versus isolation as one of early adulthood. Young adults need and want intimacy, a deep personal commitment to another. The inability to achieve such intimacy may produce isolation and self-centeredness. Moreover, the capacity for intimacy is based on a sense of identity (usually acquired in adolescence), which can serve as a source for evaluating the correctness or incorrectness of personal choices. Without a strong identity, one is unable to be intimate. Trust and intimacy are central not only to self-definition but also to successful interpersonal and counseling relationships.

Erikson limited intimacy to heterosexual relationships that produced children, having excluded other lifestyles—homosexual, celibate, single, childless—from his analysis of "healthy" development.

Despite these omissions, his understanding of identity formation and intimacy development have important implications for HIV prevention. For example, will irrational fear of HIV cause adolescents to test fewer roles, take fewer risks, and thus make it more difficult for them to discover their identity? Distrust of others, when combined with a lack of self-definition, may make intimacy difficult or impossible. Although safer sex messages that focus on sexual abstinence may keep adolescents physically healthy, such messages may have a negative impact on the healthy development of identity, trust, intimacy, and sexuality. An abstinence-based approach also fails to take into account the importance of touch as a human experience, and the physical, psychological, and social implications for people who are not able to touch, or be touched, for years at a time. Fear and distrust engendered in all these ways may be hard to overcome later in life.

Erikson also identifies a crisis of middle adulthood: "generativity" (being productive in a meaningful way; caring for children; guiding the next generation) versus "stagnation" (feeling empty and without purpose). From the standpoint of HIV prevention, a middle-aged adult in the generativity phase should be concerned with the health of young people, whereas an adult in the stagnation phase may feel no particular responsibility to the next generation. Although Erikson's approach gives some insight into the connections among generations, it does not address how this crisis could be used to guide HIV prevention efforts for adults. For example, a "stagnating" middle-aged adult—who is likely to be self-absorbed, self-indulgent, and bored—will probably focus on his or her own gratification and fail to take responsibility for actions toward sexual partners. Shifting from stagnation to generativity requires a belief in the future and the ability to care about others. Generativity and responsibility go hand in hand.

Cognitive Development: Concrete Versus Abstract Thinking

Whereas psychological development focuses primarily on a person's relationship to the self, cognitive development determines a person's relationship to the outside world. Thinking changes with age; that is, thought processes evolve over time. Jean Piaget's work demonstrated, for instance, that young people go from a period of concrete thinking to one of more abstract thinking. The central difference between these two periods is the degree to which a person is able to conceive of a reality beyond the immediate. Concrete thinkers focus on the here and now, on using logic to solve only immediate problems, and on things they can perceive. For example, concrete thinking may emphasize "things" such as consumer goods that allow a young person to compare himself or herself to others. Abstract thinkers are able to imagine—to think in terms of possibilities and the consequences of their behavior. Their comparisons with others are likely to be based more on values and ways of thinking than on immediate experiences or tangible objects. These distinctions are crucial to HIV prevention, and, in applying Piaget's theories, Roger Bibace and Mary Walsh conclude that people cannot even understand the concept of prevention, much less implement behavior change, until they reach a certain level of cognitive maturity.

What Do People Understand?

In order to understand how young people conceive of illness and, more recently, of AIDS, Bibace and Walsh have expanded on Piaget's approach. In their early work, Bibace and Walsh identified three stages—preoperational, concrete operational, and formal operational—that put conceptions of illness into the context of cognitive development (see Table 4.1).[9,10] They found that some people progressed through these developmental stages and others did not: hence, some adults may apply concrete as well as abstract approaches to thinking. A summary of their findings offers insights into how people at different ages may understand important health concepts—in particular, what causes illness.

In more recent work, Bibace and Walsh examined how children at the preoperational (ages five to seven), concrete operational (ages eight to ten), and formal operational (ages eleven to thirteen) stages think about HIV infection. The five- to seven-year-olds understand AIDS in terms of "association." That is, they explain AIDS as an association with an event, or person, or object. For example, having heard that a person with AIDS "throws up," a child concludes that the "throwing up" causes AIDS. This reflects

Table 4.1. Bibace and Walsh's Stages of Cognitive Development.

Period	Age	Example
Preoperational	2–6	Phenomenism: illness comes from external source (example: God causes colds)
		Contagion: illness comes from objects or people (example: other people cause colds)
Concrete operational	7–12	Contamination: illness due to external and harmful source (example: colds come from not wearing a hat)
		Internalization: illness is in the body but is caused by outside source (example: colds come from breathing germs)
Formal operational	12+	Physiological reasoning: external cause for internal illness (example: a virus causes colds)
		Psychophysiological reasoning: physical explanation for illness (example: virus causes cold; stress lowers resistance)

Source: Adapted from R. Bibace and M. E. Walsh, "Development of Children's Conceptions of Illness." Reproduced by permission of *Pediatrics,* Volume 66 (1980), pages 912–917.

"magical thinking" and suggests that prevention efforts for people at this stage of development need to address vague fears about being magically victimized by AIDS.[11]

Older children, ages eight to ten, who are more likely to be concrete thinkers, attribute HIV infection to a specific sequential experience that is bad for the body. Bibace and Walsh cite the child who concludes that "you get AIDS from falling into a puddle that someone with AIDS fell into before and they had a cut. And if you have a cut, it goes in yours and you get AIDS all over you." At this stage, children may describe AIDS in terms of internal body symptoms, but these descriptions are not very specific.

The oldest children, ages eleven to thirteen, understand HIV infection as an interactive process. "You get AIDS from a virus that gets into your bloodstream. It causes your immune system to stop fighting germs. Then, when another germ gets into your system, like pneumonia, the immune system can't fight it and you get very sick and may even die from the pneumonia."

Such developmental factors have been identified by other researchers as well. One study found that even though elementary school children may know the facts about AIDS, they do not necessarily understand those facts.[12] It also found that although about 25 percent mentioned drugs as a cause of AIDS, when pressed for specific examples, some listed cigarettes, alcohol, cocaine, and marijuana. Another study found that 19 percent of the high school students surveyed believed that HIV infection could be spread by sex between two uninfected people![13]

Clearly, comprehension of the symptoms of HIV disease seems to follow a characteristic developmental progression.[14] Children know and understand more about colds than they do about AIDS, probably because they have more experience with colds than they do with HIV disease. However, with increased education, it is possible to improve a child's understanding of HIV disease so that it matches his or her level of understanding of the common cold—but this can happen only if school-based HIV education programs are more closely linked to the developmental level of the child.

David Schonfeld adds to Bibace and Walsh's formulation by connecting children's explanations of illness to the concept of "immanent justice"—a belief that justice comes from inanimate objects and that misbehaviors will be punished.[15] If a child perceives illness as punishment, then he or she will likely feel guilt and shame for being sick.

Although these analyses deal primarily with the conception of illness by children, adult thinking may reside at any of these three levels. For example, for some adults, AIDS is due to immanent justice—not to HIV infection. Bibace and Walsh recount the story of a police officer who was afraid to handcuff a prostitute for fear that he might get AIDS from touching her, an example of "contamination," which reflects a form of concrete operational thinking.[16] They concluded that the police officer's cognitive development did not allow him to understand the concept of prevention. Such magical thinking occurs even among college students who are well informed of the "facts about AIDS." One study found that a majority of students believed that eating with silverware previously used by someone with AIDS would be a risky experience—even if the silverware had been washed and even if the person with AIDS had used the silverware a year earlier.[17] An obvious implication of this finding is that a one-size-fits-all approach to HIV prevention is unlikely to fit everyone equally well.

An adjunct to Bibace and Walsh's work, a survey of fifth, seventh, and tenth graders, identified two general concerns about AIDS: the disease effects and the social effects.[18] Disease effects included the lethality of AIDS, the magnitude of the disease, personal vulnerability to AIDS, helplessness if you have the disease, and uncertainty about whether someone has AIDS or not. Social effects included compassion for and victimization of those who have AIDS, phobias about people with AIDS, restrictions on sexual behavior because of fear of AIDS, ignorance about AIDS, and irresponsible behavior by people who do not take precautions. Although students at all ages were upset about the disease effects of AIDS, older adolescents tended to be more upset by its social aspects. In addition, whereas fifth graders were more concerned about the lethality of AIDS, tenth graders were more concerned about being helpless in the face of AIDS.

Even without specific education, children and adolescents are likely to form intuitive theories about AIDS, often based on their experiences with other diseases, such as the common cold. If colds can be transmitted through sneezing, why not AIDS? Two studies have shown that school-based HIV education can change the intuitive theories held by some children,[19,20] suggesting that young people's level of understanding may not be as fixed as was earlier thought.[21,22,23] This body of work suggests that young people may not progress steadily through several stages of cognitive development but may formulate and reformulate their own theories regarding HIV disease. Again, these developmental researchers argue that school-based prevention should be linked to the different kinds of intuitive theories that students apply.

Research also points to a relationship between psychological development and the decision to use drugs. A study of eighth-grade adolescents exploring this decision process found that for those students who decided to use drugs, the major factor in their decision was "personal choice."[24] They viewed drug use as a personal issue and, significantly, did not consider the perceived harm

of drugs and the social sanctions against drugs. In part, this attitude may reflect a thinking style that emphasizes certain aspects of
concrete thinking, such as a focus on the present, magical thinking, egocentrism, and a complete lack of awareness that other factors might be valid. Because these decisions are not influenced
by perceptions of harm, prevention programs that highlight the
hazards of drug use may be largely irrelevant for these youth. In
response, program developers must adopt psychologically sophis-
ticated prevention approaches that incorporate magical thinking
and egocentrism in order to reach this hard-to-teach population—
in short, to fight fire with fire.

Moral Development: Considering Convention

For many people, morality comes from religion—not from psychology. Although religious morality has influenced the content
of many HIV prevention programs, the science of moral development has had a negligible impact on program planning, implementation, and evaluation. Moral development should play a role
in prevention planning; that it does not is based more on a lack of
familiarity with developmental principles than on data showing it
to be ineffective.

Many people would like to believe that a person's morality remains the same throughout life; however, psychological research
clearly shows that moral thinking and behavior change over time,
consistent with what is known about other cognitive and psychological phenomena. From a psychological perspective, "Morality
does not consist of any specific behaviors but of a special perspective of the agent."[25] This definition suggests a very different approach from those that would categorically (and simplistically) list
"moral" and "immoral" behaviors and argue that HIV prevention
should be based on specific "right" and "wrong" behaviors. Unfortunately, such moralistic arguments are likely to fail in preventing transmission because they are based more often on the beliefs
of their proponents than on those of target populations, especially
adolescents and young adults.

Although the idea of moral development is a valuable perspective from which to examine behaviors that include some aspect of moral thinking (for example, alcohol and drug use, sexual

behaviors, and aggression), it has not been widely applied to prevention and behavior change. The standard methodology for studying moral development involves fables or stories that comprise a moral dilemma. Researchers ask participants to resolve the moral dilemma and explain why they chose the solution that they did. This methodology is applicable to AIDS prevention, which has many issues that could be described as dilemmas with no clear-cut right or wrong answers. Within this qualitative context, researchers could better determine "why" safe or unsafe decisions are made, and understand the thinking strategies that are used by people of different ages, sexual orientations, genders, and ethnicities.

Two theorists have propelled the field of moral development: Lawrence Kohlberg and Carol Gilligan. Understanding their constructs may help us to develop effective HIV prevention interventions.

Kohlberg: Laws Versus Values

Lawrence Kohlberg identified six stages of moral development organized sequentially through three levels.[26,27] Although other researchers have developed age-appropriate guidelines applying Kohlberg's theories, it must be emphasized that some people never develop beyond a particular stage. Thus, in terms of moral development—even more than for psychological and cognitive development—age per se is no guarantee that a person has progressed to a higher level of moral thinking.

Level I: Preconventional Moral Reasoning
(Primarily Ages Four to Ten)

Preconventional moral reasoning is based on external control by others. Behaviors are chosen to avoid punishment or gain rewards. This stage of moral development reflects the "concrete" thinking processes of young people: pain is bad, reward is good. A person at this level of moral thinking will probably change behaviors only if there are tangible consequences, either good or bad, of their behaviors.

In Stage 1, people ignore the motivations for a behavior and focus only on its concrete aspects (for example, how big a lie was told) or the consequences of the behavior (for example, how much property damage was done and how much it will cost to rectify). In Stage 2, individuals conform to rules out of self-interest and consideration of what others can do for them.

Level II: Conventional Moral Thinking
(Primarily Ages Ten to Thirteen)

Conventional moral thinking reflects law and social conventions. Here a person seeks approval and avoids disapproval, dishonor, or guilt by obeying laws and social expectations. People internalize the standards set by others and are capable of deciding—on the basis of these internalized values—whether their own actions are good or bad.

In Stage 3, people want to please and help others. In response to specific situations, they evaluate actions based on motivations behind the act, a thinking strategy they could not accomplish in Stage 1, and can take into account mitigating circumstances. In Stage 4, they try to meet their responsibilities, be respectful to authority, and maintain the social order. Behaviors that violate a rule and harm others are always wrong regardless of the motivation for the behavior or the circumstances surrounding it.

Conventional adolescents will act on the basis of law (either secular or religious) and social expectations. Conventional morality means "doing what you are told," especially if those instructions come from authority figures, such as parents, clergy, teachers, political leaders, or peer leaders. Young people at this level might be more likely to change their behaviors if they would gain public approval for their behaviors from relevant authority figures and role models.

Level III: Postconventional Morality (Not Before Age Thirteen;
Often Not Until Young Adulthood; Sometimes Never)

Postconventional morality represents the attainment of true morality, the ability to acknowledge conflicts between two incompatible standards and decide between them. At this point, behavioral control becomes more internalized, in terms of both standards and reasoning about right and wrong.

In Stage 5, people think more rationally and abstractly, and value majority rule as well as society's welfare. Obedience to the law is viewed as good for society. In Stage 6, the most highly developed stage, people do what they believe is right, regardless of legal standards or authoritarian demands. People in this stage have internalized standards based on abstract principles, and they must live according to their own ethical standards, or experience anxiety about being dishonest.

Because it depends on life experience to evolve, Level III may not develop until a person's twenties or even later. As experiences change, so do perceptions of right and wrong. Thus, the abstract morality of an adult is likely to be different from the concrete morality of an early adolescent. Efforts to produce behavior change among individuals with a postconventional moral perspective are likely to be ineffective if they rely on messages that emphasize simplistic right-or-wrong messages (conventional morality) or the immediate consequences of one's actions (preconventional morality).

Kohlberg assumed that people progressed through their developmental stages in a relatively orderly way, and that once a particular stage was reached, all moral decisions would be consistent with that stage. Further he assumed that behavior would always be consistent with moral reasoning. Neither of these beliefs is entirely true. Some people progress through these stages in a disorderly manner; some use reasoning from one stage to resolve one type of problem and reasoning from another stage to resolve another type of problem; and some may regress to an earlier stage under stress, for example, upon learning that they are seropositive. Kohlberg also based his analysis on research with male subjects, and commentators have questioned the generalizability of his results to women. Despite these complications, Kohlberg offers a compelling understanding of moral development in adolescence and young adulthood, one that can be helpful in developing effective behavior change strategies that are based on a reasonable theoretical foundation.

Gilligan: Moral Development Among Women and Men

Carol Gilligan pioneered the theory that female morality differs from male morality.[28] She defines male morality, which she says is what Kohlberg describes, as being based on concepts of justice and fairness, whereas female morality is based more on concepts of caring and social responsibility. According to Gilligan and Jane Attanucci, a justice orientation—that is, an external community standard—focuses on problems of inequality and oppression, with a goal of reciprocal treatment and equal respect: fairness and justice. Conversely, they define a care orientation—that is, an internal personal standard—as focusing on problems of detachment and abandonment, with a goal of attending and responding to need.[29] Gilligan and Attanucci found that although men and women applied both orientations in their moral decision making, women were much more likely to use a care orientation and men were more likely to use a justice orientation. For example, the maintenance of interpersonal relationships is a central value for women and affects their moral reasoning, decision making, and behaviors.

Gilligan identified three levels of moral development in women:

- Individual survival, in which a woman concentrates on what is best for her
- Personal value based on self-sacrifice, in which a woman sees herself as responsible for others and subordinates her needs to theirs
- Nonviolence, in which a woman's moral judgments are based on not hurting anyone, including herself

From a health promotion standpoint, it makes sense for a woman to protect herself from HIV infection by insisting that her partner use a condom. From a developmental perspective, however, enforced condom use might threaten the stability of her relationship. A man may refuse to wear a condom and may threaten to end the relationship unless his female partner agrees to unprotected sex. Depending on her stage of moral development, the woman will base her decision on the importance of maintaining her health (individual survival) or maintaining the relationship (self-sacrifice).

Applying Moral Development to HIV Prevention

Both Kohlberg and Gilligan have studied a relatively small number of subjects, and it seems premature to conclude that differences between men and women are consistent and enduring.

Their findings are also limited by their lack of focus on people of color and on the effects of chronic alcohol or drug use on moral development. Despite these limitations, the crucial lessons of these theories are that moral development is individual and that there is no lifetime standard for moral decision making.

Adolescent Development and HIV Prevention

Psychological, cognitive, and moral development affect a person's response to prevention messages and counseling, and the failure of many prevention approaches may be due to an ignorance or disregard of developmental principles. Equally significant, prevention programs that do not take development into account may advocate responses that work against psychological health and that may lead to increased HIV-related risk. These conditions are likely to be true for people of all ages but are most obvious and easiest to chart among adolescents.

Risk reduction may be difficult to accomplish during adolescence, given the many developmental changes that occur during this time and the limited number of objectives that can be addressed in even the most complete prevention program. Because adolescents (especially younger ones) do not think like adults, risk-reduction programs for adults will be less effective for older adolescents; even strategies developed for older adolescents may be less effective for younger adolescents. There are four areas in which development is crucial to adolescent prevention: risk taking, peer influence, the significance of touch, and the concept of perfection.

Is Some Risk Taking Necessary?

As mentioned earlier, some risk-taking behavior is a normal part of psychological development. Although abstinence from drugs and sex is often a desired goal, the total elimination of risk-taking behaviors during adolescence may have at least some negative consequences for some teenagers.

In a study of 101 sixteen-year-olds who had been followed since preschool, researchers found that those adolescents who had engaged in some drug experimentation (primarily with marijuana) were the best adjusted; frequent drug users were characterized by interpersonal alienation, poor impulse control, and emotional distress.[30,31] Surprisingly, the study found that adolescents who had never experimented with any drug (the abstainers) were relatively anxious, emotionally constricted, and lacking in social skills. Although these teens were chemically healthy, they were not psychologically healthy. The authors concluded that some drug experimentation, in and of itself, does not seem to be psychologically destructive. This conclusion may also apply to sexual experimentation, and it challenges the wisdom of defining abstinence as the only acceptable goal of prevention programs.

Peers Versus Friends

Many prevention programs focus on "peer pressure" as an influence on alcohol, drug, and sexual behaviors. However, peers are also friends, and educators must be careful not to advocate eliminating friendships when they try to reduce peer influences. Although peer pressure can be negative, the absence of peers can be dangerous, and the most psychologically unhealthy person may be the one who has no friends. Friendship involves identity, trust, and intimacy, all of which can be supported or discouraged by the quality of a given prevention program.

The Need for Touch

One possible outcome of an abstinence-based approach to adolescent sexuality is that some adolescents could go for years without touching or being touched. The long-term effects of touch deprivation are not yet known, but it is known that human beings need touch and that "safer sex" recommendations may be helpful in meeting that need.

In his treatise on touch, Ashley Montagu linked the lack of touching in infancy to later problems in physical, psychological, and emotional development.[32] As children move into adolescence, they are touched less often by their parents, and they seek to fulfill the need for touch through contact with friends. As they move through adolescence, sexual activity may be a primary method for touching and being touched and may be an important element of psychological and emotional development.[33] Risk-reduction programs based on scare tactics—for example, those that cause people to fear sexuality—may interfere with this progression and produce young adults who are physically healthy but psychologically isolated. In the long run, such isolation may produce a variety of psychological problems.

Perfection Versus Development

Approaching perfection is difficult and, for some, even undesirable. Although abstinence has been recommended for many years, those who recommend it often seem to be unaware of how hard it is to achieve the behavioral perfection that is the essence of abstinence. Abstinence is a common treatment goal for alcoholism, drug dependency, and cigarette smoking, yet its attainment is based on expected relapse. Simplistic recommendations for sexual abstinence that do not take into account relapse and relapse prevention will not achieve long-term success. At the very least, prevention planners should be aware of the work in relapse prevention so as to include that strategy as part of the program.

Priests take a religious vow of abstinence—perhaps the strongest and most public statement that can be made about not having sex. Even so, researchers estimate that between one-third and one-half of all Catholic priests have engaged in some form of sexual behavior, either heterosexual or homosexual.[34] Abstinence apparently works better in theory than in practice. Why should young people be expected to achieve a degree of abstinence that cannot be achieved by priests? Might the need for touch throughout the life span be related to relapse from abstinence? What role does touch play in intimacy? In self-disclosure? In identity? Although these concerns are not resolved by current research and theory, clearly they will not be answered by denying the questions.

Prevention Counseling

For some people, the counseling relationship itself can be part of a viable prevention strategy. Depending on whether the client is thinking about engaging in risky behaviors, engaging in risky behaviors, or trying to resist relapsing back into risky behaviors, the counseling experience may be a forum for primary, secondary, or tertiary prevention.

Clients can learn that caring for someone else—one's sexual partners, for example—can be a way of helping another to help oneself. Care becomes a strategy for mutual prevention. However, if people "use" other people (instead of caring about them), they jeopardize the likelihood of others being there for them when they need help. Or the person may be there if needed but, as Gilligan might frame it, only on an external level, based on community standards and expectations, rather than on an internal level, based on mutual caring and respect.

In counseling, clients may tend to judge their behaviors. Clients who apply concrete thinking (keeping in mind that concrete thinking often is the only thinking that occurs in times of crisis) may evaluate risky behavior by saying, "I did terrible things," "I shouldn't have done that," or "I'm a flawed person." As counseling progresses, therapists can help clients shift to more abstract levels of thinking, as suggested by the statements, "What's happening now in my life?" "How can I be emotionally intimate?" or "How can I take back my family?" Indeed, these three elements—current life occurrences, intimacy, and family—are key components of the counseling process itself.

A major limitation of concrete thinking is that it leads to judgment, which prevents psychological growth. After making a judgment, such as "I am a terrible person," a client is left with nowhere to go. As his or her thinking becomes more complex, the client is able to take greater emotional risks, recognize personal strengths, and accept himself or herself. Two case vignettes exemplify a developmental approach to prevention counseling.

Clem: An Obligation to Self and Others

Clem is a twenty-one-year-old White, gay male, an undergraduate at a major university in the United States. He was referred for counseling with Laura Harris, Ph.D., because of unrelenting anxiety and rage. Responding to increasing distress, Clem immersed himself in several dependent relationships with lovers who did not share his wish for long-term commitment or who were frightened by his neediness.

Clem was raised in a moderately large town. When he realized that he needed to explore his gay identity, he left home for the "big city" and college. Lacking connection and support, he quickly became homesick and desperately plunged into the relationships that were now troubling him. In order to maintain these relationships, he allowed himself to engage in unprotected anal intercourse. Although Clem did not want to become HIV-infected, he was willing to risk his own health to maintain a particular relationship, fearing that if he refused unsafe sex or insisted on safer sex his partner would reject him, ending the relationship. At this time in Clem's life, a relationship was more important than his health, and knowledge of his health risks did not lead him to behavior change.

Clem had left his hometown to avoid hurting his parents—putting their position and "good name" in jeopardy—by coming out. Clem conceived of this move as an act of "goodness." It was better to leave than to risk hurting his family or friends—and, as a result, being abandoned by them. Realizing this in therapy, Clem began to reconsider his decision to "spare" his parents in terms not only of caring for others but also of caring for himself.

At the beginning of therapy, Clem exhibited conventional moral thinking (Level II in Kohlberg's schema). He was dependent on his parents for approval and psychological support; protecting this support required protecting their reputation, even if it meant physically separating himself from them. As Gilligan notes, "Once obligation extends to include the self as well as others, the disparity between selfishness and responsibility dissolves."[35]

While working on a more mutually supportive relationship with his parents, Clem developed the skill to identify and protect his own needs and values and to make decisions based on his own well-being. His dependency on his family was a positive, motivating feature. That is, Clem realized that he could take care of his parents so that they would take care of him.

Clem was able to see the value of others and himself. Valuing his relationships meant valuing himself as well. In this way, Clem became receptive to HIV prevention and was able to integrate an appreciation of safer sex and its role in protecting him into his life.

Jeremy: Accepting Ambiguity

Jeremy is a twenty-four-year-old Asian American graduate student in philosophy at a university in the Midwest. He was born in Korea, adopted at sixteen months old, and raised by a hard-working White couple living in a large midwestern city. Jeremy was always wary and distant in his interactions with his family and peers. He said that he was not good at acknowledging and expressing feelings and described himself as having always been uncertain about his sexuality. During adolescence, Jeremy experimented a lot in his sexual relationships with a variety of partners (both men and women) and usually in the context of drinking alcohol.

In his second year of graduate school, Jeremy learned that he was HIV-infected. He was shocked, and he relied even more on alcohol to maintain denial about his condition. This led to further isolation in his social life, increasing distrust of others, and academic failure. Jeremy was thrown into a state of angry crisis, and this led to more and often random sexual encounters.

Jeremy came into therapy through a crisis visit after he repeatedly failed to meet the academic goals set by his adviser. His depressive feelings and behavioral remedies—drinking and compulsive sex—commanded too much of his time and energy. In therapy, Jeremy's counselor, Warren Simpson, M.S.W., worked to emphasize the critical nature of Jeremy's situation and used the crisis to maintain the break in Jeremy's denial that had brought him into therapy. Simpson acknowledged Jeremy's painful rage and supported Jeremy's need for relief from it. Simpson also asserted repeatedly the consequences and dangers of pursuing risky behaviors, despite Jeremy's efforts to avoid these topics, and focused discussion on practical behavior and attitudinal changes that Jeremy could make to respond to the crisis. Surprised by the attention Simpson paid to his feelings, Jeremy began to acknowledge the hurt he felt and the support Simpson provided.

Through this process, Jeremy came to believe intellectually that there were some reasons why it might be useful to more actively protect his health and safety. The crisis of his HIV diagnosis aroused the rudimentary self-protection anticipated by Kohlberg's Level I preconventional moral reasoning. Simpson's constant reinforcement led, as might have been predicted by Erikson, to Jeremy's attention to the consequences of his behavior.

As Jeremy progressed in therapy, Simpson suggested he join a support group for people with HIV, and after some consideration, Jeremy did so. Jeremy later reported that he had begun to enjoy these interactions. As other group members shared their stories and expressed genuine warmth, Jeremy began to reciprocate, at first because of the social reward (as suggested by Kohlberg's Level II conventional thinking), but later because of his success at internalizing their positive feedback. In doing so, he came to be more certain about his being gay, and increasingly less random in his sexual expression.

A close call with a major opportunistic infection served as a final turning point, at which time Jeremy found others concerned about him without expecting a specific "payback," which would suggest development in conventional moral reasoning and identity formation. He began to reflect on the varied nature of individuals. It was at this time that Simpson encouraged Jeremy to consider the ambiguity and gray areas in morality and human interaction in order to interrupt his customary all-or-nothing thinking.

Through this process, Jeremy's concrete view of the world began to give way to more flexible observations and experiences. Jeremy gradually began to see that his indiscriminate and noncommittal, risky and self-destructive behaviors were misguided quests for absolute unambiguous comfort from outside sources rather than from himself.

The Failure to Apply Theory to Prevention

Calling a program a "prevention intervention" does not make it one. One of the surprising findings from studying drug abuse prevention programs is that some interventions have actually led to an increase in use of at least a few drugs.[36,37]

When queried about the questionable efficacy of one such program—Drug Abuse Resistance Education (DARE)—one corporate sponsor said that it would continue to fund the intervention because it was popular with young people and that the sponsor would support another program only if it were as "popular" as DARE. To ensure effective prevention, providers must consider issues of ethics and the use of knowledge. Despite unimpressive outcome evaluations, DARE has been used widely throughout the United States.[38,39] Conversely, other substance abuse prevention programs that have been shown to work significantly better than DARE have not been implemented. Can the same phenomenon happen with HIV prevention?

Psychologists Jeff Stone and Elliot Aronson have applied the psychological principle of cognitive dissonance to encourage young adults to use condoms.[40] Most people like to think that they have a consistent set of values and behaviors. Confronting their own inconsistencies makes them uncomfortable, and uncomfortable feelings (cognitive dissonance) can lead to behavior change. Working with college students, Stone and Aronson provoked cognitive dissonance by first having students publicly advocate the importance of safer sex and then making the students conscious of their past failures to use condoms. The researchers expected the students to be motivated to purchase condoms to relieve the dissonance. They did.

Unfortunately, Aronson has been unable to infuse the concept into local prevention programs.[41] He notes that we are all social psychologists, with our own intuitive theories about how to get other people to change their behaviors, and that sex education has paid insufficient attention to the psychological complexity of behavior change. For example, many people—including some mental health professionals—believe that homosexuality is simply a freely chosen behavior that can be easily "cured" with the right kind of therapy. This intuitive theory, which may be strongly held, may be unchangeable, even when contradictory scientific evidence is presented.

Does enthusiasm for a program lead administrators and parents to believe that their children are being helped by interventions that are popular but ineffective? Are administrators willing even to ask tough questions about prevention programs if there is strong financial and social support for them? Who really benefits from a corporation's support—the students, the administrators, the community, the corporation? Would corporate dollars be better spent on a less visible but more effective program?

The book *Ethical Implications of Primary Prevention* addresses ethical aspects that often are overlooked in prevention programs.[42] In their efforts to help, prevention planners are sometimes unaware of the harm they may do. One type of harm may be done when a prevention program is inappropriate for its target audience. Researchers, evaluators, and policymakers may think of prevention programs simply in terms of being effective or being less effective. But do we consider the ethical implications of "less effective" programs?

Using Knowledge

Far too often, HIV-related and psychological research is not applied in developing HIV prevention. Although many have called for conceptually based interventions, most interventions have been founded not on sound psychological principles and developmental perspectives but more often on an informal combination of logic and practical experience: what the prevention planner thinks will work, hopes will work, or wants to work.[43]

This failure to apply existing theory is not unique to HIV prevention. Thomas Backer defines *knowledge utilization* as "research, scholarly, and programmatic intervention activities aimed at increasing the use of knowledge to solve human problems."[44] But using knowledge is difficult, as difficult for the person who finds out that he or she is seropositive as it is for the person planning an HIV prevention program. Although a complete analysis of this problem is beyond the scope of this chapter, Backer identified six strategies that can help organizations use knowledge in a more effective manner. Briefly, the strategies are the following:

- *Interpersonal contact.* For an innovative technique to be used in a new setting, there should be direct contact between staff members from the adopting organization with those who know about the innovation.
- *Planning and foresight.* A plan must be developed for how the innovation will be adopted in the new setting.
- *Outside consultation on change.* Outside consultants can help design the change in a more efficient way and offer an objective perspective on what should be done.
- *Information transformation.* What's known about an innovation needs to be translated into a language that can be understood by potential users. Key issues covered in such a discussion should be, Does it work? and How can I replicate it in my organization?
- *Individual and organizational champions.* The likelihood that an innovative technique will be adopted is greater if influential staff members and organizational leaders are enthusiastic about it.
- *Potential user involvement.* Everyone who will be affected by the organizational change should be part of the planning process. This will broaden the range of ideas for adopting the program and increase user ownership while decreasing user resistance.

Incorporating developmental issues into HIV prevention and counseling requires far more than merely reading this chapter or even this book. Providers should use Backer's six steps as a way of mustering the growing base of HIV-related theoretical and practical knowledge.

∽

The goal of prevention should not be to eliminate all risky behaviors from life; instead it should be to help people learn about inappropriate and appropriate risks. There is life after adolescence, and individuals who have grown up in a risk-free environment may not be able to cope with the challenges of adulthood—the workplace, parenthood, and relationships—without having had some risk-taking experience. To facilitate later psychological development, it may be more helpful to know how to take risks in a "safer" way than simply to "say no" to all potential risks.

Behavior change is difficult—and even more difficult if behavior change strategies fail to consider psychological development. How can human sexual behavior be understood without understanding identity and intimacy? How can client counseling or HIV prevention be effective without understanding cognitive or moral development? Far too often, interventions use a one-size-fits-all approach, severely limiting an intervention's efficacy.

In fact, HIV prevention needs to come in many shapes and sizes: mass media, school-based HIV education programs, and individual and couples counseling. Almost twenty years into the epidemic, most program planners have a reasonable understanding of the "facts about AIDS," but many are often totally unaware of key developmental issues. Without that awareness, prevention programs will have minimal success—when they really need to have maximum success.

Notes

1. Shedler, J., and Block, J. "Adolescent Drug Use and Psychological Health: A Longitudinal Inquiry." *American Psychologist,* 1990, *45*(5), 612–630.
2. Walsh, M. E., Buckley, M., and Bibace, R. "Conceptions of AIDS in Children and Adolescents." Presentation at the 99th annual meeting of the American Psychological Association, San Francisco, Aug. 1991.
3. Steinberg, L. "Adolescent Transitions and Alcohol and Other Drug Use Prevention." In E. N. Goplerud (ed.), *Preventing Adolescent Drug*

Use: From Theory to Practice. OSAP Prevention Monograph 8. Rockville, Md.: Office for Substance Abuse Prevention, 1991.

4. Quadrel, M. J., Fischhoff, B., and Davis, W. "Adolescent (In)Vulnerability." *American Psychologist,* 1993, *48*(2), 102–116.

5. Erikson, E. *Childhood and Society.* New York: Norton, 1950.

6. Garnets, L., and Kimmel, D. "Lesbian and Gay Male Dimensions in the Psychological Study of Human Diversity." In J. Goodchilds (ed.), *Psychological Perspectives on Human Diversity in America.* Washington, D.C.: American Psychological Association, 1991.

7. Dowsett, G. W. "Working-Class Gay Communities and HIV Prevention." *FOCUS: A Guide to AIDS Research and Counseling,* 1994, *9*(3), 1–4.

8. Bentler, P. M. "Etiologies and Consequences of Adolescent Drug Use: Implications for Prevention." *Journal of Addictive Diseases,* 1992, *11*(3), 47–61.

9. Bibace, R., and Walsh, M. E. "Development of Children's Conceptions of Illness." *Pediatrics,* 1980, *66*(6), 912–917.

10. Bibace, R., and Walsh, M. E. (eds.). *Children's Conceptions of Health, Illness and Bodily Functions.* San Francisco: Jossey-Bass, 1981.

11. Walsh, M. E., and Bibace, R. "Children's Conceptions of AIDS: A Developmental Analysis." *Journal of Pediatric Psychology,* 1991, *16*(3), 273–285.

12. Schonfeld, D. J., Johnson, S. R., Perrin, E. C., and others. "Understanding of Acquired Immunodeficiency Syndrome by Elementary School Children: A Developmental Survey." *Pediatrics,* 1993, *92*(3), 389–395.

13. Skurnick, J., Johnson, R., Quinones, M., and others. "New Jersey High School Students' Knowledge, Attitudes, and Behavior Regarding AIDS." *AIDS Education and Prevention,* 1991, *3*(1), 21–30.

14. Shoemaker, M. R., Schonfeld, D. J., O'Hare, L. L., and others. "Children's Understanding of the Symptoms of AIDS." *AIDS Education and Prevention,* 1996, *8*(5), 403–414.

15. Schonfeld, D. J. "The Child's Cognitive Understanding of Illness." In M. Lewis (ed.), *Child and Adolescent Psychiatry. A Comprehensive Textbook.* (2nd ed.) Baltimore: Williams & Wilkins, 1996.

16. Bibace, R., and Walsh, M. E. "Understanding AIDS Developmentally: A Comment on the November 1988 Special Issue on Psychology and AIDS." *American Psychologist,* 1990, *45*(3), 405–406.

17. Nemeroff, C. J., Brinkman, A., and Woodward, C. K. "Magical Contagion and AIDS Risk Perception in a College Population." *AIDS Education and Prevention,* 1994, *6*(3), 249–265.

18. Brown, L. K., Nassau, J. H., and Levy, V. "'What Upsets Me Most About AIDS Is . . .': A Survey of Children and Adolescents." *AIDS Education and Prevention,* 1990, *2*(4), 296–304.

19. Sigelman, C. K., Estrada, A. L., Derenowski, E. B., and others. "Intuitive Theories of Human Immunodeficiency Virus Transmission: Their Development and Implications." *Journal of Pediatric Psychology,* 1996, *21*(4), 555–572.

20. Sigelman, C. K., Derenowski, E. B., Woods, T., and others. "Mexican-American and Anglo-American Children's Responsiveness to a Theory-Centered AIDS Education Program." *Child Development,* 1996, *67*(2), 253–266.

21. Bibace and Walsh, "Development of Children's Conceptions of Illness."

22. Bibace and Walsh, *Children's Conceptions.*

23. Walsh and Bibace, "Children's Conceptions of AIDS."

24. Buchanan, D. R. "How Teens Think About Drugs: Insights from Moral Reasoning and Social Bonding Theory." *International Quarterly of Community Health Education,* 1990–91, *11*(4), 315–322.

25. Blasi, A. "Comment: The Psychological Definitions of Morality." In J. Kagan and S. Lamb (eds.), *The Emergence of Morality in Young Children.* Chicago: University of Chicago Press, 1987.

26. Kohlberg, L. "Stage and Sequence: The Cognitive-Developmental Approach to Socialization." In D. A. Goslin (ed.), *Handbook of Socialization Theory and Research.* Skokie, Ill.: Rand McNally, 1969.

27. Kohlberg, L. *The Philosophy of Moral Development: Essays on Moral Development.* Vol. 1. San Francisco: HarperSanFrancisco, 1984.

28. Gilligan, C. *In a Different Voice.* Cambridge, Mass.: Harvard University Press, 1982.

29. Gilligan, C., and Attanucci, J. "Two Moral Orientations." In C. Gilligan, J. V. Ward, J. M. Taylor, and others (eds.), *Mapping the Moral Domain: A Contribution of Women's Thinking to Psychological Theory and Education.* Cambridge, Mass.: Harvard University Press, 1988.

30. Sigelman, Estrada, Derenowski, and others, "Intuitive Theories."

31. Kohlberg, *Philosophy of Moral Development.*

32. Montagu, A. *Touching: The Human Significance of the Skin.* New York: Columbia University Press, 1971.

33. McAnarney, E. R. "Adolescents and Touch." In K. E. Barnard and T. B. Brazelton (eds.), *Touch: The Foundation of Experience.* Madison, Wis.: International Universities Press, 1990.

34. Sipe, A.W.R. *A Secret World: Sexuality and the Search for Celibacy.* New York: Brunner/Mazel, 1990.

35. Gilligan, *In a Different Voice,* p. 94.

36. Swisher, J. D., and Hu, T. "Alternatives to Drug Abuse: Some Are and Some Are Not." In T. J. Glynn, C. G. Leukefeld, and J. P. Ludford (eds.), *Preventing Adolescent Drug Abuse: Intervention Strategies.* NIDA Research Monograph 47. Rockville, Md.: National Institute on Drug Abuse, 1983.

37. Hansen, W. B. "School-Based Substance Abuse Prevention: A Review of the State of the Art in Curriculum, 1980–1990." *Health Education Research,* 1992, *7*(3), 403–430.

38. Rogers, E. M. "Diffusion of Drug Abuse Prevention Programs: Spontaneous Diffusion, Agenda Setting, and Reinvention." In T. E. Backer, S. L. David, and G. Soucy (eds.), *Reviewing the Behavioral Science Knowledge Base on Technology Transfer.* NIDA Research Monograph 155. Rockville, Md.: National Institute on Drug Abuse, 1995.

39. Tobler, N. S. "Meta-Analysis of Adolescent Drug Prevention Programs: Results of the 1993 Meta-Analysis." In W. J. Bukoski (ed.), *Meta-Analysis of Drug Abuse Prevention Programs.* NIDA Research Monograph 170. Rockville, Md.: National Institute on Drug Abuse, 1997.

40. Stone, J., Aronson, E., Crain, A. L., and others. "Inducing Hypocrisy as a Means of Encouraging Young Adults to Use Condoms." *Personality and Social Psychology Bulletin,* 1994, *29*(1), 116–128.

41. Shea, C. "A University of California Psychologist Investigates New Approaches to Changing Human Behavior." *Chronicle of Higher Education,* June 20, 1997, p. A15.

42. Levin, G. B., Trickett, E. J., and Hess, R. E. (eds.). *Ethical Implications of Primary Prevention.* New York: Brunner/Mazel, 1990.

43. Fisher, J. D., and Fisher, W. A. "Changing AIDS-Risk Behavior." *Psychological Bulletin,* 1992, *111*(3), 455–474.

44. Backer, T. E. "Knowledge Utilization: The Third Wave." *Knowledge: Creation, Diffusion, Utilization,* 1991, *12*(3), 226.

Chapter Five

Prevention and Culture
Working Downhill to Change HIV Risk Behavior

Amanda Houston-Hamilton
Noel A. Day

The behaviors that place people at risk of HIV infection are rarely apparent on a conscious level; rather they are rooted in basic instincts, reinforced by pleasurable sensations, and layered with cultural values. Unfortunately, the HIV prevention field has tended to view culturally embedded roles and attitudes only as obstacles to change.[1] Many cultural beliefs do present challenges to encouraging safer sex and drug use, yet the success of HIV interventions often depends on the capacity of counselors to use rather than to mitigate the power of culture.

The effects of culture on individuals are often so strong that they seem to be inborn. Harnessing such a tremendous force to influence human behavior is a strategy that counselors can use to become more efficient, effective agents of change.

Herb Shepherd, a pioneer in the field of organizational change, used to say he had the choice of "working uphill or downhill" when he was trying to modify an organization: like Sisyphus, he could roll the boulder of institutional beliefs and norms uphill, grunting, sweating with the effort only to be frustrated as it rolled back downhill, or he could take advantage of the momentum of these same values. To work downhill, he would analyze an organization's culture and identify consistent strategic interventions based on the inherent values of that organization, in this way speeding the group toward its goals.

Similarly, counselors trying to help their clients reduce their HIV risk behaviors can lose considerable time and effort working against their clients' seemingly counterproductive cultural values about sex, drugs, health, and death. This chapter presents a model for working downhill, enabling counselors to uncover the meaning each client gives to significant HIV-related issues and to work in concert with these meanings to change life-threatening behaviors.

Culture, Values, and Behavior Change

When most people use the word *culture,* they think about foods, clothing, art, or music. In fact, culture is much more than these symbols—it is the force that shapes a person's core, that tells each of us how *to be,* how to survive. A successful culture is not static: these ways of being and the rules that surround them have evolved over time to meet needs specific to particular environments and circumstances, new conditions, or the assimilation of other groups and their precepts.

A culture is a group's design for living, which defines the perception and interpretation of *the group's* experience of being human: the inherent quality of human beings (good, evil, or both), the relation of humans to nature (harmony, subjugation, or mastery), the rules of human relationships (individualistic, collateral, or lineal), the temporal focus (past, present, or future), and the basic purpose and direction of human activity (doing, being, becoming).[2] Shared meanings and values develop not only within ethnic groups but also within affinity groups—those based, for example, on social class, gender, and sexual orientation. Spoken and written language are only two of the many ways to communicate effectively. Behavior is culture made manifest, giving visible form and expression to beliefs, values, and attitudes of both client and counselor.[3,4,5] Movement, art, spatial sensibility, color, and audio tone are among the other explicit languages of culture.

Perhaps because the stakes in HIV prevention counseling are high, many clinicians avoid interventions with clients whose cultures seem at face value different from their own and, in this way, avoid interactions that risk failure. The diversity of the populations at risk for HIV infection requires different sources and deeper levels of inquiry, but one of the best models for working downhill with cultural values lies in the fundamental premise of client-focused work: the client is at the center of the interaction, and the therapist as facilitator of change collaborates with the client, listening for the meanings and metaphors that can establish and promote the intervention plan the therapist and client have developed together.

If it is hard, in many cultures, to talk about risk behaviors, it is even harder to change them. Counseling interventions are dependent not only on appropriate and precise language but also on rules of courtesy, sequencing, familiarity, assertiveness and candor, phrasing, grammar, and medium. Each aspect involves an exchange of expectations determined by a combination of personal experience and cultural messages. Clear communication of these expectations and the correct interpretation of cultural meanings in turn develop the rapport necessary for uncovering and harnessing the attitudinal norms that are central to behavior. They also instill trust, a prerequisite to accepting and incorporating protective health measures into everyday life.[6,7] Violating cultural expectations, on the other hand, may compromise the therapist-client relationship and hazard negative judgments of being rude, dangerous, uneducated, untrustworthy, or incompetent.

HIV counselors are pilots in cross-cultural communication, seeking the modes, form, pace, and meanings that will best promote healthy behaviors. They rely on clients' guidance as well as their own careful study to make the correct interpretations and use of their cross-cultural tools. Some people have argued that such efforts are a burden to already stretched resources. But the initial energy and motivation required to reconsider the limitations of prevention activities are more than offset by the eventual downhill momentum gained in efficient communication and by the ultimate success of prevention interventions.

The Challenge to Counselors

The pervasiveness and intransigence of cultural lessons can keep counselors from putting clients at the core of risk-reduction counseling. Culture is like your skin: you're not aware of it until it itches. Most people have no consciousness of the ways in which culture influences their every perception and expectation. Some uphill interventions, in fact, deny cultural differences for the sake of a global "people are people" approach that professes the benefits of an impartial, culture-free intervention. But as Vicente Navarro notes, "Culture-free service delivery is nonexistent—the counselor's objectivity is tempered by the subjectivity of his or her own norms and values."[8] Working downhill toward the client does not demand negation of the counselor's cultural contribution to the interaction. Rather it presents an opportunity to enhance the counselor's knowledge of self and of what he or she brings to the interaction.

Counselors who want to increase their understanding of the meanings of HIV disease in other cultures will find little help in the literature. In the scant qualitative work published, African Americans, American Indians, Latinos, as well as people of Asian and Pacific Island descent have been considered inherently "hard to reach,"[9] a term that serves simply to distance populations with whom professionals are unfamiliar. The descriptions of numerous cultural barriers provide neither solutions nor more positive cultural elements with which counselors can build prevention strategies. Appropriate interventions for many groups have been hindered more by this marginalization than by the cultural attributes that researchers ascribe to the groups. It is true, for instance, that access to men of color is sometimes limited by their high rates of institutionalization and mortality in the United States,[10] but a more frequent impediment is the inability of institutions charged with targeting prevention efforts to distinguish among the heterogeneity of experience, class, and language within racial groups.[11,12,13]

Paradoxically, there is evidence in the literature of both stereotyping—"Latino men are macho"—and invisibility. Again men of color provide an example: despite reports that the characteristics of homosexuality are different in different cultures,[14] most researchers generalize about the attitudes and behaviors of all gay and bisexual men from samples consisting largely of men of European descent.[15,16] In this way, useful cultural variables are ignored or treated as exceptions in the creation of normative scales.

The narrowness of information in the literature points even more to the need for counselors to listen consciously for cultural lessons communicated continually in their own lives. The success of cross-cultural work relies, in particular, on the counselor's sharp, active assessment of professional and personal relationships that may provide insights into how to affect safer sex and drug behaviors.

The Cultural Context of HIV Counseling Models

Counseling requires the use of *self* as a tool for the change of others. HIV disease further challenges counselors in a downhill mode to examine their own feelings about the existential, metaphorical, and practical aspects of such issues as disability, death, homosexuality, race, age, gender, class, and ethnicity. In the counseling relationship, the parties involved may not share beliefs about these issues or about fundamental concepts in counseling, medicine, and even the science of HIV. Until we assess our own belief systems, we can neither understand the gaps between ourselves and our audience nor appreciate the tenacity of cultural norms and values.

Cultural concepts central to mainstream American beliefs determine both the substance and the structure of HIV prevention interventions and affect the counselor-client relationship in the context of power and powerlessness. The most influential behavior change models in the HIV counseling arena reflect Anglocentric, pedagogical notions. Indeed, the idea of changing cultural attitudes—a central HIV education method—reflects a largely doomed strategy tantamount to cultural hegemony and is the epitome of working uphill.

In terms of the substance of prevention approaches, these principles value individual responsibility and control, assume that the medical system is trustworthy, and propose that client-based issues like low self-efficacy or denial are the primary obstacles to behavior change. In terms of the structure of prevention strategies, the models suggest that single interventions are appropriate and that information—the more the better—should be presented in a didactic form with knowledge passing in one direction, from presenter to audience. The issue of power and powerlessness affects both the substance and the structure of interactions, plays a particularly important role in HIV prevention models and in the counseling relationship, and is central to the reality of living outside the mainstream.

Substance: Uncommon Ground

Among the ideas that relate to HIV disease and vary most from culture to culture are the role of the individual, definitions of sex, the motivation to take the HIV antibody test, and perceptions about the medical system. Although most HIV prevention strategies value taking active, measurable control of one's health, other worldviews are fatalistic or reliant on outside forces; for example, some cultures see prayer as a practical, dynamic intervention, not a passive strategy. Many HIV prevention interventions focus on individual responsibility, although many ethnic cultures in the United States are oriented toward collective behavior in which the target of a prevention activity may be the entire family. Some groups attribute illness to an imbalance in life or in the environment rather than to a pathogenic agent like HIV. Reticence to talk about HIV disease may be wrongly interpreted by a counselor as homophobia or denial rather than, possibly, the desire to ward off bad omens, the shame of the death of children before a parent (an attitude in many Asian cultures), or the need to maintain the expected boundaries around private versus public behavior.[17,18,19] The existence of such distinct perceptions highlights the importance of seeking life-saving strategies within the context of a client's worldview and the utility of taking time to define meanings within this worldview that will suggest authentic motivations for risk reduction.

Although guidelines for safer sex attempt to standardize definitions, individual conceptions of what is and is not "sex" can affect behavior change counseling. Similarly, in a number of ethnic groups, men who have sex with men as well as with women do not envision their same-sex behaviors as linked to a sexual identity. In uphill interventions, this attitude is sometimes misread as a rejection of self and targeted as an obstacle to behavior change. In fact, it may instead represent a separation of behavior, role, and sense of self that has long been common in many cultures throughout the world.[20]

Fundamental differences both in biological beliefs and in perceptions of medicine may influence decisions to undergo antibody counseling and testing. For instance, people from some Asian cultures believe blood tests upset the balance of yin and yang in the body or diminish *chi,* the vital life force. People from some disadvantaged groups have learned that it is appropriate, even essential, to distrust the health care system. Modesta Orque and colleagues note that "Blacks [for example] entering health care programs automatically exhibit more 'paranoid responses' than other patients," based on their past experiences or on their perceptions of the health care system as unsafe.[21]

Such distrust reflects a body of historical fact. American medicine is replete with well-documented evidence of an impersonal and self-serving medical system, a history that taints the current beliefs of whole groups of people regarding the causation and prevention of illness. Examples include the use of clinical diagnoses of rebellious slave behavior to justify beatings, the forced sterilization of many African Americans, the performance of lobotomies to "cure" homosexuality, the release of viruses into the New York subway to study their viral paths and life spans, and the Tuskegee Institute's experimentation on Black men and their partners, which left them untreated for syphilis for forty years. Considering this legacy, it is easy to understand the pervasiveness of conspiracy theories in the dialogue on HIV among African Americans, who have so often been viewed as expendable in these "research" efforts.[22,23,24] Studies have found that many African Americans including college-educated and churchgoing men and women—hardly radical or marginalized groups—distrust information they have heard about both the source and impact of HIV, instead viewing the epidemic and even standard prevention measures such as condom use as part of a larger genocidal plot against African Americans.[25] White counselors might be surprised by the number of their Black colleagues who share some of this same skepticism about the source or the implications of the disease.[26]

Counselors can choose either to dismiss such responses as dysfunctional or to explore the meaning of such beliefs, acknowledging the credibility of such suspicions and joining with clients to discover what each sees as the implications of such a history for HIV prevention. Typically the substance of HIV education negates alternative theories regarding, for example, disease etiology; these approaches are therefore destined to alienate a significant part of their intended audience. Despite the goodwill of providers, clients may view theories about the origins of HIV as a kind of provocation or intellectual imperialism. Counselors should reconsider the

purpose of presenting information that does not directly assist behavioral negotiation. It is unclear, for example, what purpose communicating the theory that HIV originated in Africa serves, except
to offend African Americans and deflect their attention away from
the more critical prevention messages.

In the counseling interchange, offering information about the
virology and etiology of HIV similarly may help providers feel
grounded in their cultural assumptions, but the time spent on disseminating this information might be better spent building empathy and rapport. There is already so much to be done to maintain
the most basic elements of an HIV intervention, it makes sense to
allow individuals their particular understanding of illness as long as
these ideas do not impede the movement of counselor and client
toward an agreement on safer behaviors.

Structure: One Size Fits All?

Terry Tafoya and Doug Wirth, psychologists experienced in HIV-
related cross-cultural training, point out limitations in the Anglo-
Saxon belief in rationalism and the power of knowledge, a belief
that is at the foundation of HIV prevention education: "It is a common American cultural belief and communication strategy that if
enough information is presented, an audience or client will automatically reach the same conclusion as the presenter or practitioner."[27] Laurence Green calls the same belief the "empty vessel
fallacy." He suggests that this fallacy leads "health educators to behave as if all they have to do to ensure the success of their programs is to pour health information into the empty minds of an
eagerly awaiting target population. As an extension, technologies
are sought that will transmit the most information to the most people by and large regardless of their differing beliefs, attitudes, values, and perceptions."[28]

Green identifies two other shortcomings in health education
practice born of mainstream American values. One he calls the
"fallacy of the more, the better." This notion, consistent with the
value placed in our society on accumulation, assumes "that positive outcomes will increase proportionately with more time, more
television coverage, more media equipment, more personnel, or
more contacts." The second he calls the "fallacy of the inherent

superiority or inferiority of some methods."[29] By that he means that many practitioners advocate particular methods regardless of whether those methods are appropriate for the particular population they are serving—truly a one-size-fits-all assumption. In this vein, Tafoya and Wirth caution, "Techniques and effectiveness will always vary along a bell-shaped curve with any given population as long as one uses only one approach, intervention or curriculum."[30]

Counselor-Client Power Relationships

For traditionally oppressed groups such as ethnic minorities, "A strong determinant of world views is very much related to racism and the subordinate position assigned to them in society."[31] Therefore, interventions that work downhill with individuals from any historically oppressed group should begin by assessing both real and learned powerlessness, the source of many cultural adaptations and survival mechanisms that seem to oppose HIV prevention strategies.

This assessment also should acknowledge the distinct effects of class, generation, and other elements that bestow privilege or diminish social status. Many beliefs and behaviors attributed to ethnic culture are, in fact, values of a drug-using lifestyle or what Elaine Pinderhughes calls "the victim system," a set of shared norms and survival strategies developed in response to being the objects of abuse within a society. An African American woman who is only able to discuss immediate issues and dismisses prevention as "I'll deal with it when it comes up" is not expressing a value inherent to her ethnic culture; she is expressing a victim-system belief, focusing on her limited power in the here and now while leaving tomorrow to fate or chance.[32]

In such instances, HIV counseling might well borrow from twelve-step programs, which turn tomorrow into a series of "todays." This approach can permit people who have adapted to their absence of control to limit their expectations to momentary gains. In doing so, it offers them small doses of experience in the power of behavior change—in the present and one day at a time. This kind of intervention is difficult for many HIV counselors because it requires resisting provider-culture values about planning and future orientation. Instead, the strategy accepts the client's in-the-moment values, remembering that these may nonetheless lead to behavior change.

Providers too often stereotypically assume powerlessness among whole populations. For example, presumed absence of power among low-income, immigrant women of color is cited by many HIV counselors as a reason to avoid prevention efforts with these populations.[33,34] Describing these women as passive, obedient, and "traditional," and emphasizing the potential physical danger for women in taking the initiative in sex, this theory suggests that the unequal distribution of power in these cultures is the primary obstacle to protective behavior. Although there is sometimes truth in these concerns, misreading the power balance in relationships may be just as damaging to HIV prevention efforts as failing to acknowledge power interplay at all.[35,36] In some cases, counseling a woman to be sexually assertive may be working uphill against her values if she is, in fact, acculturated to be submissive to her partner in such decision making.[37] For instance, a culture that seems to support a passive role for women may also possess dynamics that can foster HIV protection through matriarchal components that enable certain women to speak with authority or exert dominance in certain contexts.

Even a minimal effort to uncover the innate cultural features that define and support HIV protective measures ultimately eases the HIV prevention task. For example, clients who have been subjected to war, political repression, torture, domestic abuse, or other traumas may experience residual power imbalances, which may play out in their risk behaviors; these imbalances need to be made explicit in order for prevention interventions to be effective.

Finally, HIV prevention messages are themselves delivered and heard within a power framework, because

the helping relationship is in itself a power relationship in which the dynamics of power and lack of power are operating. . . . The cross-racial and cross-ethnic helping encounter compounds the consequences of this power differential. For the client, intervention by a member of a group he or she regards as the oppressor may reinforce the powerlessness felt in a moment of need. Intervention by a worker whom the client sees as inferior may also reinforce the client's sense of helplessness. Power issues related to differences in ethnicity, class, sex, age, and other social markers may exaggerate the power inherent in the helping role in a way that causes the worker to misperceive the client. With an awareness of the influence of power in complementary relationships, [the counselor] is better prepared to guard against occurrences that may result in destructive use of the worker's power or the client's lack of power.[38]

Clients tolerate a great deal to come to providers: they give up personal information, time, and transportation costs; they sustain the potential dissonance regarding information presented in the session; and they endure the demands counselors make on them based on organizational rules or bureaucracy. At the same time, they risk shame, stigma, and judgment. It is a sacrifice counselors too often take for granted because they hold all the cards. Consider HIV prevention, a topic that is already likely to be culturally charged in this power context, and it is clear why the onus is on counselors to adapt.

For counselors to employ the power in the client's culture to reach prevention goals, his or her empathy and acceptance of the social context are critical. An awareness of this context can help counselors gain a true picture of clients' capabilities and endowments and identify both the sense of powerlessness clients may feel in relationships and the sources of power on which they rely for health promotion.[39]

The Power of Culture and Working Downhill

Barbara Solomon defines the attributes of the nonracist counselor quite simply: "the ability to perceive in any behavior—other's or one's own—alternative ways to explain that behavior, particularly those [behaviors] which the self might most strongly reject as false."[40] Counselors establish cross-cultural credentials with clients not by showing off bits of knowledge about the traditional behaviors or beliefs of a group but by regularly demonstrating an openness to learning about the forces that affect clients and influence their HIV-related risk or protective behaviors. Francesca Farr concurs: "The minority patient will respect and appreciate your acknowledgment of cultural differences. . . . It is not how much one knows about the culture that determines the success of the clinical encounter, but the clinician's overt recognition that the patient's culture is important and as deep and rich as anyone's culture."[41]

To seek alternative explanations and, thereby, more effective prevention strategies, counselors can learn to wonder before they speak—to question the meaning of a client's behaviors in the context of the function of these behaviors. Thus, working downhill in HIV prevention counseling consists of four steps:

1. Find ways to acknowledge regularly to oneself and to the client that each human being comes with both cultural and personal histories and that both of these are integral to a sense of self and a shared worldview. These histories are especially important when dealing with elements, such as sexual activity, that are essential to one's identity, well-being, and social role.
2. Rather than limiting communication to the verbal mode favored in psychotherapy, incorporate a full range of sensory information and expressive resources to uncover the style and medium that makes prevention approaches most accessible, understandable, and acceptable to the client.
3. Don't be afraid to modify prevention messages, modes, and materials on the spot in the counseling session as new information emerges that may make culturally biased prevention concepts clearer to clients with different worldviews.
4. Account for the cultural dynamics on both sides of the therapeutic engagement, exploring not only the client's barriers to change but also the meanings of power, sex, drugs, and other HIV-related issues to the counselor.

This last point is crucial and often minimized: counselors must be aware of their own values and beliefs if they are to consider the effect their behaviors might have on the cross-cultural message. This requirement parallels the general responsibility of therapists to sort through motivations, emotional determinants, and countertransference through the processes of supervision and consultation.

To this end, it may be useful for providers to consider every client interaction to be cross-cultural and to wonder out loud and without interpretation when they encounter behaviors that seem inappropriate or incomprehensible. For example: "I don't know what it means, but I've noticed you haven't made eye contact with me during the discussion of condoms. [Pause to leave room for client if he or she wishes to respond.] I mention this because I want to be as useful as I can in helping you to decide what to do. I always want to know if there something I might be doing differently to help you feel supported, so you can ask or do what you need."

This is not a script; an interchange like this one will involve the counselor's perception in the moment, risk taking, the forestalling of behavioral interpretation, and most important, the willingness to accept whatever the client communicates.

It is essential to go through an explicit process of uncovering expectations and determining with the client the parameters of an appropriate exchange. Overlooking this process will open the door to blaming the client and his or her culture for failing to fulfill a contract that was never made apparent. If this process is undertaken honestly, the counselor will realize that he or she too expects to get something from these contacts: the recognition of his or her words with a nod or a question, a greeting and farewell, even a thank you. To maximize the momentum of these interactions requires counselors to be aware of their own expectations of each intervention— for example, "I want her to make a verbal commitment to me to use condoms and take several home to try." Some counselors will want to give or get more, and others less, so they must continually grapple with their own met and unmet expectations.

Another principle, almost self-evident yet rarely heeded, is to spend time learning something about the cultural worldviews and HIV-related behavioral taboos of clients. The ability to engage in a humble and honest acknowledgment of difference is not part of therapeutic training. In fact, such discussion is traditionally discouraged in American culture in favor of the concept of a cultural melting pot, a concept that labels difference as bad and sameness as unifying.[42] This exploration requires a major expansion of social and professional circles, contact with a range of consultants, and the development of referral and support networks before cross-cultural contacts occur.

Credibility is critical to working downhill and to the therapeutic relationship. A study by Jacquelyn Flaskerud found that effectiveness and trust depend on the client perceiving the counselor as credible.[43] This too may seem obvious, but mainstream American providers often assume that credibility accompanies degrees or job titles. Although such achievement may indeed be critical to credibility with some clients, many groups confer status only in terms of the quality of each interaction or a person's reputation for delivering something of value to others in the group. Thus a counselor may gain credibility and respect only in response to his or her prior success as a healer, as someone able to offer tangible aid well beyond the abstractions of HIV prevention. Counselors need to attend carefully to the measures of credibility clients use and to how they as providers can meet these expectations. Beyond the usual medical, sexual, and drug-use histories, effective counselors learn by observation, inquiry, and study of a client's cultural identity, which counselors integrate to different degrees into the assessment and resolution of a "problem." Cultural identity includes aspects of "Old World," American mainstream, and victim-system worldviews.

The LEARN Model

LEARN is one of the structural models useful in acknowledging a client's culture and developing insights into how she or he conceptualizes a problem or concern.[44] The acronym LEARN stands for

Listen with sympathy and understanding to the client's perceptions of the problem—an active process of soliciting in many ways the information necessary to understand what a person feels he or she needs.

Explain your view of the problem, which may or may not be different from the client's but is expressed in terms that relate to previously learned information.

Acknowledge and discuss the differences and similarities between these two views—as you heard them.

Recommend a response.

Negotiate agreement about what both client and counselor will do and about who else should be involved in the process.

Psychologists representing diverse ethnic cultures endorse LEARN, but some of them caution that it is not a shield against ethnocentrism. Tafoya and Wirth recognize the validity of the

LEARN model, but suggest that all too often focus is taken away from the client through the practitioner's failure to effectively manage the five components. For instance, the client's perception of events is glossed over or ignored in the Explain state as the practitioner focuses on preparing to Recommend a response. This failure to Acknowledge leads directly to an inability to Negotiate, and demonstrates "a lack of understanding of the critical importance and attention that must be given to process when working with culturally-diverse clients."[45]

This process represents the route by which both provider and client can integrate cultural perspectives into the clinical response.

The components of LEARN should lead to HIV counseling strategies and tactics that work downhill with culture rather than uphill against it. The caption from an AIDS education poster targeting one element of the gay male subculture epitomizes the absolute synchrony of the message with this subculture's values and behaviors, and serves as a model for working downhill: "If you're dominant, demand a condom. If you're submissive, beg for one."

&

When human beings lived in small, isolated, homogenous settlements, they tended to be culturally similar and to behave in the same ways. However, as the human experience became more complex, the number of reference groups with which people could identify increased, and people identified not only as male or female but also as a member of a particular racial or ethnic group, age group, social class, religious denomination, nationality, region, and profession or occupation. The cultural mandates of each of these reference groups overlay each other like a series of lenses through which to view the world. For this reason, counselors must guard against stereotyping and assuming that all members of a cultural group can, and should, be approached using exactly the same methods. Stereotypes serve only to separate counselors from their clients and to limit the view of who needs prevention counseling and services and how to reach them.

Cultural awareness requires the time and interest to go beyond stereotypes to uncover the realities and the meanings behind a client's behaviors, the prevention approaches the therapist wishes to implement, and the therapist's own behaviors. Dangers lurk in this work: the downhill momentum can carry the therapist beyond the evidence at hand. It can also obscure the principle that each person is a unique individual with combinations of emotional and social risk factors specific to him or her, and that these differences require personalized interventions recognizing the distinct skills, resources, and limitations each client brings to the counseling experience.

In the face of so many differences in interpersonal rules and the charged content of AIDS risk, it is easy to feel paralyzed by the potential mistakes that may seem to lurk in the HIV counseling relationship. To paraphrase a wise clinical supervisor, however, "Our patients are willing to forgive mistakes of the head. Mistakes of the heart are more difficult. Our job is to know as much as we can and to know the difference between our mistakes."

When therapists view clients as full participants in the HIV intervention, they worry less about the inevitable cultural mistakes, because in these moments, the message that the counselor communicates most clearly is that both client and counselor are engaged in a learning experience that aims toward the shared goal of ensuring the client's health. In acknowledging and exploring cultural mistakes openly without devaluing the skills they bring to the intervention, counselors further communicate the message that everyone makes errors, a message easily applied to HIV-related behavior change. Further, a counselor's sensitive response to crossing cultures can model for clients how to handle the anxiety and awkwardness of attempting new behaviors. For counselors working with HIV disease, the experience of taking risks to reach across to clients who are culturally different offers lessons applicable to all clients and a perspective that makes them more effective counselors to everyone they serve.

Notes

1. Bayer, R. "Commentary–AIDS Prevention and Cultural Sensitivity: Are They Compatible?" *American Journal of Public Health*, 1994, *84*(6), 895–898.
2. Kluckhorn, F. R. "A Method for Eliciting Value Orientations." *Anthropological Linguistics*, 1960, 2(2), 1–23.
3. Bayer, "Commentary."

4. Hall, E., and Hall, M. *Understanding Cultural Differences.* Yarmouth, Maine: Intercultural Press, 1990.

5. Woodworth, R. "The Puzzle of Color Vocabularies." In I. Al-Issa and W. Dennis (eds.), *Cross-Cultural Studies of Behavior.* Austin, Tex.: Holt, Rinehart and Winston, 1970.

6. Bayer, "Commentary."

7. Hall and Hall, *Understanding Cultural Differences.*

8. Pinderhughes, E. *Understanding Race, Ethnicity, and Power: The Key to Efficacy in Clinical Practice.* New York: Free Press, 1989, p. 315.

9. Freimuth, V. S., and Mettger, W. "Is There a Hard-to-Reach Audience?" *Public Health Reports,* 1990, *105*(10), 232–238.

10. Milburn, G., Gary, L., Booth, J. A., and others. "Conducting Epidemiological Research in a Minority Community: Methodological Considerations." *Journal of Community Psychology,* 1991, *19*(1), 3–12.

11. Ibid.

12. Mays, V. M., and Jackson, J. S. "AIDS Survey Methodology with Black Americans." *Social Science and Medicine,* 1990, *33*(1), 47–54.

13. Mays, V. M., Cochran, S. D., Bellinger, G., and others. "The Language of Black Gay Men's Sexual Behavior: Implications for AIDS Risk Reduction." *Journal of Sex Research,* 1992, *29*(3), 425–434.

14. Mays and Jackson, "AIDS Survey Methodology."

15. Mays, Cochran, Bellinger, and others, "Black Gay Men's Sexual Behavior."

16. Peterson, J. L., Coates, T. J., Catania, J. A., and others. "High-Risk Sexual Behavior and Condom Use Among Gay and Bisexual African American Men." *AIDS Education and Prevention,* 1995, *7*(1), 1–9.

17. Hsu, J. "Asian Family Interaction Patterns and Their Therapeutic Implications." *International Journal of Family Psychiatry,* 1983, *4*(4), 307–320.

18. Aoki, B., and Ja, D. "AIDS and Asian Americans: Psychosocial Issues." Presentation at the 95th Annual Meeting of the American Psychological Association, New York, Aug. 1987.

19. Flaskerud, J. H. "The Effect of Culture-Compatible Intervention on the Utilization of Mental Health Service by Minority Clients." *Community Mental Health Journal,* 1986, *22*(2), 127–141.

20. Day, N., Houston-Hamilton, A., Taylor, D., and others. *A Report on the First Tracking Survey of AIDS Knowledge, Attitudes, and Behaviors in San Francisco's Black Communities.* Vol. 1. San Francisco: Polaris Research and Development, 1989.

21. Orque, M., Bloch, B., and Monrroy, L. *Ethnic Nursing Care: A Multicultural Approach.* St. Louis, Mo.: Mosby-Year Book, 1983, p. 101.

22. Thomas, S., and Quinn, S. C. "The Tuskegee Syphilis Study, 1932 to 1972: Implications for HIV Education and AIDS Risk Reduction

Programs in the Black Community." *American Journal of Public Health,* 1991, *81*(11), 1498–1499.

23. Jones, J. *Bad Blood: The Tuskegee Syphilis Experiment.* New York: Free Press, 1993.

24. Kirp, D. L. *Rethinking the Legacy of Tuskegee in the Era of AIDS.* Working Paper no. 208, Graduate School of Public Policy. Berkeley: University of California Press, 1994.

25. Kirp, D. L., and Bayer, R. *The Politics of Needle Exchange for AIDS Prevention.* Working Paper no. 199, Graduate School of Public Policy. Berkeley: University of California Press, 1993.

26. Turner, P. *I Heard It Through the Grapevine: Rumor in African American Culture.* Berkeley: University of California Press, 1993.

27. Tafoya, T., and Wirth, D. "The Second Decade of AIDS, Training for Cultural Competence: Vow Not to Repeat Old Mistakes." In T. Eversole and J. R. Anderson (eds.), *Psychology, HIV, & Communities of Color Trainer's Manual.* Washington, D.C.: American Psychological Association, 1996, p. 85.

28. Green, L. "Health Education Today and the PRECEDE Framework." In M. Dreuter, S. Deeds, and K. Partridge (eds.), *Health Education Planning: A Diagnostic Approach.* Palo Alto, Calif.: Mayfield, 1980, p. 6.

29. Ibid.

30. Tafoya and Wirth, "Training for Cultural Competence," p. 88.

31. Sue, D. W. *Counseling the Culturally Different: Theory and Practice.* (2nd ed.) New York: Wiley, 1990.

32. Pinderhughes, *Understanding Race, Ethnicity, and Power.*

33. Kline, A., Kline, E., and Oken, E. "Minority Women and Sexual Choice in the Age of AIDS." *Social Science and Medicine,* 1992, *34*(4), 455.

34. De La Cancela, V. "Minority AIDS Prevention: Moving Beyond Cultural Perspectives Toward Sociopolitical Empowerment." *AIDS Education and Prevention,* 1989, *1*(2), 141–153.

35. Sue, *Counseling the Culturally Different.*

36. Kline, Kline, and Oken, "Minority Women and Sexual Choice."

37. Marin, B. "Hispanic Culture: Effects on Prevention and Care." *FOCUS: A Guide to HIV Research and Counseling,* 1993, *6*(4), 1–4.

38. Pinderhughes, E. "Teaching Empathy in Cross-Cultural Social Work." *Social Work,* 1979, *24*(4), p. 315.

39. Pinderhughes, *Understanding Race, Ethnicity, and Power.*

40. Solomon, B. "Empowerment: Social Work in Oppressed Community." *Journal of Social Work Practice,* 1987, *2*(4), 79–91.

41. Farr, F. "Somatization." In A. Lopez, E. Lee, and F. Farr (eds.), *Immigrants and Refugees: A Handbook of Clinical Care.* San Francisco: University of California Press, 1991, p. 11.

42. Glazer, N., and Moynihan, D. *Beyond the Melting Pot.* Cambridge, Mass.: MIT Press, 1963.
43. Flaskerud, "The Effect of Culture-Compatible Intervention."
44. Berlin, E., and Fowkes, W. "A Teaching Framework for Cross-Cultural Health Care." *Western Journal of Medicine,* 1983, *139*(6), 934–938.
45. Tafoya and Wirth, "Training for Cultural Competence," p. 87.

Chapter Six

Substance Use Case Management, Harm Reduction, and HIV Prevention

Miriam Garfinkel

Substance use—through needle sharing and sexual contact with seropositive injection drug users—still accounts for one-third of cases of HIV disease in the United States.[1] But there have been notably successful efforts to reduce transmission among substance users, a group of people perceived to be unreachable. The most effective interventions have applied harm reduction, an approach to protect against transmission in the absence of abstinence. Guided by two key principles—self-efficacy and incremental change—harm reduction has manifested primarily in the form of drug treatment, especially methadone maintenance; needle exchange; and instruction regarding cleaning needles.

One particularly successful means of implementing harm-reduction principles has been clinical case management. Holistic in nature, this approach emphasizes as a therapeutic tool the relationship between client and case manager, at the same time acknowledging the importance of providing linkage to practical resources and other service providers. This type of case management integrates substance use and HIV prevention interventions, incorporating aspects of psychodynamic theory and harm-reduction theory to create a comprehensive model of care and change.

This chapter details the clinical case management approach and asserts its advantages in the context of HIV prevention for substance users. It also proposes a case management model—based on harm-reduction strategies—to protect injection drug users and their sexual partners.

Harm-Reduction Theory

Harm reduction was adopted in the United States in response to the HIV epidemic. It assumes that a using addict can make positive changes in his or her life despite continued drug use and melds ideas from behavior change theory with understandings of dependency and addiction. Harm reductionists posit the obvious but often overlooked axiom that people use substances—just as they engage in risky sexual behaviors—for a reason. Substance use is adaptive, a way to cope with real circumstances, past or present, such as poverty, racism, and abuse. Change must begin with understanding and accepting an individual in relationship to a behavior, helping him or her identify the harm that results from that behavior, and working with him or her to make small, incremental changes in the behavior to decrease that harm.

The *Diagnostic and Statistical Manual of Mental Disorders* of the American Psychiatric Association *(DSM-IV)* defines substance abuse and dependency as follows:

- A cluster of cognitive, behavioral, and physiological symptoms indicating that the individual continues use of the substance despite significant substance-related problems.
- A maladaptive pattern of substance use manifested by recurrent and significant adverse consequences related to the repeated use of substances.[2]

In contrast, harm-reduction theory conceptualizes drug use along a spectrum from casual use to controlled use to chaotic use, rather than in more general terms of dependency or addiction. A "casual" user is the equivalent of a recreational user, someone who truly uses a drug on a social basis with no signs of physical or physiological addiction. "Controlled" users may be dependent, physically or psychologically, but are able to use in a way that does not create adverse consequences in their lives. A "chaotic" user is an individual who is physically or psychologically dependent and continues to use despite adverse consequences in his or her life.

Harm-reduction theory values the role abstinence may play in the lives of some users, acknowledging that whereas some users have the ability to move from chaotic use to controlled or casual use, some chaotic users may need to achieve abstinence in order to stop the damage in their lives. Other users may also benefit optimally from abstinence, but given the opportunity—through respectful, clinical engagement and the experience of improved quality of life—many active users have the ability to mitigate both HIV- and substance-related harm without achieving abstinence.

The Harm Reduction Coalition in Oakland, California, defines harm reduction in the following way: "A set of strategies and tactics that encourage users to reduce the harm done to themselves and communities by their licit and illicit substance use. In allowing users access to the tools with which to become healthier, we recognize the competency of their efforts to protect themselves, their loved ones and their communities. . . . You don't remove a person's primary coping mechanisms until others are in place. It starts wherever a person is at, and moves at the pace of the individual. . . . The operating principle is any positive change."[3]

Although some harm-reduction interventions, such as needle exchange and methadone maintenance, have received a great deal of attention, effective harm reduction is dependent on creativity and innovation in program development to meet individual needs. This perspective easily fits within the theoretical foundations of clinical case management.

Clinical Case Management

Although the concept of clinical case management preceded the formulation of harm reduction, it mirrors the key concepts in harm reduction: self-efficacy and incremental change. According to Robert Surber, clinical case management establishes and uses the relationship between the case manager and the client to achieve change in the client, within the client's environment, and in the relationship between the client and the environment.[4] The case manager–client connection becomes a vehicle through which clients can better understand themselves, their interpersonal relationships, and their life goals. Surber describes this type of case management as, "as much a way of thinking about care as it is providing specific interventions. . . . What is therapeutic is what is helpful."[5] Successful interventions are defined by their ability to help clients improve the quality of their lives.

A clinical case management intervention is one in which the ongoing case manager–client relationship is a key component in creating small, positive changes. When developed in the 1960s through work with chronic psychiatric populations, such a change might have been an improvement in medication compliance. In working with active users, change may comprise increasing compliance with medical appointments by limiting drug use on the day of the appointment, or reducing HIV-related risk by increasing intermittent use of clean needles or condoms. Preliminary results of a research project comparing HIV-infected substance users receiving clinical case management with those receiving usual care showed a greater than 50 percent reduction in positive urinalysis results after six months in case management.[6]

Linkage is a central function of case managers. Linkage includes a set of interventions ranging from referral to actually taking clients to appointments or helping them negotiate bureaucracies. These interventions are designed to facilitate access to resources. Case managers provide a combination of links to practical resources—housing, food, medical care—and to peer and social service support. In addition, case managers help with skills-building and may provide individualized counseling. The result of this menu of options is the opportunity for a comprehensive, individualized, client-centered treatment approach. Client participation is always voluntary, and goals are defined through a collaboration between case manager and client. Ideal results are outcomes that are meaningful on a practical as well as intrapsychic level. In other words, clients build a sense of self-efficacy and self-esteem through participation in developing and then realizing a concrete plan for change.

Case managers often come from the communities they are serving, as the importance of peer intervention has been proven over and over again in interventions with active users.[7] Because clinical case management, unlike other types of peer relationships,

relies on a psychodynamic understanding of the interactions between the case manager and the client, it is essential that case managers have formal education in the foundations of psychodynamic
theory or on-the-job supervision and training in this perspective.
Understanding of such issues as transference and countertransference and maintaining boundaries are important for case managers to apply in their work with clients.

Working with Addiction

There are many theories of why people become addicted to substances. Substance use has been blamed on moral weakness, bad
habits, a gene, a disease, and unresolved familial issues. In studying either active or abstinent users, it can be difficult to weed out
etiology from the ravages of the addiction itself. It is not uncommon for retrospective histories to show evidence of preexisting
character disorders, affective disorders, or thought disorders. In
addition, the alluring power of the substances themselves cannot
be dismissed.

Although people may have a variety of these psychiatric symptoms, some substance users become addicted partly by chance: they
are young and impulsive, and they want to "fit in"; they fall into
drug use because of peer pressure; and the power of the experience itself starts to take over. The sweet honor roll student becomes anxious, suspicious of others because he or she is hiding
something; and as the person gives more and more attention to
drugs, guilt takes over, grades slip, fear of getting "caught" leads to
lying, and the road forks toward a very different life.

Regardless of his or her level of functioning prior to beginning
use, once a user becomes dependent or addicted, or chaotic in his
or her use, the addiction itself becomes a primary disorder with its
own set of behavioral and psychological characteristics. Addicts generally have difficulties with self-esteem, are sensitive to the actions
and thoughts of their peers, may present a somewhat grandiose external self (in order to manage a fragmented internal self), and can
have difficulty "holding" or managing their emotions.[8]

From a treatment perspective—and to apply a self psychological construct—the presence of an idealized, usable "selfobject"
over a significant period of time is essential if the client is to man-

age internal change. Selfobjects, in this instance, are other people who provide the mirroring necessary for the development and internalization of healthy self-esteem and self-ambition. This suggests why community and peer interventions have proven to be essential components of both addiction treatment and HIV prevention. The centrality of self-esteem also poses a powerful argument for the addition of a therapeutic relationship within a client-centered framework in order to optimize harm-reduction or case management interventions. From the case manager's vantage point within this ongoing therapeutic relationship, it is also easier to sort out a client's coexisting psychiatric disorders, which may benefit from evaluation and treatment.

Maintaining a psychodynamic framework can be particularly challenging, as case managers have the freedom to work with clients outside of traditional social service provision sites such as agency offices, which furnish natural boundaries and role expectations. An essential tool to reach substance-using populations and develop trust with them, case management in San Francisco has included outreach in hospital emergency rooms, methadone maintenance clinics, and housing shelters, as well as on street corners where drug dealing and prostitution occur. Delivering services in these settings has several advantages. It helps case managers find clients and develop trust. In settings where there are other service providers, it allows case managers the opportunity to link with these providers. Linking with providers enables case managers to become "translators" between client and provider or service system, facilitating mutual understanding and the effective use of the system. Finally, by being present in these settings, case managers are able to foster connections among clients, facilitating natural peer support and creating formal peer support groups of users interested in making similar changes.

Barriers to HIV-Related Case Management

Drug users pose significant challenges to HIV prevention work, and much has been written about effective approaches to reach them.[9–12] There are many potential barriers to this work. First, for many drug users, involvement in illegal activity to support addiction leads them to be suspicious of "outsiders," including outreach workers or social service personnel not well known to them. Second, African American and Latino users, who are disproportionately represented among injection drug and crack users, are more likely to distrust larger systems because of their experiences with institutional racism and classism.[13] Third, drug users are reliant on community norms that may not support safer practices. Lastly, more pressing needs take precedence over HIV prevention; these can include maintaining an addiction and dealing with economic and social concerns, housing, food, and more acute medical problems.

Despite the challenges of overcoming these barriers, it is notable that education is not the predominant prevention difficulty when reaching out to this population. Injection drug users have, to a large degree, been successfully educated about safer needle-sharing practices. As has been shown time and again in many populations, however, education alone does not facilitate behavior change. Despite their knowledge about the dangers of HIV and the ways to protect themselves from these dangers, users continue to participate in unsafe drug-using behaviors. The reasons for this disparity are often connected to economics or interpersonal difficulties, circumstances that can supersede information.

The integration of case management focused on reducing both HIV and substance-using risk is a sensible one. Case managers can address some of these issues through linkage to needle exchange or skills-building programs. In addition, there is evidence that injection drug users are not as educated about safer sexual practices—in particular for those who are heterosexually identified—as they are about needle-cleaning practices.[14,15] Case managers, through the fostering of ongoing, trusting relationships with active users, have the opportunity to create a venue for talking about sexual practices. The goal of this approach might be developing common understandings of HIV-related risks and implementing client-centered interventions designed to help lower these risks.

HIV Prevention Efforts: The Current Scene with Substance Users

A review of current prevention efforts can help illuminate which have been successful and which have not, informing decisions about applying comprehensive clinical case management as a necessary component of care. These efforts can be divided into those aimed at users seeking treatment and those aimed at active users.

Working with Users Seeking Treatment

Substance use treatment remains the most effective way to prevent HIV transmission as a direct result of substance use. At the very least, it secures a "captive" audience. At best, treatment provides an arena for a reevaluation of and recommitment to an individual's life and well-being. Treatment can encompass a variety of approaches, including methadone maintenance, residential treatment, outpatient programs, and detoxification units.

Methadone Maintenance Treatment

For decades, methadone maintenance has been an effective and somewhat controversial method to decrease heroin use. Early on in the epidemic, methadone maintenance clinics, with their daily access to known injection drug users, became obvious venues for prevention messages. Since that time, methadone maintenance sites have delivered not only HIV prevention messages but also HIV-related counseling and medical care. The development of ongoing relationships with mental health or medical providers opens the potential for HIV prevention through work on self-esteem, increased health, and skills-building.

The obvious drawback of this type of treatment is that it reaches a small population of substance users: heroin addicts who wish to use methadone to manage, or detoxify from, their addiction. Case managers, working in conjunction with methadone maintenance clinic staff, have the ability to access a wide array of substance users in a variety of settings beyond methadone maintenance treatment programs, reinforcing prevention messages and facilitating linkage to services outside the clinic.

Residential Drug Treatment

Residential treatment settings, or "therapeutic communities," offer ongoing behavioral and peer reinforcement for drug and alcohol users that can have long-lasting effects. They also have high attrition rates[16] and can have waiting lists that are prohibitive for the user seeking treatment. In other words, they can work very well, but only for a small number of people.

In an environment where the examination of an individual's drug use and life issues is continually reinforced, it is logical to introduce HIV prevention efforts—although historically this integration has been challenging. Staff and program administrators, in their enthusiasm to help clients manage addiction, have feared losing that focus by introducing other issues, such as HIV prevention. In addition, staff are often recovering addicts, and it can be difficult for them to address HIV-related risk with clients if they have not explored these issues themselves. Funding streams have historically mirrored this compartmentalization of issues. It was not until 1997 that the Centers for Disease Control and Prevention allocated funds to ensure that treatment program staff understand HIV-related issues and have the skills necessary to work with clients regarding HIV risk behaviors and prevention.

As residential treatment programs move toward integrating prevention interventions, they will increasingly provide linkage resources for case management. In addition, case managers can work with clients who are on waiting lists for residential treatment, laying a groundwork of harm-reduction messages, both HIV and drug related, that residential settings will reinforce after a client enters the program.

Outpatient Treatment Programs

Outpatient treatment programs, settings that require attendance ranging from weekly to daily, have become popular as lower-cost interventions. In San Francisco, outpatient programs target a variety of types of substance use as well as specific populations such as African Americans, Asian Americans, Latinos, gay men, lesbians, and sex workers. Such a focus is an attraction for users and a strength for the program, building on the importance of community and peer reinforcement of norms.

Outpatient programs employ both group and individual counseling and education related to substance use. This combination offers a rich source of HIV prevention opportunities. A San Francisco study, in which researchers compared two HIV interventions with substance users seeking treatment, suggests how some of these approaches might be shaped.[17] The first intervention was a psychoeducational group focused on information; the second was a series of individual sessions combining education and skills-building in preparation for the high-risk situations that clients would most likely encounter. The group approach resulted in increases in HIV-related knowledge and self-efficacy that were retained three months later; the individual approach, augmenting education with skills-building related to real-life situations, resulted in even more frequent safer needle-sharing and sexual practices.

As with residential treatment, the HIV prevention opportunity in outpatient settings has been fettered for several reasons. Outpatient treatment staff may have difficulty knowing how to talk with clients about HIV risk and how to help clients explore such issues as deciding to take an HIV test, if they themselves have not explored these issues in their personal lives or received training in how to do so. Again, lack of prevention funding has historically reinforced the lack of service integration. Finally, because outpatient treatment is aimed at users who remain functional in their communities and daily lives, the most chaotic clients attend only sporadically and may have difficulty benefiting from the ongoing reinforcement necessary for successful change.

Clinical case managers have the ability to duplicate the best prevention efforts outpatient treatment offers. Case management is predicated on the idea of integrated service delivery, using the relationship with the case manager to address substance use as well as HIV prevention concerns. Case managers are educated and trained in providing comprehensive care, ensuring a focus on all aspects of harm-related activity in a client's life. These providers can work with clients in their own environments and facilitate engagement with the most chaotic of users. With the development of an ongoing relationship, case managers can educate clients about HIV prevention issues and work with them to problem-solve in risky situations. As is true with linkage to residential treatment, case managers can work with clients who are waiting to enter outpatient treatment, laying the groundwork for a comprehensive approach to treatment.

Detoxification Units

Detoxification units, inpatient settings for those in acute withdrawal, respond to drug-related physical or emotional crises, usually among individuals who have not considered seeking drug treatment. To the outside observer, a detoxification program may seem like a revolving door as clients enter on short notice, stay three to seven days, and leave once the crisis seems resolved.

A detox unit, however, can become an important point of contact for the disenfranchised, chaotic substance user and can therefore provide an important HIV prevention opportunity to clients at highest risk—a route to counseling and testing and linkage to other HIV-related services.[18] Case managers can facilitate linkage within detox units, begin to establish relationships with users in the program, and continue that relationship once the client is discharged.

Reaching Out to Active Users

Successful prevention can and must take place outside of formal drug treatment settings if rates of infection are to be reduced among active users—those clients who are by definition the most likely to put themselves at risk. Current prevention efforts with this population have had some success and provide important lessons for a clinical case management model. Among the most notable out-of-treatment efforts are information dissemination, interventions performed by community health outreach workers, client contact in social service venues, and needle exchange programs.

Information Dissemination

Although education does not equal prevention, education is an essential component of risk reduction. Despite assumptions to the contrary, active users can learn to reduce risk. But it is even more useful to help these individuals understand how they can apply knowledge to real-life situations.[19]

Prevention efforts in the early years of the epidemic were focused almost exclusively on education about needle sharing and cleaning—messages disseminated primarily through posters and leaflets, billboards and bus placards. Later, these messages became more comprehensive, including information about the dangers of sharing works—cotton and water—as well as needles. By the 1990s, surveys showed that injection drug users were relatively well educated about the likelihood of HIV transmission through the sharing of injection equipment. Far fewer were aware of HIV-related sexual risk.[20]

In a 1991 study of injection drug users in Cleveland, 91 percent of respondents knew that HIV is not eliminated by cleaning needles with water alone.[21] In contrast, only 46 percent knew that latex condoms provided better protection than other types of condoms. A 1992 Puerto Rican study found that although injection drug users knew about the HIV risk inherent in needle sharing, they knew less about the dangers of sharing works and having unprotected sex. The study found that users had little skill in negotiating situations that would challenge their abilities to use this knowledge—for example, dealing with pressure from partners to have unsafe sex.[22]

Case managers can use the information clients have absorbed through HIV education campaigns as a springboard to deepen and broaden levels of understanding, ensuring that drug users are familiar with all the aspects of HIV-related risk. In addition, case managers can use their relationship to help clients increase their abilities to negotiate difficult situations—in other words, to apply their knowledge.

Community Health Outreach Workers

Community involvement and peer support are significant components of effective risk-reduction interventions, and the most successful efforts are performed by peers who are former or current users themselves.[23] In the 1990s, HIV and substance abuse treatment providers have increasingly emphasized the efforts of community health outreach workers (CHOWs) in order to forge the connection between service providers and users within the community. CHOWs, generally most effective if they are members of the communities they serve, deliver prevention messages to drug users wherever they may be. CHOWs have the ability to spend days, weeks, or months in communities or neighborhoods building relationships and trust with drug users, relationships that reinforce and legitimize their prevention messages.

Outreach workers can also provide information and referral and, more recently, street-based HIV antibody counseling and testing through the use of oral testing methods. Antibody testing is difficult to sell to people living precarious lives one day at a time, who have no desire to discover they have a "fatal" disease. Studies have shown that even participants in paid studies have a difficult time returning for their disclosure session to receive test results.[24,25] CHOWs can provide drug-using clients the ongoing support necessary for them to learn their serostatus. This is crucial both for prevention efforts and for care for seropositive clients, who can benefit from early antiviral intervention with combination therapy.

Some of the most important functions of outreach workers are similar to those of case managers, though more limited in scope. CHOWs work with clients in their communities, focus on building relationships and trust, and provide information and referral. Case managers are able to take these functions several steps further through their ability to function in a broader array of settings, link their clients to resources, and apply a psychodynamic understanding of the relationship to further behavior change and self-understanding.

Client Contact in Social Service Venues

HIV prevention is most effective if the social and medical services to which drug users have access are integrated, ensuring that everywhere active users go, HIV prevention messages are introduced and reinforced. Most disenfranchised drug users come into regular contact with various social and health service delivery providers, for example, public health clinics, emergency rooms, and public assistance offices. Although these settings increasingly offer a forum for HIV prevention messages through written materials and structured client education programs, they themselves may frustrate prevention efforts by treating drug users in negative ways within such institutions. These perceptions may discourage clients from accessing services, or they may sabotage the provider-client alliance necessary to undertake the difficult conversations that accompany effective HIV prevention counseling. Case managers, through their ability to be physically present in these settings, can both reinforce prevention messages and act as "translators" between other providers and their clients, helping to interpret communications and facilitate relationships.

Needle Exchange Programs

Real-life concerns often take precedence over hypothetical HIV risk, and people are better able to make changes when their basic needs are met. Recent studies have shown that most needle users have no desire to share needles.[26] Needle sharing usually occurs because of socioeconomic factors, such as the scarcity of new needles, rather than because of "subcultural norms" such as the ritual of using or the need for intimacy.

In study after study, needle exchange programs have demonstrated their role in preventing the spread of HIV disease. Needle exchange programs are generally mobile, with an emphasis on easy access by drug users; sites move to different neighborhoods on different nights of the week. Users bring in their "dirty" needles and are allowed to swap, one-for-one, for clean ones. The programs make establishing consistency and trust a top priority, laying the groundwork for other types of interventions.

Needle exchange programs are extremely popular among addicts themselves. In San Francisco, where the injection drug using population is estimated to be somewhere between twelve thousand and fifteen thousand, the needle exchange program distributes more than one million needles a year.[27] Needle exchange programs directly prevent HIV transmission by deterring needle sharing and by providing an opportunity for further HIV education regarding safer needle sharing practices and sexual activity. In recognition of their access to users who may otherwise remain invisible to traditional service systems, San Francisco needle exchanges have begun to provide medical care and HIV counseling and testing.

Needle exchange is effective for some of the same reasons that clinical case management is: easy access, an emphasis on practical resources, the development of trusting relationships as foundations for dissemination of information and behavior change, and respectful engagement. Case managers have the opportunity to deepen these relationships.

∽◦∾

Despite treatment advances, as we approach the end of the second decade of the epidemic we remain far from a cure for HIV. The virus continues to spread, people continue to die, and communities continue to be ravaged. In this atmosphere, it is difficult to acknowledge the prevention successes.

Over the years, prevention efforts have grown. Both success and failure have led to greater understandings of how people change behaviors. Interventions have increasingly emphasized skills-building and the influence of community norms. There has been a greater integration of HIV prevention efforts both within services for specific communities and in the general population. Divisions within social and medical service provision systems, which arose to address HIV-related needs in the 1980s, have begun to dissolve, and the goal is shifting toward providing quality HIV treatment and prevention in the contexts of all medical and social service settings.

From this ground have grown harm-reduction strategies and HIV prevention clinical case management services. These two treatment approaches combine to form a holistic and comprehensive model with achievable objectives—an ideal approach for working with populations of substance users, who are at the highest risk for HIV infection but are the least likely to be reached.

Notes

1. Centers for Disease Control and Prevention. *HIV/AIDS Surveillance Report*, 1997, *9*(1).

2. American Psychiatric Association. *Diagnostic and Statistical Manual of Mental Disorders.* (4th ed.) Washington, D.C.: American Psychiatric Association, 1994.

3. Report from the meeting of the National Harm Reduction Working Group, Oakland, Calif., Oct. 21–23, 1993.

4. Surber, R. W. "An Approach to Care." In R. W. Surber (ed.), *Clinical Case Management: A Guide to Comprehensive Treatment of Serious Mental Illness.* Thousand Oaks, Calif.: Sage, 1994.

5. Ibid, p. 3.

6. Sorensen, J. L., Dilley, J. W., Delucchi, K., and others. "Case Management of Substance Abusers with HIV/AIDS: Preliminary Results." Abstracts from the conference of the College of Problems of Drug Dependency, Scottsdale, Ariz., June 1998.

7. Guydish, J., and Sanstad, K. H. "Behavior Change Among Intravenous Drug Users: The Role of Community-Based Interventions." *Psychology of Addictive Behaviors*, 1992, *6*(2), 91–99.

8. Levin, J. *Treatment of Alcoholism and Other Addictions.* Northvale, N.J.: Aronson, 1991.

9. Guydish and Sanstad, "Behavior Change Among Intravenous Drug Users."

10. Anderson, J. E., Cheney, R., Clatts, M., and others. "HIV Risk Behavior, Street Outreach, and Condom Use in Eight High-Risk Populations." *AIDS Education and Prevention*, 1996, *8*(3), 191–204.

11. Finlinson, H. A., Robles, R. R., Colon, H. M., and others. "Recruiting and Retaining Out-of-Treatment Injecting Drug Users in the Puerto Rico AIDS Prevention Project." *Human Organization*, 1993, *52*(2), 169–175.

12. Schilling, R. F., El Bassel, N., Serrano, Y., and others. "AIDS Prevention Strategies for Ethnic-Racial Minority Substance Users." *Psychology of Addictive Behaviors,* 1992, *6*(2), 81–90.

13. Ibid.

14. Donoghoe, M. C. "Sex, HIV and the Injecting Drug User." *British Journal of Addiction,* 1992, *87,* 405–416.

15. Finlinson, H. A., Guberti, B., Robles, R. R., and others. "'What We Want to Know About HIV/AIDS': An Analysis of Questions Asked by Substance Abuse Clients Attending AIDS Education Classes in Puerto Rico." *Human Organization,* 1996, *55*(3), 370–378.

16. Schilling, El Bassel, Serrano, and others, "AIDS Prevention Strategies."

17. Sorensen, J. L., London, J., and Morales, E. "Group Counseling." In J. L. Sorensen, L. Wermuth, D. Gibson, and others (eds.), *Preventing AIDS with Drug Users and Their Sexual Partners.* New York: Guilford Press, 1991.

18. Schilling, El Bassel, Serrano, and others, "AIDS Prevention Strategies."

19. Ibid.

20. Donoghoe, "Sex, HIV and the Injecting Drug User."

21. Feucht, T. E., Stephens, R. C., and Gibbs, B. H. "Knowledge About AIDS Among Intravenous Drug Users: An Evaluation of an Education Program." *Journal of AIDS Education and Prevention,* 1991, *3*(1), 10–20.

22. Finlinson, Guberti, Robles, and others, "'What We Want to Know About HIV/AIDS.'"

23. Friedman, S. R., Neaigus, A., Des Jarlais, D. C., and others. "Social Intervention Against AIDS Among Injecting Drug Users." *British Journal of Addiction,* 1992, *87,* 393–404.

24. Finlinson, Robles, Colon, and others. "Recruiting and Retaining Out-of-Treatment Injecting Drug Users."

25. Catania, J. A., Kegeles, S. M., and Coates, T. J. "Psychosocial Predictors of People Who Fail to Return for Their HIV Test Results." *AIDS,* 1990, *4,* 261–262.

26. Carlson, R. G., Siegal, H. A., Wang, J., and others. "Attitudes Toward Needle 'Sharing' Among Injection Drug Users: Combining Qualitative and Quantitative Research Methods." *Human Organization,* 1996, *55*(3), 361–369.

27. Personal communication with René Durazzo, director of programs, San Francisco AIDS Foundation, 1998.

Part Two

Transformation and Psychotherapy
Helping Clients Live with HIV

It is a cliché—and a sentimental one at that—that HIV transforms the lives of people whom it touches. But like all clichés, this one carries a grain of truth, perhaps even a nugget: HIV is an agent of change. The cliché of transformation developed early on in the epidemic, around the time that "AIDS victims" became "people living with HIV." Both of these concepts—transformation and living with AIDS—suggest that the powerful experience of HIV is one that leads not necessarily to death or only toward death but also toward some deeper understanding of life.

That is what psychotherapy is all about. It is a tool not to negate the horror of AIDS but to find some way of living with it, to change perspective in response to altered circumstances. At a time of hope, it is exciting to consider a future when we might treat HIV as a chronic, manageable disease—something that can be combated, requiring adaptation but perhaps little effort of self-discovery and understanding in order to come to terms with its effects.

But despite recent advances in treatment, that day seems distant. As long as there is illness and disability, loss and grief, fear and isolation, confusion and uncertainty; and as long as there is also recovery and rejuvenation—new beginnings and new challenges—we will continue to rely on the empathic and transcendent power of counseling to help people adjust to unpredictable and sometimes unthinkable circumstances. Part Two provides insights into this process.

Chapter Seven

HIV Disease as an Agent of Transformation
A Survey of Therapeutic Approaches

Israel Katz
James W. Dilley

Since the early days of the epidemic, many of us—both seropositive and seronegative—have been challenged by the experience of living and working with HIV. In most cases, challenge has wrought change—some good, some bad, but nonetheless some transformation in the way we live, interact with others, and perceive ourselves.

If, in this way, HIV is a catalyst for transformation, psychotherapy is one of the most effective crucibles for safely engaging in such change. On a practical level, psychotherapy can improve self-esteem, provide emotional support, and teach coping skills—all central tasks for people coping with HIV disease. On a more fundamental level, psychotherapy can help people come to terms with basic existential issues: mortality, disability, spirituality, interpersonal relationships and intimacy, and change itself, whether adjusting to a threat to life or, at a time of exciting treatment advances, to renewed life. Sometimes an HIV diagnosis brings a person into therapy; other times it is one of many issues, coexisting with maladaptive behavioral patterns that preceded HIV disease and with dysfunctional views of the self and of relationships.

Up to now, no one psychotherapeutic approach has proven more effective than any other; and most therapists, regardless of their theoretical approach, can treat the person with HIV disease with only some modifications to their basic techniques and an awareness of the HIV-specific concerns that emerge. The literature on psychotherapy for people with HIV disease has grown as knowledge about the psychological, biological, social, and cultural aspects of the epidemic has increased. Given the prevalence of HIV disease in the United States, therapists are increasingly likely to encounter one or more clients who are facing these challenges. This chapter begins to explore the psychological issues HIV disease raises and the psychotherapeutic techniques available to respond to these issues. Following this introduction, it presents four case studies as a survey of both clinical themes and theoretical approaches.

A Complex Psychological Circumstance

HIV disease is clearly a complicated medical condition, but it is also, perhaps more than any other illness, a complex social, cultural, and psychological circumstance. The literature bears this out. Many authors have written about the psychological challenges of living and coping with HIV, and an articulate and in-depth account of psychotherapeutic issues that arise for people with HIV disease has recently been published. Among these issues are rejection by others, social isolation and ostracism, initiating or maintaining intimate relationships, loss of cognitive functioning, shortened life span and "unfinished business," grief and loss, potential job loss, and financial security and health costs.[1]

Jeffrey Weiss discusses the use of a psychodynamic approach with seropositive gay men, and notes the common themes of loss, uncertainty, the evolution of HIV as self-identity, and the search for meaning.[2] Peter De Roche explores issues of stigmatization and homophobia, the metaphorical meanings of contagion, helplessness and loss of control, fears of abandonment, fear of death, and the loneliness that many of his clients with HIV disease experience while in psychotherapy.[3]

Several studies point to similarities between the psychological reactions of people with HIV disease and people with cancer. These studies found that structured group interventions that provided emotional support helped reduce depression and anxiety, and taught clients better ways of coping with their illness.[4] Clinicians should also be aware of special issues that come up in the course of treating diverse populations affected by HIV disease. Most of the research literature pertains to White gay men, but there is a growing literature on psychotherapies for women, lesbians, people of color, the chronically mentally ill, and pediatric and geriatric populations.

Psychological adjustment to HIV disease may require making peace with the life a person has lived and to work through the stages described by Elisabeth Kübler-Ross in dealing with a terminal illness: denial, anger, bargaining, depression, and acceptance. Bereavement, multiple loss, and survivor guilt are particularly pertinent issues for people with AIDS.[5]

The Therapist's Stance

Therapists working with seropositive clients must be aware of these concerns and be able to shift treatment approaches as determined by their clients' needs. They must also be familiar with the medical consequences of HIV disease and be willing to adapt to the physical and psychological needs of their clients as these unfold. In the context of this unpredictability, strict adherence to a theoretical model may limit the efficacy of therapy.

Therapists must maintain a flexible therapeutic frame that allows clients to work through problems and enables therapists to maintain an empathic and supportive stance. Fees as well as the timing, frequency, and location of the sessions may have to bend. For example, home and hospital visits, or shortened or postponed visits, may become necessary in response to physical or cognitive changes.

In this context, therapists will have to be especially cognizant of the client-therapist boundary and of countertransference, including all of the therapist's emotions and thoughts related to the client during and between sessions. Therapists working with seropositive clients need to be aware of their own reactions to death, physical deterioration, the loss of cognitive abilities, helplessness, hopelessness, the stigma of HIV disease, fears of contagion, and a variety of other issues. Awareness of these issues and a therapist's reactions will help him or her to monitor thoughts and feelings during psychotherapy and promote the optimal therapeutic environment. (See also Chapter Sixteen, "Present in the Balance of Time.")

The work of Eugene Farber and others examines helplessness in mental health professionals who treat people with HIV disease.[6,7] He recommends solutions to combat this sense of helplessness, including reminders of the overwhelming biopsychosocial influences on a client's functioning that place limits on how much the therapist can be expected to do, the maintenance of realistic and balanced professional expectations, and the exploration of death anxiety and crises of meaning for the therapist.

Psychotherapeutic Approaches

Clinicians will find that HIV-related psychotherapy—even insight-oriented approaches—will often have to be combined with more practical support, reassurance, empathy, help in coping with decisions, problem solving, and other factors related to the client's daily functioning. It is also common for individual therapy to be combined with couples therapy, group therapy, emotional support groups, and other modalities based on the client's needs and goals in therapy. As a result, the therapist often works collaboratively with social workers, psychologists, psychiatrists, physicians, and other clinicians in the multidisciplinary care of the client. The four case studies following this introduction illustrate common issues that arise in the treatment of people with HIV disease. They advocate different approaches to treatment and are based on different theoretical models, yet all provide support, help increase self-esteem, and help clients cope with HIV disease. The four approaches are described in the sections that follow.

Interpersonal Psychotherapy

Kathleen F. Clougherty and John C. Markowitz apply an interpersonal psychotherapeutic approach to the case of Albert, a seropositive, gay, Jewish man with major depression. Therapy occurred over the course of sixteen fifty-minute sessions, during which time the therapist emphasized the connection between the client's mood and his social environment, and therapy explored the client's interpersonal patterns as manifested in his relationships.

Central to this approach is the "interpersonal formulation," which links the client's depression to one of four interpersonal problem areas: grief, role dispute (disagreements with significant others), role transition (for example, diagnosis with HIV disease, and demotion or promotion at work), or interpersonal deficits (long-standing difficulties in maintaining relationships). In contrast to the therapist's role in a more conventional psychodynamic approach, the interpersonal therapist is active, offering the client suggestions about what to do, refraining from exploring the client's transference, and encouraging a problem-solving approach in the here and now—with a focus on one of the four interpersonal problem areas. The interpersonal approach does not encourage an exploration of the past as currently reflected in the present and focuses less on intrapsychic factors than on interpersonal relationships.

Self Psychology

Sharone Abramowitz applies self psychology to the treatment of a White heterosexual couple, Anthony and Helen, both of whom are in their thirties. Anthony has recently seroconverted; Helen remains HIV-negative. The couple enters therapy to deal with Anthony's low libido and Helen's frustration with the infrequency of their sexual relations.

The self psychological approach, based on the writings of Heinz Kohut and his followers, views the self as the center. In self psychology, symptoms and defenses are seen as attempts to attain cohesion of a threatened and fragmented self, and the approach emphasizes understanding the client's subjective experience rather than the interpretation of unconscious conflicts. The theory suggests that the failures of parents and significant others to mirror the child's healthy and age-appropriate needs to idealize others and to experience grandiosity lead to an arrested stage of self-development. The therapist can counteract this by providing "empathic attunement" and interpretation of the inevitable ruptures in the cohesion of the self that result when narcissistic injuries occur.

Self psychology emphasizes the environment and its capacity for mirroring the infant or the infant's capacity for mirroring the environment, deemphasizing a view of the infant as being born with conflicts among drives or instincts. The purpose of psychotherapy is to understand and empathize with the client's subjective experience and to help the client explain this experience in terms of his or her self's attempt to recruit from the environment what it needs to feel whole. Self psychology considers transference and past relationships, and the therapist maintains therapeutic distance while empathizing with the client's experience.

Psychodynamic Psychotherapy

Israel Katz presents a more "classical" ego-psychological psychodynamic model in the treatment of Robert, a White seronegative man who was putting himself at risk by having unsafe sex with his partner and by failing to assert himself in the relationship with his partner. In the psychodynamic approach, instincts such as aggression and sexuality fail to be expressed directly because of prohibitions from the superego, which embodies rules and regulations from parents and society, and because of anxieties about expressing these instincts. These anxieties include fear of loss of the significant relationship and of the other's love, fear of bodily harm, and fear of punishment. The ego mediates between the id and the superego and erects defense mechanisms to deal with the anxieties engendered by sexuality and aggression.

Psychodynamic psychotherapy emphasizes conflict between instincts and defenses rather than deficit (the failure of psychic features to develop) and deemphasizes the lack of empathic attunement from important figures in the creation of psychopathology. The main purpose of psychotherapy is to explore transference, that is, how the past reflects itself in the present relationship with the therapist, and to examine the anxieties and fantasies connected to the expression of aggression and sexuality—the goal being the freeing of the ego to be able to express these instincts appropriately. The psychodynamic psychotherapist tries to avoid giving direct advice or suggestions to the client.

Time-Limited Psychotherapy

In another case study, Israel Katz describes time-limited dynamic psychotherapy in his discussion of Enrique, a thirty-year-old seropositive Latino man who is mandated to enter therapy by the court. Time-limited dynamic psychotherapy (TLDP) is based on a formulation comprising the client's actions, the client's expectations of how others will act toward him or her, the acts of others in relation to the client, and the self-perception of the client and its corroboration by others. Psychotherapy using this approach attempts to raise the client's awareness of how he or she actively participates in creating maladaptive cycles by behaving toward others in ways that precipitate reactions that, in turn, confirm the client's expectations of himself or herself and of other people.

For example, Enrique tends to withdraw from or be unusually submissive around others because he expects them to take advantage of him and reject him if he were to be more assertive. Consequently, other people either ignore Enrique or take advantage of him, which confirms Enrique's view of himself as a helpless person. The therapist explores this maladaptive cycle as it manifests in the relationship between the client and the therapist and the client and others.

HIV Recedes into the Background

In these cases, HIV remains a component of psychotherapy and a catalyst for change, but many times it recedes into the background while interpersonal, intrapsychic, familial, and societal issues come to the fore. In the interpersonal psychotherapy case, Albert has difficulties adjusting to being infected with HIV, yet the psychotherapy also deals with Albert's change of careers, his setting of appropriate limits with friends, and his ability to express his needs to others. In the self psychology case, Anthony's HIV infection confronts him with his substance abuse and helps him attain sobriety. Yet it is the couples' intimate relationship and their self-esteem that becomes the focus of therapy.

The psychodynamic case deals with Robert's difficulty asserting himself with his partner, which puts him at risk for HIV. However, therapy focuses on Robert's difficulty asserting himself in everyday life. In the time-limited dynamic therapy case, Enrique's unresolved anger toward his mother becomes the central issue of his therapy.

HIV disease always requires adjusting, but adjustment and change always occur in the context of other issues. Change is the result of the catalytic properties of HIV—and HIV-related concerns are resolved as a result of this catalytic process. But the ultimate re-sult seems to be a transformation of some kind that is more basic than an adjustment to the epidemic's many challenges.

∽

Other approaches may be used in conjunction with the approaches covered in this chapter. Among these are cognitive-behavioral ther-apy, existential therapy, object-relations therapy, other brief psy-chodynamic therapies, and group therapy and support groups. In addition, most therapists, even those whose practice is more insight oriented, employ supportive elements in their approaches.

There is not enough empirical research in the area of psy-chotherapies for HIV disease, yet clinical experience and the stud-ies that do examine the relationship between psychotherapy and HIV confirm that psychotherapy can be enormously helpful for clients with HIV disease. With the awareness of special concerns that emerge in the treatment of people infected with HIV disease, most therapists can provide support and help as clients seek to work through the many issues they face. All of these approaches share the concern for the individual, the attempt to understand the individual and his or her relationships, and the effort to pro-vide better coping tools for dealing with HIV disease.

Interpersonal Therapy: Albert

Kathleen F. Clougherty
John C. Markowitz

Albert, a forty-two-year-old divorced gay White Jewish male insurance adjuster, came to his therapist, Ron Hammonds, L.C.S.W., complaining that he felt depressed and "overwhelmed" in his personal and professional life. Albert had tested HIV-positive two years before, and he had recently experienced a 300-point drop in his CD4+ cell count to 211, a jump in his viral load to 10,000, job dissatisfaction, the ending of a romantic relationship, and the death of his grandmother in the previous year.

Albert presented with complaints of depressed mood, loss of interest in activities he normally enjoyed, social isolation, decreased libido, difficulty falling and staying asleep, anxiety attacks, and suicidal ideation (without attempts). His initial Hamilton Depression Rating Scale score was 25,[8] indicating significant symptom severity.

Albert told Hammonds he had no previous depression or psychiatric treatment but had a long history of alternative psychological treatments such as meditation, affirmation (chanting positive thoughts), and astrology. He had used alcohol and drugs socially in the past but not recently. He had no family history of psychiatric disorder, substance abuse, or suicide. Medically asymptomatic, Albert had refused antiviral medications, whose side effects he feared outweighed any possible benefits, but he did visit his physician regularly.

Personal and Psychiatric History

Raised in a major northeastern city, Albert was the middle of three siblings and the second son in a middle-class family. His father singled him out for physical and emotional abuse from childhood through adolescence, calling him a "wimp" and a "fag" from early on. His father was close to Albert's elder brother, but without provocation hated Albert "from the day I was born." Albert was close to his mother, and particularly to his maternal grandmother, who died nine months before his presentation. His grandmother, but not his mother, protected him from his father.

Six months prior to entering treatment, when Albert's father forbade his mother to buy Albert a special birthday present, Albert stopped speaking to the father, even though his parents lived in his building and he saw them daily. This decision pleased Albert but did not diminish the rage he felt toward his father.

Albert was notably reliant on friends, calling many of them each day. Several had died of AIDS. He felt close to his friends, but remarked that although he willingly extended himself on their behalf, he worried that he could not expect reciprocal support and was reluctant to express his needs to them. This same pattern was evident in the three romantic relationships he had had. The last, a relationship that lasted two years, had ended about a year before treatment, when his lover became sexually involved with Albert's good friend and expected Albert to tolerate this situation. When Albert could not, his lover left him. Another close friend of seventeen years, whom Albert had supported through a series of crises, reacted to the news that Albert was seropositive by abandoning him. Albert commented that the emotional pain he endured in these relationships paralleled the abuse he had received from his father.

A college graduate, Albert had been reasonably successful in a variety of business ventures, and had worked at his current job for more than three years. Although the work was financially secure, Albert found it unstimulating, and he disliked his colleagues.

Formulation and Initial Treatment Plan

Albert met *DSM-IV* criteria for major depression without psychotic features. Having applied for treatment in a research program offering brief therapy for depressed HIV-positive clients, he was randomized to receive a course of sixteen weekly fifty-minute sessions of interpersonal psychotherapy.[9] He was pleased by this selection, saying he might have refused antidepressant medication, which had been one of the other treatment alternatives.

Interpersonal psychotherapy (IPT) is a time-limited psychotherapy for treating depression, which has also been adapted to nonmood disorders.[10,11,12]

By ascertaining where a client's interpersonal functioning is impaired, determining what the client wants in affectively laden situations, and identifying what options the client has to achieve these desires, the therapist can help to resolve both the interpersonal problem and its associated symptoms of depression.

In obtaining a client's history, the therapist compiles an interpersonal inventory of key relationships, interpersonal patterns, and client expectations and outcomes. Therapists give clients the diagnosis of depression and with it the "illness" role.[13] Seropositive clients are told they have *two* medical conditions, depression and HIV infection, and they are encouraged to become experts on both.[14,15]

The therapist links the mood disorder to one of four interpersonal problem areas:

- Grief (complicated bereavement)

- Role dispute (disagreement with intimate partners or coworkers)

- Role transition (for example, the beginning or ending a relationship or job, a demotion or promotion, the loss of an ideal, or diagnosis of a significant medical illness such as HIV disease)

- Interpersonal deficits

The last, the least conceptually developed problem area and a residual category for clients who fall into none of the first three problem areas, defines clients with long-standing difficulties in maintaining relationships.

Once therapist and client agree on the focus of therapy, the therapeutic process involves using specific strategies to address the interpersonal problem area. Therapists are active, supportive, and non-neutral, and they address issues in the "here and now" rather than in terms of developmental antecedents. Albert's history suggests a role transition to accommodate to chronic infection with HIV: in his words, "making the most of the life I have left." Within that framework, there were also clear role disputes with friends and family. Albert found this formulation reasonable and helpful.

Treatment

Albert felt trapped in an unrewarding job at a point in life when he had no time to waste. Early in treatment, he explored his career options. Many years before, he had been active in the theater but left it for better pay. Now he wanted to return to what had been a more fulfilling life. He pursued old contacts and was negotiating for a position at the time therapy concluded. This was a liberating decision that had a marked effect on his mood and depressive symptoms.

His success in changing careers and his increased self-esteem provided momentum to tackle his interpersonal disputes. Discussion and role playing with Hammonds helped him set appropriate limits with friends, even risking their anger and rejection. On dates, where he had previously "felt like damaged goods," he learned when to express his needs and to initiate discussion of HIV status—both his own and the other person's—at the appropriate juncture. Although not every encounter went smoothly, Albert recognized that addressing such issues early helped clarify whether a potential relationship was worth pursuing. Therapy also explored his dispute with his parents, including his mother's role in his abuse. He maintained his distance from his father but stayed in daily, intimate contact with his mother, albeit avoiding discussing his anger with her.

His Hamilton depression score dropped to less than 6, indicating remission of the depressive episode. Close friends remarked on how much happier he seemed to become during the sixteen weeks of treatment. Visiting a dying relative in a hospice raised issues of Albert's own mortality but did not hinder pursuit of his goals or cause a relapse.

On completing therapy, Albert faced the future with some excitement and anxiety, and he recognized that the role transition caused by HIV infection would be ongoing. During the final sessions, Albert and Hammonds acknowledged his considerable therapeutic gains, reviewed warning signs of depression, and discussed interpersonal maneuvers to avert its recurrence. This included setting clear expectations in relationships and asserting his own needs—for example, asking friends to call at least once a week so that he would not feel he was doing all the work in the relationships.

Discussion

There is a risk that therapists may feel overwhelmed in treating depressed clients who are seropositive. Infection with HIV may appear to provide a concrete "reason" for being depressed, hopeless, and helpless. Yet it is important to recognize that most people with HIV are *not* depressed[16,17,18] and that those who are often respond to treatment with antidepressant medication[19] or psychotherapy.[20]

Given the time pressure that many seropositive clients feel, brief, focused antidepressant therapies such as interpersonal psychotherapy are well suited for their treatment.[21,22] Seropositive clients are also beset by the interpersonal problems that interpersonal psychotherapy addresses: they are frequently grieving many deaths, and adjusting to HIV disease defines an inevitable role transition.

Albert was pleased to have a time-limited intervention that offered him practical techniques to deal with his life. Returning for his second interpersonal session, he told Hammonds, "You won me over when you told me you'd give me tools for helping myself." For him these tools eventually included the recognition of depression as a treatable medical illness rather than a characterological paralysis; recognition of the link between mood and environment; and the galvanizing demonstration that although depression made him feel helpless, he could in fact capably pursue his desires, choose among his options, and exercise effective control over his relationships, career, and life.

HIV disease does affect life course and outlook and necessitates reassessment of one's priorities. Under the pressure of time and illness, people with HIV are often willing to make dramatic changes in the course of therapy, to transform their lives as Albert did. The success of interpersonal psychotherapy in addressing depression and HIV should alleviate feelings among psychotherapists that they have nothing to offer in treating such clients.

Self Psychology: Anthony and Helen

Sharone Abramowitz

Anthony and Helen, a couple in their thirties, began their relationship in the fog of Anthony's alcohol and drug use. They enjoyed passionate sex and good times as they kept their relationship casual. Married once, Anthony preferred keeping his commitments to a minimum, and he approached life with an ex-hippie "live and let live" philosophy. He offered Helen a pleasurable and undemanding escape from the pain of her recent divorce. For a while their casual lust was enough. Maybe it was the discovery of Anthony's seropositive status or a growing attachment, but each began to want something more out of the relationship.

Given his newly detected HIV status, Anthony was confronted with a stark choice. He could continue his drug-dependent lifestyle and die sooner, or stop and die later. He began to compare his lifestyle to Helen's ambitious writing career and full social life. Anthony's life of occasional landscaping and frequent drug use left him feeling inadequate beside this formidable woman. The choice became clear; he entered a twelve-step program. Recovery opened him to a profound spiritual awakening. A dream began to take hold of him. He envisioned designing, planting, and building a magnificent garden. With the program's philosophy guiding him, he entered into a "clean and sober" partnership with Helen. To be responsible and present in a relationship while not relying on the numbing effects of drugs challenged him. He worked hard at this new commitment, but the sizzle of passion died and his desire for sexual intimacy waned.

Anthony's transformation from a high and passionate lover to a sober man with low libido both encouraged and troubled Helen. She tremendously respected Anthony's efforts at recovery. His new ambition to create a wonderful garden inspired her. She joyfully helped organize the garden's plans, and while he planted and cared for the garden, she paid the bills. Helen's love for Anthony grew as she saw his emerging depth of character. What pained her was his sexual distancing. She wanted more, not less, intimacy as their relationship deepened.

Helen believed she could master all problems. At her urging, she and Anthony joined a support group. Then, wanting more focused attention, Helen searched for a therapist who had experience both with HIV issues and couples. With great hope and a willingness to work hard, Helen and Anthony entered psychotherapy.

Personal and Psychiatric History

Helen, born in South Africa, was the eldest child of an industrious mother and an ambitious but less than successful painter father. In her White, middle-class culture, appearances were all-important, a family's value depended on professional and monetary successes, and vulnerabilities and excesses were private.

Helen's mother carried out these cultural expectations. When her father's work did not sell, her mother supported the family. Helen was expected to help, and under her mother's tutelage she learned to manage a household efficiently and keep up appearances. Helen gained her parents' respect if she hid her needs and remained productive. Forced out of childhood before it really began, Helen grew up quickly.

Despite her father's failure as a provider, he offered a route out from the numbing conformity of their culture by encouraging Helen into the creative arts. Through the arts, Helen met rebellious intellectuals and received affirmation for her individuality. This support enabled her to move to the United States and distance herself from the suffocating expectations of White South African culture.

Anthony was the only son and youngest child of a lower-middle-class, third-generation Italian American family. His mother and older sisters blanketed him with attention. He felt special but also smothered. Anthony's father was as distant as his mother was doting. Although Anthony wished he could be closer to his father, his father's strict Catholic morality alienated him. Living up to these rigid expectations was a losing battle, and as a result Anthony frequently felt inadequate.

As Anthony entered adolescence, America of the late sixties greeted him. "Sex, drugs, and rock and roll" promised an escape from his father's bible and his mother's hugs. Although the counterculture affirmed that which his father condemned, it could not completely repair his core sense of inadequacy. The problem became compounded by his growing involvement with alcohol and drugs. On the one hand, drugs offered self-enhancing functions: on cocaine, he could sexually dominate a woman, overcome his fear of female suffocation, and, until the high wore off, enter a moment of intense intimacy. On the other hand, drugs locked him into a meaningless life where his ambitions suffered, his values plummeted, and his self-esteem remained low, finally threatening his life—first by exposing him to HIV and then by compromising his infected immune system.

Treatment

Anthony and Helen entered couples therapy as they began the third year of their relationship and as Anthony entered the second year of sobriety. Their chief complaint was sexual dysfunction, a problem common among serodiscordant couples.[23] Treatment was conducted in sixty-minute sessions, twice a month, for two years. Anthony remained free of HIV symptoms throughout the course of the therapy, and Helen remained seronegative. Their therapist, Renata Pascal, Ph.D., employed a psychoanalytic self psychological approach.

Rather than assume that the couple's sexual symptoms were motivated by unconscious defenses against conflicts about HIV, self psychology emphasizes that it is first necessary to gain an empathic understanding of the clients' subjective experience. One of the first therapeutic tasks was to explore how the couple saw the relationship of Anthony's HIV infection to their sexual problems. Although they felt frustrated with how safer sex (which they assiduously practiced) interfered with spontaneity, neither believed that the virus was at the root of their sexual dysfunction: Helen wanted more sex, not less, and Anthony felt sure that his HIV status did not underlie his inhibitions.

The next goal of therapy was to assess Helen's and Anthony's stages of self-development. The self, according to self psychology, is the intrapsychic organization or internal structuring of subjective experience; it is the center of a person's initiative and provides a sense of cohesion and an experience of continuity in space and time.[24] To assess each client's stage of self-development, it was necessary to determine which dimensions of self-experience were most vulnerable to disruption and which were most secure. What complaints or successes did they each bring to the hour? It was also important to observe the types of *selfobject experiences* that the couple had of each other and of the therapist.

According to self psychology, the emergence and maintenance of the self require more than the inborn tendency to organize experience; they also require the presence of others.[25,26] A selfobject experience is the intrapsychic experience of an "other" (a person, idea, or behavior) that provides nurturance and support to the self. To assess the partners' selfobject experiences, Pascal sought to discover what most soothed or upset each partner about the other's behavior. What behaviors did each rely on to soothe himself or herself after feeling injured? What was it that each most wanted from the other? In addition, Pascal explored how the couple's dynamics recapitulated or repaired the successes and failures of the selfobject experiences that they had with their families as children.

As part of this process, Pascal assessed the transferences each partner had with the other and their transference expectations of the therapist. For self psychologists, transference has two dimensions: a *repetitive* aspect (the negative transference) and a *restorative* aspect (the positive transference). The repetitive dimension is the client's fearful expectations that the partner or therapist will again fail to provide the selfobject functions that the client's caregivers originally failed to provide. The restorative dimension is the client's longing to receive from the partner or therapist the missing, insufficient, or once unavailable selfobject functions of the formative years.[27,28]

The Intact Self and the Fragile Self

Helen presented with an intact self. Her ambitions were solid, and she was a strongly principled woman. What plagued Helen was a sense of insecurity concerning whether others would successfully provide her with idealized selfobject experiences. As a result, Helen followed in her mother's footsteps, becoming involved with a man less outwardly organized and competent than herself.

When Anthony began treatment, his self state was fragile. He suffered from bouts of self-depletion and fragmentation anxiety, not infrequently requiring long hours of total quiet. At times he withdrew into transient depressive states accompanied by wishes to die. It was important for the couple for Anthony to discuss the self-disruptive events that precipitated these states and to explore in what ways he then restored himself. Anthony needed mirroring (affirming affective attunement), and Helen needed to see the therapist model this. An appreciation of mirroring counteracted Helen's belief that action is the cure for all ills. At the same time, the therapist was careful to validate how worrisome it was for Helen to see Anthony in these states. Over time, as Anthony's sense of self strengthened, these states abated.

To break the cycle of discontent between Helen and Anthony, most graph-ically played out in their sex life, Pascal had to be the transferential repository of selfobject functions that the partners could not yet provide one another. By emphasizing process, not immediate behavior change, Pascal worked with each partner's wish that the other would immediately gratify his or her unmet selfobject needs.[29] As Solomon suggests, "If the goal is a healing of the central disturbance and development of a cohesive self, it is very important for the therapist to avoid instructions that suggest changes in actions or behavior toward each [partner of the couple]."[30] Pascal initially offered a few sugges-tions, not as solutions but as a way to illustrate the dynamics of their relation-ship, particularly because sexuality is "the arena in which fundamental relational issues and struggles are played out."[31]

Pascal initiated a basic self psychological technique: first the part-ners sought to empathically *understand* each other's position; then, they *explained* why their respective positions were their selves' best attempts to re-cruit what they needed.[32] An important component of this process was helping the couple to see how their responses and expectations of each other reflected the dynamics from their early years. In this way, they began to view the inade-quate responses of the other not as purposefully persecutory but as coming out of early developmental deficits. As each partner's self strengthened through the therapeutic process, each could begin to provide the other with the needed self-object functions.

Discussion

Self psychology views symptoms (for example, sexual dysfunction) and defenses not as "resistance" but as the client's best attempt to maintain the cohesion of a threatened self.[33] The therapeutic task in the case of Helen and Anthony was to understand how each partner threatened and supported the other's sense of self, and how this was played out through their sexual dynamics.

While a part of Helen yearned to be taken care of, she also disavowed these needs. *Disavowal* is a defense prevalent in clients with the narcissistic dynamics of overt self-competence hiding a fragile and shame-ridden inner self.[34] Helen disavowed her dependency needs because she came from a family that discouraged her from expressing these needs. To contain the anxiety and shame that these unmet needs caused her, she consciously disavowed the unmet needs while unconsciously deceiving herself that she felt little about them.[35] When Anthony was not there for her, Helen believed, "It doesn't really matter, because I can take care of it."

Helen's yearning to be taken care of presented itself in the form of an idealized selfobject transference. Feeling overburdened with her self-expectation to be a consummate caretaker, she wanted to lean on what she imagined to be the therapist's omniscience. She often asked for direction and frequently commented on Pascal's skill. By not undermining Helen's idealized view of the therapist, the idealized selfobject experience allowed Helen to accept encouragement to expose her disavowed vulnerabilities to Anthony. She began to trust that her dependency needs could also be responded to.

Therapy also allowed Anthony to provide important self-enhancing opportunities for Helen. As a seropositive man, Anthony was fighting for his life through his recovery process, while trying to create his dream garden and realize a life's ambition before it was too late. By providing practical support to a man driven by such a quest, Helen could feel that she was an efficacious partner in a meaningful journey. Anthony also provided a vital counterpoint to Helen's upbringing. He actively lived the philosophy of living life one day at a time. This view directly conflicted with Helen's goal-directed upbringing. At times it made her insecure and pushed her to become more controlling. At other times, this philosophy, along with Anthony's capacity to be open to her feelings, offered Helen a mirroring selfobject milieu in which she could begin to integrate the vulnerability her background had forced her to disavow.

Helen's self-assured style anchored Anthony, who experienced a confusing array of feelings. Relating to Helen was, in good and bad ways, like relating to the women in Anthony's family. She played "the eldest sister" to his "youngest brother." She provided him with idealized selfobject functions such as guidance and structure, and modeled ambition. But her formidable will also easily overpowered Anthony's fragile sense of self-assertiveness.

Fortunately the route away from drugs led Anthony to a twelve-step recovery program, a relationship that counterbalanced Helen—the kind of counterbalance to his mother that his distant father was unable to provide him as a boy. Although Anthony rejected his father's Catholicism, he did respect his father's love of Christ. The twelve-step movement provided the "twinship" self-object experience that Anthony yearned for as a boy but could not obtain from his father. He found a way to share in his father's spirituality while at the same time connecting to other men like himself. The pride he felt through his participation in the recovery program also allowed him to combat the shame that his father's religious dogma engendered.

Anthony's and Helen's sexuality played out the range of these interpersonal dynamics. Anthony's unavailability caused Helen to fantasize about Anthony dominating her. Embedded in this image was her wish to merge into the arms of a strong male figure and to be taken care of. The more she expressed this desire, the more Anthony felt unable to meet it. Because cocaine was no longer available to rescue him from his fear of female engulfment, he turned to fantasies of anonymous sex with distant men and objectified sex with diminutive women more passive than Helen.

Anthony's shame and guilt led him to request meeting with Pascal alone so that he could initially discuss these fantasies outside of Helen's presence. Helen consented to this arrangement. Although this technique is controversial, in this case it proved to be quite helpful. Because shame propelled Anthony to hide these issues from Helen, it remained inaccessible to the couple's work. For Anthony to deal with these fantasies and their implications, he required active encouragement from Pascal to expose this hidden material. After a few one-on-one sessions, Anthony was able to bring into the couples work underlying interpretations of the fantasies without directly exposing their contents. This both saved face for Anthony and protected Helen.

⁓

With the twelve-step program and therapy bolstering him, Anthony increasingly asserted himself with Helen. Helen, at first unsure of her value to Anthony if he did not need her directiveness, felt relieved that he was becoming a stronger and more dependable figure. In the meantime, Anthony acquired a more empathic understanding of Helen's background and grew less reactive to her directiveness. Helen responded by acknowledging that she, and not only Anthony, needed recovery. She joined Al-Anon and retreated from only focusing on what Anthony should and should not do. She began to pay more attention to the vulnerable states that her other-directedness was defending against. As Helen backed off, Anthony moved forward. Finally, Anthony could feel like a grown man when facing Helen's "big sister" persona, and Helen could stop being the only adult. Needless to say, their sex life improved.

Psychodynamic Psychotherapy: Robert

Israel Katz

Robert was a twenty-four-year-old White gay man, the son of a Russian immigrant mother and a German American father. A few months before he started therapy, he had relocated from the Midwest to Southern California to join his thirty-four-year-old Asian American lover. Robert sought treatment because he was scared that his feeling down all the time was threatening his relationship with his partner.

Robert had a hard time enjoying himself with his partner and didn't quite believe that he deserved a loving relationship. His partner, Frank, in turn withdrew from Robert and got irritated when Robert berated himself and his life. Robert worried that he was not attractive enough and was not satisfying Frank sexually. He was afraid that Frank would abandon him or look for outside sex and bring HIV into the relationship. He was also afraid that if his current relationship did not survive he would become a "sex-starved cruising junkie" who would contract HIV and be doomed to loneliness for the rest of his life. Finally, Robert felt "out of sync" with gay people and intimidated by "handsome buffed men," whom he believed looked down on him.

Robert had a lot of difficulty asserting himself and verbalizing his desires to Frank. He was afraid that he would sacrifice the relationship if he did assert himself and did not please Frank. Robert wanted to understand why he felt so bad about himself even after moving away from his religious family, whom he perceived as being very homophobic and judgmental. He wanted to feel better and more confident.

Martin McCombs and Graciela Morales developed an earlier version of this case, for which the author is indebted to them.

Personal and Psychiatric History

On arriving in the United States, Robert's family joined relatives in Ohio and became active in the leadership, administration, and management of the local evangelical church. Robert's father was a middle-management supervisor at an auto parts plant; his mother was a homemaker. Both parents had finished high school and worked hard to ensure that their children succeeded.

Robert's parents already had a fifteen-year-old daughter when they decided to have Robert, a second child. Robert perceived both parents as strict and withdrawn people who expected him to be powerful and masculine in fairly stereotypical ways; his father encouraged him almost unceasingly to play sports and to keep a lid on his feelings.

As a child, Robert was withdrawn and isolated, had few friends, was obese, and felt alienated from his peers, partly because his mother did not speak English proficiently and his community had very few "foreigners." Despite his father's pressure, Robert did not like to play sports, and he avoided male friendships. He recalled adolescent homoerotic fantasies, which were extremely painful and disconcerting to him; homosexuality had been so unacceptable that it was an inconceivable alternative to these fantasies.

During his adolescence, Robert had fantasies of suicide as a relief from his psychological pain, but he never acted on them because of his fears of afterlife damnation. Robert did not date in high school, although he maintained social contact with girls through the youth activities at his church. After he graduated from high school, Robert lived at home with his parents and worked as an administrative assistant in his father's company—so assiduously that he successfully avoided having a social life. Robert met Frank while Frank was visiting Ohio on a business trip. The two men stayed in contact for several months before Robert decided to move to Los Angeles to join Frank and get away from his parents. Robert had not come out to his parents and, in fact, secretly doubted his homosexuality.

Once in Los Angeles, Robert sought treatment from Jonathan Cooper, L.C.S.W., a therapist he had found listed in a gay newspaper. Robert told Cooper that he felt bad about his sexuality and was terrified that he would contract HIV.

Formulation and Treatment Plan

During his first session, Robert talked about "feeling down," his inability to assert himself, and his terror that one way or another he would get HIV. Because he had the capacity to look at himself and was motivated to try to understand why he felt so bad about himself, he connected well with his therapist. During the initial visit, Cooper concluded that Robert did not have problems with impulse control, suicidality, homicidality, or substance abuse, any of which would have made it more difficult for Robert to respond to an insight-oriented approach. Cooper also noted that Robert could tolerate some anxiety and could focus on himself and his internal world. For all these reasons Cooper believed that a psychodynamic approach could help his client.[36,37]

Cooper developed a psychodynamic formulation, which included a conflict among three elements: Robert's wanting to express his assertiveness, anger, and sexual impulses toward others; his fear that if he showed these impulses he would be punished, damaged, and abandoned; and the defense of turning his aggression on himself and hating himself as a way to deal with the anxieties connected to being more sexually confident with his partner and being more assertive with his parents and with other people. In some ways Robert exhibited a classical Oedipal conflict: he feared the expression of aggressive and sexual instincts toward his father (and other important figures in his life) because of fears of the bodily damage and punishment that would follow were he to express these instincts. He also had pre-Oedipal fears of abandonment and loss of the "object" (mother or father or both) if he expressed his sexuality and aggression.[38]

Cooper believed that Robert could benefit from exploring the conflict between his need to assert himself and his fear of being punished or abandoned. Perhaps if Robert experienced and understood this anxiety within the context of the therapeutic relationship, he could come up with better ways to assert himself appropriately and feel better about himself.

Treatment

Cooper saw Robert once a week for forty-five-minute sessions in an office setting over the course of twenty-one months. During this period, Cooper tried to establish a therapeutic alliance by listening attentively to Robert and empathizing with the difficulties he presented. However, because Robert felt bad about himself and because he had internalized a disapproving father, he saw male figures as condemning. As a result, Robert often interpreted Cooper's empathy as condescension, feeling that Cooper was judging him as not being "good enough" instead of trying to understand his life. At one point Robert said to Cooper, "You don't really care about me. All you want is to judge me." Cooper tolerated these attacks and tried to explore Robert's perception of the therapist as judgmental. Cooper pointed out the connection between Robert's childhood experiences and his assumption that the therapist would behave as Robert's father had.

Cooper also was attentive to material that centered on the theme of Robert's anxiety about asserting himself in his outside relationships, in the therapeutic relationship, and, to a limited extent, with his parents. Robert had an easier time talking about his difficulties asserting himself with his partner, Frank. For example, Robert recounted the time he wanted to go to a particular restaurant that Frank did not like. Robert backed down because he believed that Frank would punish him by withdrawing if Robert asserted himself. Robert described such scenarios often, even though he was never able to offer an example of this feared result having occurred.

Cooper tried to explore Robert's anxiety and fantasies about asserting himself with Frank. Whenever he was questioned in this way, however, Robert changed the subject, saying that he did not want to "talk about it." At times Cooper persisted, which made Robert irritable. However, Robert had difficulty expressing this irritation toward Cooper and was able only once to let Cooper know how upset he was during therapy. When encouraged to elaborate on his feelings, Robert stated that perhaps something "bad" would happen if he were to be more assertive with the therapist. When Cooper asked Robert what he meant by "bad," Robert said that he was too nervous to discuss the subject anymore. Robert successfully rebuffed Cooper's further attempts to talk about the therapeutic relationship, instead focusing discussion on his relationship with Frank.

After about a year of psychotherapy, Robert shamefully acknowledged that he had been lying to Cooper about practicing safe sex with Frank and that neither partner had been tested for HIV. Robert and Frank frequently had un-protected anal intercourse, and Frank never used a condom. Robert also had lied to Cooper about successfully and assertively communicating either his dis-comfort with this practice or his suspicion that Frank may be having sex with other men. Robert was afraid that if he "removed" the "special offering" of unprotected sex, Frank would punish him, spending more time with other men outside the relationship or leaving Robert altogether.

Cooper confronted Robert about the riskiness of his behavior. Robert's lack of self-respect was palpable as he stated with all sincerity that he believed if he complained, he would lose Frank or be punished for speaking out about his own needs. Cooper pointed out the price Robert was paying—possibly getting HIV—and described it as "self-destructive." He and Robert discussed that it was possible to refuse to have unsafe sex and yet maintain a relationship; it was possible to have a good relationship in which both partners communicated and in which one of the partners did not have to suffer or be afraid of asserting himself. Robert began to practice safer sex even though he continued at times to have sex without a condom. He tested HIV-negative and continued to be HIV-negative during the remainder of therapy.

❧

Robert decided to stop therapy after twenty-one months. From Cooper's perspective, Robert had made some modest gains and still had several areas to work on. Robert felt a bit more comfortable asserting himself with Frank, had a better sense of self-esteem, and could enjoy sex more. He still struggled with his passivity and tended to go along with others a lot of the time, but he was more aware of this pattern. Robert and Frank practiced safer sex most of the time, and Robert felt less depressed overall. (Robert also said that Frank had become a little more patient with Robert's downswings now that Robert was more assertive and less self-denigrating.)

Cooper believed that Robert became more anxious as their relationship grew closer, but Robert did not agree with Cooper's interpretations that Robert was seeking to flee psychotherapy in order to avoid confronting Cooper.

Robert was able to make some gains in the psychotherapy while still struggling with his fears of assertiveness and sexual confidence. Through psychotherapy, Robert gained a better understanding of his fears of assertiveness and sexual confidence and grew to appreciate how these issues affected other areas of his life, largely through the repeated experiences of analyzing his transference feelings toward Cooper and his expectations of him.

Time-Limited Psychotherapy: Enrique

Israel Katz

Enrique was a thirty-five-year-old seropositive Mexican American man who entered therapy under court mandate. His story began as he was helping to clean a local park. An older woman approached him and started yelling at him, telling him not to pick up the trash. Enrique and the woman got into an argument, and he ended up pushing the woman twice and calling her names. Enrique was arrested for battery and did not defend his actions at that point. Furthermore, he did not go to court to follow up on the charges, because he "did not feel like it." The court found him guilty but agreed to a plan of requiring at least twelve sessions of psychotherapy rather than sending Enrique to jail.

Enrique started therapy with Mark Krimsky, M.D. He reported no history of violence and said that this was the only time in his life in which he had fought with someone; he described himself as always being "in control" and peaceful and basically in good health despite his HIV status. Initially, his only motivation to attend therapy was the court order, but soon he said he was looking forward to understanding his behavior in the park. He was puzzled and wanted to understand why the altercation occurred. He wanted to feel less irritated about this incident, to be happier, and feel better about himself.

Personal and Psychiatric History

Enrique was born in San Francisco, the seventh of eight children. Both parents were Mexican. His father developed leukemia when Enrique was nine months old, and he decided to move the family back to Mexico to be closer to their extended family. Enrique's father had a series of low-paying, blue-collar jobs, while his mother stayed at home taking care of the children. His parents did not get along with one another; his father drank a lot of alcohol and beat up his mother. Enrique got along much better with his father, who died when Enrique was eleven years old, than he ever did with his mother.

Enrique said that he was never a "masculine" boy and that his mother disliked him because of this, preferring his older brother, who was more conventionally "macho." Enrique remembered having erotic fantasies involving men since the age of eight and felt that he had never been typically male. He was not out as a gay man to any of his family, and he feared that if he told his mother he was gay that it would kill her. Enrique's mother did not go to his elementary or high school graduation ceremonies, never hugged him or touched him, and neglected him emotionally. He felt that he could never express any feelings toward his mother, because she would respond by telling him that men "were not supposed to go on about their feelings."

Enrique left Mexico at the age of eighteen and came back to San Francisco for a better life. He worked as a bartender for a few years, when he developed major depressive symptoms: depressed mood, anhedonia, difficulty sleeping, low energy, low self-esteem, and psychomotor retardation—but no suicidal or homicidal ideation and no psychotic or manic symptoms. There was no medical cause, substance abuse or dependency, or acute psychosocial stressor that could account for Enrique's depression, so he started seeing a psychiatrist, Celia Hauser, who prescribed Zoloft. At the time of the incident in the park, Enrique had been in complete remission from his depression for several months. He had no history of psychiatric hospitalizations, suicide attempts, homicide, or any other troubles with the law.

After he was mandated by the court to seek psychotherapy, Enrique saw two other therapists, both of whom were women. He did not like either of these therapists because "they were women and reminded me too much of my mother." He said that they only pretended to be caring but in fact were just doing their job. In both cases, he quit therapy without talking to the therapists about his dissatisfactions. He had no other experiences in psychotherapy.

Enrique believed that he got HIV from Bob, a White man from Texas whom he met in 1985. Enrique and Bob were together for one and a half years. In late 1986, Enrique noticed that Bob had an eye infection and suspected Bob was HIV-positive. However, he did not want to "hurt" Bob by asking him about this and so withdrew from him, never seeing him again. Enrique was angry with Bob but did not want to speak to him. Several years afterward, Enrique saw Bob in the subway but fled before his former partner could reach

him. He later found out that Bob died from AIDS. Enrique had been seropositive since 1986; his CD4+ cell count was in the 400s, his viral load was less
than 5,000, and he had no history of opportunistic infections.

Enrique had one other relationship that lasted for six months in 1997.
Enrique was not attracted to Randy, a White man who also had HIV, but was
afraid to let him know this, because it might "hurt him." Enrique said that
he was also uncomfortable with Randy's frequent insistence that they have unprotected anal intercourse, something that Enrique felt was terribly risky, even
though they were both seropositive. As a result, Enrique drew back from Randy.
Enrique also described a pattern of interaction with his friends and lovers in
which he would try very hard to please others but would end up "being taken
advantage of," at which point he would become angry and then withdraw
from these relationships.

Formulation of a Treatment Plan

After hearing this history and listening for behavioral and psychological
patterns, Krimsky, who was trained in the use of time-limited dynamic psychotherapy (TLDP),[39,40] conceptualized Enrique's interpersonal style as follows:

- Acts of self. In general, Enrique withdrew from others; when he was around
  others he was overly compliant—acting submissive, then resenting the
  other, becoming angry, and withdrawing.

- Expectations of others. Enrique expected others not to care about him or to
  care about him only to take advantage of him. He said that others would
  reject him if he were to assert himself or his needs.

- Acts of others. Some people would ignore Enrique altogether; others would
  strike up a friendship with him only, in fact, to take advantage of him, and
  Enrique would let them. When others would try to understand Enrique's
  needs, he pushed them away, causing them to become bewildered and
  irritated.

- Introject (or self-perception). Enrique experienced himself as a defective,
  helpless human being who could never express his own needs or assert
  himself and who got taken advantage of by other people.

Krimsky saw Enrique nine times, applying a time-limited psychodynamic approach. Enrique came to every session and seemed to be engaged
in the process of psychotherapy. The first two sessions consisted of a recapitula-

tion of the incident in the park, his developmental history, and the arrangement of an agreement for brief psychotherapy. Enrique resented the court mandate to be in therapy, but he also realized that the process might help him feel better about himself and understand the park incident. The sessions took place in English, even though Krimsky was bilingual and had lived in Latin America. Enrique said Spanish reminded him of his childhood and of being with his mother; he felt that English was more "neutral," less threatening, and would help him control his emotions. In the end, Enrique ended up interspersing English with Spanish during the sessions and eventually spoke only Spanish during the last five sessions.

Treatment

Early on in therapy, Enrique expressed his distrust of Krimsky, saying that the therapist listened only because it was his job and that in "real life" the therapist would dismiss Enrique as "boring." Enrique was able to recognize that he was reacting to Krimsky as he would interact with mother, and Krimsky pointed out that it was indeed easier to see the therapist as not caring for him, because this had been his way of experiencing other people in the past. Enrique agreed and said that it was hard to feel all the time that no one cared for him.

As therapy progressed, it focused on Enrique's need to please others in his relationships, even if he resented the need to please all the time. He and Krimsky discussed how this need applied in the case of his relationship with Randy. Enrique also acknowledged that he wanted to please Krimsky, and the pair explored what would happen if Enrique expressed his needs in relation with Krimsky. Enrique said that he was scared to look at what he wanted from therapy and what he needed from his therapist.

Enrique observed that perhaps this had something to do with what happened in the park with the woman, that perhaps the anger he expressed had been bottled up inside for a long time. Krimsky pointed out Enrique's tendency to conceive of his relationships in only two ways: he either had to please others or have an outburst. Enrique began to understand the price he paid for this attitude: his estrangement from Bob, his lack of relationships and communication with others, and his legal trouble. Enrique said that he felt terrified that he would "hurt" them if he were to express anger toward his friends. Enrique was able to recognize that this fear of "hurting" others made it very difficult for him to negotiate anything with them or to express his desires, and that perhaps the situations would unfold differently from what he imagined.

As the sessions went on, Krimsky wondered whether Enrique's insights into his patterns and emotional understandings were forced, articulated merely to please Krimsky just as he had pleased others. Did Enrique, in fact, resent psychotherapy, or had he realized on some level that by participating he was taking care of himself and figuring out his maladaptive patterns? The pair discussed this issue during session number six, and Enrique identified with both perspectives. He was playing the "good patient," and he also had a sense that he did deserve to feel better.

Later on during that session, Enrique said that he was asserting himself a little bit more with his friend John, for whom he had routinely done many chores and tasks. Enrique felt anxious while confronting his friend, but noticed that he felt better afterwards and that John did not retaliate against him, punish him, or leave him.

Enrique also said that he felt more comfortable with Krimsky, seeing the therapist as more than just a "part of the system." Enrique then admitted that he was angry with Krimsky for not giving him enough and for not meeting with him more than once a week. He seemed to be confronting his neglectful mother in the transference and finally letting himself know how angry he had been for all these years. As he talked about his neglectful mother, he began to recognize the feeling as similar to how he felt while fighting with the woman in the park; he put a name on it, identifying it as anger. Krimsky asked Enrique whether he felt it was safer to be angry with a stranger than with his mother. Enrique said yes, remembering his mother's angry outbursts and his childhood fears for his own life.

Shortly after this session, Enrique began to talk about his impending move to Florida. He had decided before psychotherapy began (but after the incident in the park) that he was going to move away from San Francisco to Miami since he had a better support network and life was cheaper there. He felt bad and guilty about having to leave Krimsky and the psychotherapy but also experienced some relief at stopping the process, fearing that if he truly felt better about himself, something terrible might happen. He was not able to articulate what that might be, but Krimsky suspected that further improvement would entail Enrique's confrontation of his anxieties about asserting himself and a range of consequent fears regarding loss of his mother and her love, castration anxieties, change of lifetime patterns in his relationships, and modification of his object relationships, especially those with his mother.

During session number eight, the pair discussed the move and Krimsky's upcoming two-week vacation, which would take place after session number nine. Eventually, Enrique admitted that he felt Krimsky was being selfish and that Enrique resented the therapist's vacation. Enrique surmised that Krimsky was leaving because Enrique had been "bad," which meant not being "macho" and being gay. Krimsky observed that perhaps Enrique felt afraid to express his anger toward the therapist, so he expressed it toward himself. Enrique said that it was much easier to see Krimsky as abusive and neglectful than as caring, which might mean that he, Enrique, would have to confront the fact that he deserved to be cared for, despite his feelings of "badness."

Enrique talked about the pain he felt in not being able to tell his mother how much he had loved and needed her when he was young. He said he could never express his irritation toward her because he felt she was already overloaded with a large family. Krimsky noted this pattern and helped Enrique understand that he was an adult and could have more choices about what to do in his relationships; in fact, he could confront others in ways that might actually deepen these relationships instead of destroying them. Enrique said that he felt comfortable asserting himself even with Krimsky and expressing his anger about Krimsky not being more available to him.

During session number nine, Enrique reported that he was realizing that many of his "friends" had taken advantage of him and that he was beginning to be able to confront them about this. The pair also discussed Krimsky's upcoming vacation, Enrique expressing feelings of disappointment and a return of his feeling that perhaps Krimsky was just part of the "system." Enrique did not show up after Krimsky's two-week vacation and did not return calls. Enrique had left for Miami prematurely and had been afraid to tell Krimsky.

⚬⚬⚬

Even though they did not see each other again, Krimsky believed that Enrique benefited from expressing some of his anger and exploring his fears about expressing anger. Enrique learned that he could have needs and that he could ask for things from others while still maintaining a relationship. Perhaps his leaving prematurely was a way to act out his underlying resentment toward the therapist and the feeling that he had to comply with the therapist and the therapy because of the court system and the therapist's needs. He might also have been unable to tolerate the anger he felt about Krimsky's vacation and could have decided to retaliate by abandoning the therapist, perhaps because of his fears that Krimsky might be abandoning him.

Enrique did make significant gains in exploring his difficulties, asserting himself, getting in touch with his anger toward his mother, and becoming aware of the patterns in his interactions with others. Enrique realized that he could let others know about his desires and that others could accept his needs without being angry at him or leaving him. Enrique also realized that he did not have to go along with whatever other people wanted to do; he could establish a dialogue with other people and negotiate his relationships. He could express his anger toward others rather than turn it inward, and actually improve his relationships as a result.

Notes

1. Schwartzberg, S. *A Crisis of Meaning: How Gay Men Are Making Sense of AIDS*. New York: Oxford University Press, 1996.
2. Weiss, J. J. "Psychotherapy with HIV-Positive Gay Men: A Psychodynamic Perspective." *American Journal of Psychotherapy*, 1997, *51*(1), 31–44.
3. De Roche, P. L. "Psychodynamic Psychotherapy with the HIV-Infected Client." In P. B. Jacques and P. Crits-Christoph (eds.), *Dynamic Therapies for Psychiatric Disorders (Axis I)*. New York: Basic Books, 1995.
4. Fawzy, F. I., Namir, S., and Wolcott, D. L. "Structured Group Intervention Model for AIDS Patients." *Psychiatric Medicine*, 1989, *7*(2), 35–45.
5. Blechner, M. J. (ed.). *Hope and Mortality: Psychodynamic Approaches to AIDS and HIV*. Hillsdale, N.J.: Analytic Press, 1997.
6. Farber, E. W. "Psychotherapy with HIV and AIDS Patients: The Phenomenon of Helplessness in Therapists." *Psychotherapy*, 1994, *31*(4), 715–724.
7. Sadowy, D. "Is There a Role for the Psychoanalytic Psychotherapist with a Patient Dying of AIDS?" *Psychoanalytic Review*, 1991, *78*(2), 199–207.
8. Hamilton, M. "A Rating Scale for Depression." *Journal of Neurology, Neurosurgery and Psychiatry*, 1960, *25*, 56–62.
9. Klerman, G. L., Weissman, M. M., Rounsaville, B., and others. *Interpersonal Psychotherapy of Depression*. New York: Basic Books, 1984.
10. Ibid.
11. Markowitz, J. C., and Weissman, M. M. "Interpersonal Therapy." In E. Beckham and W. Leber (eds.), *Handbook of Depression*. (2nd ed.) New York: Guilford Press, 1995.
12. Klerman, G. L., and Weissman, M. M. (eds.). *New Applications of Interpersonal Psychotherapy*. Washington, D.C.: American Psychiatric Press, 1993.
13. Parsons, T. "Illness and the Role of the Physician: A Sociological Perspective." *American Journal of Orthopsychiatry*, 1951, *21*, 452–460.

14. Markowitz, J. C., Klerman, G. L., and Perry, S. W. "Interpersonal Psychotherapy of Depressed HIV-Positive Outpatients." *Hospital and Community Psychiatry,* 1992, *43*(9), 885–890.
15. Markowitz, J. C., Klerman, G. L., Perry, S. W., and others. "Interpersonal Psychotherapy for Depressed HIV-Seropositive Patients." In G. L. Klerman and M. M. Weissman (eds.), *New Applications of Interpersonal Psychotherapy.* Washington, D.C.: American Psychiatric Press, 1993.
16. Perry, S. W., Jacobsberg, L., Ashman, T., and others. "Severity of Psychiatric Symptoms After HIV Testing." *American Journal of Psychiatry,* 1993, *150*(5), 775–779.
17. Ostrow, D. G., Monjan, A., Joseph, J. G., and others. "HIV-Related Symptoms and Psychological Functioning in a Cohort of Homosexual Men." *American Journal of Psychiatry,* 1989, *146*(6), 737–742.
18. Williams, J. B., Rabkin, J. G., Remien, R. H., and others. "Multidisciplinary Baseline Assessment of Homosexual Men with and Without Human Immunodeficiency Virus Infection. II. Standardized Clinical Assessment of Current and Lifetime Psychopathology." *Archives of General Psychiatry,* 1991, *48*(2), 120–123.
19. Manning, D., Jacobsberg, L., Erhart, S., and others. "The Efficacy of Imipramine in the Treatment of HIV-Related Depression." *Abstracts of the World Health Organization Sixth International Conference on AIDS, San Francisco, 1990.* Geneva: World Health Organization, 1990.
20. Parsons, "Illness and the Role of the Physician."
21. Markowitz, Klerman, and Perry, "Interpersonal Psychotherapy of Depressed HIV-Positive Outpatients."
22. Markowitz, Klerman, Perry, and others, "Interpersonal Psychotherapy for Depressed HIV-Positive Outpatients."
23. Cohen, J., and Abramowitz, S. "AIDS Attacks the Self: A Self-Psychological Exploration of the Psychodynamic Consequences of AIDS." In A. Goldberg (ed.), *Progress in Self Psychology.* Vol. 6. Hillsdale, N.J.: Analytic Press, 1990.
24. Kohut, H. *How Does Analysis Cure?* (ed. A. Goldberg and P. Stepansky). Chicago: University of Chicago Press, 1984.
25. Wolf, E. *Treating the Self.* New York: Guilford Press, 1988.
26. Kohut, H. *The Restoration of the Self.* New York: International Universities Press, 1977.
27. Stolorow, R., Brandchaft, B., and Atwood, G. *Psychoanalytic Treatment: An Intersubjective Approach.* Hillsdale, N.J.: Analytic Press, 1987.
28. Ornstein, A. "The Dread to Repeat and the New Beginning: A Contribution to the Psychoanalysis of the Narcissistic Personality Disorders." *Annals of Psychoanalysis,* 1974, *2*, 231–248.

29. Solomon, M. "Treatment of Narcissistic Vulnerability in Marital Therapy." In A. Goldberg (ed.), *Progress in Self Psychology.* Vol. 4. Hillsdale, N.J.: Analytic Press, 1988.

30. Solomon, M. *Narcissism and Intimacy.* New York: Norton, 1988.

31. Mitchell, S. *Relational Concepts in Psychoanalysis.* Cambridge, Mass.: Harvard University Press, 1988.

32. Ornstein, P., and Ornstein, A. "Clinical Understanding and Explaining: The Empathic Vantage Point." In A. Goldberg (ed.), *Progress in Self Psychology.* Vol. 1. Hillsdale, N.J.: Analytic Press, 1985.

33. Kohut, *How Does Analysis Cure?*

34. Kohut, H. *The Analysis of the Self.* Madison, Wis.: International Universities Press, 1971.

35. Basch, M. *Understanding Psychotherapy.* New York: Basic Books, 1988.

36. De Roche, "Psychodynamic Psychotherapy."

37. Weiss, J. J. "Psychotherapy with HIV-Positive Gay Men."

38. Blechner, M. J. (ed.). *Hope and Mortality: Psychodynamic Approaches to AIDS and HIV.* Hillsdale, N.J.: Analytic Press, 1997.

39. Levenson, H. *Time-Limited Dynamic Psychotherapy: A Guide to Clinical Practice.* New York: Basic Books, 1995.

40. Strupp, H., and Binder, J. *Psychotherapy in a New Key: A Guide to Time-Limited Dynamic Psychotherapy.* New York: Basic Books, 1984.

Chapter Eight

The Role of Psychotherapy in Coping with HIV Disease

John Devine

As with cancer, heart disease, and other chronic and life-threatening conditions, responding to HIV disease is as much an emotional endeavor as it is a physical one. This is true not simply because studies suggest that emotional health may directly affect the body's ability to respond to disease but also because facing a life-threatening disease requires a capacity for coping that goes far beyond the mechanisms we use to deal with everyday life.

Unlike the response to other life-threatening diseases, however, there has been an appreciation of the importance of mental health services for people with HIV disease since the beginning of the epidemic. Although research into specific HIV-related mental health interventions has lagged, providers on the front lines nonetheless can draw on a wealth of experience to help their clients.

The psychosocial issues raised by HIV disease follow the progression of the condition, from learning that one is seropositive through to the dying process. They also encompass the concerns of uninfected family, partners, friends, coworkers, and acquaintances, who watch as this course extends beyond life into bereavement. In response to this range of emotional difficulties, therapists have successfully employed a variety of psychotherapeutic approaches—including individual psychotherapy and group, family, and couples therapy. They have also employed technical variations with respect to the duration and frequency of therapy and have used diverse frameworks of treatment determined by therapeutic stance and informed by a specific theoretical orientation.

This chapter defines the range of HIV-related stressors, reviews the current literature on psychotherapy and HIV disease, and addresses the most commonly applied treatment modalities, focusing in particular on short-term psychotherapy, an increasingly common approach. For many therapists, brief psychotherapy is an outgrowth of pressure from insurance companies or institutional providers, which limit the number of sessions for each client. Short-term therapy can, however, be seen as an effective and efficient tool for managing particular emotional difficulties that arise in the context of HIV disease and may be more congruent with a client's plans to address a focused issue in a timely manner. The theoretical underpinning of time-limited therapy will be reviewed later in this chapter.

Early in the course of HIV disease, clients face the challenges of recognizing that they are seropositive and, in response, of accepting and incorporating this fact into their lives. (About 20 percent of people with HIV disease discover they are infected later in the course of disease when they experience severe symptoms, and therefore need to adjust immediately to physical disability.) As time passes, clients confront fears regarding disclosure to employers, friends, family, and lovers, and, despite new treatments that have reduced rates of disease progression and death, begin to reassess goals for work and relationships in light of potential disability and a foreshortened life span. Clients face frustration in terms of the onset and uncertain progression of physical illness, the difficult process of making treatment decisions, the assumption of the role of "patient," and the complexity of medical treatment regimens. If antiviral treatment is effective, clients must come to terms with having a chronic illness, being dependent for long periods on medications, and redefining themselves as "able." If medical treatment does not work or if clients are unable to access these treatments, clients face existential tasks as they anticipate and ultimately confront mortality and death. People with HIV disease are especially at risk for adjustment, anxiety, and depressive disorders, and for suicide.

Such stressors may affect both emotional and physical health. Although psychoneuroimmunology remains a field of study in its infancy, and the literature is complex and often contradictory, research has suggested a relationship between emotional well-being and immune status.[1] For example, using self-report measures, a recent study found a significant association between depression and a more rapid decline of CD4+ cells, suggesting increased disease progression.[2] Another study demonstrated the ability of psychiatric interventions to reduce affective distress, enhance effective coping strategies, and increase survival among cancer patients.[3] These reports, however, conflict with other data from a four-year longitudinal study at Columbia University that employed both self-report and interviewer-derived data; the study did not support a significant association between depression and CD4+ cell count decline or clinical progression to AIDS.[4]

Whether or not there is a direct correlation between mental health and increased longevity, appropriate psychotherapy helps serve the overall goal of mental health care: responding to emotional difficulties, decreasing the symptoms of emotional distress, and improving overall quality of life. Psychotherapeutic interventions can help develop and strengthen coping strategies for people living with HIV disease, improve a person's ability to relate to others, define and correct unhealthy psychological defenses and maladaptive behavior patterns, and replace feelings of isolation, hopelessness, and despondency with a renewed sense of intimacy, purpose, and optimism.

Lessons from the Literature

The professional literature on psychiatric treatment of people with HIV disease has focused primarily on the assessment and management of neuropsychiatric problems, practical interventions for psychosocial stressors, and education and disease prevention. Relatively little has been written on understanding specific psychotherapeutic techniques in the treatment of HIV disease, and given the current changing paradigms regarding treatment and prognosis, what has been written may require revision. A brief overview of some of the literature provides the foundation for the more detailed discussion of specific psychotherapeutic techniques that follows.

The "Phases of Illness" Framework

One way to conceive of the goals of HIV-related psychotherapy is to consider the emotional issues and needs specific to each phase of illness. Gary Lomax and Jeffery Sandler suggest a framework for this examination,[5] basing their formulations on earlier work on the psychosocial challenges at each stage of HIV disease.[6,7] The advent of successful combination antiviral therapy may change the ways in which individuals proceed through these stages, but for many, the psychological challenges outlined here remain.

The initial phase, HIV diagnosis, is characterized as an emotional crisis, with early reactions ranging from shock, denial, and emotional numbing to marked anxiety and panic. In addition, clients may experience catastrophic expectations, including fears of disfigurement, physical pain, disability, and rejection by loved ones. The therapist's goal during this phase is to support a client's appropriate coping reactions while identifying and challenging dysfunctional defenses. Tasks at this phase include providing an empathic, supportive, and reality-based presence, making appropriate referrals to medical and social services, and assessing and monitoring levels of subjective distress, including suicidal ideation. In the context of the success of combination antiviral treatment, the crisis during this initial phase may be diminished. Nevertheless, learning that one is HIV-infected still means catastrophe for most individuals, and the need to adjust to the painful loss of one's identity as uninfected and healthy is an important one.

Following the initial phase, clients go through a period of gradual acceptance, and they refocus on the need to formulate new meanings about life and goals for living. During this period, which includes what Lomax and Sandler call a "honeymoon phase," clients gradually come to believe that they are not going to die immediately and, during this asymptomatic phase, that they may "beat this disease." Therapeutic tasks include exploring and working through fear, anger, guilt, loss, and sadness; supporting "adaptive denial"—the psychological mechanism that allows a client to develop a healthy distance from negative events; and confronting maladaptive denial—a mechanism by which a client refuses to accept his or her illness and, for example, avoids necessary medical care. These tasks have become more complex in light of the success of combination antiviral treatment. There are many concrete reasons for clients to be hopeful, related to actual and dramatic improvements in health, as well as many more opportunities for them to deny in dysfunctional ways the risks of untreated or inadequately treated HIV disease.

The third phase is heralded by the development of debilitating illness and is marked by physical deterioration and the letting go of certain aspects of one's life (for example, work), which may exert a great emotional toll. Loss of hope and preoccupation with death and dying become prominent, and therapy may shift to more supportive contact. Improved prognosis has meant for many people not only that the second phase may stretch out for many years but also that many clients are cycling back from the third phase to the second as treatment success reverses previous debilitation. Clients may respond with ambivalence to these developments because of uncertainty regarding the duration of improvements in physical health and an inability to cope with adhering to rigorous treatment regimens.

During the final phase of illness—a phase that progress in treatment has not yet eliminated—the primary clinical goal is to maintain a supportive connection, which may require hospital, home, and hospice visits and telephone contact in addition to routine therapy sessions. Extreme physical decline and the onset of cognitive impairment may limit the degree to which communication can occur; nevertheless, clients can benefit from the continued presence of a supportive contact to help cope with the process of end-stage illness and death and the psychological issues it evokes.

Examining the Therapeutic Alliance

The literature on HIV-related psychodynamic psychotherapy is useful in considering approaches to the issues raised by the stages of HIV progression. It examines the therapeutic relationship and the effects and uses of transference, countertransference, and identification with both seropositive and seronegative clients (see Chapter Sixteen). One commentator highlights the need for a strong therapeutic alliance because HIV infection is often clouded by overwhelming feelings of isolation and alienation.[8] In this context, HIV disease may also be viewed as a narcissistic injury; self-precepts

derived from the sense of oneself as physically intact and healthy
and illusory beliefs in apparent invulnerability to disease are shat-
tered by an HIV diagnosis. This is particularly true for those HIV-
infected individuals who previously had little contact with serious
illness. The client's overall sense of both physical and psychological
self may be threatened, particularly as changes in health status
occur, and may strongly influence and reinforce negative self-
images of being flawed or deficient. For many gay men, these perceptions reinforce preexisting ones.

Transference and countertransference reactions may also arise
in terms of the client's need to idealize an omnipotent figure—the
therapist—in order to manage anxiety related to the loss of control.[9]
In addition, clients with HIV disease may unconsciously use other
defensive strategies, including projective identification, in order to
rid themselves of feelings of helplessness and rage.[10] In this case the
therapist may find his or her own feelings of frustration and inadequacy targeted by the client's projections, leading the therapist to
feel a heightened sense of futility. In a commentary on the psychoanalytic treatment of a woman dying of AIDS, Diane Sadowy also
identifies powerful transference- and countertransference-based fantasies concerning the omnipotence of the therapist. She goes on to
discuss the need, as both the therapist and client face the very real
prospect of the client's death, to disengage and shift from "a rapidly
dying external reality and to enter a living vibrant internal reality."[11]
In this context, Sadowy also addresses the need to modify the usual
therapeutic parameters—for example, to make changes in the therapeutic "frame" related to session length, telephone contacts, and
involvement of significant others in the therapy.

Leon McKusick emphasizes the importance for both seronegative and seropositive therapists of analyzing the nature of their
countertransference reactions.[12] Seronegative therapists should be
alert to responses of distancing, fears of contagion, survivor guilt,
and judgmental attitudes toward their clients' sexual or drug-
related behaviors. Seropositive therapists, on the other hand, must
be wary of overidentifying with their clients. In either case, psychodynamic therapists in particular need to examine fully the potential transference issues regarding their serostatus and determine
if exploration and possibly self-disclosure of this information would
be beneficial or detrimental to the work.

Other models of psychotherapy have been reviewed in the literature, including a study of the efficacy of interpersonal psychotherapy and cognitive-based therapy, the utility of grief and bereavement theoretical paradigms to understand the meaning of loss in the treatment of those affected by HIV disease, and the applicability of self psychology.[13-17] (See Chapters Seven and Twelve for more information on all of these theoretical stances.)

The Value of Group, Couples, and Family Psychotherapy

A number of studies demonstrate the efficacy of group psychotherapy and describe its role in HIV-related care. Fawzy Fawzy examines the effect on mood state of a time-limited educational and support group and found a significant decrease in total mood disturbance scores and an improvement of coping skills.[18] Similarly, a study of a psychoeducational cognitive-based group therapy intervention measured decreased levels of depression and anxiety and improvement in coping among people with asymptomatic HIV infection.[19] Jeffrey Kelly found that depressed HIV-infected clients treated in either cognitive-behavioral or social support groups achieved greater reductions in feelings of depression and anger when compared to clients who were not treated, and that group therapy helped these clients shift the focus away from physical symptoms.[20] It is notable that the social support group—in which members discussed feelings associated with their illness and adopted encouraging and supportive roles toward others in their group—resulted in a greater clinical improvement than did the cognitive-based group. This suggests the importance of formally addressing the interpersonal aspect of therapy.

Researchers have also studied the utility of group psychotherapy to treat specific populations. HIV-infected women in group therapy raise gender-specific issues, including the following: isolation and a greater sense of being unsupported in their illness than are seropositive men, a greater tendency of caregivers to dismiss the severity of their medical complaints, changes in their role within the family as a result of illness, and the potential loss of reproductive choice.[21] Other researchers focus on the needs of other specific groups, including ethnic minorities, other disenfranchised populations, and dual-diagnosis clients. Finally, other commentators

outline the atmosphere and process of ongoing HIV psychotherapy groups.[22,23]

Couples and family therapy are crucial adjuncts to individual
therapy, because HIV disease is so intimately related to interpersonal relationships and because these relationships can create significant stress among people affected by HIV disease. Pertinent
articles regarding these approaches include a pilot study of the efficacy of cognitive-behavioral-based couples therapy[24] and a discussion of family therapy and HIV disease.[25] (See also Chapter
Seven, "HIV Disease as an Agent of Transformation.")

Another set of articles addresses the specific legal and ethical
dilemmas therapists face in conducting HIV-related psychotherapy, which can arise in the setting of individual, couples, family, or
group therapy. Among these challenges are knowing when and
how to confront a client's denial regarding his or her illness and
its consequences, and understanding the ethical and legal duties
of psychotherapists with regard to their clients' behaviors, including the duty to disclose.[26,27,28]

Selecting a Therapeutic Approach

A number of factors can influence the mode and nature of the psychotherapy for clients with HIV disease.[29] Among these are the
client's stage of illness, his or her past experiences in therapy, the
presence of significant characterological problems, and the extent
of social support available. Other important determinants are the
presence of other psychiatric illness, any existing psychopharmacological interventions, and the nature of a therapist's training and
practice. This section and the next review the most commonly used
psychotherapeutic approaches—group, family, and individual—
highlighting their specific strengths and weaknesses and the problems best suited to each approach.

Group Psychotherapy

Joining a support group is often the first step a person will take in
responding to HIV-related distress. When it is not the doorway to
individual therapy, it is frequently an adjunct. For these reasons, it
is appropriate for us to begin a discussion of psychotherapeutic

modes with group therapy. Group therapy for people with HIV disease is particularly effective in providing social support and education, improving coping skills, and decreasing emotional distress. Groups vary considerably with regard to theoretical orientation, composition, duration, setting, and the roles of facilitators and members. In terms of content, however, several issues are common to nearly all groups for clients with HIV disease. These include a focus on physical symptoms (including comparisons among group members), uncertainties regarding disease treatment and progression of illness, stigma and shame associated with risk behaviors, and a central focus on death and dying. Broaching such issues and discussing them with others who share similar experiences can be remarkably healing. Groups can also provide clients a forum in which to explore issues related to medical treatment decisions and to share experiences that can help them navigate this complex area.

We can derive several guidelines regarding group formation and composition from the HIV-related group experience. Groups that are homogenous in terms of sexual orientation, gender, and risk history provide members with the necessary safety and mutual identification to facilitate group cohesion. Homogeneity alone, however, does not ensure cohesion, and the group psychotherapist needs to be particularly attentive to the various stages of group development, including the degree to which group trust and safety has been established, in order to handle anxiety-provoking issues as they arise.

Stage of illness is also an important consideration, because the issues raised by group members will vary depending on where clients are in their illness; too much variation can potentially overwhelm or isolate members. It is difficult, however, to form groups in which all members are at an identical stage in their illness, and it is impossible to maintain such homogeneity over time. There may also be therapeutic advantages to having group members who are at varying stages of illness and who share their experiences of HIV disease, alternately giving and obtaining support from other members.

Conversely, at a time when some people with HIV disease are experiencing sudden improvements in health, the gulf between group members who are able and those who are disabled may complicate this already complex dynamic. It can be a challenging task for therapists to make room for the group to focus on the needs both of members who are more directly facing disability and death and of those who are focused on living and renewed health. Therapists can achieve the necessary balance between individual and group needs through an open exploration of differences among group members—whether these are related to health status or to other issues—and how both difference and commonality may be influencing the group process.

Members new to the group should agree to a standard contract regarding group attendance, confidentiality, specific group goals, overall group functioning, and time commitment. The introduction of an overly ambivalent member or one who might challenge the contract can destabilize group cohesion and safety and thwart the development of a therapeutic group process. In monitoring contracts, particularly regarding absences from the group, therapists need to do their best to distinguish client resistance from the physical factors that may impinge on the client's ability to attend and participate. Therapists should also examine the effect of absences on the group as a whole, as these may resonate for other members with issues of rejection and abandonment in addition to specific fears regarding failing health.

Whereas outside contact is discouraged in more analytically focused psychotherapy groups, contact among group members outside a support group may be condoned. Contact allows for continuity of support between sessions and may provide practical support—specifically, transportation to and from group sessions. Nonetheless, therapists need to consider potential complications that might result from out-of-group contacts; for example, issues raised in the group by a client could possibly be processed outside the group with another member, denying the group the opportunity to grow through the experience of working through the issue, and interrupting continuity from one session to the next.

As in individual therapy, group members' transference wishes often emerge for an omnipotent therapist to magically cure their physical illness. Concerns relating to trust and acceptance may motivate clients to ask about their therapist's sexual orientation, HIV infection status, and knowledge of HIV disease. Some clients may want to work with therapists who are different from them—for example, who are heterosexual or seronegative—in the belief or fantasy that these people are "healthy" and unaffected by HIV disease. Countertransference reactions, including the therapist's feeling that only he or she is "healthy" enough to treat group members, may also impede the group's development and may limit the therapist's awareness and use of group process. There may instead be a temptation to focus inordinately on the individual, thereby interfering with the engagement of other group members.

HIV group therapists face ongoing therapeutic decisions about balancing discussion between attitudes toward death and dying with life-affirming topics, especially given the impact of new treatments on disease course. A basic rule that is helpful in directing interventions in this regard is to listen for what is *not* being expressed by the group; for example, is the group avoiding death and dying by focusing only on the positive advances in treatments? If the group seems to be avoiding this subject, the therapist may need to point out the resistance as well as explore the reasons why the group may be finding it difficult to give voice to their concerns.

In striking this balance, it is important for the therapist to keep in mind the stage of group development, including the degree to which trust and cohesion exist among members. Early in group development, the group may experience the rigorous exploration of anxiety-provoking issues as threatening to group integrity. During this phase it might be necessary to support the group's denial of thoughts and emotions related to death and dying in order to promote an environment in which group members can safely develop trust and acceptance. Once this group culture has been established, and especially if physical decline and death occur among members of the group, it is crucial to promote an active discussion of feelings raised by these events.

Family Therapy

As is true for group therapy, family therapy can increase the availability of support for the client and help him or her deal with significant interpersonal relationships. Family therapy seeks to understand the ways in which an individual's concerns affect and are affected by the family system, and to determine how these problems relate to preexisting conflicts and compromises among family members. It is an effective treatment modality for clients with HIV disease whose primary supportive relationships with family and with significant others have been weakened as a consequence of the client's HIV status. For example, clients may be experiencing the stressor of being in a serodiscordant relationship, or a family may be dealing with the issues associated with caring for a client with end-stage disease.

Family therapy has received little attention in the literature on HIV disease and psychotherapy, and it is underused in HIV clinical practice.[30,31,32] This may be due in part to the distant relationships that many gay or bisexual men have with their families of origin. It may also relate to anxieties about terminal illness and premature death, as people with HIV disease seek to protect their families (and themselves) from potential shame and stigma. However, by bringing family members together and helping them identify mutual problems and reaffirm their love and concern for each other, therapy can be instrumental in facilitating understanding and support. In addition, therapy can help family members come to terms with illness and death and ease potential bereavement. In working-class and particularly poor families, family therapy focused on problem solving and advocacy can also help ensure the stability of the family system.

The therapist's role as an educator may be particularly important, because families may be uninformed about HIV disease prognosis, treatment, and transmission. By allaying irrational fears and clarifying rational ones, and by allowing family members to express their emotional responses—including anger, blame, regret, and sadness—the family therapist can help clients and their families reach understanding and acceptance.

Individual Psychotherapy

Individual psychotherapy has been used to treat a wide range of emotional difficulties associated with HIV disease. Although severe mood disorders may require psychopharmacological interventions in addition to therapy, the more common and milder affective disturbances and adjustment reactions are primarily addressed through psychotherapy. As noted earlier, these adjustment reactions are best understood in relation to the phase of a client's illness. Initial concerns include ambivalence regarding antibody testing; response to the news of seroconversion; assessment of life goals in the area of work and relationships; disclosures of illness to family, friends, and coworkers; and strengthening or development of social support systems.

As HIV disease progresses and clients develop physical symptoms, limitations on the ability to work and to pursue personal interests and clients' increasing dependency on medical and social supports become prominent issues in therapy. For clients whose successful treatment has suddenly halted disease progression, issues of working and short-term and long-term goals become central; these issues are challenging HIV-related psychotherapy in new ways. At advanced and terminal stages of disease, clients' decisions regarding aggressiveness of medical treatments and hospice and palliative care and their existential concerns regarding death and dying arise as therapeutic goals. As has always been true—and particularly so in the context of new antiviral treatments—clients may move in nonlinear ways through this progression, returning to health after severe illness, experiencing new symptoms after a period of health, confronting a host of serious side effects, and even believing that they have been "cured."

The decision to embark on either a time-limited or an open-ended course of therapy is an important initial consideration in treatment. An open-ended course may be helpful for the client who has limited social support and wants or needs an ongoing connection for support and who is not primarily limited by time or money. With the growth of managed care and an increasing demand on public resources, clients are affected more and more by these limitations. For these clients and for others who feel more comfortable with therapy that has a perceptible beginning, middle, and end, brief psychotherapy may be an attractive alternative.

Delineating individual psychotherapy into time-limited and open-ended approaches may obscure other crucial variations in psychotherapeutic approach that may have particular relevance for seropositive clients; for example, although "insight-oriented" psychodynamic psychotherapy is an approach often used with clients with HIV disease, variations include the use of cognitive-behavioral therapy, "problem-solving" therapy, and existential therapy.

Open-ended psychodynamic psychotherapy may be appropriate for clients who have a number of issues they want help in understanding, as well as for those clients who present without clear-cut goals for treatment. Often it can take a period of months before the most salient features of a client's interpersonal or intrapsychic difficulties emerge. An open-ended or long-term individual therapy may also be more suitable for

- Clients with more severe character-based disorders, including severe personality disorders, if the goal of the therapy is to induce changes in the client's defensive strategies and character structure
- Clients in need of ongoing, primarily supportive therapy
- Clients who wish to engage in a treatment that will provide them with a continuing forum for self-exploration
- Clients, particularly people with HIV, for whom the continued presence of the therapist in their lives provides a sense of stability

For clients with HIV disease, the essential principles of treatment are no different from those of other clients. The therapist assumes a nondirective stance and allows for the gradual unfolding of themes related to psychological conflict. The therapist not only listens to how those themes manifest in current and past relationships but also attends to their reenactments within the therapeutic relationship through transference. Eventually the therapist will direct the therapeutic work toward the goal of analyzing the transference, and in doing so will seek to help resolve the specific conflicts that are creating difficulties in the client's life.

In the HIV-specific setting, the therapist, particularly over the course of long-term therapy, may need to shift from an insight-oriented stance to a more supportive one in the face of changes in health status. At this time of significant change in HIV-related medical treatment, therapists should also be sensitive to changes in therapeutic goals. Clients who have focused in therapy on coming to terms with losses in functional status may now be finding that their goals have, at least temporarily, shifted toward concerns regarding "reentry" and renewed health. These shifts can be unsettling for both the client and the therapist; they both will be affected by the uncertainties and ambiguities that changing treatment paradigms present. In particular, therapists may find that some clients who have embarked on long-term psychodynamic therapy may want to change to a more short-term, problem-oriented approach that focuses on immediate back-to-work issues and termination of the therapeutic relationship.

Using Brief Psychotherapy

The remainder of this chapter defines two forms of brief psychodynamic psychotherapy, identifies applications for these approaches to clients with HIV disease, and illustrates the utility of these models with several case examples. In the process, it clarifies the overall goals of HIV-related psychotherapy. This focus more specifically on brief psychotherapy makes sense in light of a number of factors. Many therapists who work with seropositive clients currently find themselves operating in systems mediated by managed care service limitations or in institutional or program settings faced with shrinking resources and increasing demand. In addition, many clients with HIV disease come to therapy desiring shorter-term approaches. Although it may seem counterintuitive that clients with emotional distress related to a life-threatening illness could be effectively treated in brief therapy, many therapists find that advances in the theory and practice of brief therapy are applicable to clients with HIV disease and can result in enduring improvements in emotional health.

Writing in the earlier part of the twentieth century, Sandor Ferenczi and Otto Rank[33] and Franz Alexander[34] referred to short-term approaches to analytic therapy, recommending that therapists take a more active stance than was usual for the standard psychoanalytic approach in use at the time. They described the advantages of setting finite limits to the number of sessions, emphasizing a more rapid emergence of transference and countertransference issues and a heightened motivation on the part of the client to work actively in the treatment process.

In the 1960s and 1970s, other theorists, working independently, developed brief therapy models that varied considerably in terms of the type of client treated but shared a reliance on certain key features:[35,36,37]

- The therapist's assumption of an active and optimistic stance
- The relatively rapid assessment of the client's problems with an emphasis on the "here and now," specifically focusing on current problems in psychosocial functioning rather than on the slower emergence of historical content
- The development of an interpersonal versus an intrapsychic focus, by which the therapist helps the client understand his or her important relationships, thus providing an identifiable foundation on which to base treatment
- Prompt intervention
- A heightened focus on and need to address termination issues throughout treatment

Current "third generation" models of brief dynamic individual therapy include time-limited dynamic psychotherapy, developed by Hans Strupp and Jeffrey Binder,[38,39] and short-term dynamic therapy, developed by Mardi Horowitz specifically to treat Post-Traumatic Stress Disorder (PTSD).[40] Both approaches have specific applications to clients with HIV disease.

Time-Limited Dynamic Psychotherapy

Time-limited dynamic psychotherapy is an interpersonal model of treatment based on a psychodynamic approach. It allows for the examination of "cyclical maladaptive interactional patterns" within a fifteen- to twenty-session format. Time-limited dynamic psychotherapy posits that although maladaptive ways of relating to others are typically learned in childhood, they are maintained in the present through relations with significant others and can cause symptoms of anxiety and depression.

In treatment, clients will unconsciously press for reenactment of their dysfunctional style with the therapist.[41] The therapist's goal is to respond to the client in unanticipated ways, thereby providing a "corrective" emotional experience and revealing to the client a new emotional and cognitive understanding of the dysfunctional style. As in long-term psychodynamic therapy, the therapist is guided by the "dynamic focus," a method of organizing and formulating his or her observations. In the case of time-limited therapy, the dynamic focus describes the "pattern of interpersonal roles in which clients unconsciously cast themselves, the complementary roles in which they cast others, and the maladaptive interaction sequences, self-defeating expectations, and negative self-appraisal that result."[42] The dynamic focus provides a "blueprint for therapy," helping to define the goals of treatment as well as anticipating problems that will occur within the therapeutic relationship. Unlike therapeutic interactions in longer-term models of treatment, the time-limited psychotherapist is more active in communicating interpretations, which are limited in their scope to the specific dynamic focus; he or she diverges more often from the "blank screen" model of therapeutic neutrality typical of classical psychoanalysis and actively acknowledges the time limit, thereby accelerating the pace and urgency of the therapy.

Interpersonal conflict is an ideal focus for time-limited psychotherapy, as the problem is especially suited to the strengths of this approach. Among the conflicts that may arise in the setting of HIV infection are social isolation and the exacerbation of preexisting difficulties (stemming from underlying characterological problems) in making and sustaining interpersonal relationships. A manifestation of this conflict might involve a client with borderline personality disorder who, under the stress of a recent HIV diagnosis, enters a cycle of stormy relationships that leave him feeling angry, rejected, and alone.

Clients without significant preexisting interpersonal difficulties may also experience conflicts as a result of an HIV diagnosis. These can take a variety of forms, including depressive reactions following the loss of autonomy and in anticipation of disability. For instance, a client may be reluctant to develop new interests and relationships out of the fear that he or she may become dependent on others. By examining conflicts concerning dependency, the therapist can help the client relinquish firmly held views about the need for absolute self-sufficiency and dispel irrational and catastrophic beliefs regarding his or her illness. Conversely, therapists might use this approach to help clients with preexisting passivity, which may worsen in the context of HIV, to develop a more active stance toward themselves and their treatment.

Time-limited dynamic psychotherapy is also effective in mediating the emotional reactions and interpersonal disturbances that may result from experiencing HIV infection as a narcissistic injury.

Clients may come to view themselves as flawed, imperfect, and un-deserving of health, medical treatment, or meaningful relation-ships. This self-denigrating view can result from guilt regarding drug-use behavior or internalized homophobia, or may relate to core feelings of worthlessness and shame in clients with narcissis-tic character disturbances. Time-limited dynamic psychotherapy in this situation can respond to these self-denigrating views and help clients regain a healthy narcissistic investment in themselves and their lives. A case study will clarify how time-limited dynamic ther-apy operates in practical terms.

Tom: HIV Infection and Feelings of Inferiority

Tom is a thirty-five-year-old single gay man who requests "a few sessions" to help him deal with symptoms of mild depression and anxiety. Tom tested HIV-positive a year ago and initially blamed himself and felt guilt-ridden. During the year, he has remained asymptomatic but has become increasingly isolated from his friends and family. He feels unable to enter into relationships and has stopped dating to avoid "burdening anyone" with his condition.

Tom is a freelance graphic artist and has grown concerned about his ability to embark successfully on new projects. He describes occasional insom-nia but denies using drugs or alcohol or having any consistent symptoms of major depression. Tom was raised by emotionally distant parents who readily expressed their disappointment in him. He has had several significant rela-tionships with men in his adult life, which he believes ended because he felt that they lost interest in him.

Tom's therapist, Helen Carter, works initially to define a dynamic focus that will guide the therapy. She does this by actively listening to the issues Tom raises during the first few sessions and, in contrast to open-ended therapy, re-lies less on a wealth of historical detail and more on Tom's description of cur-rent problems. Carter notes a maladaptive interpersonal pattern that recurs in Tom's relationships with his friends and family and sees a similar process oc-curring in Tom's approach to initiating relationships. Critical to the workings of this therapeutic model is the identification of ways in which such a mal-adaptive pattern manifests within the therapeutic relationship.

In this case, the dynamic focus centers on how infection reinforces Tom's long-standing feelings of inferiority and expectations of rejection. These atti-tudes surface in transference: Tom feels that he is taking up "valuable time" and that he doesn't deserve the fifteen sessions Carter proposes. He appears exquisitely sensitive to the actions on the therapist's part that might imply disinterest or even rejection. For example, when Carter has to cancel a session, Tom responds in the next session by talking about ending therapy, as Carter "probably has other client's who could use the time with her."

Carter works to reveal how Tom's self-denigrating views are affecting current interpersonal interactions, including those in the therapy. She asks Tom about why he feels that she would be better off seeing other clients and offers an interpretive link between this interaction and Tom's assumptions that his relationships ended due to his own inadequacies. She helps Tom understand his current feelings in light of his past relationships, including those in his family of origin, while providing support and demonstrating genuine interest in him in order to enhance his feelings of self-worth. In this way the therapist actively works to provide Tom with a "new experience," through which he is able to feel positive regard from the therapist and consequently is able to challenge previously held beliefs that others will reject him. In this case, the termination of therapy will likely induce a similar negative transference, but Carter discusses this with Tom in a way that helps him understand his feelings in light of his personal history.

Short-Term Dynamic Therapy

Following a traumatic event—for example, rape or combat exposure—people experience dramatic shifts in previously held views, or "schemata," of themselves and the world. They will also undergo changes in states of mind, both undermodulated, expressed as denial and emotional numbing, and overmodulated, expressed as intrusive ruminations. The resulting adjustment difficulties—manifested as painful feelings and dysfunctional behaviors—arise due to a failure to integrate the meaning of the traumatic event into a variety of self-held schemata.

According to Mardi Horowitz, the goal of the twelve-session short-term dynamic therapy model is "to help the patient complete the cycle of ideational and emotional responses to a stress event." The result is to diminish the "severity and frequency of intrusion-denial phases" and facilitate the "integration of the meaning of the traumatic event into the patient's view of themselves and their world."[43] Horowitz underscores the importance of acknowledging the contributions of a client's personality style to the persistence of the client's maladaptive coping. In contrast to Strupp's time-limited therapy model, Horowitz's short-term therapy focuses more on intrapsychic processes than on interpersonal difficulties. In addition, the model deemphasizes the significance of transference and countertransference patterns and concentrates on understanding the client's characteristic defensive style.

HIV-related applications of this model follow from the conceptualization of HIV disease as a series of potentially devastating stressors. A variety of stressors—the initial response to being seropositive, the development of severe and debilitating medical illness, the letting go of career aspirations, the grief resulting from the deaths of loved ones, the immediacy of one's mortality, and more recently, the challenge of rejoining life after regaining health—may contribute to a series of significant adjustment reactions, which may elicit a clinical stress response syndrome that can resemble PTSD. Feeling overwhelmed and anxious, alternating with periods of feeling emotionally disengaged and in denial, corresponds with the stress-response phases Horowitz describes; these phases interfere with a client's ability to cope and to live a meaningful life.

Therapists using the short-term dynamic approach can help clients modify preexisting internal schemata and modulate dysfunctional patterns arising from HIV-related stressors. This modification in turn allows a functional integration of initial and continuing HIV-related stressors.

Blanca: Denial and Overwhelming Emotion

Blanca is a thirty-year-old divorced mother of two, referred for psychotherapy to treat severe anxiety and insomnia, which had developed over the preceding month. She has been seropositive for several years but had had only mild physical symptoms until she was recently diagnosed with AIDS because of a sudden drop in her CD4+ cell count.

Blanca feels "overwhelmed," anxious, and afraid that she will be unable to care for her ten-year-old son and eight-year-old daughter. Prior to her AIDS diagnosis, she had "tried not to think" about her illness and had been inconsistent about her medical care. She has been reluctant to tell her extended family about her HIV disease for fear that they would ostracize her, and in general she has felt isolated.

Blanca's therapist, Howard McDonald, identifies elements of a stress response syndrome in Blanca's denial of her illness followed by her feeling overwhelmed and incapacitated by it. He focuses therapy initially on Blanca's blunted emotional responses and helps her express her most pressing fears in order for her to gain a sense of control over her feeling states. In doing so, McDonald is mindful of Blanca's underlying cognitive style, which includes a tendency toward jumping to conclusions, impulsivity, and thinking the worst. He works in therapy to counter that style by employing a more reasoned problem-solving approach.

Over the course of twelve sessions, McDonald allows Blanca to voice her greatest fears, which center on her concerns regarding her children's welfare. He helps Blanca formulate specific plans for identifying those members of her extended family from whom she would feel comfortable asking for assistance if her health deteriorated further. Through this approach, Blanca is able to integrate her illness into her life and, as a result, is able to be more open with her family, who in turn are able to offer her emotional and practical support.

As the epidemic moves into its second decade, there is a continuing need to identify and refine forms of psychotherapeutic intervention so as to better understand and help patients cope with illness. Aside from this evolution in technique, an essential component of the work remains the ability to convey personal qualities of compassion, caring, and positive regard. Despite difficulties, frustrations, and sadness, helping those who are struggling to cope with HIV disease can be among the most gratifying, rewarding, and exhilarating of our endeavors as psychotherapists. Greater clarity about when and for whom to use particular techniques can only improve the lives of clients and deepen the satisfaction of providers.

Notes

1. Leiphart, J. "Psychoneuroimmunology: A Basis for HIV Treatment." *Focus: A Guide to AIDS Research and Counseling,* 1997, *12*(3), 1–4.
2. Burack, J., Barrett, D., Stail, R., and others. "Depressive Symptoms and CD4 Lymphocyte Decline Among HIV Infected Men." *Journal of the American Medical Association,* 1993, *270*(21), 2568–2575.
3. Fawzy, F. I., Fawzy, N. W., Hyun, C. S., and others. "Malignant Melanoma: Effects of an Early Structured Psychiatric Intervention,

Coping, and Affective State on Recurrence and Survival 6 Years Later." *Archives of General Psychiatry,* 1993, *50*(9), 681–689.

4. Rabkin, J. G., Goetz, R. R., Remien, R. H., and others. "Stability of Mood Despite HIV Illness Progression in a Group of Homosexual Men." *American Journal of Psychiatry,* 1997, *154*(2), 231–238.

5. Lomax, G., and Sandler, J. "Psychotherapy and Consultation with Persons with AIDS." *Psychiatric Annals,* 1986, *18*(4), 253–259.

6. Dilley, J. W. "Treatment Interventions and Approaches to Care of Patients with Acquired Immune Deficiency Syndrome." In S. Nichols and D. G. Ostrow (eds.), *Psychiatric Implications of AIDS.* Washington, D.C.: American Psychiatric Press, 1984.

7. Nichols, S. "Psychiatric Aspects of AIDS." *Psychosomatics,* 1983, *24*(12), 1083–1089.

8. Dilley, "Treatment Interventions."

9. Feldmann, T. "Psychotherapy with AIDS Patients." *Journal of the Kentucky Medical Association,* 1989, *87*(8), 368–370.

10. Kermani, E., and Weiss, B. "AIDS and Confidentiality: Legal Concept and Its Application in Psychotherapy." *American Journal of Psychotherapy,* 1989, *43*(1), 25–31.

11. Sadowy, D. "Is There a Role for the Psychoanalytic Psychotherapist with a Patient Dying of AIDS?" *Psychoanalytic Review,* 1991, *78*(2), 199–207.

12. McKusick, L. "The Impact of AIDS on Practitioner and Client." *American Psychologist,* 1988, *43*(11), 935–940.

13. Markowitz, J. C., Klerman, G. L., and Perry, S. W. "Interpersonal Psychotherapy of Depressed HIV-Positive Outpatients." *Hospital and Community Psychiatry,* 1992, *43*(9), 885–890.

14. Kelly, J. A., and Murphy, D. A. "Psychological Interventions with AIDS and HIV: Prevention and Treatment." *Journal of Consulting and Clinical Psychology,* 1992, *60*(4), 576–585.

15. Kaal, H. "Grief Counseling for Gay Men." *FOCUS: A Guide to AIDS Research and Counseling,* 1992, *7*(7), 1–4.

16. Grothe, T., and McKusick, L. "Coping with Multiple Loss." *FOCUS: A Guide to AIDS Research and Counseling,* 1992, *7*(7), 5–6.

17. Abramowitz, S., and Cohen, J. "The Psychodynamics of AIDS: A View from Self Psychology." In S. A. Cadwell, R. A. Burnham, and M. Forstein (eds.), *Therapists on the Front Line: Psychotherapy with Gay Men in the Age of AIDS.* Washington, D.C.: American Psychiatric Press, 1994.

18. Fawzy, F. I., Namir, S., and Wolcott, D. L. "Structural Group Intervention Model for AIDS Patients." *Psychiatric Medicine,* 1989, *7*(2), 35–45.

19. Levine, S. H., Bystritsky, A., Baron, D., and Jones, L. D. "Group Psychotherapy for HIV-Seropositive Patients with Major Depression." *American Journal of Psychotherapy,* 1991, *45*(3), 413–424.

20. Kelly, J. A., Murphy, D. A., Bahr, G. R., and others. "Outcome of Cognitive-Behavioral and Support Group Brief Therapies for Depressed, HIV-Infected Persons." *American Journal of Psychiatry*, 1993, *150*(11), 1679–1686.

21. Chung, J., and Magraw, M. "A Group Approach to Psychosocial Issues Faced by HIV-Positive Women." *Hospital and Community Psychiatry*, 1992, *43*(9), 891–894.

22. Beckett, A., and Rutan, J. "Treating Persons with ARC and AIDS in Group Psychotherapy." *International Journal of Group Psychotherapy*, 1990, *40*(1), 19–29.

23. Tunnell, G. "Complications in Group Psychotherapy with AIDS Patients." *International Journal of Group Psychotherapy*, 1991, *41*(4), 481–498.

24. Usher, J. "Cognitive Behavioral Couples Therapy with Gay Men Referred for Counseling in a AIDS Setting: A Pilot Study." *AIDS Care*, 1990, *2*(1), 43–51.

25. Curtis, J. "Treating AIDS: A Family Therapy Perspective." In C. Kain (ed.), *No Longer Immune: A Counselor's Guide to AIDS*. Alexandria, Va.: American Association of Counseling and Development, 1989.

26. Kermani and Weiss, "AIDS and Confidentiality."

27. Adler, G., and Beckett, A. "Psychotherapy of the Patient with an HIV Infection." *Psychosomatics*, 1989, *30*(2), 203–208.

28. Wood, G. J., Marks, R., and Dilley, J. W. *AIDS Law for Mental Health Professionals*. San Francisco: UCSF AIDS Health Project, 1992.

29. Zegans, L. S., Gerhard, A. L., and Coates, T. J. "Psychotherapies for the Person with HIV Disease." *Psychiatric Clinics of North America*, 1994, *17*(1), 149–162.

30. Walker, G. *In the Midst of Winter: Systemic Family Therapy with Individuals, Couples, and Families with AIDS*. New York: Norton, 1991.

31. Walker, G. "Supportive Counseling for HIV-Infected Drug Using Women." *FOCUS: A Guide to AIDS Research and Counseling*, 1995, *10*(10), 1–4.

32. Walker, G. "Eco-Systemic Family Therapy." *FOCUS: A Guide to AIDS Research and Counseling*, 1993, *8*(12), 5–6.

33. Ferenczi, S., and Rank, O. *The Development of Psychoanalysis*. New York: Nervous and Mental Disease Publishing, 1925.

34. Alexander, F., and French, T. *Psychoanalytic Therapy: Principles and Applications*. New York: Ronald, 1946.

35. Mann, J. *The Limited Psychotherapy*. Cambridge, Mass.: Harvard University Press, 1973.

36. Sifneos, P. *Short-Term Dynamic Psychotherapy: Evaluation and Technique*. New York: Plenum, 1987.

37. Davanloo, H. (ed.). *Short-Term Dynamic Psychotherapy*. Northvale, N.J.: Aronson, 1980.

38. Strupp, H., and Binder, J. *Psychotherapy in a New Key: A Guide to Time-Limited Dynamic Psychotherapy.* New York: Basic Books, 1984.
39. Levenson, H. "Time-Limited Dynamic Psychotherapy: A Guide to Clinical Practice." New York: Basic Books, 1995.
40. Horowitz, M. "Short Term Dynamic Therapy of Stress Response Syndromes." In P. Crits-Christoph and J. Barber (eds.), *Handbook of Short-Term Dynamic Psychotherapy.* New York: Basic Books, 1991.
41. Levenson, "Time-Limited Dynamic Psychotherapy."
42. Strupp and Binder, *Psychotherapy in a New Key,* p. 68.
43. Horowitz, "Short Term Dynamic Therapy."

Chapter Nine

HIV Disease over the Long Haul

Hope, Uncertainty, Grief, and Survival

Avi Rose

Since the beginning of the epidemic in the early 1980s, the history of HIV treatment has been marked by intermittent flurries of excitement based on rumors, anecdotal stories, clinical trials, and a deeply shared longing for hopeful news to sustain people's spirits. Over time, new treatments have been able to check the progress of the virus, to protect immune-compromised people against various opportunistic infections, and to strengthen the immune system itself. Increasingly, people with HIV are living longer and healthier lives than they would have a decade or even a few years ago.[1]

In the course of the epidemic, however, many promising developments ended in disappointment or, at least, fell short of initial expectations. The roller-coaster of HIV treatment, as pioneering HIV therapist Michael Shernoff has called it,[2] is long, steep, and unpredictable, and riding it remains a daily reality for those who are living with HIV as well as for all those who care for them.

In the mid-1990s, with the advent of protease inhibitors and triple combination therapy, hopes and expectations rose to new heights. Among those who have had access to these powerful drugs, many have responded remarkably well: their viral loads have plummeted to lower than detectable levels, their immune system measurements have rebounded, and they have experienced surges of new vitality and dramatic reductions in opportunistic infections and moderate to severe symptoms. In 1998, this trend continues for some, although both clinical studies and anecdotal evidence reveal that many individuals are not able to remain at the plateaus they had reached. Many are managing difficult side effects, switching to new combinations, waiting for the newest drug to get approved, and continuing to live with hope and uncertainty. Although the roller-coaster continues, there has been a paradigm shift: the language and assumptions of hope have been firmly incorporated into the vocabulary of the epidemic.

For those who are doing well, living with HIV disease as a chronic manageable condition is not necessarily as simple as "the epidemic is over for me, and I'm getting on with my life." First, although some have asserted otherwise, the epidemic is not over.[3] As Shernoff has said, "The epidemic is only over for those who have died."[4] Second, even those who are doing well face a complex set of issues in going about the profound task of reconstructing the future. This challenge is the primary focus of this chapter; it addresses some of the psychosocial issues that accompany this process, primarily issues of hope, uncertainty, meaning, and survival.

Before beginning, however, it is important to express a caveat, already implied. Globally, the vast majority of the twenty-nine million people currently living with HIV disease[5] do not have access to any basic medical care, much less the expensive new medications that, for some, have transformed the epidemic. Many of these people do not have access to simple antibiotics, and some also lack resources for adequate nutrition, clean water, and other basic preconditions for maintaining good health.

In the United States, statistics that show declining death rates and drops in the incidence of opportunistic infections also reveal significant disparities: the new hope and the new treatments fail to benefit many women and people of color, particularly African Americans. Although we acknowledge improved treatment and prospects for survival, we must also be mindful of these differences and remain committed to advocating for access to hope for everyone.

Reclaiming the Future

For the global minority who do have access to care and are doing well with combination therapy, there are many positive and hopeful developments to acknowledge and celebrate. Many of these people are feeling a renewed energy and strength they have not felt in years. Some are returning to work or school or are seriously contemplating such life changes, making long-term plans they had expected never to make again. Some people are building new relationships with new life partners, while others are mustering the courage to leave relationships that have been unhealthy. Some are experiencing joy and pleasure in their resurgent sexuality. Some are feeling much more motivated to confront their addictions to alcohol, tobacco, and other drugs, as well as other forms of addictive behavior. Others are engaging in or increasing various kinds of physical and recreational activity. Overall, many people are reclaiming a future, representing a profoundly hopeful shift away from the despair and resignation many have understandably felt in the past.

There have always been seropositive people who lived with a tremendous amount of energy and spirit, believing that they would survive for a long time, or at least that they would make the most of whatever time they were going to have.[6] For some of these people, the new surges of hope have not changed their lives dramatically. However, the breadth and intensity of these new hopes have influenced everyone affected by the epidemic, even on its periphery. Our ideas about and images of the epidemic are being reshaped. In the industrialized world, everyone's expectations have been heightened.

The Spectrum of Experience

Heightened expectations are, of course, experienced differently by different groups of people. For those doing well with the new medications, these expectations can spur them on to make, or at least consider, major life changes. But for those who are having problems due to viral resistance or to troubling side effects, it is difficult to avoid succumbing to panic or despair. Feelings of failure and self-blame are common as people struggle to come to terms with not doing as well as others. It is not new for groups of seropositive people to experience wide disparities of success with treatment, often for no apparent reason. However, now the stakes of success or failure seem higher than ever, so the attendant feelings of inadequacy, shame, or despondency sometimes run deeper.

Especially in communities hardest hit by the epidemic, such as the gay and bisexual men's community, where many have been sustained by the camaraderie of shared adversity as well as shared hopes, these disparities in treatment success are difficult to manage. In general, the atmosphere has become more optimistic since the advent of combination therapy, although it has grown more cautiously so. In this context, it has been hard for some who are not doing well to speak up; as someone recently said at a public forum, "I don't want to spoil the party for everyone else." Among those who are doing well, some feel self-conscious or guilty about the failed hopes of friends. It remains a challenge for both individuals and communities affected by HIV disease to continue to make room for the whole range of emotions, from exhilaration to despair, that people experience. The solidarity that has sustained so many people through this epidemic is as important as ever, possibly more so. Special attention must be directed to ensuring the inclusion and sustenance of those who are not doing well, who may inadvertently be avoided or even abandoned by care providers and others who feel powerless to restore their health.

Disparities in treatment success are best faced directly. When people are able to speak openly about the awkwardness and pain regarding these differences, it is usually a relief to everyone involved, an opportunity to share the pain that may have become a taboo topic. This kind of openness is, of course, easier to achieve and more likely to be successful in the context of an ongoing support group or a retreat for seropositive people, where participants have the opportunity to develop a sense of caring and community. It is important to note that with current treatments, individuals may move back and forth between "success" and "failure," rendering categories fluid and requiring participants and facilitators to be inclusive of every experience.

Living with Uncertainty

The relative success of combination therapy has been exhilarating. Although exhilaration is hopeful and exciting, it can also leave people feeling dizzy and disoriented. For everyone affected by HIV disease, the underlying current of uncertainty still runs strong and deep. Questions abound regarding how long new treatments will remain effective, whether particular strains of the virus will become resistant, what short-term or long-term side effects might develop, whether the next wave of treatment alternatives will come along in time, and whether these new alternatives will be made available to all who need them. Some people fear that they will make major life changes, get sick again, and then feel more vulnerable—physically, emotionally, and financially—than ever.

People living with HIV disease do not necessarily expect answers to these questions, but they need to ask them. They do deserve full acknowledgment and empathy for the feelings behind the questions: fear, skepticism, anger, weariness. Those who provide care to seropositive clients may not always have sufficient time to address this spectrum of emotions. However, providers do carry the responsibility at least to acknowledge the unanswerable questions, to avoid fending them off out of discomfort, and to understand how frightening it might be not to have the answers.

Coming to terms with uncertainty as a basic existential fact of life is an ongoing challenge for all people. To do so while diagnosed with a life-threatening illness is especially challenging. Yet it is crucial for people with HIV disease to address uncertainty if they are to cope with HIV infection over time. Denial may be an effective coping mechanism for a period, but as it wears down, the stressful nature of uncertainty requires a more mature and effective stance toward living in the face of a full range of possibilities.

A seropositive woman I knew for years—I'll call her Sharon—was extremely hopeful about her prospects for long-term survival. She actively engaged in pursuing various treatment alternatives, was an extremely well informed and demanding consumer of health care services, and spoke publicly about her experiences, giving strength and hope to herself and to others. For several years, Sharon felt angry and sabotaged by any hint that she might not live a long life. Over time, however, she was able to integrate the possibility of death without feeling threatened by it and as a result was able to make guardianship plans for her daughter. Sharon was able to make peace with the uncertainty of her own future without feeling compromised or as though she were giving up. The power of her positive thinking had a major impact on the quality of her life and possibly on her physical health as well, and she was strengthened by being able to embrace her serostatus in a more grounded, less defensive manner.

Through the years, I have seen people like Sharon find relief and comfort in facing uncertainty head-on and learning to live with it. Especially in the early stages of coming to terms with a HIV diagnosis, it can be too overwhelming to confront the possibility of death. But beyond this initial period, it becomes important for someone who is relatively intact psychologically to confront the whole range of his or her possibilities. As Steven Schwartzberg writes in *A Crisis of Meaning: How Gay Men Are Making Sense of AIDS,* "Coping effectively with HIV . . . involves allowing yourself to experience grievous loss along with bittersweet growth."[7] Whereas Sharon tended toward the hopeful and discounted potential illness and death, some clients on the other end of the spectrum firmly expect only the worst of outcomes. This distortion may help some feel less vulnerable to feelings of disappointment and better prepared for health crises, but they run the risk of not noticing that life is unfolding in the meantime.

Control and Change

Uncertainty inevitably brings up the issue of control, one that tends to be surrounded by myth and illusion. Schwartzberg discusses the importance of distinguishing (within environmental, health, and economic constraints) between what can be controlled—for example, current and future life decisions, health care choices, and personal goals—and what cannot be controlled—the past, other people's behavior, and who our parents or siblings are. Further, he discusses the cultural meaning of control, which some pursue unrealistically and others abandon out of a sense of despair or defeat.[8] Clearly, issues of control tend to run deep into a person's psyche. To the degree a person can learn to relate to control realistically and in a relaxed way, he or she can also develop an easier relationship with issues of uncertainty.

Related to the twin issues of uncertainty and control is the difficulty of adjusting to change. There are many people with HIV disease whose basic expectation was that over the years, they would gradually get sicker and die. They had planned the rest of their lives according to this scenario. Not that they were looking forward to these outcomes, but the process of reformulating the scenario in order to prepare for a future of new possibilities was a profound and difficult one.

In the process of assisting people who are facing the whole range of issues related to uncertainty, care providers need to be scrupulously honest about what they do and do not know. For some this means dealing with their own discomfort about uncertainty, their desire for control, and their feelings of responsibility to "fix" things far beyond their control. When providers take these appropriate steps and do not pretend to have the answers to unanswerable questions, they need to be prepared to deal with their clients' anger in reaction to uncertainty, trusting that clients will ultimately be more reassured by honesty than by pretense. This is crucial: facing something difficult or disturbing does not mean that a person has to like it. It can be helpful for people to have the opportunity to rail at the cosmic unfairness of living in a world where so much remains unknown and uncontrollable. Ironically, in coming to terms with uncertainty and lack of control, people usually end up feeling more empowered.

Facing the Past, Facing the Future

Re-creating a sense of having a future is an awesome, complex task. Much of it is joyful, but much depends in part on what the future looked like before one's life was transformed by HIV disease. No adult came to this experience as a blank slate; each already had his or her own history, circumstances, and character. For those fortunate enough to have had a sense of purpose and direction in life, to have felt generally good about themselves, to have had positive and fulfilling relationships with family and friends, to have done meaningful work, and to have felt connected to a community, the opportunity to recreate a future will most likely be experienced as joyful and exciting.

However, for the growing numbers of seropositive people who felt chronically isolated, anxious, or depressed, struggled with major addictions, had limited job skills and opportunities or were doing work they did not like, or were barely able to make ends meet, re-creating the future is likely to be a fearful and problematic process. For an increasing number of people with HIV disease, dealing with these long-standing problems as well as with current governmental policies regarding welfare, health care coverage, and immigration makes it difficult to feel hopeful about the future, no matter how promising new treatments may be. Care providers need to look far beyond the traditionally defined parameters of "HIV issues" in order to assist the full spectrum of clients.

Seropositive people have always needed practical assistance as well as emotional and psychological support. Earlier in the epidemic, practical assistance often focused on tasks related to serious illness and death—for example, arranging for wills and durable powers of attorney to protect the life partners of gay men, or organizing networks of family and friends to provide enough care to enable a person to die at home. These needs still exist, but there are many new tasks related to living for longer periods of time: arranging for long-term housing subsidies; supporting people through long-term substance abuse treatment and recovery; and, increasingly, assisting people in the process of going back to work. This process is both psychological and practical: people need counseling to realistically assess their own skills and work and education history, to protect their own confidentiality and appropriately disclose HIV serostatus, and to face fears of failure. In addition, clients may need help understanding disability benefits, health insurance, and legal protections against workplace discrimination. As clients prepare to take such major steps, it is crucial that they be helped to take them successfully.

Facing the future is further complicated for some by having felt left behind by uninfected peers in the past. For a large number of seropositive people, HIV infection interrupted their lives during a stage of life when they ordinarily would have been building the foundation for a seemingly secure future. When viewing seronegative friends who have settled down to careers, families, financial security, or retirement planning, seropositive people find it difficult not to feel envious, even resentful. It is important to offer clients opportunities to express and face these feelings. It is important, as well, for them to mourn the lost opportunities of the past in order to move forward into a reconstructed future.

The History and Meaning of Survival

Even though the epidemic is not over, successful combination therapy has encouraged growing numbers of seropositive people to contemplate living a normal life span, to confront the prospect of survival and its implications. Some are thinking about posttraumatic stress, even as they acknowledge that we are not yet "post." This epidemic will end at some point, and it is not too early to face the challenge of envisioning a future beyond AIDS and preparing people to live in it.

In speculating about the nature and future of HIV survival, one source of wisdom is the experience of others who have survived or witnessed ongoing life-threatening trauma. Throughout human history, people have experienced both natural and human-made disasters, and some have managed to survive against great odds. In recent memory, one cannot help but think of the Holocaust—an opportunity not to compare such starkly different phenomena but to learn from the experiences of people who survived.

One lesson from the experiences of these survivors is that "back to the future" is not the same as "back to normal." Life after a massive trauma is never the same. That is not at all to say that healing is impossible. It is to emphasize, however, the importance of acknowledging the reality and power of trauma as well as the task of rebuilding afterwards.

Another lesson is that it is difficult to reconstruct life when so many people from one's past have not survived. Mourning such losses is a lifelong process that will be reactivated at all life stages, especially at times of separation or loss. The prospect of aging without one's peers, for example, is a common issue for many people with HIV disease. Looking at the experience of past survivors, we see that it is possible to build new families and communities and that there can arise a tremendously powerful feeling of triumph in doing so. However, the loss of those with whom we have a shared history is permanent; honoring that history and those who did not survive is crucial.

In order to survive trauma, particularly the effects of massive cumulative grief, survivors defend against becoming psychically overwhelmed by learning how to numb themselves. This "psychic numbing" is one of the five themes enumerated by Robert Lifton as an outgrowth of his work with survivors of massive death experiences; the others are "death imprint," survivor guilt, "suspicion of counterfeit nurturance"—that is, a mistrust of the depth of understanding or even the motives of those who offer comfort—and the struggle for meaning.[9] Numbing can become habitual, and it can be very difficult for a survivor to feel psychologically prepared to reopen himself or herself to the whole spectrum of human emotions. Survivors may fear that in allowing themselves to experience any feeling, they may get flooded by horrific images and emotions, and intrusive thoughts are common among those who have survived trauma. Sometimes the most compassionate and intelligent approach to treating trauma is to help a client contain rather than express these emotions, with the hope that over time, the client can build enough psychic strength to dip into the well of horror and grief. Not all wounds heal, and not all should be reopened. People learn to live with scars, and some are able to do so with great wisdom and grace.

Studies of Holocaust survivors teach us that those who resisted and stood up for themselves and for others, even very privately and quietly, often did better afterwards. To a remarkable degree, many people who have lived with HIV disease have done so with the aid of their own great altruism and powerful activism. The experience of helping others and feeling connected to the larger world reduces isolation and expands feelings of mastery and empowerment both in the present and the future. Survivors also teach us that it helps to stay connected to the community of others who have gone through the traumatic experience, although people sometimes feel compelled to dissociate from these connections in order to build new lives.

Finally, survivors teach us about the importance of memory. Whereas some survivors need to contain their emotions about and images of the trauma, many others need to recount their stories to people who will listen with honor and respect. Although the HIV epidemic has been documented in many ways and with much creativity, there are potential oral and video history projects, for example, that could have great value and meaning in the years to come. The community of people affected by HIV has been well served by the NAMES Project Memorial Quilt, but we need additional communal rituals of remembrance, affirmation, and renewal.

As a powerful image of the kind of ritual we require, Schwartzberg movingly describes the Onion Cellar, a fictitious nightclub in Günter Grass's postwar novel, *The Tin Drum:*

> The Onion Cellar is an unusual place. It serves no food or drink, offers no conventional entertainment. Instead, well-heeled patrons sit at crude tables, where they are given cutting boards, paring knives, and onions. They wait obediently until the club owner

instructs them to cut and peel the onions. They start timidly. But then they cut and peel with abandon.

And they begin to cry. Their crying soon turns to wailing, a communal grief mirrored in a skein of individual tears. The patrons turn to their friends and to strangers, weeping and comforting each other. They confess their sins, their hurts, their guilt. They use the onions to gain access to the pain they carry but cannot otherwise express. They come to the Onion Cellar to share this pain publicly, because the experience is less fulfilling if one cuts onion at home and cries alone. Some patrons come only once, others repeatedly, until exhausted of their tears. And somehow, in the process, they feel healed.[10]

We face a similar situation with the AIDS epidemic right now. We need Onion Cellars. As a community, as shared witnesses and bearers of so much loss, we must find ways to express the pain, the grief, the despair that feels increasingly out of our scope—and to do so safely, emotionally, repeatedly. And we must do so communally, so that others may be there to support and witness, so that we may each serve as comforter and mourner.[11]

❦

Survivors of any trauma never form a homogenous group; this is certainly true about people living in the shadow of HIV. To say that they are uniformly resilient or heroic would be untrue, although many have shown both characteristics to a remarkable degree. It would also be untrue to romanticize AIDS as a transformative experience, without acknowledging the depth of the losses so many have suffered.

We will continue to suffer losses. Some people will demonstrate dazzling resilience, and some will not. The degree to which we will as individuals and as a society be transformed by this epidemic remains to be seen. The hope, courage, humor, resourcefulness, and determination that have sustained so many to this point will be crucial for the rest of our lives. Therapists will be challenged to persevere over a completely unpredictable and long haul, to summon the full depth and breadth of their skill and their humanity in the process of helping seropositive clients face the past, live in the present, and reinvent the future. May we all have the strength to continue until the epidemic really is over.

Notes

1. "Monthly Update." *AIDS Reference Guide,* 1996, *113,* 1.
2. Shernoff, M. "A History of Hope: The HIV Roller Coaster." *FOCUS: A Guide to AIDS Research and Counseling,* 1997, *12*(7), 5–7.
3. Sullivan, A. "When Plagues End: Notes on the Twilight of an Epidemic." *New York Times,* Nov. 10, 1996, p. 52.
4. Shernoff, M. Unpublished remarks at the HIV and Social Work conference, Los Angeles, June 1997.
5. World Health Organization. *The World Health Report: Conquering Suffering, Enriching Humanity.* Geneva: World Health Organization, 1997.
6. Among the many sources on the issue of long-term survivors of HIV disease are the following: Sally, J. "Psychosocial Issues of AIDS Long-Term Survivors." *Families in Society,* 1994, *75*(6), 324–332; Callen, M. *Surviving AIDS.* New York: HarperCollins, 1990.
7. Schwartzberg, S. *A Crisis of Meaning: How Gay Men Are Making Sense of AIDS.* New York: Oxford University Press, 1996, p. 201.
8. Schwartzberg, *Crisis of Meaning.*
9. Lifton, R. J. "The Concept of the Survivor." In J. E. Dimsdale (ed.), *Survivors, Victims, and Perpetrators: Essays on the Nazi Holocaust.* Washington, D.C.: Hemisphere, 1980.
10. Grass, G. *The Tin Drum* (trans. R. Manheim). London: Secker & Warburg, 1962.
11. Schwartzberg, *Crisis of Meaning.*

Chapter Ten

Beyond Stereotypes
Stigma and the Counseling Process
Mindy Thompson Fullilove

In 1996, the *New Yorker* published a special issue, "Black in America."[1] The issue included the usual trenchant cartoons, but, for the occasion, each examined an aspect of Black life. A number of cartoons depicted the ways in which stereotypes create alienation between Black and White America.

For example, one cartoon contained the image of a laboratory bench where three White and one Black scientist sit side by side working away. The dialogue bubbles reveal their thoughts. The first White man is thinking, "I wonder how he feels about O.J.?" The second White man is thinking, "I wonder how he feels about Farrakhan?" The next person, a White woman, is thinking, "I wonder how he feels about affirmative action?" The bubble of the fourth person, who is Black, is filled with complex mathematical equations. He is focused on the work—as the others should be.

Another cartoon depicts an upscale New York party, where a White woman says to a Black man, "I've seen most of Spike Lee's movies, so I know what you must be going through." The offense is amplified by the fact that the reserved, middle-aged, soberly dressed Black man appears to be anything but the typical character of a Spike Lee film. Yet the cloak of sameness is applied willy-nilly.

The author would like to thank Keith Cylar, who offered helpful comments on an earlier version of this chapter.

In a society structured by intergroup enmity, whether between Blacks and Whites, gays and straight people, or between other diverse groups, every interaction runs the risk of replacing genuine engagement with stereotypical interchange. Stereotyping can be harmful in all human interchanges, but its presence in therapy is particularly destructive. Therapy ought to provide individuals with opportunities to explore and reorder the ways in which they experience the self. To provide these opportunities requires the therapist to get to know and react to each individual as an individual. It is impossible to do this if stereotyping comes into play. Stereotypes replace an understanding of the individual with imaginary characteristics of the group to which the individual belongs. Stereotypes concretize images of groups, preventing exploration of a complex reality. Stereotypes applied to individuals in therapy effectively block exploration of self. This chapter looks at the origins of stereotypes and, through three scenarios, explores ways in which stereotypes emerge in HIV-related therapy. It also instructs therapists on how to ensure they do not damage their therapeutic relationships through stereotyping.

How Stereotyping Happens

Few would disagree that stereotypes and stereotypical interactions are harmful in therapy. But this acknowledgment does not mean we have effectively eliminated them, and our failure to do so is a result of a confluence of several forces, as described in the sections that follow.

Believing in Stereotypes

First of all, we all believe in stereotypes and use them in everyday life. A 1994 national survey of people in the United States found that members of all groups endorsed stereotypes about each other.[2] For example, 46 percent of Hispanic Americans and 42 percent of Blacks agreed with the statement that Asians were "unscrupulous, crafty and devious in business." Asian Americans, in turn, endorsed stereotypes about others: 68 percent endorsed the statement that Hispanics "tend to have bigger families than they are able to support," and 31 percent agreed that Blacks "want to live on welfare."

Although the White people polled were somewhat more cautious than others in endorsing stereotypes, a large majority felt that minorities were given the same opportunities as Whites to get a good education, a skilled job, or decent housing.

Stereotyping appears to be a universal human activity, practiced from all sides of every marker of social difference—race, class, region, sexual orientation, gender, religion, and language—providing a kind of social shorthand for otherwise complex intergroup differences. It is, admittedly, easier to think of all Asians as having the same slanted eyes than it is to look carefully at the thousands of variations on eye configuration that exist in the world. Stereotypes are the stuff of our jokes ("How many Poles does it take to change a light bulb?"), our rage ("Fuck you, faggot!"), our dreams ("This big, black buck of a man was panting after me"). Stereotypes change with the times, taking on the nuances of the moment, emphasizing the "outgroups" of the moment, but never disappearing from our social strategies for intergroup relations.

Malcolm Gladwell, a Jamaican who had lived in the United States and in Toronto, was struck by the social construction of "Jamaican" in those two places. In the United States, people from the West Indies were widely believed to be "model Blacks" and were accorded greater respect and opportunities than other Black people. In Toronto, by contrast, West Indians were tagged with all the stereotypes given to African Americans in the United States: they were shiftless, lazy, and prone to living on welfare, and they deal drugs and abandon their children. How could one group of people fit such distinctly different social images? Gladwell wondered, "Didn't Torontonians see what was special and different in West Indian culture? But that was a naive question. The West Indians were the first significant brush with Blackness that White, smug, comfortable Torontonians had ever had. They had no bad Blacks to contrast with the newcomers, no African Americans to serve as a safety valve for the prejudices, no way to perform America's crude racial triage. . . . In America there is someone else to despise. In Canada, there is not. In the new racism, as in the old, somebody always has to be the nigger."[3]

Considering the constancy of stereotyping as a feature of human life, psychoanalysts and others have argued that it represents the workings of a basic psychological process common to all

people.[4,5] Some have proposed that the creation of stereotypes occurs as the result of the projection of hated parts of the self on to
others. The projection of these shadow parts creates the illusion
of a wholly "good" self that can be accepted with equanimity. In effect, stereotyping reduces anxiety for the individual. At its foundation, stereotyping is useful as a way of reinforcing group
boundaries and increasing an individual's sense of belonging.
Human beings strive for membership in human communities.
When healthy avenues of cooperation are blocked by social upheaval or other processes, people may turn to shared hatreds as a
source of bonding.

OBSERVATION 1: We all construct stereotypes, and then we believe
   in them. Therefore, we must know which stereotypes we endorse and in what ways they may interfere with helping others.
   We must also know which stereotypes of our own group we
   have internalized.

Our Unconscious Judgments

The second force that nurtures stereotyping is an individual's unconscious judgments. We make judgments from inside culture-
bound value systems, but we are often blind to this process. Each
of us is a product of a particular culture, and we operate within the
rules of that culture. Each culture's rules are based on a set of
principles that in general are never enunciated but are assumed
to be correct. A corollary to these principles is the assumption that
the rules of other cultures are wrong.

In order to understand this problem, consider the array of
rules various cultures have regarding personal introductions.
Should people bow on being introduced? If they bow, how low
should they bow? Who should bow to whom? Perhaps people
should shake hands rather than bow? If so, how hard is the hand
to be held, and in what manner is it shaken? Raised to perform
greetings in a certain manner, we will unquestioningly infer bad
manners or disrespect on the part of strangers who fail to act as required by our culture. That they may be acting with perfect pro-
priety as defined by a different set of rules is an interpretation
unlikely to occur to the average citizen. Because cultural censure

can be quite severe, a stranger's "social errors" might lead to estrangement or even death.

The growing complexity of our world has made it more likely that we will meet people from disparate parts of the world. The historical diasporas of African and Jewish peoples are matched today by people fleeing war, famine, drought, poverty, and oppression. Women are fleeing genital mutilation; gay men and lesbians search for sexual liberty. The diasporas of our day have created a whirlwind, mixing together people from every isolated hamlet on earth. Susan Sontag observed, "Like the effects of industrial pollution and the new system of global financial markets, the AIDS crisis is evidence of a world in which nothing important is regional, local, limited; in which everything that can circulate does, and every problem is, or is destined to become, worldwide."[6]

By implication, we must be prepared to meet people of many cultural traditions. We will not always know the meaning of the words, behaviors, and gestures to which we are reacting. We must therefore train ourselves to inquire constantly: Did that act or word or gesture mean what I thought it did?

OBSERVATION 2: Because we are blind to the assumptions of our own culture, we must show our work to colleagues from different backgrounds so that they may act as our eyes and ears—that is, as our interpreters.

The Role of Events in Shaping Psychology

Acting as a third force, our models of individual psychology have undervalued the importance of trauma and other stressful events in shaping character and mental distress. A part of what distinguishes people is the event structure of the individual's life. Minority people, for example, will experience acts of oppression, as well as life conditions, that result from social structures that define and confine them to the margins of society. A gay man growing up in a small town will search in vain for images that affirm his sexuality. In his longing for support and succor, he may eventually accept exile from his birthplace as the price he has to pay to live with some measure of dignity and freedom. John Preston, in an autobiographical essay titled "Medfield, Massachusetts," described what it felt like to have to leave home in search of a place for himself: "In some ways I moved into my new life with great joy. There was real excitement in it, certainly there was a great passion. . . . I also experienced rage over what was happening to me. I was being taken from Medfield and everything it stood for. I was the one who should have gotten a law degree and come home to settle into comfortable Charles River Valley politics—perhaps with a seat in the Great and General Court. . . . But I was no longer one of them. I had become too different."[7]

Events like this shape the life course of a gay man. His efforts to make sense of his experience will define his philosophy and the issues he might bring to therapy. In order for therapy to be meaningful, it must have the tools and the sensibilities to explore the event structure of the individual's life.

OBSERVATION 3: If we undervalue events, we might miss the key turnings in a person's life story. Instead, we must study the great and small happenings in the lives of our clients.

The Fragmented Society

The final force that generates and maintains stereotypes arises because society is structured to keep groups apart, giving people few opportunities to get to know each other. It may well be impossible to appreciate the nuances of the life of a house queen or a rap artist unless one has met a few. But it is nearly impossible to accomplish that in U.S. society, structured as it is with visible and invisible boundaries erected around each group.

In 1986, Richard Simon wrote "Across the Great Divide," an article about the services offered at a mental health clinic in the South Bronx, a poor, underserved area of New York City.[8] The title ostensibly referred to the Harlem River, which separates Manhattan from the Bronx, but really referred to the social chasm between wealthy White family therapists (the writer and his audience) and the poor clinic in the South Bronx. Why was it so important to signal that a social boundary had been crossed? Clearly it had nothing to do with understanding how the clinic served its community, as both clinic and community were located on the "other" side. It is more likely that the title was directed at the stereotypes of the largely White, middle-class readership of the magazine who would never venture into the South Bronx and thought of it as an awful place. Simon meant to entice them on an exotic journey into "otherness," a little bit like taking a tour with *National Geographic*.

If the only way a therapist—or any person—gets information about the "other" is through a lens tinted in this fashion, he or she will remain forever in the dark. Rather, therapists must get to know other settings and the people in them if they are to help. An example of this is the effort to understand African American gay men who were "raised" in the church. They are often very religious people for whom the church was a second home. They are also often tortured by the homophobia in the church, which is alienating and confusing. The dual feelings—loving the church but hating being denounced by the clergy—battle within the self of many Black gay men. This conflict undermines self-esteem and interferes with HIV risk reduction and HIV care.

Whether or not there is damage to self-esteem, attacks on gay men and lesbians in the church have meant that many do not know how to apply religious teachings to their own lives. One gay man admitted being baffled by his relationship to the church, which he said spawned in him a "kind of schizophrenic child." He continued, "Part of me says that I need [religion] to keep me in order, because [I] will push every single limit, and there has to be something keeping me in check."[9] On the other hand, he said, he recognized the barriers the church had created for him, and this made it difficult for him to accept it. Understanding the setting of the African American churches is key to understanding the experience of many African American gay men. The same can be said of other people and other settings.

OBSERVATION 4: It is hard to get to know people outside of our own group, but we must expand our horizons and our venues.

These four forces not only act independently to keep people ignorant about each other but also act together. For instance, a White man who believes in stereotypes and never meets someone whose family origins are in Asia is unlikely to know how to have a conversation that will reveal a new reality. Each of the forces acts to shape the history and content of the therapeutic relationship.

It is possible for these stereotypical interactions to undermine the therapeutic alliance. But it is also possible that genuine engagement will promote individual recovery.

Confronting Stereotypes in Therapy

Treatment occurs in the context of the therapeutic relationship. That relationship, among other functions, serves as a model for exploring past relationships and re-creating present ones. It is the therapist's task to ensure that this relationship brings into consciousness the stereotypes that both client and therapist may believe in. Assuming that stereotypes are a part of everyone's thinking, the work in therapy is to identify these stereotypes and make them part of the healing process. The three case examples in this chapter depict therapists and clients working with stereotypes.

Like any other relationship, the therapeutic alliance may incorporate intolerance and insensitivity: it may become a reenactment of other oppressive relationships. How is the therapist to know when the relationship has gone astray? What do relationships look like when they are fraught with negation? Instead of the stuttering progress—from uncovering to working through—that normally characterizes therapy, oppressive therapeutic relationships become stuck in one spot. The therapist's eager efforts to help the client feel better are undermined by his or her alienating acts—imposing stereotypes, making unwarranted assumptions, radiating fear of the client's "badness"—that negate the client's sense of self. Often the client will take on the shadow that is being projected by the therapist. In these cases, the client will become highly symptomatic, exhibiting inconsolable sadness and uncontrollable anxiety.

What does this process of alienation sound like? The following dialogues from fictitious psychotherapy sessions help illustrate the interactions in an oppressive relationship.

A Loving Man

Sam is an asymptomatic seropositive gay man who has been making progress in developing a stable intimate relationship. His therapist, Paul, is also a gay man, but one troubled by guilt and doubt about his homosexuality.

Sam: Yeah, Mario's what I never thought I'd find. Each day I discover new levels of thinking and feeling in the presence of somebody else. It's probably the first time that I'm not constantly on guard.

Paul: No?

Sam: You know how I've always talked about the tension. The tension that something's going to happen. I guess because, in my life, something always did happen, my mother—I just never knew what would happen with her health. Actually, Mario started coughing the other day and I got really scared. I started to see visions of him lying in the hospital all filled with tubes. But what happened then—and this was the surprising part—I thought, well, I'll be there to share it with him. And I wanted to just be part of whatever happens in his life. He's not even HIV-positive, so I was really bugging. Anyway, that was when I decided I wanted him to move in with me.

Paul: (Coughs) Isn't that a little fast?

Sam: Fast? What do you mean?

Paul: Well, how long have you known him?

Sam: Twenty years.

Paul: You know what I mean.

Sam: Well, it's still true. I've known him since I was ten. We were in Boy Scouts together. I mean, yeah, we've only connected as lovers in the past two months. But it doesn't feel fast because of all that shared history.

Paul: OK, lovers, but live together? I mean, have your boss to dinner with the two of you?

Sam: I'm not out to my boss, so how could I do that?

Although the problems of any therapeutic intervention are many— what to say, when, and how—the issue here is that the therapist takes exception to the client's plan to live with his lover. Because Sam has been working in therapy to develop a relationship, it seems logical that he move forward to consolidate the affair. The therapist, speaking from his own internalized homophobia, attacks the proposal. Further, he depicts a frightening scenario, which changes the tone of the session from one of confidence to one of fear. He reintroduces dread which, for a moment, the client had escaped.

Such a statement is one of thousands of statements made in the course of therapy. The parties separate, think about what has happened, and meet again. Let us assume that Paul shares his cases with Jim, a trusted colleague. Paul, who is aware that his own fear might be interfering in his work, plays a tape of his session with Sam. In the following conversation, Paul and Jim review the dialogue.

Jim: (Stopping the tape just as Sam says, "How could I do that?") What do you think that last intervention was about?

Paul: You know, at the time, I felt that I had to protect him. I was really worried that he would leap into this relationship and ruin everything.

Jim: Has that been his pattern?

Paul: (Thinks about it.) No, not really.

Jim: I was a little surprised listening, because it's not like you. Especially what you said about his boss. I could hear the fear in his voice; why did you want to frighten him?

Paul: Frighten him?

Jim: (Waits. Paul is clearly struggling.)

Paul: Oh God! Is this my stuff getting into the therapy?

Jim: Hey! Sure sounded like it to me. I mean I thought you'd be jumping for joy that the guy's made so much progress, and instead you beat him up.

Paul: That's a little extreme!

Jim: I'm sorry I have to push on this, but listen again.

Jim supports Paul in hearing and acknowledging that, in his statements to Sam, he has reacted to his own disgust at the idea that men could live together. As a child, Paul knew two men who lived together and were the object of many crude jokes in his small town. They were viewed as ridiculous. Paul lived in dread that his own homosexuality might make him equally ridiculous, and this fear was especially linked to the idea of men living together. As Jim and Paul talk about that fantasy and its meaning, Paul is able to see how he reacted in a way that might injure his client. Jim and Paul also work through various scenarios about how to mend the damage. Although Paul cannot undo his earlier statements, he does use the insights gained in his discussion with Jim to provide appropriate support to Sam.

The recognition of the pernicious role of stereotypes has the potential not only to prevent harm but also to promote individual growth and survival strength. The thrust of this example is to suggest that client and therapist must act as monitors, sharing the vigilant watch for homophobia or other kinds of prejudice that might derail the therapy. This is a new kind of equality in the therapeutic relationship, an essential ingredient for cross-cultural work.

A Woman on Her Own

Sandra, a Black woman with AIDS, works with her therapist, Peter, an Asian American gay man. Peter is very comfortable in cross-cultural work and is able to explore differences in a manner that promotes his client's growth.

Sandra: I hated that group. I did not belong in that group with the welfare mother crack heads. Like what was I supposed to do there? Say I'm sorry you're homeless, I just closed a million-dollar real estate deal, and I have AIDS too? It was awful. I was so angry I wanted to rip open every cell in my body and tear out the virus. This virus is taking everything from me!

Peter: What made you most angry?

Sandra: I was looking around the room at all these dope fiends and I was like, I don't think so. This is not me.

Peter: Who are you?

Sandra: What is it with you and this "Who are you" question? I was thinking about you the other day. I said, I know he's gonna ask me this question. I was thinking up smart aleck things to say. But then I thought this is supposed to help me.

Peter: Yeah. It's supposed to help you.

Sandra: Who am I? I'm sad. Can a person be a feeling?

Peter: Why are you sad?

Sandra: It's funny, it's not the AIDS or anything. I mean, it doesn't make sense to me, even. But there was a time when I fit in. I mean if I walked into that room I would have felt close, like I fit, like it was OK—I'm not sure this is clear even to me. It's like I wasn't a self all alone, I was just part of. When I walked in that room I wanted to scream, I'm not this—I'm not poor! I'm not pathetic!—I'm—I don't know, a real estate mogul. (Snorts in disdain.)

Peter: In my culture, the individual hardly matters compared to the group. To separate, as you have done, is difficult. One loses a lot.

Sandra: (Silent; starts to cry) Isn't that silly? What do a bunch of homeless women have that I need?

Peter: What?

Sandra: Oh just everything. Just love.

> *Peter:*   What might a woman do that would let you know she loved you?
> *Sandra:*   Comb my hair, cook with me, hold me. Say something like, "Don't worry, it'll be all right."

Sandra, an ambitious and successful career woman, is enraged at the potential loss of class status she expects to experience as a result of her illness. At the same time, attaining that status has meant moving out of her community to function in a man's world—in reality, a White man's world. She yearns for the oneness of her youth but is horrified at contact with other women who lack her social and economic achievements. Peter is aware of Sandra's use of stereotypes to distance herself from others. Peter's style in therapy is to keep a focus on unraveling her emotions. In order to trace her feelings accurately, he describes a feature of his culture. Although he is asking about differences between their two cultures, the question reveals the special value both place on the life of the group. It helps Sandra recognize that she is yearning for contact with other women.

Peter follows with a question about the ways in which women express concern. This is a key feature of his therapeutic style. He is constantly searching for detail in Sandra's life. It helps him to understand her; it prevents mistakes that he might make were he to assume commonalties across race, gender, and sexual orientation. This kind of question might appear to be less necessary in an established therapeutic relationship, but, on the contrary, it continues to be of great importance as the relationship matures, reinforcing the connection through the process of discovering the small but real differences between the two parties.

My Therapist, My Friend

This final scenario examines the interaction between Fred, a homeless Puerto Rican man living with HIV disease, and his therapist, Patricia, who is a White lesbian. In this scenario, again, a client expresses stereotypical views, this time directed at the therapist herself.

> *Patricia:*   Fred, *como esta?*
> *Fred:*   *Muy bien,* Patty. But like wait a minute, Patty. Patty, I heard something. I was real upset. I didn't even want to come talk to you about it. But like you been good to me so I gotta say. Patty, they are saying that your boss is a faggot. What's up with that?
> *Patricia:*   It's true, Fred. And me, too, Fred. I'm a dyke.

Fred: Patty, why you gotta talk like that? That's not nice. You should watch your mouth. You a nice lady, talking that nasty stuff.

Patricia: Fred, what's so nasty? Don't you call yourself a spic sometimes?

Fred: That's not the same. That's a bad word, but it's not nasty.

Patricia: So what makes *dyke* a nasty word?

Fred: You know.

Patricia: What? What makes it nasty?

Fred: You know, girls be doing nasty things that they shouldn't be doing.

Patricia: Fred, did you ever do any nasty things?

Fred: I did bad things, but I didn't do no nasty things.

Patricia: What's the difference?

Fred: Like drugs, shooting up, that's bad. I was like an addict and all that. But I like have like with women you know, natural sex. Why you got to say those things to me? You got me all upset and you my friend.

In this scenario, Patricia is confronted with Fred's homophobia. She opens a dialogue that challenges his beliefs about homosexuality as something bad, while at the same time conveying her affection and commitment to him. He is clearly agitated and upset by the news that this person he trusts is "nasty" in a manner that is difficult for him to accept. Yet his acceptance of Patricia could open the way for him to deal with many of the problems that are troubling him. Although he says that he is untroubled by his past needle use, in fact he struggles with shame and guilt about his drug use. Gays are an easy target, allowing Fred to externalize some of his own self-hatred. Patricia must use the strong foundation of her relationship with Fred to get past his prejudices.

Patricia: Fred, remember last week when we had to go to the welfare office?

Fred: So?

Patricia: When we were there, you remember that lady was screaming at that mother? She was saying, "You Indians have too many babies. Why don't you get on birth control?" You said—you remember—you said one thing you were proud of was that you treat people the same. So Fred, how about me? I'm a people.

Fred: You a people. Yeah. And I treat you good. We talk and I got you a card for your birthday. You can't say I don't treat you nice. But you shouldn't do bad things.

Patricia: But Fred, you don't have to be in my business, do you? I thought
we respected that we're both adults. You do things I think are bad.
I do things you think are bad. But we can still be friends; we're just
different.

Fred: I got to like what you do to like you.

Patricia: Well, then maybe you won't like me anymore now that you know
I'm lesbian. I'll still be here to help you. If you don't want my help,
I'll get somebody else in the agency to work with you. But Fred, I
feel upset that you would throw away all the good times so easily.

Fred: That's not what I'm doing. I'm not saying I don't want to work
with you. It's just not what I'm used to.

Patricia: Fred, remember the first time you told me how you robbed old
people to get money for drugs? I got to tell you it wasn't what I was
used to either. But I had to get over it because it's part of what's
been your life. You, your life, I want to help. I'm not here to judge.

Fred: Patty, another thing, we got to talk about. I want to go talk to the
doctor about this sore on my hand.

Fred's abrupt change of subject signals to Patty that she has made her
point: he is arguing on weak ground and realizes it's not a fight worth fighting. Has Fred given up his homophobia? No, he hasn't. But he has acknowledged that an important person in his life is a lesbian. He also recognizes that
Patty has treated him with respect and affection that have been rare in his life.
Returning the favor is not much to ask.

In an interesting way, Patricia's acknowledgment of her homosexuality
creates a more level playing field between client and therapist. As a member of
a despised group—a group often more reviled than addicts are—Patricia appears vulnerable. Fred has the power to hurt or to protect her. Given the long-
standing relationship, he becomes her protector and defender, to himself as
well as to others. Her unflinching avowal of her homosexuality impresses him:
he never thought she was a wimp, but now he's even more sure that she's got
the "right stuff." In his eyes, Patricia becomes "one of the guys."

❧

In some ways this emphasis on stereotypes must be seen as contra-
dicting the recommendations that cultural sensitivity be attained
by learning key facts about the culture of others. The "factoid" ap-

proach emphasizes that Puerto Ricans visit spiritualists and believe in "hot-cold" theories of illness, that Native Americans recognize more than two genders, and that men from New Guinea might run amok. Arthur Kleinman related an anecdote that points out the pitfalls of this quickie anthropology.[10] An eager medical student, having recently completed a course on medicine and culture, asked his patient, a prominent Black banker, if he carried a mojo (traditional folk medicine sack). The banker chuckled at being asked such a preposterous question; the student was chagrined.

Brief descriptions of cultures cannot be applied to individuals. Cultures are created and sustained by the interactions of groups of people in a particular place at a particular time. The beliefs of the group may govern the actions of the individual, but they cannot be assumed to define the individual. Although learning from the individual about his or her cultural background is indispensable, learning about the culture and applying that to the individual is counterproductive.

In an increasingly complex world fraught with racial hatred and other divisions between groups, we must commit ourselves to a plan of work that takes seriously the task of getting to know the individuals in our care. Careful attention to an individual's life story, philosophy, and worldview must be the basis for a therapy that goes beyond stereotypes.

Notes

1. The cartoons mentioned in the text are from "Black in America," a double issue of the *New Yorker,* Apr. 29 and May 6, 1996, pp. 90, 101.
2. Holmes, S. A. "Survey Finds Minorities Resent One Another Almost as Much as They Do Whites." *New York Times,* Mar. 3, 1994, p. B-8.
3. Gladwell, M. "Black like Them." *New Yorker,* Apr. 29 and May 6, 1996, pp. 74–81.
4. Gilman, S. L. *Differences and Pathology: Sexuality, Race, and Madness.* Ithaca, N.Y.: Cornell University Press, 1985.
5. Herek, R. M., Burris, S., Chesney, M., and others. "AIDS and Stigma: A Conceptual Framework and Research Agenda." *AIDS and Public Policy Journal,* forthcoming.
6. Sontag, S. *AIDS and Its Metaphors.* New York: Farrar, Straus, and Giroux, 1989, p. 92.
7. Preston, J. "Medfield, Massachusetts." In J. Preston (ed.), *Hometowns.* New York: Dutton, 1991, p. 8.

8. Simon, R. "Across the Great Divide." *Family Therapy Networker*, Jan.-Feb. 1987, pp. 22–30, 74.
9. Fullilove, M. T., and Fullilove, R. "Homosexuality and the African American Church: The Paradox of the 'Open Closet.'" In J. Walker (ed.), *Though I Stand at the Door and Knock*. New York: Balm in Gilead, 1997, p. 6.
10. Kleinman, A. "Culture and Medicine." Paper presented during the Grand Rounds of the New York State Psychiatric Institute, 1993.

Part Three

Distress and Disorder
Helping Clients with Psychiatric Conditions

Adjusting to living in the HIV epidemic is a complex process. For many, it is made even more complicated by preexisting psychiatric conditions or by psychiatric disorders that may arise out of the experience of having HIV disease or of facing multiple loss.

Therapists working on the front lines of the epidemic need to be aware of HIV-related psychiatric disorders and be prepared to identify problems as they arise. They need not feel that they should be able to treat all of these conditions; in fact, without special training, counselors should refer these clients to other providers.

As we head into the third decade of HIV disease, HIV-related psychiatric disorders have changed less in substance than in form. For example, HIV-associated dementia is less common today than was once anticipated, and it is more amenable to treatment. Other disorders express themselves in terms of current HIV-related issues—for example, treatment failure and adherence, or an ever-deepening and unresolved bereavement—and the use of psychopharmacological agents has become much more complex in the context of combination antiviral treatments. Other challenges—in particular, working with those with triple diagnoses—are complexes of familiar symptoms or disorders that combine to create new conditions that may or may not be treatable using old interventions.

The fact remains, however, that many of these disorders *are* familiar, defined as they have always been by the *Diagnostic and*

Statistical Manual. As with everything related to HIV disease, such familiar characteristics can help providers ground treatment in what they know (and their sense of their own abilities to treat clients), which is a boon as long as such confidence does not obscure the complicating effects of a life-threatening disease. Part Three serves to remind providers of the most common HIV-related psychiatric disorders and highlights important treatment protocols.

Chapter Eleven

Anxiety and Depression
Mood and HIV Disease

Dan H. Karasic
James W. Dilley

Despite promising advances in the medical treatment of HIV, people living with the disease must learn to cope with a variety of stressors and frequently find themselves struggling to manage shifts in mood—some related to HIV disease and some related to underlying affective disorders. Mood states commonly associated with HIV-related coping range from momentary sadness and anxiety or anger to major depressive or full-blown anxiety disorders. In addition, because HIV infects the central nervous system, people with HIV can develop mood disorders associated with primary brain infections; these are classified as organic mood disorders.

Distinguishing mood states directly related to HIV from those that underlie and are exacerbated by it is crucial to treatment, and therapists must be prepared to assess a client's presentation, determine the cause, and employ a combination of psychotherapy and psychopharmacology to respond. The good news is that major depression, in particular, once believed to be synonymous with HIV disease, is now known to be much less common among seropositive people than previously thought; the less-than-good news is that

An earlier version of the material on anxiety disorders in this chapter originally appeared in D. H. Karasic, "Anxiety and Anxiety Disorders," *FOCUS: A Guide to AIDS Research and Counseling*, 1996, *11*(12), 5–6.

when it does exist it can be devastating and can complicate not only quality of life but also medical care. This chapter reviews known information about the relationship between HIV disease and depression, organic mania, and anxiety disorders, and describes currently accepted treatment approaches.

Prevalence of Depression and Anxiety

Early in the course of the AIDS epidemic, several researchers reported significant rates of "depression" among adults with HIV disease. These rates ranged from 1.4 percent to 43 percent for major depression and 13 percent to 54 percent for diagnoses of adjustment disorder with depressed mood.[1-6] Citing the stress and uncertainty of living with a stigmatizing, life-threatening disease that was previously unknown, these reports were based largely on data collected from hospitalized patients. However, because they reported on clients referred for psychiatric evaluation, some early studies overestimated the prevalence rates of depression in people with HIV disease, leaving the perception that significant depression was an almost inevitable result of living and coping with HIV disease.

More recent studies have shed new light on the subject of depression in people with HIV, and their results have greatly altered this perception. For example, longitudinal studies of nonhospitalized individuals reported much lower rates of clinically significant depression than did earlier samples.[7] Self-report data from a population-based sample of gay and bisexual men in San Francisco found a 20 percent rate of depression among 257 seropositive gay and bisexual men.[8] These findings are similar to a New York study that also found on self-report a 32 percent rate of depression among a more diverse sample of 106 seropositive men and women one year after each received a positive test result.[9] In the New York study, however, elevated depression scores were not associated with whether subjects tested seropositive or seronegative; rather, they were associated with preexisting depression and were higher in female, heterosexual, and injection drug–using subjects.

A study of sixty-one gay men, all of whom were examined at the time of HIV antibody testing, found that the twenty men who tested seropositive showed no more psychological distress one year

later than those who tested seronegative.[10] A study of fifty heterosexual men and women found no difference in anxiety or depression scores between asymptomatic seropositive subjects and
seronegative subjects.[11] Finally, another study of fifty-seven seropositive women found low rates of psychiatric disorders.[12]

Standardized Diagnostic Interviews

In studies using standardized diagnostic interviews to make the diagnosis of major depression, trained clinical interviewers examined
nonclinical samples and found considerably lower rates of major
depression. For example, a small San Diego study using the Structured Clinical Interview for Diagnosis (SCID) found that 11 percent of 45 seropositive gay and bisexual men rated a diagnosis of
major depression.[13] A study of 442 seropositive men in the military
found higher rates of preexisting mood and substance use disorders but also found that 15 percent had current anxiety or depressive symptoms necessitating mental health referral.[14] The study
also found that 17 percent of those testing seropositive had serious
suicidal ideation and 6 percent qualified for a diagnosis of major
depression. Another study of 43 seropositive women found low
rates of psychiatric disorder, except sexual dysfunction.[15]

Also using the SCID, a Columbia University study found a 6
percent rate of major depression in a longitudinal study of 124
seropositive gay and bisexual men.[16] Similarly, low rates (also 6 percent) of depression occurred in a sample of 53 "long-term survivors" recruited through the Gay Men's Health Crisis in New
York.[17] These men may not be completely representative of people
with HIV disease, but they present an important reference group:
they had lived with an AIDS diagnosis for at least three years; they
all had had at least one opportunistic infection; most of the men
had been told on one or more occasion that he had only a few
months to live; most were unable to work; and many had watched
friends die from AIDS. Despite these characteristics, nearly all
"maintained the conviction that good times lay ahead and that
their lives were worthwhile."

Not surprisingly, higher rates of major depression have been
found among injection drug users with HIV disease. Unpublished
data from New York found that 23 percent of roughly equal-size

groups of seropositive and seronegative subjects, including both men (147 subjects) and women (76 subjects), had a current depressive disorder.[18] Although the rates of depressive and anxious symptoms were greater than those of the general population, they were no greater than rates for injection drug users in other studies. The authors suggest that HIV status may be less critical in determining mood disorder among injection drug users than the overall degree of psychopathology in this population.

Stability of Mood Symptoms over Time

There is disagreement over the stability of mood over time among people with HIV disease. In a recently published study of 112 seropositive men, researchers demonstrated that over the course of nine semiannual evaluations and despite substantial HIV disease progression, there was no significant increase in clinical or symptomatic depression or anxiety.[19,20] The study also found that psychopathology did not predict death. Similarly, a study of 436 gay and bisexual men found that psychiatric symptoms did not increase over three years of living with HIV disease.[21]

In contrast, among 911 seropositive men in the Multicenter AIDS Cohort Study (MACS) followed as they progressed to AIDS, there was a significant increase in depressive symptoms beginning twelve to eighteen months prior to a subject's AIDS diagnosis.[22] Clinicians at the San Francisco General Hospital AIDS Clinic have observed that the onset of new HIV-related physical symptoms, especially pain, often relates to the onset of a depressive disorder. An increase in depressive symptoms associated with pain has also been noted by other researchers.[23]

Taken together, these data strongly suggest that the rate of depressive and anxiety disorders among nonclinical samples of gay men with HIV is lower than initially believed. It appears that the rates of depression found in these samples of people with HIV are consistent with studies of other life-threatening illnesses, notably cancer.[24]

Although the psychological and physical challenges of living with HIV and possibly a shortened life span may cause transient symptoms of sadness and anxiety, it is clear that clinical disorders of depression and anxiety in this population are the exception, not the rule. In light of new antiviral treatments, it is possible that mood disorders caused by failing health may diminish in number. However, as is becoming more clear each day, other challenges to mood emerge as some clients feel better physically yet struggle to cope with the realities of other problems in their lives that had been eclipsed by their failing health. (See Chapter Nine for more on the psychosocial implications of the new treatment paradigm.)

Because the negative consequences of depressive and other mood disorders on quality of life and on social and occupational functioning can be severe, clinicians working with HIV disease must be alert for symptoms and signs of depression and anxiety in their clients. For those clients in whom mood or anxiety disorders are suspected, clinicians should initiate treatment promptly.

Diagnosis and Treatment of Mood Disorders

Changes in mood are a natural part of living. People normally feel sadness and elation in response to the range of experiences and thoughts that occur daily. There are times when the expected emotional response may be a prolonged period of depressed mood: for example, when grieving the loss of a loved one.

A depressive disorder occurs when sadness persists, is out of proportion to the degree of stress experienced, or when everyday functioning deteriorates. Mood states with persistent sadness become clinical syndromes when they pass certain thresholds for severity and duration and are categorized by the *Diagnostic and Statistical Manual of Mental Disorders (DSM-IV)* as bereavement, major depression, adjustment disorder with depressed mood, and dysthymia.[25] These categories are necessary because each has implications for defining illness, prognosis, and treatment. A brief review of each category offers providers descriptions to inform clinical practice.

Bereavement

Bereavement encompasses a common range of reactions to the death of a loved one. Its symptoms are similar to those of major depression; for example, periods of sadness, loss of appetite or weight, and difficulty sleeping may be present. The survivor may also have feelings of guilt about things he or she "might have done," and thoughts may focus on wanting to be dead, perhaps to be joined with the deceased. The proportion of the day preoccupied with the deceased and with feelings of sadness tends to decrease with time; however, it is common that these thoughts and feelings will recur at times, months and years later, rekindled by reminders of the loss. Bereavement usually does not result in a depressive disorder. However, if persistently depressed mood lasts more than two months, or if impairment of everyday functioning, suicidal ideation, or preoccupation with feelings of guilt and worthlessness persists, bereavement may be complicated with major depression(see Chapter Twelve for a more in-depth discussion).

Bereavement may be particularly difficult for people living with HIV disease. The grieving process for some seropositive people may be near-continuous at times, as one friend, partner, or family member after another dies. The seropositive person also grieves for the continuing losses in his or her own life. He or she may lose career, goals, home and other possessions, a positive body image, and a sense of autonomy, as well as a community and support system. An initial response to such loss may be numbness, when the alternative emotion is to feel overwhelmed with grief or anxiety. This sense of numbness may persist as losses accumulate faster than a person can assimilate prior losses.

In a study of bereavement in gay men, researchers found that common grieving processes occurred but usually did not result in major depressive episodes, and depressive symptoms were not related to the number of loved ones lost.[26] However, bereaved people living with HIV disease may suffer greater distress than those who are seronegative.[27] In addition to the cumulative load of both interpersonal and individual losses, the death of a loved one brings up the issue of a seropositive bereaved person's own mortality. A death perceived as painful or humiliating may provoke fear that the grieving person's dying process will be similarly difficult. The seropositive caretaker of a partner with HIV disease may also fear that he or she will die alone.

Although symptoms diminish with time and without treatment for most bereaved people, psychotherapy, medication, or both may alleviate discomfort and facilitate a return to normal functioning. For the bereaved person who alternates between repressing grief and feeling overwhelmed by it, the psychotherapist may work on improving coping skills. Research has long demonstrated that people with HIV disease who are able to take direct action to address life stressors ("active-behavioral coping"), rather than evading confrontation with these issues ("avoidance coping"), suffer less anxiety and depression.[28] Therapists can work to strengthen their clients' problem-solving skills and can teach relaxation techniques so that clients feel better able to manage the grief process without feeling overwhelmed and to master feelings of anxiety. For some clients, a focus on past or present interpersonal relationships may be helpful, for example, when there are ambivalent or hateful feelings toward the deceased or when the bereaved person needs help adjusting old relationships or developing new ones. Bereavement groups may be a source of psychosocial support, and group members may model adaptation skills for one another.

Short-term use of medications may also reduce suffering during bereavement. Benzodiazepines such as lorazepam or clonazepam can be used to treat persistent or overwhelming anxiety. Benzodiazepines—such as temazepam—trazodone, or other sedatives such as zolpidem can be used to treat short-term insomnia commonly related to bereavement.

Major Depression

When depressed mood persists and affects functioning and outlook in a pervasive way, a client may be suffering from a major depressive episode. It is critical to quality of life that this clinical syndrome not be missed, because major depressive episodes respond readily to treatment. Symptoms include loss of interest in usually pleasing activities or interests; insomnia; decreased energy; loss of appetite or eating more than usual—resulting in weight loss or gain; crying spells; suicidal ideation; loss of libido; and difficulty concentrating. (See Exhibit 11.1 for a more detailed description.) It is important to note that several symptoms of depression may be due to HIV disease rather than mood:

- Weight loss may be caused by wasting syndrome or other physical illness.
- Loss of appetite may be caused by gastrointestinal disease or nausea from medications.

Exhibit 11.1. Diagnostic Criteria for Depression.

A. Five (or more) of the following symptoms have been present during the same two-week period and represent a change from previous functioning; at least one of the symptoms is either (1) depressed mood or (2) loss of interest or pleasure. *Note:* Do not include symptoms that are clearly due to a general medical condition, or mood-incongruent delusions or hallucinations.

1. Depressed mood most of the day, nearly every day, as indicated by either subjective report (for example, feels sad or empty) or observation made by others (for example, appears tearful). *Note:* In children and adolescents, can be irritable mood.
2. Markedly diminished interest or pleasure in all, or almost all, activities most of the day, nearly every day (as indicated by either subjective account or observation made by others)
3. Significant weight loss when not dieting, or weight gain (for example, a change of more than 5 percent of body weight in a month), or decrease or increase in appetite nearly every day. *Note:* In children, consider failure to make expected weight gains.
4. Insomnia or hypersomnia nearly every day
5. Psychomotor agitation or retardation nearly every day (observable by others, not merely subjective feelings of restlessness or being slowed down)
6. Fatigue or loss of energy nearly every day
7. Feelings of worthlessness or excessive or inappropriate guilt (which may be delusional) nearly every day (not merely self-reproach or guilt about being sick)
8. Diminished ability to think or concentrate, or indecisiveness, nearly every day (either by subjective account or as observed by others)
9. Recurrent thoughts of death (not just fear of dying), recurrent suicidal ideation without a specific plan, or a suicide attempt or a specific plan for committing suicide

B. The symptoms do not meet criteria for a Mixed Episode.
C. The symptoms cause clinically significant distress or impairment in social, occupational, or other important areas of functioning.
D. The symptoms are not due to the direct physiological effects of a substance (for example, a drug of abuse, a medication) or a general medical condition (for example, hypothyroidism).
E. The symptoms are not better accounted for by Bereavement; that is, after the loss of a loved one, the symptoms persist for longer than two months or are characterized by marked functional impairment, morbid preoccupation with worthlessness, suicidal ideation, psychotic symptoms, or psychomotor retardation.

Source: Reprinted with permission from the *Diagnostic and Statistical Manual of Mental Disorders, Fourth Edition.* Copyright 1994 American Psychiatric Association.

- Sleep may be affected directly by HIV disease[29] and also by HIV-related medications.
- HIV-related cognitive impairment may cause psychomotor slowing and difficulty thinking or concentrating.
- Fatigue may surface either early or late in the course of HIV disease.
- Recurrent thoughts of death may arise as new physical symptoms amplify fears of mortality.

In diagnosis, focus on the client's history and on symptoms not likely to be related to HIV disease. Does the client feel sad most of the time? Is he or she uninterested in or unable to enjoy the usual activities that he or she is physically able to do? Has he or she been more focused on negative thoughts? Do any of the symptoms have a discrete time course that is not explained by physical illness? Does the client have a history of major depression? Is there a familial history of depression?

It is possible to confuse the apathy and blunting of affect caused by HIV-related cognitive impairment with depression. However, organic brain disease may cause a bonafide depression. To differentiate between depression and cognitive impairment, look for persistent feelings of sadness and negative thoughts, which indicate depression, or more prominent and persistent cognitive problems such as memory loss or disorientation, which indicate cognitive impairment (see Chapter Fourteen).

Alcohol and stimulant (cocaine or amphetamine) abuse, and sometimes opiate withdrawal, can also mimic symptoms of depression. A period of sobriety is usually necessary to distinguish whether or not the depression is directly substance induced or whether treatment for depression, in addition to substance abuse, is necessary. The client who has not used drugs or alcohol in the previous month but continues to meet symptom criteria for a major depressive episode merits treatment specific for depression (see Chapter Fifteen).

Finally, because it is sometimes impossible to fully differentiate among the depressive symptoms caused by various underlying medical disorders and those caused by depression, providers should give clients the benefit the doubt. In other words, diagnose depression independently of the medical problem if it appears the client is depressed. Because newer antidepressants with relatively few side effects are available, antidepressant treatment can be initiated, and the clinical outcome of this treatment can be quickly assessed. If the client does not respond, antidepressant medication can always be stopped. The client will not have been harmed by this intervention and will likely have benefited. The depressed client who is not treated because of uncertainty about whether he or she completely fulfills diagnostic criteria will continue to suffer needlessly.

Adjustment Disorder with Depressed Mood and Dysthymic Disorder

Adjustment disorder with depressed mood is diagnosed when clinically significant depressive symptoms develop within three months of an identifiable stressor, but the symptoms are not sufficient enough to meet criteria for a major depressive episode.[30] Treatment usually centers on psychotherapy rather than medication. Short-term cognitive-behavioral therapy emphasizing improving coping skills, as described later in this chapter, may be particularly useful. Dysthymic disorder refers to chronic depressive symptoms lasting more than two years (often present since childhood or early adulthood) that are not severe enough to meet criteria for a major depressive episode. Antidepressant medication and psychotherapeutic approaches may be useful; however, dysthymic symptoms often respond poorly to treatment.[31]

Treating Major Depression

Psychotherapy and pharmacotherapy are often used together to treat depression. For many clients, these different modes of treatment can work synergistically. Similarly, symptoms that do not respond to one modality may respond to the other. Clients with severe, persistent depression, however, should always be assessed for pharmacologic treatment.

Antidepressant Medications

There is an ever-expanding selection of antidepressant medications, and more are being developed or improved upon. Among those now available are tricyclics, selective serotonin reuptake inhibitors (SSRIs), bupropion, trazodone, venlafaxine, nefazodone, and mirtazapine. Clients with asymptomatic HIV disease may be treated with the same dosages as seronegative patients; however, those with more advanced illness should be treated initially with half the usual starting doses, raising dosage only after it is clear the client is tolerating the medication.

SSRIs are the most commonly prescribed antidepressants. They include fluoxetine (Prozac), sertraline (Zoloft), paroxetine (Paxil), and fluvoxamine (Luvox). SSRIs are very safe drugs and even in overdose situations do not threaten life. They are just as effective for depression as the tricyclic antidepressants, without the latter's difficult side effects. However, SSRIs can cause nausea, jitteriness, insomnia, and sexual dysfunction. The most common sexual dysfunction is delayed ejaculation, but impotence and loss of sexual desire also occur. These side effects frequently diminish with time or if the dosage is reduced and cease when the drug is stopped. In addition, other medications may be prescribed to treat sexual dysfunction.

For most clients, however, side effects are mild and tolerable when compared to the benefits of improved mood. Because side effects are often most bothersome early in treatment and because significant improvement of depressive symptoms takes two to six weeks of treatment, clinicians need to encourage clients to remain on their medications during this early period. Clinicians should also be ready to switch clients to an antidepressant with a different side-effect profile.

Among the tricyclic antidepressants, it is best to avoid those with greater anticholinergic side effects (causing dry mouth and sometimes constipation) and orthostatic side effects (causing dizziness or faintness when blood pressure falls abruptly after a person rises from lying to sitting or standing), like amitriptyline (Elavil). Desipramine and nortriptyline have fewer of these side effects and are effective for depression as well as for treating the pain associated with peripheral neuropathy. Although most clients tolerate desipramine and nortriptyline well, tricyclic side effects may include anticholinergic and orthostatic side effects, urinary retention, lightheadedness on standing up, increased heart rate, and cognitive impairment, and the drugs may cause the heart to stop on overdose.

For clients in whom insomnia is the most prominent symptom, trazodone (Desyrel) is helpful, but its side effects of morning grogginess and orthostatic hypotension may prevent an effective antidepressant dose from being reached. Bupropion (Wellbutrin) is a stimulating antidepressant, without the sexual dysfunction caused by SSRIs. It is somewhat more likely to lower seizure threshold. The newer slow-release form (Wellbutrin SR) has reduced seizure risk and has been well tolerated by clients at the San Francisco General Hospital AIDS Clinic. It may be helpful for clients who do not respond to the SSRIs, for clients who discontinue SSRIs due to sexual dysfunction, and for those with fatigue accompanying depression. Bupropion may also aid in smoking cessation.

Nefazodone (Serzone) is an SSRI as well as a postsynaptic serotonin blocker and has a low rate of sexual dysfunction side effects. Nefazodone may be helpful with anxiety accompanying depression but sometimes causes excessive sedation or nausea. Mirtazapine (Remeron) is also less likely to cause sexual dysfunction and is helpful for insomnia accompanying depression. Venlafaxine (Effexor) is a serotonin as well as norepinephrine reuptake inhibitor and may be useful for people who do not respond to SSRIs. In people with advanced AIDS and with apathetic withdrawal as the most prominent depressive symptom, the psychostimulant methylphenidate (Ritalin) may improve functioning or mood.

Psychotherapy

Psychotherapeutic treatment for depression may be effective for motivated patients who prefer not to take antidepressants, or it can be used in conjunction with antidepressants. There are a variety of cognitive and behavioral approaches that are appropriate to the full range of depression-related issues. Structured group therapy emphasizing active-behavioral coping skills and teaching relaxation techniques and problem-solving skills has been effective in treating depression in people with HIV disease.[32] Long-standing changes in coping skills have also been achieved through brief psychotherapeutic interventions,[33] other cognitive-behavioral and supportive group psychotherapies,[34] and interpersonal psychotherapy, which focuses on role transitions and interpersonal losses, on acquiring social support, and on improving problem solving.[35]

A wide variety of issues may affect a person's ability to cope with HIV disease and with depression. Among these are adapting to loss (as discussed previously); disclosing HIV status to family, friends, employers, or intimate partners; facing dependency—including loss of control, reemergence of childhood issues, and rage at caregivers; addressing long-standing self-esteem issues; and examining suicidal feelings. Suicidality may be a symptom of a treatable depression or of a pain syndrome. Most commonly, thoughts of suicide help clients maintain a sense of control, a sense that there is a means to end their suffering if necessary. Usually these feelings remain theoretical, in the distance. Imminent suicidal feelings, especially if a client has made concrete plans, require immediate assessment and intervention.

Relationship issues are often a focus in psychotherapy for mood disorders. Maintaining stable relationships in an environment of bereavement and loss is a challenge, and illness may further disrupt long-standing roles in a relationship. Sexual dysfunction may disrupt patterns of physical intimacy. Finally, career loss and financial difficulties may create stress within a relationship.

Organic Mania

An organic manic syndrome has been associated with HIV disease.[36,37] Its symptoms include elevated or irritable mood, insomnia, pressured speech, grandiosity, racing thoughts, distractibility, rapid speech, restlessness, and reckless or disinhibited behavior. In clients with no prior history of affective illness, this manic syndrome is often accompanied by HIV-related cognitive impairment and other evidence of a physical basis, such as abnormalities that would show up on a magnetic resonance image of the brain.[38,39] It has been suggested that these manic episodes are caused by the process that leads to HIV-associated dementia.[40]

In other clients, manic episodes are likely exacerbations of preexisting bipolar disorder and are not usually accompanied by dementia. They may also follow the routine administration of high-dose steroids for *Pneumocystis carinii* pneumonia in patients hospitalized for medical reasons. Other cases of manic syndromes are associated with amphetamine and cocaine abuse and with antidepressant medications, and there have been case reports of mania associated with ZDV treatment.[41]

Clinicians should seek to investigate and treat the underlying organic causes of mania. Neuroleptic drugs may bring about the fastest resolution of manic symptoms and are effective in treating the condition's initial agitation. Newer "atypical" neuroleptics (for example, olanzapine) are particularly useful in controlling psychosis and manic agitation and have a much lower risk of extrapyramidal side effects (stiffness and muscular rigidity) than older neuroleptics. Conventional medium-potency neuroleptics (for example, perphenazine), which are generally well tolerated, may be started at low doses; higher doses of high-potency neuroleptics, such as haloperidol, frequently cause extrapyramidal side effects in people with AIDS.[42]

Neuroleptic drugs, if well tolerated, may be used for long-term treatment but may result in tardive dyskinesia (a nonreversible neuromuscular disorder characterized by lip-smacking or chewing motions and seen in the chronically mentally ill who have taken high doses of neuroleptics over time). Clinicians therefore use mood-stabilizing medications for ongoing management. For example, divalproex sodium is well tolerated and effective,[43] although its side effects include stomach discomfort, sedation, and an increase in liver enzymes. Lithium carbonate is also effective; however, because there appears to be a greater sensitivity to lithium side effects in clients with organic mania, initial blood levels of the drug should be targeted slightly lower than usual. In addition, clinicians should monitor lithium serum levels carefully, because clients with AIDS are particularly susceptible to toxicity secondary to dehydration or renal disease.

Finally, carbamazepine (Tegretol) may also be used to treat mania; however, among clients with preexisting bone marrow suppression, it may reduce the capacity or efficiency of the bone marrow in creating new blood cells. Newer anticonvulsants such as lamotrigine and gabapentin show promise, but there is insufficient evidence yet to recommend these except as second-line treatments.

Anxiety Disorders

People with HIV disease may be attempting to cope with social losses, family conflicts, occupational transitions, financial uncertainty, and the uncertainty of the disease process. Under these circumstances, periods of anxiety are normal. Although there is a wide range in the amount of anxiety a person may experience—some people having by nature an "anxious temperament"—most people are able to respond psychologically and behaviorally to the stress of living with HIV disease and limit the impact of anxiety on the quality of their lives. Only a minority of people—those with anxiety disorders—suffer anxiety of an intensity and duration that causes prolonged impaired functioning. In addition, persons with AIDS with poor coping skills tend to be more anxious.

Anxiety and Coping

Active-behavioral coping—taking direct action to address the stressor—is the most effective coping style for reducing anxiety. Active-cognitive coping—forming a mental framework or strategy to respond to the stressor—is of intermediate effectiveness. Avoidance coping—attempting not to address the stressor, for example, by increasing substance use or isolation—is least effective.

The anxious client can learn to cope more effectively with illness-related stressors, often through brief psychotherapeutic interventions. By identifying both overt and covert sources of anxiety and responding to maladaptive defenses, therapists can help clients develop coping tools. Studies in cancer patients have shown that changes in coping style are long lasting and can affect not only anxiety but also the course of illness.[44]

Structured group therapy has demonstrated efficacy in teaching and encouraging active-behavioral coping techniques.[45,46] Among these techniques are problem-solving and communication skills, and relaxation—for example, progressive muscle relaxation, guided imagery, and self-hypnosis. Problem-solving and communication skills training give clients tools to allow them to address stressors more directly. Relaxation techniques foster a sense of internal control over anxiety that helps prevent anticipatory anxiety, which may inhibit clients from actively addressing stressors. The group format allows members to practice newly learned coping skills through role-playing stressful situations, facilitates learning adaptive skills from other group participants, and helps reduce social isolation and thus may encourage more active coping.

Severe Anxiety

Severe, persistent anxiety, affecting day-to-day functioning, may be a symptom of a *DSM-IV* anxiety disorder. Anxiety disorders include generalized anxiety disorder, panic disorder, agoraphobia, specific and social phobia, obsessive-compulsive disorder, acute stress disorder, substance-induced anxiety disorder, anxiety disorder due to a general medical condition, adjustment disorder with anxious mood, and Post-Traumatic Stress Disorder.[47] Accurate diagnosis is helpful in determining treatment, which varies somewhat between the different disorders.

Panic Disorder

Panic disorder is characterized by the sudden onset of severe anxiety, with a fear of losing control or dying, and somatic symptoms.[48] Although they may be infrequent, these episodes are so traumatic that the person develops a persistent worry or anticipatory anxiety that the attacks will recur. Agoraphobia is the fear of being in places in which escape would be difficult in the event of panic symptoms, such as in a crowd, on a bus, or in a car on a bridge. An agoraphobic person avoids these situations, often by staying home.

Panic disorder and agoraphobia respond well to treatment. Cognitive-behavioral therapy has been particularly effective. Antidepressants, including SSRIs and tricyclics, are also effective in preventing or reducing the number of panic attacks. Dosages are similar to those for treatment of depression; if a more stimulating antidepressant such as fluoxetine or desipramine is used, clients should start at a lower than usual dose. Benzodiazepines have the advantage of working more quickly than antidepressants and may be used for immediate relief until the antidepressant takes effect. Long-term benzodiazepine use has the disadvantages of creating dependency and of rebound anxiety with discontinuation.

Generalized Anxiety Disorder

In generalized anxiety disorder, there is excessive worry or anxiety present most days for at least six months. A range of psychotherapies may be effective in response. Relaxation techniques may also be helpful. Pharmacologic treatment includes using buspirone (Buspar); although it takes days to weeks to be effective, it can treat anxiety without affecting cognition or creating dependency.

Adjustment Disorder with Anxious Mood

Adjustment disorder with anxious mood is similar to adjustment disorder with depressed mood described earlier. Treatment includes individual or group psychotherapy; cognitive-behavioral therapies for depression also reduce anxiety symptoms.[49,50] Training in relaxation techniques can increase a client's sense of internal control. Buspar or short-term benzodiazepine therapy may also be helpful.

Post-Traumatic Stress Disorder

In Post-Traumatic Stress Disorder (PTSD), the client has symptoms for more than a month after experiencing a severe trauma. The symptoms are of three types:

- Reexperiencing the event—for example, through flashbacks, dreams, or in response to a cue that raises memory of the traumatic event
- Engaging in avoidance and numbing
- Experiencing increased arousal or feeling "edgy"

Treatment includes individual and group psychotherapy, and antidepressants. Acute Stress Disorder is similar to PTSD but lasts less than a month; dissociative symptoms are prominent.

Obsessive-Compulsive Disorder

Obsessive-compulsive disorder usually precedes HIV infection, but HIV disease may become a focus for the obsessive thoughts. The SSRIs—at higher doses and for longer periods than when used for depression—deliver effective treatment, preferably in combination with behavioral therapy. Phobias, which are anxiety disorders characterized by fear and avoidance of particular situations, respond well to behavioral therapy.

Substance-Induced Anxiety Disorder and Anxiety Disorder Due to a General Medical Condition

The key to treating substance-induced anxiety disorder and anxiety disorder due to a general medical condition is to identify and treat the underlying cause. Alcohol or benzodiazepine withdrawal and amphetamine and cocaine intoxication are common causes of anxiety. Hypoxia, or decreased oxygen in the blood, as caused by *Pneumocystis carinii* pneumonia, may present with symptoms of anxiety. Steroids used in the treatment of pneumonia may also exacerbate the anxiety. In addition, other cardiorespiratory disease as well as central neurological conditions may present with anxiety.

Drug Interactions

Protease inhibitors and medications used to treat mood and anxiety disorders may interact. Protease inhibitors, ritonavir (Norvir) in particular, are powerful inhibitors of the various P450 isoenzymes that metabolize antidepressants, benzodiazepines, and neuroleptics. For example, people on tricyclic antidepressants should cut their dosages by one half to two thirds, at least initially, and check blood levels to establish a safe and effective dose. Bupropion is completely contraindicated with ritonavir. SSRIs and nefazodone may also increase protease inhibitor blood levels; however, the clinical significance of this interaction is not known. Although the SSRIs have a very wide therapeutic window, without the danger of overdose of tricyclics, SSRI doses should initially be cut also by one half to two thirds, then increased again as needed for therapeutic response.

The benzodiazepines lorazepam (Ativan), temazepam (Restoril), and oxazepam (Serax) do not interact with ritonavir. Other benzodiazepines such as diazepam (Valium) or clonazepam (Klonopin) do, so clients should switch to lorazepam prior to beginning ritonavir treatment. Those on other benzodiazepines, such as triazolam (Halcion) and flurazepam (Dalmane), should switch to temazepam for treatment of insomnia.

Neuroleptic doses should be decreased prior to starting ritonavir, and clients should be closely monitored. Pimozide (Orap) is contraindicated. Among mood stabilizers, carbamazepine levels are affected by ritonavir, but valproic acid and lithium levels are not. Other protease inhibitors have much smaller effects on psychotropic drug levels. However, triazolam and pimozide may interact with other protease inhibitors and should be avoided.

～

Transient sadness and anxiety are a normal part of living, and especially of coping with the stresses of living with HIV disease. Mood symptoms that are severe and persistent and affect daily functioning are much less common. Because mood disorders can severely affect quality of life and also respond well to treatment, it is critical that these disorders not be overlooked. Clinicians working with people with HIV disease should be aware of characteristic symptoms and make appropriate referrals for treatment when they suspect a psychiatric disorder.

Finally, considering the safety and efficacy of treatments for depression and anxiety disorders, it is advisable to err on the side of treatment. Medications can always be stopped if they are not helpful, but a client with an untreated mood disorder is left to suffer in silence.

Notes

1. Dilley, J. W., Ochitill, H. N., Perl, M., and others. "Findings in Psychiatric Consultations with Patients with Acquired Immune Deficiency Syndrome." *American Journal of Psychiatry,* 1985, *142*(1), 82–86.
2. Forstein, M. "The Psychosocial Impact of the Acquired Immune Deficiency Syndrome." *Seminars in Oncology,* 1984, *11*(7), 77–82.
3. Bialer, P. A., Wallack, J. J., and Snyder, S. L. "Psychiatric Diagnosis in HIV-Spectrum Disorders." *Psychiatric Medicine,* 1991, *9*(3), 361–375.
4. Seth, R., Granville-Grossman, K., Goldmeier, D., and others. "Psychiatric Illnesses in Patients with HIV Infection and AIDS Referred to the Liaison Psychiatrist." *British Journal of Psychiatry,* 1991, *159,* 347–350.
5. Snyder, S., Teyner, A., Schmeidler, J., and others. "Prevalence of Mental Disorders in Newly Admitted Medical Inpatients with AIDS." *Psychosomatics,* 1992, *33*(2), 166–170.
6. Bialer, P. A., Wallack, J. J., Prenzlauer, S. L., and others. "Psychiatric Co-Morbidity Among Hospitalized AIDS Patients vs. Non-AIDS Patients Referred for Psychiatric Consultation." *Psychosomatics,* 1996, *37*(5), 469–475.
7. Rabkin, J. G., Goetz, R. R., Remien, R. H., and others. "Stability of Mood Despite HIV Illness Progression in a Group of Homosexual Men." *American Journal of Psychiatry,* 1997, *154*(2), 213–238.
8. Hays, R. B., Turner, H., and Coates, T. J. "Social Support, AIDS-Related Symptoms, and Depression Among Gay Men." *Journal of Consulting and Clinical Psychology,* 1992, *60*(3), 463–469.
9. Perry, S. W., Jacobsberg, L., Card, C., and others. "Severity of Psychiatric Symptoms After HIV Testing." *American Journal of Psychiatry,* 1993, *150*(5), 775–779.

10. Pugh, K., Riccio, M., Jadresic, D., and others. "A Longitudinal Study of the Neuropsychiatric Consequences of HIV-1 Infection in Gay Men. II. Psychological and Health Status at Baseline and at 12-Month Follow-Up." *Psychological Medicine,* 1994, *24*(4), 897–904.

11. Pergami, A., Gala, C., Burgess, A., and others. "Heterosexuals and HIV Disease: A Controlled Investigation into the Psychosocial Factors Associated with Psychiatric Morbidity." *Journal of Psychosomatic Research,* 1994, *38*(4), 305–313.

12. Pergami, A., Gala, C., Burgess, A., and others. "The Psychosocial Impact of HIV Infection in Women." *Journal of Psychosomatic Research,* 1993, *37*(7), 687–696.

13. Atkinson, J. H., Jr., Grant, I., Kennedy, C. J., and others. "Prevalence of Psychiatric Disorders Among Men Infected with Human Immunodeficiency Virus. A Controlled Study." *Archives of General Psychiatry,* 1988, *45*(9), 859–864.

14. Brown, G. R., Rundell, J. R., McMinis, S. E., and others. "Prevalence of Psychiatric Disorders in Early Stages of HIV Infection." *Psychosomatic Medicine,* 1992, *54*(5), 588–601.

15. Brown, G. R., and Rundell, J. R. "A Prospective Study of Psychiatric Aspects of Early HIV Disease in Women." *General Hospital Psychiatry,* 1993, *15*(3), 139–147.

16. Williams, J. B., Rabkin, J. G., Remien, R. H., and others. "Multidisciplinary Baseline Assessment of Homosexual Men with and Without Human Immunodeficiency Virus Infection. II. Standardized Clinical Assessment of Current and Lifetime Psychopathology." *Archives of General Psychiatry,* 1991, *48*(2), 124–130.

17. Rabkin, J. G., Remien, R. H., Katoff, L., and others. "Resilience in Adversity Among Long-Term Survivors of AIDS." *Hospital and Community Psychiatry,* 1993, *44*(2), 162–167. Published erratum appears in *Hospital and Community Psychiatry,* 1993, *44*(4), 371.

18. Rabkin, J. G., Williams, J. B., Neugebauer, R., and others. "Maintenance of Hope in HIV-Spectrum Homosexual Men." *American Journal of Psychiatry,* 1990, *147*(10), 1322–1326.

19. Ibid.

20. Rabkin, Goetz, Remien, and others, "Stability of Mood."

21. Joseph, H. G., Caumartin, D. G., Tal, M., and others. "Psychological Functioning in a Cohort of Gay Men at Risk for AIDS." *Journal of Nervous Mental Disease,* 1990, *178*(10), 607–615.

22. Lyketsos, C. G., Hoover, D. R., Guccione, M., and others. "Changes in Depressive Symptoms as AIDS Develops." *American Journal of Psychiatry,* 1996, *153*(11), 1430–1437.

23. Singer, E. J., Zorilla, C., Fahy-Chandon, B., and others. "Painful Symptoms Reported by Ambulatory HIV-Infected Men in a Longitudinal Study." *Pain,* 1993, *54*(1), 15–19.

24. Derogatis, L. R., Morrow, G. R., Fetting, J., and others. "The Prevalence of Psychiatric Disorders Among Cancer Patients." *Journal of the American Medical Association,* 1983, *249*(6), 751–757.

25. American Psychiatric Association. *Diagnostic and Statistical Manual of Mental Disorders.* (4th ed.) Washington, D.C.: American Psychiatric Association, 1994.

26. Neugebauer, R., Rabkin, J. G., Williams, J. B., and others. "Bereavement Reactions Among Homosexual Men Experiencing Multiple Losses in the AIDS Epidemic." *American Journal of Psychiatry,* 1992, *149*(10), 1374–1379.

27. Martin, J. L., and Dean, L. "Effects of AIDS-Related Bereavement and HIV-Related Illness on Psychological Distress Among Gay Men: A 7-Year Longitudinal Study, 1985–1991." *Journal of Consulting and Clinical Psychology,* 1993, *61*(1), 94–103.

28. Namir, S., Wolcott, D. L., Fawzy, F. I., and others. "Coping with AIDS: Psychological Implications." *Journal of Applied Social Psychology,* 1987, *17,* 309–328.

29. Wiegand, M., Moller, A. A., Schreiber, W., and others. "Nocturnal Sleep EEG in Patients with HIV Infection." *European Archives of Psychiatry and Clinical Neuroscience,* 1991, *240*(3), 153–158.

30. American Psychiatric Association, *DSM-IV.*

31. Wells, K. B., Burnham, A., Rogers, W., and others. "The Course of Depression in Adult Outpatients." *Archives of General Psychiatry,* 1992, *49,* 788–794.

32. Targ, E. F., Karasis, D. H., Diefenbach, P. N., and others. "Structured Group Therapy and Fluoxetine to Treat Depression in HIV-Positive Persons." *Psychosomatics,* 1994, *35*(2), 132–137.

33. Fawzy, F. I., Cousins, N., Fawzy, N. W., and others. "A Structured Psychiatric Intervention for Cancer Patients. I. Changes over Time in Methods of Coping and Affective Disturbance." *Archives of General Psychiatry,* 1990, *47*(8), 720–725.

34. Kelly, J. A., Murphy, D. A., Bahr, G. R., and others. "Outcome of Cognitive-Behavioral and Support Group Brief Therapies for Depressed, HIV-Infected Persons." *American Journal of Psychiatry,* 1993, *150*(11), 1679–1686.

35. Markowitz, J. C., Klerman, G. L., and Perry, S. W. "Interpersonal Psychotherapy of Depressed HIV-Positive Outpatients." *Hospital and Community Psychiatry,* 1992, *43*(9), 885–890.

36. Boccellari, A., Dilley, J. W., and Shore, M. D. "Neuropsychiatric Aspects of AIDS Dementia Complex: A Report on a Clinical Series." *Neurotoxicology,* 1988, *9*(3), 381–389.

37. Kieburtz, K., Zettelmaier, A. E., Ketonen, L., and others. "Manic Syndrome in AIDS." *American Journal of Psychiatry,* 1991, *148*(8), 1068–1070.

38. Lyketsos, C. G., Hanson, A. L., Fishman, M., and others. "Manic Syndrome Early and Late in the Course of HIV." *American Journal of Psychiatry,* 1993, *150*(2), 326–327.

39. Halman, M. H., Worth, J. L., Sanders, K. M., and others. "Anticonvulsant Use in the Treatment of Manic Syndromes in Patients with HIV-1 Infection." *Journal of Neuropsychiatry and Clinical Neuroscience,* 1993, *5*(4), 430–434.

40. el-Mallakh, R. S. "AIDS Dementia-Related Psychosis: Is There a Window of Vulnerability?" *AIDS Care,* 1992, *4*(4), 381–387.

41. Maxwell, S., Scheftner, W. A., Kessler, H. A., and others. "Manic Syndrome Associated with Zidovudine Treatment." Letter. *Journal of the American Medical Association,* 1988, *259*(23), 3406–3407.

42. Hriso, E., Kuhn, T., Masdeu, J. C., and others. "Extrapyramidal Symptoms Due to Dopamine-Blocking Agents in Patients with AIDS Encephalopathy." *American Journal of Psychiatry,* 1991, *148*(11), 1558–1561.

43. Halman, Worth, Sanders, and others, "Anticonvulsant Use."

44. Fawzy, F. I., Fawzy, N. W., Hyun, C. S., and others. "Malignant Melanoma: Effects of an Early Structured Psychiatric Intervention, Coping, and Affective State on Recurrence and Survival 6 Years Later." *Archives of General Psychiatry,* 1993, *50*(9), 681–689.

45. Targ, Karasis, Diefenbach, and others, "Structured Group Therapy."

46. Fawzy, F. I., Namir, S., and Wolcott, D. L. "Structured Group Intervention Model for AIDS Patients." *Psychiatric Medicine,* 1989, *7*(2), 35–45.

47. American Psychiatric Association, *DSM-IV.*

48. Ibid.

49. Targ, Karasis, Diefenbach, and others, "Structured Group Therapy."

50. Kelly, Murphy, Bahr, and others, "Outcome of Cognitive-Behavioral and Support Group Brief Therapies."

Chapter Twelve

The Clinical Management of AIDS Bereavement

Peter B. Goldblum
Sarah Erickson

Despite new treatments that prolong the lives of people with HIV disease, deaths continue to occur, and the burden on caregivers remains significant.[1] Like the epidemic of HIV, the epidemic of HIV-related grief is far from over. Even with a 12 percent decline in mortality, twenty-two thousand Americans died of AIDS in the first six months of 1996.[2] It is still too early to determine the long-term effect of medical breakthroughs on mourners, but if anecdotal evidence is accurate, recent accounts suggest that mourners experience dismay at the idea that their loved ones may have just missed the opportunity to extend their lives.[3]

Although AIDS bereavement presents some unique challenges, the human experience of grief is universal. A recent New York study found that people mourning HIV-related losses experience grief symptoms—including numbness, denial, and preoccupation with the deceased—similar to those faced by other bereaved individuals.[4] To the extent that we allow ourselves to develop strong emotional attachments to others, we open ourselves to the experience of loss when these ties are severed.

In addition to the stigma associated with AIDS, homosexuality, and substance abuse, the likelihood of multiple losses due to the epidemic increases the burden for people with HIV disease and those who care for and mourn them. Further, and in contrast to

most life-threatening illnesses, HIV disease has affected disproportionate numbers of young and middle-aged people. The resulting premature death may increase the risk of prolonged or
pathological grief reactions in loved ones.[5]

In the gay and bisexual community, the experience of HIV-
related bereavement is not a randomly distributed event.[6] Those
men who have a history of high-risk sexual behavior are not only
more likely to be infected but are also more likely to lose one or
more friends to the disease. In fact, men who are HIV-infected are
almost twice as likely to have lost a loved one than are uninfected
men.[7] This places HIV-infected gay and bisexual men in a dilemma:
on one hand, the gay community can provide support and assistance in facing the epidemic; on the other, integration into the gay
and bisexual community increases one's risk for multiple losses due
to the disease. Likewise, uninfected people who are closely connected to the gay and bisexual community may seek community
support to face the challenges of HIV-related bereavement and
multiple loss and at the same time risk further grief. Although research evidence is lacking, this dual aspect of community integration is probably similar for other groups with high infection rates,
such as injection drug users.

This chapter proposes a coherent clinical model for assessing
and treating HIV-related bereavement. The model is based on general bereavement theory and HIV-specific research, including
preliminary findings from the Stanford AIDS Caregiving and Bereavement Study.[8] Throughout the chapter, the term *bereavement*
refers to the emotional and behavioral reaction to a loss due to the
death of a loved one and encompasses both grief and mourning.
Grief refers to the subjective emotional experience that follows the
psychological recognition of a loss. Normal grief is often difficult
to distinguish from a range of psychological disorders, most often
depressive disorders. *Mourning* refers to the process in which individuals strive to adapt to loss and attenuate grief.

Several authors have described the mourning process and ways
individuals successfully manage bereavement. In his classic work
Attachment and Loss, John Bowlby identified four stages in the typical mourning process: numbing, yearning and searching, disorganization or despair, and reorganization.[9] In contrast to describing
stages of mourning, J. William Worden identified four tasks that

must be accomplished before mourning is complete. By focusing on tasks, Worden emphasized intentional change on the part of the mourner, rather than the passage of time, as the most important factor in successful resolution of grief.[10] Worden emphasizes intentional change to complete the mourning process, an approach that differs from Bowlby's and others' stage theories, which describe the passage of time as leading to a natural resolution of grief. Worden's four tasks are to accept the reality of the loss, to experience the pain of grief, to adjust to an environment in which the deceased is missing, and to withdraw emotional energy and reinvest it in another relationship.

Within the context of these theories, this chapter outlines a model that separates responses to the loss of a loved one into four bereavement outcomes: uncomplicated mourning, uncomplicated mourning with risk factors, complicated mourning without psychological disorders, and complicated mourning with psychological disorders. Uncomplicated mourning is the adequate management of the bereavement process; the mourner successfully moves through the stages and tasks of mourning consistent with his or her own values and cultural norms. The chapter also identifies ten risk factors of bereavement distress.

Clinical Assessment of AIDS Bereavement

Although differential diagnosis of psychological disorders requires a mental health specialist, primary care professionals and community members are frequently called on to identify and respond to problems arising from bereavement. The assessment model described here can also be used to develop a full spectrum of services for people dealing with HIV-related bereavement.

Risk Factors for AIDS Bereavement Distress

Certain relationships, behaviors, or personal characteristics place people at risk for *bereavement distress,* a term that encompasses as separate entities both complicated mourning and the psychological disorders that may be associated with bereavement. The risk factors outlined in this section and summarized in Exhibit 12.1 have been compiled from empirical studies on both HIV-specific and general bereavement.

Exhibit 12.1. Risk Factors for AIDS Bereavement Distress.

1. Being a caregiver, primary partner, parent

2. Experiencing multiple losses

3. Being HIV-infected

4. Experiencing interpersonal conflict and perceiving a lack of social support

5. Engaging in substance abuse or experiencing substance dependency

6. Experiencing guilt and low self-esteem (including internalized homophobia)

7. Being pessimistic

8. Engaging in avoidance and ineffective coping (including ruminative coping)

9. Experiencing cumulative life stressors

10. Having preexisting psychological disorders

Being a Caregiver, Primary Partner, or Parent

Although AIDS caregiving responsibilities often fall to primary partners, a variety of caregiving arrangements include parents, friends, and community volunteers. Research with gay men suggests that caregivers, both the partners and mothers of HIV-infected people, are at increased risk for psychological distress.[11] The Stanford study found that gay male caregivers in all HIV categories—seropositive, seronegative, with AIDS, and untested—had high levels of depressive symptoms, regardless of their own health status.[12] Further, their risk for psychological distress was independent of their having many close friends affected by HIV disease (including deaths and diagnoses). These results suggest that the demands of the caregiving role supersede any palliative or deleterious effect of personal health or multiple loss.[13]

Although there is little empirical data, clinical observation suggests there is added strain on parents who mourn a loss to HIV disease, and it is notable that parental mourning is, in itself, a predictor for complicated bereavement. Parents of both gay men and injection drug users may be estranged from their children due to lifestyle conflicts, and this estrangement may lead to an exacerbation of guilt and remorse after the death of a child. In addition, parents of young children in the injection drug–using community are likely to be infected themselves. In fact, many have transmitted HIV to their children perinatally, a situation that may represent the most difficult and high-risk bereavement, replete with self-blame and increased or renewed drug use.

Experiencing Multiple Losses and Being HIV-Infected

Mourners living in epicenters of the epidemic are likely to have experienced multiple losses due to the disease. A large proportion of them are likely to be HIV-infected, to have lost the core of their support networks, and to worry about who will be there to take care of them. To add to the concrete losses of loved ones and their own physical health, many mourners suffer from a variety of symbolic losses due to the epidemic. For example, many gay men lament the loss of sexual freedom. This accumulation of losses may overwhelm the mourner.

Research related to multiple loss and bereavement remains preliminary. In a study conducted early in the epidemic, John Martin and Laura Dean at Columbia University found that multiple bereavement had a negative impact on survivors, many of whom experienced symptoms of traumatic stress, demoralization, sleep problems, sedative use, and recreational drug use.[14] On a more hopeful note, Martin and Dean found that gay men who survived the first ten years of the epidemic experienced fewer negative psychological symptoms two years after the loss of a loved one than did similar men tracked in their earlier study. However, they also found that those men who were both bereaved and HIV-infected continued to report high levels of psychological distress throughout the epidemic.[15] Another Columbia University research group found that, although bereavement symptoms—notably preoccupation with and searching for the deceased—were related to the number of AIDS deaths reported by subjects, diagnosable psychological disorders were not.[16]

Experiencing Interpersonal Conflict and Perceiving a Lack of Social Support

Perhaps the area of greatest agreement between the clinical and research literature on bereavement relates to the importance of perceived social support in mediating psychological health. An accumulation of research suggests that the perception of social support is more important than any quantitative measure of support.[17,18]

The Stanford study found that among gay caregivers, overall satisfaction with caregivers' support systems was associated with lower depression symptomatology. However, structural aspects, such as the total number of friends or number of gay and nongay friends, were not related to depression.[19] Another aspect of social support—affirmation by others—has been found to be helpful to mourners.[20,21] Affirmation includes approval of one's beliefs, feelings, and decisions by important others. This may be particularly important to gay men and lesbians who are new to, or live outside of, supportive gay communities.

Conflict and friction within the social network may have a negative impact on emotional well-being. In fact, the Stanford study found that the amount of friction in a gay male caregiver's networks, the frequency of unpleasant encounters, and social isolation were the most consistently and strongly related support measures related to depression.[22]

Experiencing Guilt and Low Self-Esteem

For some mourners, guilt may arise in response to their own negative evaluation of their caregiver performance; for others, it may be the result of long-standing psychological problems. In addition, many gay and bisexual men experience lower self-esteem related to internalized homophobia.[23,24] Even those who have lived for years feeling good about their sexuality may be revisited by negative self-images and accompanying anguish after the loss of a loved one.

Being Pessimistic

In general, people with an optimistic appraisal style demonstrate better emotional well-being than those who are more pessimistic.[25,26] The Stanford study found that gay male caregivers who reported greater levels of both general optimism and HIV-related optimism reported less distress.[27] Although it would appear to make intuitive sense that men who were seronegative or untested would differ from HIV-infected men, all three groups of caregivers expressed similar self-appraisals regarding their ability to cope with the disease.

Engaging in Avoidance and Ineffective Coping

Coping refers to the cognitive and behavioral strategies individuals employ to manage specific demands they appraise as taxing or exceeding their resources.[28] Coping has two major functions: to manage or alter the problem that is causing distress (problem solving) and to regulate the emotional response to the problem. Using ineffective methods to cope with bereavement-related problems or emotions may relate to the nature of current stressors or to a more generalized deficit in coping abilities. Many mourners fall back on old patterns of overeating, substance use, or inappropriate sexual behavior in attempts to avoid the pain of grief.

Although much of the research on coping with negative emotions has focused on people who deny or avoid their negative emotions, a large caregiving and bereavement study of nongay mourners conducted by Susan Nolen-Hoeksema demonstrated that people who are overly focused on their emotions are at risk for more severe and lengthy periods of distress.[29] In a pattern described as ruminative coping, people worry excessively but passively about their depression, its symptoms, the implications of their depression, and the consequences that being depressed has on their lives. Although this rumination may appear to be a method to solve problems ("What am I going to do now?"), the ruminative person is less likely to engage in active problem-solving behavior.

Experiencing Cumulative Life Stressors

The study of nongay mourners also found that the sheer number of stressors one month following the death of a loved one predicted depressive symptoms five months later. These stressors may include financial, occupational, or health problems.[30] For many AIDS-bereaved individuals who are seropositive themselves, their own health status serves as an additional stressor.

Having Preexisting Psychological Disorders

People with preexisting psychological disorders may find it more difficult to adequately manage the loss of a loved one.[31,32] For example, a person who is chronically anxious or depressed may be overwhelmed by the addition of a significant loss in his or her life. Similarly, people with personality disorders—for example, borderline or avoidant—may have difficulty coping with the burdens of bereavement.

Complicated Mourning

Bowlby believed that pathological or complicated mourning is best understood as an exaggeration or distortion of the normal process of mourning.[33] He asserted that pathological mourning and psychiatric illness are more likely to occur in individuals who experienced a significant loss as children and subsequently developed a personality disturbance characterized by a hypersensitivity to loss. Three variants of complicated mourning are widely discussed in the clinical literature: absent mourning, delayed mourning, and chronic mourning.

Absent Mourning

Absent mourning suggests the lack of grief reaction after a significant loss. In some cases, the absence of grief may indicate that an individual was well prepared for the loss, as in response to the death of an aged and gravely ill parent. At other times, however, it is an indication of an impeded mourning process usually stemming from psychological defenses, conscious or unconscious, such as denial or repression. Some people have the self-perception that they are emotionally fragile and are unable to tolerate the pain of grief. Others worry that grief may stimulate overwhelming fears of their own death and dying.

Delayed Mourning

Delayed mourning, like absent mourning, manifests as a lack of grief symptoms. There are some circumstances in which delayed mourning processes may be adaptive. For example, a person who has experienced multiple losses may need to delay mourning less significant losses in order to process those of a greater magnitude. Similarly, a person battling acute exacerbation of his or her own HIV disease may delay mourning the loss of a friend until he or she feels strong enough to handle it.

Chronic Mourning

Chronic mourning involves the undesired persistence of grief reactions, including shock, yearning, searching, disorganization, and despair. Even after the passage of an appropriate length of time (six months is one marker frequently used in the United States), a person's subjective experience of the loss continues to be as salient as if the loss had occurred yesterday. In its most severe form, painful memories and thoughts intrude into consciousness and interrupt occupational and social functioning. Although chronic grief often is unremitting, it is not unusual for these mourners to vacillate between periods of absent and acute grief.

Psychological Disorders and AIDS Bereavement

Whether they precede loss or arise from it, psychological disorders complicate the bereavement process. Among the disorders that commonly occur are mood disorders, anxiety disorders, Post-Traumatic Stress Disorder, and substance abuse.

Mood Disorders

A high proportion of gay men who have experienced the loss of a lover meet the criteria for major depression or Post-Traumatic Stress Disorder.[34] A general bereavement study found three results related to loss-induced depression. First, full depressive episodes are common throughout the first year after the death of a spouse. Second, depressive episodes may occur not only in the early months of bereavement but also later in bereavement. Third, four groups appear to be at highest risk for having depressive episodes thirteen months after their loss: younger widows and widowers; those with a past history of depressive episodes; those still grieving at two intervals—two and seven months after the loss; and those who perceive themselves as being in poor physical health. Contrary to clinical lore suggesting that early intense grief is the normal and healthy response to loss, Sidney Zisook and Stephen Shuchter found that intense early grief reactions are associated with later complications, such as chronic mourning, unresolved grief, or depression.[35]

These findings highlight the value of a careful evaluation of depression in mourners. Although this evaluation may be complicated by the overlap of depression and grief symptoms, it is important to offer early psychotherapeutic interventions whenever a client meets criteria for depression. Clinicians should consider antidepressant medication if symptoms are intense, include vegetative signs or ruminative coping, last for more than six months, or when there is a past personal or family history of major depression (especially if previous depressions were helped by medication).[36]

Anxiety Disorders

Although anxiety is an expected and normal response to loss, anxiety disorders may require psychotherapeutic or pharmacological intervention. Anxiety reactions are often overlooked and may be overshadowed by depressive reactions.[37] Studies have found that both panic disorders—with and without agoraphobia—and generalized anxiety disorders may be associated with bereavement,[38] as may the onset or exacerbation of obsessive-compulsive symptoms. Although anxious avoidance of situations that remind mourners of their losses is not unusual, clinicians should consider whether these reactions are evidence of anxiety disorders when these behaviors significantly interfere with social or occupational functioning.[39]

Post-Traumatic Stress Disorder (PTSD)

Post-Traumatic Stress Disorder is the development of characteristic symptoms following exposure to an extreme traumatic stressor involving direct experience of an event that involves actual or threatened death or serious injury or other threat to a person's physical integrity. This may include learning about an unexpected death. To merit a diagnosis, the person's response must involve intense fear, helplessness, or horror. Furthermore, characteristic symptoms include persistent reexperiencing of the traumatic event, persistent avoidance of stimuli associated with the trauma, and numbing of general responsiveness. Finally, people with PTSD may also suffer from persistent symptoms of increased arousal such as irritability, hypervigilance, and exaggerated startle response.[40] While most AIDS mourners experience some of the symptoms of PTSD, including intrusive thinking and affective numbing, few meet the complete criteria for a diagnosis of PTSD.

Substance Abuse and Dependency

The relationship between substance abuse and HIV-related bereavement is a complex one. Substance abuse can be both a risk factor for bereavement distress and a negative outcome of painful bereavement. A sizable and growing proportion of people with

HIV disease have been infected as a result of unsafe injection drug use, and clinical observation suggests that those mourning the loss of these individuals are at increased risk for psychological distress. Because these mourners are more likely to have a current or past history of substance abuse and may also be HIV-infected, they are more likely to be isolated and stigmatized and to experience financial difficulties.

Research has documented an increased prevalence in alcohol, tobacco, and prescription and nonprescription drug use among mourners—including new users but more often among people already using substances.[41] The heavy use of mind-altering substances may interfere with successful bereavement in several ways. Using drugs and alcohol to anesthetize the pain of grief may block, delay, or prolong the mourning process. In short, substance dependency may be a maladaptive avoidance coping behavior that is used in lieu of more productive problem-solving and emotion-focused strategies.

AIDS Bereavement Interventions

In most cases of AIDS bereavement, individuals are able to manage the emotional and physical impact of grief with the support of their friends, family, and community. However, clinicians may be called on to assist individuals at every level of bereavement distress: uncomplicated mourning, uncomplicated mourning with risk factors, complicated mourning without psychological disorders, and complicated mourning with psychological disorders. Bereavement interventions available include preventive and educational approaches; small-group and individual counseling; grief-related psychotherapy; and medical and psychiatric treatment. As outlined in Table 12.1, clinicians should apply bereavement interventions according to the type of mourning a client experiences.

Preventive and Educational Approaches

Bereavement education—emphasizing the nature of bereavement, defining effective coping strategies, and encouraging a community-wide norm of support for mourners—can go far to assist mourners in coping with their grief and preventing bereavement-related

Table 12.1. Bereavement Intervention Based on Level of Distress.

Level of Distress	Bereavement Interventions			
Level One: Uncomplicated mourning without risk factors	AIDS bereavement education			
Level Two: Uncomplicated mourning with risk factors	AIDS bereavement education	Individual or group counseling		
Level Three: Complicated mourning without psychological disorder	AIDS bereavement education	Individual or group counseling	Grief-related psychotherapy	
Level Four: Complicated mourning with psychological disorder	AIDS bereavement education	Individual or group counseling	Grief-related psychotherapy	Psychiatric evaluation and treatment

problems. In the early stages of mourning, people often say that they are unprepared for the intensity of their feelings and the level of disruption and are relieved to hear that these experiences are normal.

Bereavement education, which is often provided through spiritual sources, may help mourners place death within an over-all religious or philosophical context, thus reducing the sense of alienation. Secular counselors must be sensitive to religious and cultural differences among mourners and should encourage mourners to find ways to cope with mourning consistent with their own religious, cultural, and personal values. A recent doctoral dissertation, completed as part of the Stanford study, found that of those mourners who considered themselves religious or spiritual, the ones who frequently participated in religious or spiritual activities coped better with bereavement than those who did not.[42]

Community-wide efforts to remove the stigma of HIV disease may decrease the reluctance of some mourners to request support. Programs designed to reduce the isolation of mourners, especially those who live outside the epicenters of the disease, are also important. Community-wide rituals, such as memorial services and candlelight parades, may offset the sense that those who have died have been devalued and forgotten.

Education of health care professionals should encourage sensitivity toward the loved ones of persons with HIV disease. Discussions with partners, family, and close friends early in the course of illness are helpful not only in assessing the quality of a patient's support system but also in validating the important role of loved ones in the patient's life, an act that can facilitate future grieving.

Problem-Oriented Individual and Group Counseling

In general, bereavement counseling seeks to help the survivor accept the reality of loss and express the feelings that accompany this realization. As a survivor is allowed to grieve at his or her own pace, in his or her own way, the emotional bond between the survivor and the deceased gradually changes, allowing the survivor to form new relationships with the living.

Time-limited, problem-oriented individual counseling—focused on tasks of grieving and on mitigating any risk factors—may be helpful to clients at all levels of bereavement distress. Shuchter and Zisook suggest that rather than viewing the goal of bereavement counseling to be the resolution of psychological attachment to the deceased, which may take several years, counseling should address specific grief-related problems with the understanding that the client can return if additional problems arise in later stages of bereavement.[43]

A common feature of AIDS bereavement counseling is addressing the issue of multiple loss or "bereavement overload."[44] Many mourners come to counseling feeling overwhelmed by the number of losses and may need assistance organizing their bereavement to focus on the most important losses. Others may need to separate losses in order to fully grieve each. Counselors should listen for hidden or unacknowledged losses, such as the sense of diminished freedoms or the loss of enjoyable sexual activities. Sometimes the fatigue of grief, in part due to the extended nature of the epidemic, wears individuals down. In such cases, mourners may welcome the suggestion of taking a "bereavement holiday" to focus on other matters for a period of time.

A range of small-group counseling strategies—from one-time lectures or workshops to ongoing counseling groups—can assist mourners. Research on the effectiveness of small groups in preventing bereavement complications has shown that interventions are most successful when they target mourners who demonstrate high levels of distress or specific risk factors. This research stresses the importance of the timing of the intervention: group intervention provided too soon—that is, within the first couple of weeks after loss—may have no positive effects or, as illustrated in one study, may even delay or interfere with the bereavement process.[45] Some programs provide group support for individuals in the later stages of mourning, for example, after the first year subsequent to the loss. These groups may be particularly helpful for people living in HIV epicenters where whole support systems have been decimated.

Bob: Multiple Loss

Bob, a thirty-nine-year-old seronegative gay man, came to counseling six months after the loss of his partner of twelve years, Tom. Bob was disturbed by periods of anguish, grief, and longing, interspersed with times when he felt emotionally numb. Bob had been a devoted caregiver during Tom's two-year illness with AIDS. Even so, at times he felt he had not done enough. During the time of Tom's illness, three close friends of Bob's died—two from AIDS and one from breast cancer.

Bob despaired. "Everyone's gone—there's no one left. I was so busy with Tom that I didn't have time for Quentin, Charlie, and Sarah. Now it's too late. I just wish life was the way it used to be."

Bob was estranged from his family of origin: "They never really accepted my being gay." During Tom's illness, Bob had isolated himself from other friends. Now, as he began to pick up the pieces of his life, he felt too embarrassed to reach out to them. Further, many of these friends were HIV-infected, and Bob reluctantly admitted that he did not feel up to the challenge of getting involved with people who might get sick. He felt alone, angry, stuck, and confused.

At his first session with his therapist, Paul Carpenter, L.C.S.W., Bob was surprised to hear himself express that at times he wished he had AIDS. "I can't stand the idea that I am going to spend the rest of my life taking care of and grieving for my friends." Carpenter listened empathically; Bob was relieved that Carpenter was not offended by these ideas, which Bob found shocking. Carpenter helped Bob recognize the risk factors that added to the distress of his mourning: isolation, multiple loss, caregiving exhaustion, shame and guilt, and the paradoxical effect of being seronegative. As the two spoke, Bob began to experience a wider range of emotions and to feel validated for his losses. At the end of the initial session, Bob agreed to participate in an eight-week course of bereavement counseling spread over a period of three months, and to attend an AIDS bereavement class to learn about the stages of mourning and about bereavement tasks and overload.

During his sessions with Carpenter, Bob reviewed each of the important losses, including his sense that his life as a gay man had been permanently altered. As he began to focus on each loss individually, he was surprised by some of the deep emotions he had suppressed. As Bob gained awareness of these emotions, he was relieved to find that he once again was able to experience strong feelings of affection for his deceased friends—even though he had not been able to participate in their final days.

Toward the end of the three-month course of counseling, Bob spent his final sessions with Carpenter developing ways to reach out to old friends as well as new ones. Bob joined a bereavement group to help him continue to work through his conflicted feelings about being seronegative and about his urge to avoid people with HIV disease. As he was ready to leave counseling, Bob noticed that he had a new level of energy and a cautious optimism for the future. He left knowing that there was still much mourning ahead of him yet feeling confident that help was available if he needed it.

Grief-Related Psychotherapy

Mourners who present with preexisting or recent onset of psychological disorders or those for whom the bereavement process is disrupted may require more intensive forms of psychotherapy. Grief-related psychotherapy may follow shortly after a death or may be required to treat delayed or chronic mourning, for which the loss may have occurred many years before.

Mardi Horowitz and his colleagues at the University of California, San Francisco, developed a time-limited (twelve-session) psychodynamic psychotherapy model to assist people experiencing instances of complicated mourning.[46] According to this model, in the aftermath of any stressful life event, certain processes must occur to facilitate assimilation, accommodation, and healthy resumption of living. Individuals must resolve the personal meanings of the stressful event, including its implications for relationships, self-image, and behavior. This process entails the individual's reappraising the event and revising his or her core models of self, role relationships, and future plans.

The primary goal of this intervention is to reduce the need for psychological defenses against awareness of ideas and images that lead to stress and intolerable emotional states. Therapy accomplishes this goal by helping mourners consciously connect their ideational responses to stressful events and their associated emotional responses. For clients experiencing denial or numbing, the therapeutic task is to encourage reexperiencing grief; for those who experience intrusive-repetitive thoughts or emotions, the task is to promote resolution or in some cases conscious distraction. One technique designed to give clients a sense of mastery is called "dosing," which entails reexperiencing a bereavement event and its meanings for a specific time, putting it out of mind for a period of time, and once again recalling the event.

Therese Rando describes the benefits of using rituals to enhance psychotherapy with mourners, both those who are in denial of their grief and those overwhelmed by grief.[47] A grief ritual is a formal activity that provides a time and a place to honor an important loss. Mourners may develop their own or opt to use rituals prescribed by their religious or cultural traditions. Through rituals, clients may combat the sense of helplessness accompanying grief and may find a legitimate form to express strong feelings. Clients blocked in their awareness and expression of grief may find that rituals provide a safe context in which to recall memories and the emotions associated with them. For clients having difficulty modulating the intrusion of strong memories or images, rituals may help delimit grief by providing a specific time and place for these painful mental phenomena.

Ralph: Ritual and Grief-Related Therapy

Ralph, a forty-seven-year-old Asian gay man, came to therapy four months after the death of Martin, his lover of five years, and three weeks after being discharged from the hospital for his first bout of *Pneumocystis carinii* pneumonia. Ralph exhibited intense grieving and rumination, repeatedly asking, "What am I going to do now? Who is going to take care of me?" Sometimes he sat motionless, numb beyond emotion. At other times, feeling out of control, he experienced extreme anxiety. Ralph spent much of his day crying and longing for his departed partner.

A thorough psychiatric assessment concluded that Ralph was suffering from major depression. After conferring with Ralph's primary physician, his therapist, Karen Morley, prescribed an antidepressant medication. She also began building rapport by undertaking a sympathetic review of Ralph's current medical situation. Through these discussions, Ralph began to understand the relationship between his grief and his own health predicament. Together Ralph and Morley developed a way for Ralph to spend some portion of the day honoring the memory of Martin; during the rest of the day Ralph was to redirect his attention away from painful memories. Each morning Ralph sat for thirty minutes in an area he had designated as a "shrine" and had consecrated with photographs and other items that elicited memories of Martin. Morley encouraged Ralph to speak—in a sense, to carry on a dialogue—with Martin or to write him letters. At the end of the thirty minutes, Ralph

was to say good-bye to Martin and remind himself that he would return
tomorrow.

Ralph was comforted by the ritual, which he saw as consistent with
his cultural tradition. The therapy sessions were used to assist Ralph in understanding the personal meanings of his loss and in coping with negative
thoughts and affects, and to encourage his reaching out to new people
through involvement in community bereavement groups.

After twelve sessions spread over sixteen weeks, Ralph felt more in control
of his life, his depressive symptoms were greatly reduced, and he was dating a
man he met at a bereavement group. He continued to use his shrine to mourn
his beloved partner.

Psychiatric and Medical Intervention

In order to respond to bereavement distress, providers must determine the relationships among mourning, psychological disorder, and physical disease. A thorough assessment, including a
careful history of physical and psychiatric symptoms, is crucial to
identifying preexisting disorders or vulnerabilities to disorder.

Although it is important to encourage mourners to experience
grief, some people may become emotionally overwhelmed and
may need assistance to tolerate intense grief. Whenever possible,
clinicians should apply nonpharmacological interventions such as
general relaxation exercises to reduce stress or behavioral approaches to reduce insomnia. When these approaches are not sufficient, judicious use of tranquilizers and sleeping medication may
be indicated.[48]

The use of psychotropic medications in the clinical management of bereavement is an area of great debate. Given the historic
misuse of medication to "calm" mourners, there is general suspicion about this approach among bereavement experts. "Although
some might argue that the use of psychotropic medications during bereavement is maladaptive in that these substances prevent
the bereaved from 'getting in touch with their true feelings' and
thereby block the resolution of grief, this position has not been validated by empirical data."[49]

Rando contends that failure to recognize and respect the reality that some mourners require psychotropic medication is as

detrimental as forcing medication without just cause.[50] She suggests that a treatment plan should include a careful medical examination as well as appropriate psychological and pharmacological management. If clinicians suspect suppression of or interference with grief, they should reconsider medication use, keeping in mind that medication should be used as an adjunct to psychological treatment and social support, not as a replacement for them.

☙

This chapter reviews the universal and unique challenges of HIV-related bereavement. Nowhere is the dual nature of bereavement so pronounced as it is for providers who assist people who mourn HIV-related losses. Many providers come from communities hardest hit by the epidemic and are themselves bereaved, mourning the loss of personal relationships and clients. Given the magnitude of the epidemic and the special circumstances surrounding AIDS, the potential for bereavement overload is immense. On the other hand, many providers have found ways to incorporate the profound universal lessons of life and death they have learned through the process into helping their clients and themselves find personal meaning in their lives.

Notes

1. Folkman, S., Chesney, M., Collette, L., and others. "Post-Bereavement Depressive Mood and Its Pre-Bereavement Predictors in HIV+ and HIV– Gay Men." *Journal of Personality and Social Psychology*, 1996, *70*(2), 336–348.

2. Centers for Disease Control and Prevention. "Update in Trends in AIDS Incidence, Deaths, and Prevalence—U.S., 1996." *Morbidity and Mortality Weekly Report*, 1997, *46*(8), 165–173.

3. Personal communication with clients and other mental health providers.

4. Lennon, M. J., Martin, J. L., and Dean, L. "The Influence of Social Support of AIDS-Related Grief Reaction Among Gay Men." *Social Sciences and Medicine*, 1990, *31*(4), 477–484.

5. Parkes, C. M., and Weiss, R. S. *Recovery from Bereavement*. New York: Basic Books, 1983.

6. Martin, J. L., and Dean, L. "Risk Factors for AIDS-Related Bereavement in a Cohort of Homosexual Men in New York City." In B. Cooper and

T. Helagason (eds.), *Epidemiology and the Prevention of Mental Disorders.* London: Routledge, 1989.

7. Ibid.

8. Erickson, S. "Social Support as Mediator of Emotional Well-Being in Gay Male Caregivers of Loved Ones with AIDS." *Dissertation Abstracts International,* 1993, *55*(7B), 3011.

9. Bowlby, J. "Loss: Sadness and Depression." In J. Bowlby, *Attachment and Loss.* Vol. 3. London: Hogarth Press, 1980.

10. Worden, J. W. *Grief Counseling and Grief Psychotherapy: A Handbook for the Mental Health Practitioner.* New York: Springer, 1982.

11. Martin, J. L., and Dean, L. "Effects of AIDS-Related Bereavement and HIV-Related Illness on Psychological Distress Among Gay Men: A 7-Year Longitudinal Study, 1985–1991." *Journal of Consulting and Clinical Psychology,* 1993, *61*, 94–103.

12. Ibid.

13. Erickson, "Social Support."

14. Martin and Dean, "Risk Factors for AIDS-Related Bereavement."

15. Ibid.

16. Neugebauer, R., Rabkin, J. G., Williams, J. B., and others. "Bereavement Reactions Among Homosexual Men Experiencing Multiple Losses in the AIDS Epidemic." *American Journal of Psychiatry,* 1992, *149*(10), 1374–1379.

17. Erickson, "Social Support."

18. O'Brien, K. "Primary Relationships." Unpublished manuscript, Department of Psychology, Portland State University, 1992.

19. Erickson, "Social Support."

20. O'Brien, "Primary Relationships."

21. Nolen-Hoeksema, S., Parker, L., and Larson, J. "The Blessings and Burdens of Social Ties: Social Support and Well-Being in Family Members of the Terminally Ill." Unpublished manuscript, Department of Psychology, Stanford University, 1992.

22. Erickson, "Social Support."

23. Herek, G. M. "Psychological Heterosexism in the United States." In A. R. D'Augelli and C. J. Patterson (eds.), *Lesbian, Gay, and Bisexual Identities over the Lifespan.* New York: Oxford University Press, 1995.

24. Ibid.

25. Bandura, A. *Social Foundations of Thought and Action.* Upper Saddle River, N.J.: Prentice Hall, 1986.

26. Peterson, C., and Seligman, M.E.P. "Causal Explanations as a Risk Factor for Depression: Theory and Evidence." *Psychology Review,* 1984, *91*, 347–374.

27. Erickson, "Social Support."

28. Lazarus, R. S., and Folkman, S. *Stress Appraisal and Coping.* New York: Springer, 1984.
29. Nolen-Hoeksema, S., Parker, L., and Larson, J. "Coping with Negative Emotion Following Loss." Unpublished manuscript, Department of Psychology, Stanford University, 1992.
30. Ibid.
31. Martin, J. L., and Dean, L. "Bereavement Following the Death from AIDS: Unique Problems, Reactions, and Special Needs." In M. Stroebe, W. Stroebe, and R. Hansson (eds.), *Handbook of Bereavement: Theory, Research, and Intervention.* Cambridge: Cambridge University Press, 1993.
32. Nolen-Hoeksema, S., and Morrow, J. "A Prospective Study of Depression and Post-Traumatic Stress Symptoms After a Natural Disaster: The 1989 Loma Prieta Earthquake." *Journal of Personality and Social Psychology,* 1991, *61*(1), 115–121.
33. Bowlby, "Loss."
34. Martin and Dean, "Bereavement Following the Death from AIDS."
35. Zisook, S., and Shuchter, S. R. "Depression Through the First Year After the Death of a Spouse." *American Journal of Psychiatry,* 1991, *148,* 1346–1352.
36. Ibid.
37. Rando, T. A. *Treatment of Complicated Mourning.* Champaign, Ill.: Research Press, 1993.
38. Jacobs, S., and Grim, K. "Psychiatric Complications of Bereavement." *Psychiatric Annals,* 1990, *20,* 314–317.
39. Rando, *Treatment of Complicated Mourning.*
40. American Psychiatric Association. *Diagnostic and Statistical Manual of Mental Disorders.* (4th ed.) Washington, D.C.: American Psychiatric Association, 1994, p. 428.
41. Osterveis, M., Solomon, F., and Green, M. (eds.). *Bereavement: Reactions, Consequences, and Care.* Washington, D.C.: National Academy Press, 1984.
42. Costello, C. L. "Religion and AIDS-Related Bereavement: A Study of Partners and Family Members." *Dissertation Abstracts International,* 1993, *54*(6B), 3335.
43. Shuchter, S. R., and Zisook, S. "Hovering over the Bereaved." *Psychiatric Annals,* 1990, *20,* 327–333.
44. Rando, *Treatment of Complicated Mourning.*
45. Osterveis, Solomon, and Green, *Bereavement.*
46. Horowitz, M. J. *Stress Response Syndromes.* (2nd ed.) Northvale, N.J.: Aronson, 1986.
47. Rando, T. A. "Creating Therapeutic Rituals in the Psychotherapy of Bereaved." *Psychotherapy,* 1985, *22,* 236–240.

48. Barton, D. "The Process of Grief." In D. Barton (ed.), *Dying and Death: A Clinical Guide to Caregivers.* Baltimore: Williams & Wilkins, 1977.
49. Zisook, S., Shuchter, S. R., and Mulvehill, M. "Alcohol, Cigarette, and Medication Use During the First Year of Widowhood." *Psychiatric Annals,* 1990, *20,* 318–326.
50. Rando, *Treatment of Complicated Mourning.*

Chapter Thirteen

Personality Disorders and HIV Disease

The Borderline Patient

Michele Killough Nelson
Rochelle L. Klinger

Clients with mental disorders may face significant barriers to obtaining and maintaining care for their HIV disease. Mental disorders can, by themselves, create impediments to accessing HIV-related medical care and antiviral treatment, complicate the doctor-physician relationship, and decrease adherence to complicated drug combinations. Because mental disorders may also reduce impulse control, clients with these disorders may also have difficulty conforming regularly to safer sex and needle-sharing practices.

Among those people with mental disorders who face the greatest challenge both in terms of prevention and care are people with personality disorders.[1,2,3] Using the borderline personality disorder as a lens, this chapter offers a view of what it is like to interact with seropositive clients with serious mental disorders. It reviews the epidemiology, etiology, and clinical manifestations of borderline personality disorder and emphasizes the role and process of psychotherapy with borderline clients. It also examines the ways in which the health care team working with these clients can maximize the delivery of appropriate services and minimize the occurrence of problems.

Defining Borderline Personality Disorder

Borderline personality disorder is characterized by volatile emotional states and emotional emptiness, poor impulse control, difficult and often stormy interpersonal relationships, and problems with anger management. These characteristics make borderline clients difficult to treat in psychotherapy. Borderline clients typically require more planning, structure, emotional energy, and time than other clients and may therefore strain therapists and drain a disproportionate amount of resources away from psychologically healthier clients.

Epidemiological studies estimate the prevalence of borderline personality disorder as 0.2 percent to 10 percent in the general population and 15 percent among psychiatric clients.[4,5,6] Approximately 76 percent of borderline clients are female.[7,8] A 1993 study found a 33 percent incidence of personality disorder (mostly borderline) among HIV-infected gay men versus 15 percent among seronegative gay male controls.[9] The investigators concluded that borderline individuals may be more prone to contract HIV due to impulsive, unsafe behaviors. This finding also suggests that the problem of borderline personality disorder in HIV-infected clients will continue to be significant.

Borderline clients seldom come into psychotherapy on their own unless they are in crisis. Once the crisis has passed, however, they often flee. It is more likely that HIV-infected borderline clients will be pushed into psychotherapy by their health care providers, who feel frustrated and angry with them. Mental health workers who practice in medical settings, therefore, may have longer periods of contact with borderline clients than providers who work in other settings. Borderline clients may also present for treatment in private practice settings if they have adequate financial resources or if they want to avoid seeing a therapist at their medical center.

Given the difficulties inherent in working with these clients, it is important to be familiar with the most common forms of their psychopathology. This familiarity can help therapists better understand the undeveloped personality structure common among these clients and use this knowledge to develop an appropriate and focused treatment plan. Taken as a group, people with borderline personality organization can span the spectrum from relatively high functioning to low functioning, but a common feature is that their lives are constantly troubled by difficulties in relating to others. Although this difficulty often impedes their ability to form healthy working relationships with therapists, it does not preclude the possibility of significant progress in psychotherapy. But it does necessitate careful evaluation of a client's level of functioning in order to set appropriate goals and to understand the strengths that can be used as foundations to help the client reach these goals.

Personality disorders are inflexible, maladaptive ways of perceiving or relating to the interpersonal environment that cause functional impairment or subjective distress in an individual. These disorders—including, for example, narcissistic, antisocial, and histrionic personality disorders—are long-standing, characteristic ways of relating to the world, typically emerging in childhood or adolescence and continuing throughout adult life. They are enduring characteristics, not present only at times of distress. This makes a longitudinal history essential to the diagnosis of personality disorders, especially if a person is first seen at a time of great distress such as during HIV-related illnesses.[10] All of these disorders represent exaggerated styles of interacting with others and significantly interfere with a person's ability to have positive, lasting relationships and to have accurate self-concepts.[11,12]

The *DSM-IV* categorizes borderline personality disorder under Cluster B Personality Disorders, which include clients who are often dramatic, erratic, or emotional.[13] The diagnostic criteria include a pervasive and long-standing pattern of instability of mood, identity, and relationships. Identity disturbance leads to feelings of emptiness and boredom; mood instability manifests as rapid swings in demeanor. Impulsive, self-destructive behaviors can also be part of this constellation. (See Exhibit 13.1 for the *DSM-IV* diagnostic criteria for borderline personality disorder.) Although all personality disorders involve chronic maladaptive behavior patterns, borderline personality disorder is characterized in particular by disturbed interpersonal relationships, poor impulse control, a heightened potential for repeated self-injury, and an increased fear of being alone.[14]

Borderline personality disorder is often coupled with substance abuse or uncertainty about sexual orientation or gender. These may offer additional signs of a client's feelings of emptiness

Exhibit 13.1. Diagnostic Criteria for Borderline Personality Disorder.

A pervasive pattern of instability of interpersonal relationships, self-image, and affects, and marked impulsivity beginning by early adulthood and present in a variety of contexts, as indicated by five (or more) of the following:

1. Frantic efforts to avoid real or imagined abandonment. (Does not include suicidal or self-mutilating behavior covered in Criterion 5.)

2. A pattern of unstable and intense interpersonal relationships characterized by alternation between extremes of idealization and devaluation

3. Identity disturbance: markedly and persistently unstable self-image or sense of self

4. Impulsivity in at least two areas that are potentially self-damaging, for example, spending, sex, substance abuse, reckless driving, and binge eating. (Does not include suicidal or self-mutilating behavior covered in Criterion 5.)

5. Recurrent suicidal behaviors, gestures, threats, or self-mutilation behavior

6. Affective instability due to a marked reactivity of mood, for example, intense episodic dysphoria, irritability, or anxiety, usually lasting a few hours and only rarely more than a few days

7. Chronic feeling of emptiness

8. Inappropriate, intense anger or difficulty controlling anger, for example, frequent displays of temper, constant anger, recurrent physical fights

9. Transient, stress-related paranoid ideation or severe dissociative symptoms

Source: Reprinted with permission from the *Diagnostic and Statistical Manual of Mental Disorders, Fourth Edition.* Copyright 1994 American Psychiatric Association.

and difficulties with coping. Adjustment disorders and Major Depression are also often seen in clients diagnosed with borderline personality disorder.[15] This is especially true for HIV-infected borderline clients, who must cope with a threat to life and who may harbor repressed anger toward others and themselves for their current health situation.

Psychodynamic and object relations theorists postulate that the disorder is rooted in the child's unsuccessful struggle to separate and differentiate during the first eighteen months of life. This failure may be the result of constitutional aspects of the child, or of the behavior of a parent or parents or other primary caregivers (for example, custodial grandparents). Many, but not all, borderline clients come from families with a history of extreme neglect or abuse. In addition, within these families there is frequently a historic inability on the part of caregivers to let the child grow up independently.[16,17]

Another theory, which has gained less acceptance in the literature, suggests that borderline personality disorder is a subtype of the affective disorders, with mood instability manifesting as dysfunctional behavior. In response, theorists who propose this explanation advocate vigorous pharmacological treatment for affective pathology in borderline clients.[18,19]

Diagnosing Borderline Personality Disorder

Unfortunately, few borderline clients present clinically with a neat list of *DSM-IV* criteria. More frequently, the borderline pathology declares itself in a dramatic and unexpected fashion. Certain features, however, can tip off therapists to the borderline personality disorder.

One clue is that borderline clients often present with stories of other institutions and providers who have "done them wrong." In characteristic fashion, they may idealize a new provider or clinic at first, saying things like, "I know you can help me. . . . You're the only doctor who understands me." Providers should be wary of this kind of idealization, especially if it comes early in the course of the provider-client relationship, and they should be prepared for a later devaluation of their relationship. Initially inflating the value of therapists allows clients to feel more comfortable asking for help and expecting results. Their sense of emptiness and fear of rejection make them sad and frightened, and attaching to someone else (such as a therapist) is a way to fill this void. The overwhelming needs of borderline clients, however, make it impossible for providers to live up to clients' expectations. If these issues are not addressed early in the course of therapy, it is likely that clients will feel abandoned when they are inevitably disappointed by their therapists.

When members of a treatment team are split about whether a client is likable, this may be a clue that the client is borderline. Borderline clients who engender strong opposing feelings in members of the team are often using projective identification, a mechanism by which a client projects irreconcilable conflicts onto others, who then act them out for him or her. Thus, one member of the team may defend the client while another berates him, resulting in a struggle within the team.

It is interesting to note that the term *borderline* was originally used to define clients who seemed to fall between the categories of neurotic and psychotic. This heterogeneous grouping included clients with early schizophrenia or affective disorders, as well as clients who would be defined with borderline personality disorder by current standards. Often these were people who had brief episodes of psychosis under stress, particularly interpersonal stress. However, psychosis did not have to be present for a client to fulfill borderline criteria.[20,21,22] The following case example illustrates a common presentation of a person with borderline personality disorder. The case will be revisited in the treatment section of this chapter.

Maurice: Presentation

Maurice is a thirty-four-year-old gay African American man who presented to Anne Graham, a psychologist, for an intake interview. He was referred by the staff at the infectious disease clinic because of problems with missed appointments, demanding behavior, volatile mood, difficulties getting along with the staff, and vague but recurrent suicidal threats.

Maurice arrived early and was surprised when told that Graham could not see him until his appointment time. When she came out for him, he commented on how he had waited in the lobby for a long time, but then began talking about how good it was to meet her and how many nice things he had heard about her. He told her that his life had been difficult because "everyone's gone out of their way to do me wrong." He went on to describe several situations in which others had taken advantage of him.

Maurice was upset about his recent AIDS diagnosis and, consistent with his perceptions of the past, felt that everyone was abandoning him. He said that no one came to visit him in the hospital when he was ill, and he complained that he felt constantly misunderstood by his friends and most of his family, who had rejected him when he disclosed his homosexuality. The only positive relationships he described were with his grandmother, who had died, and a new lover, who was "wonderful" and whom he had been dating for two weeks. Maurice also told Graham that he had had many lovers in the past and described a series of intense relationships cut short as each boyfriend disappointed him. Maurice said it was no wonder that he had been driven to drink and use drugs—everything from speed to heroin.

Maurice acknowledged difficulties getting along with the staff at the infectious disease clinic. He felt they saw him as "just another number." He boasted that skipping appointments was a good way to let them know that he did not care about them either. Maurice said he sometimes felt suicidal, primarily because of loneliness and frustration over his declining health. He said he told the staff at the clinic about this but did not believe they cared enough to do anything about it.

Maurice thought psychotherapy might help him deal with all these feelings. His goal was to confront people who had wronged him. He said that he might be interested in having a session with his parents so that he could tell them how much they had hurt him and to see if they could work things out. Maurice was also concerned that he might become depressed during the course of his illness and hoped that therapy might stop this from happening. Finally, he wanted to talk about dying, which sometimes "terrified" him, particularly when he was trying to go to sleep at night.

Clinical Features and Challenges in Treatment

Most psychotherapists feel challenged and frustrated when working with clients diagnosed with borderline personality disorder. These clients are difficult and time-consuming to manage, and the literature is unclear about whether anything other than limited improvement can be expected even with the best treatment. Clients with both borderline personality disorder and HIV disease often experience a magnification of borderline symptoms because they have difficulty coping with the added emotional, financial, and interpersonal stressors that a serious medical illness imposes. There are four key clinical issues for therapists treating borderline clients with HIV disease:

- Helping the client secure whatever resources—medical, financial, or social—that will help minimize stressors
- Improving interpersonal skills to facilitate the development of healthy relationships
- Teaching the client ways to reduce self-injurious behaviors and increase positive, adaptive ones
- Addressing the client's feelings in a way that promotes open discussion and exploration of issues

Interpersonal relationships are difficult for all borderline clients to maintain. Volatile mood, tendencies toward splitting (pitting one provider against another), poor impulse control, and a demanding nature preclude healthy, lasting relationships and instead result in alienation from others. HIV-infected borderline clients experience new and increasing needs, including the need for regular medical care and for external financial support because of their decreased ability to work. They are, however, often unable to work effectively within the social services system to get their needs met because they alienate even the most patient professionals.

HIV-infected borderline clients have more trouble maintaining positive relationships than other borderline clients because of HIV-related stigma and rejection. Their problems with impulse control and desire for immediate gratification may cause others to fear that these clients will act irresponsibly and spread the virus. This injects skepticism and anxiety into the clinical relationship, sabotaging trust. In addition, health concerns and legitimate needs for attention are often camouflaged by the chaos of the client's life and his or her anger about having become infected.

This profile is especially trying for mental health professionals because these clients have difficulty processing and resolving issues. It can seem as if the same themes—for example, "I am the victim"—

repeatedly play out in therapy, leaving therapists with the sense that there has been no real progress. As clients get more frustrated with their declining health or with the perceived lack of cooperation and support from others, it is likely that they will create chaos and conflict in an attempt to avoid dealing with these painful issues. Such chaos may take the form of calling repeatedly, missing appointments, or behaving in a seductive fashion toward the therapist. Exploring these actions with clients will be helpful, but it may also be beneficial to make appropriate accommodations to the physical realities of declining health, for example, hospital or home visits.[23]

HIV-infected borderline clients are often more sensitive to abandonment issues than other people with borderline personality disorder; in order to get their needs met, they may try to play physicians, nurses, and therapists against one another, alternately devaluing and idealizing these practitioners. This "splitting" may be the only way that borderline clients can deal with their inability to see the middle ground between the extremes of good and bad in themselves and others.[24,25] It is important to note that there need not be a treatment team for splitting to occur. Clients may introduce other people from their lives—a lover or parent—and use them against the therapist. For example, a client may complain that his lover gives him insufficient attention in hopes of having the therapist respond by increasing the number or length of sessions.

Although society has become more understanding and less condemning of people with HIV disease, there remains an expectation that clients will behave responsibly to protect their own health and that of others. This is difficult for HIV-infected borderline clients, because they do not like to be told what to do. Borderline clients tend to live in the moment and have difficulty planning ahead. They often express resentment that HIV-specific resources are linked to expectations about their behavior. These clients see authority figures and resource allocators as biased against them and, at best, have ambivalent relationships with such people. These same issues are usually played out during therapy sessions, and the attachments between these clients and their therapists are fraught with ambivalence, resentment, and strong dependency needs.

Feelings of emptiness and boredom are typical for all borderline clients. As borderline clients begin to grapple with HIV disease, however, many experience these feelings in a new way, often recognizing that their lives have not been what they had hoped. Some clients describe themselves as "hollow" or "empty" and express great sadness about this realization. They also realize that their lives will be shorter than they expected and that they may not have the chance to make changes they would have liked to make. For some clients, dealing with these existential issues can precipitate a major depression or a desire to escape from what they perceive as the futility of their lives. It is important to monitor these feelings because such borderline clients can easily become suicidal; and because they have difficulty controlling their impulses, they are more likely to act on these inclinations.

Other clients may respond to their illness by experiencing an existential shift that promotes positive change and growth. It is also important to note, however, that even when clients desire to make positive changes, they frequently do not have the coping skills to implement these changes.

Finally, in considering treatment issues, psychopharmacology offers some options that should not be completely forgotten. As noted previously, the affective instability and chronic dysthymia so common in these clients can lead to the development of major depressive disorders. In such instances, treatment with antidepressants is often helpful. Similarly, complaints of severe anxiety and difficulties with insomnia can sometimes be helped by neuroleptic drugs.

Psychotherapy and the Therapeutic Relationship

There is limited research on the effectiveness of psychotherapy with borderline clients. Controlled outcome studies are rare, and at present no single approach is generally accepted to be more or less effective than other approaches. Otto Kernberg, who has written extensively about his experiences with traditional and nontraditional psychoanalytic psychotherapy with borderline clients, suggests that focusing on transference and the clinical manifestations of defense mechanisms is most useful.[26,27,28] Aaron Beck, a cognitive-behavioral psychotherapist, focuses more on developing a working relationship with the client, decreasing dichotomous and distorted thinking, gaining control over emotions and impulses that often lead the client to participate in self-destructive behaviors, and strengthening the client's self-concept.[29] Neither author, however, presents significant empirical data to support his position.

Considering how frustrating and difficult it can be to work with borderline clients with HIV disease, it is helpful to remember that it is unlikely that therapy will alter a client's basic personality structure. Instead, the therapy process generally seeks to strengthen adaptive behaviors and coping mechanisms to improve quality of life. The therapist accomplishes this by providing constant feedback to help clients identify and generalize acceptable behaviors. During this process, the therapist also labels maladaptive behaviors and coping mechanisms and encourages clients to avoid them. It is also beneficial for the therapist to help clients learn to anticipate the consequences of their behaviors. For example, if a client asks for money from her mother to pay the rent and does not act appropriately appreciative—that is, she does not say thank you or try to make arrangements to pay it back—then it is unlikely her mother will want to lend her money again. Introducing clients to basic social skills and simple social situations can help them understand similar and more complex situations.

It is important to remember that although most clients desire to live more positive, productive lives, this desire is insufficient to effect true change. Good intentions without good coping skills usually lead to feelings of frustration and disappointment, which often result in a resumption of previous maladaptive behaviors. Basic social and coping skills are a necessary foundation for achieving long-term change.

The therapeutic relationship is perhaps the most significant tool in the treatment of clients with personality disorders. Although HIV-infected borderline clients commonly have numerous difficulties with interpersonal relationships, they usually do not understand their roles in these interactions. Therapists can use the safety of the therapeutic alliance to help clients explore their feelings about relationships.

Therapists need to give clients constant and carefully phrased feedback and to remain open to feedback from clients. Being mindful that clients will relate to therapists in the same way they relate to others can enable therapists to respond appropriately when clients express ambivalent, conflicted, and angry feelings toward them. This knowledge can also help therapists provide immediate feedback to clients when they begin to inject chaos into the therapeutic relationship; this feedback allows clients to examine the emotional origins of their behaviors, which in turn helps clients understand the angry, rejecting responses of others and allows them to alter the situation and move forward. It is most easily undertaken by commenting on the therapeutic process rather than by directly addressing the content of what clients are saying or doing. For example, if the client misses two appointments and shows up late to the third, it is best not to engage in an argument but instead to ask what was happening that the client was avoiding psychotherapy.

Interpersonal group psychotherapy has also been useful in treating some HIV-infected borderline clients. These groups focus on helping clients learn how to interact with others in appropriate ways by providing feedback about interpersonal style and encouraging participants to modify these styles within the group. Despite the pain this process may elicit, clients usually find that this immediate feedback helps them understand the effects of their behaviors on others. Providing both positive and negative constructive feedback can minimize the emotional resistance. Borderline clients may find these groups difficult, because they must "share" the therapist with others and do not receive the therapist's undivided attention. It is important for therapists to prepare individual clients ahead of time about what is expected from them and what they can expect from the group.

Some clients will benefit from both group and individual psychotherapy, either concurrently or sequentially. In these situations, it is best to have two therapists involved so that clients do not feel that their individual therapists owe them special favors within the group and so they understand that the confidentiality of their private sessions is being preserved. In such a situation, clients should be informed that the individual and group therapists will regularly communicate, both to provide a unified treatment approach and to limit opportunities for splitting.

Finally, it is important to recognize that most therapists, no matter how patient, become frustrated working with borderline clients. Recognizing and exploring negative countertransference allows therapists to use their reactions to better understand clients' effects on others and to gain additional information for treatment planning. It is also necessary for therapists to process these feelings in formal or informal supervision, consultation, or personal psychotherapy, and to discuss them with the other team members.[30] Failing to do so may lead to frustration with the client and the therapeutic process.

Maurice: Treatment

During their first session, when Maurice told Graham about his terror of dying, his hope of reconciling with his parents despite his anger toward them, and his desire to confront those who had wronged him, Graham encouraged Maurice to discuss these feelings. She listened supportively, asked questions to clarify his statements as necessary, and learned more about his previous relationships, his substance use, and his family. The last fifteen minutes of the session were spent planning treatment goals, including considering ways to improve Maurice's medical compliance, discussing how to get his needs met by others in more appropriate ways, and talking about improving his relationship with his family.

Maurice agreed to compile a list of his concerns and questions about his medical condition for the next session. Maurice signed a release so that Graham could talk to his health care providers. Graham made it clear that she wanted to coordinate with the treatment team and share information as appropriate. Maurice asked if they could set up a meeting with his team in the near future. Graham encouraged him to wait until he had discussed his list of concerns with her first.

Graham and Maurice also discussed options to improve his social support, and Graham agreed to get information about local support groups for him and bring it to the next session. The two agreed to meet weekly and focus on helping him both process his feelings and better manage some of his practical concerns.

Graham recognized that working with Maurice would require a slow and careful approach. She knew her task would be to try to sustain his good feeling toward her; at the same time, she acknowledged to herself that she would inevitably disappoint him whenever she did not comply with his wishes or "failed" to intervene with his medical team to get him what he wanted. Graham hoped, however, that by anticipating problems, by explaining to Maurice what she could and could not be relied on to do, and by being explicit and consistent in her approach, she would be able to help him manage his feelings.

Responding to Chaos

In approaching borderline clients with HIV disease, therapists should consider paying special attention to two central issues. First, it is important to stay calm and aloof from the chaos borderline clients create. To minimize the effects of the chaos clients will inject into the therapeutic relationship, therapists must set firm and consistent limits with clients and carefully outline the client's and therapist's responsibilities. This is often done by using contingency contracts. Therapists may use these contracts to outline specific client requirements, including that the client be on time, call at least twenty-four hours in advance to cancel or change an appointment time, or complete homework assignments. The contract should clearly spell out the consequences of compliance or noncompliance. For example, clients may have to pay for missed sessions, or psychotherapy may be terminated if an individual misses three or more sessions.

Second, if clients bring chaos into the therapeutic relationship, they may succeed in baiting the therapist into conflict, thereby gaining inappropriate control. Often, the end result of such conflict is that negative countertransference obliterates an objective view of the situation. Arguing with clients, even borderline clients at their most contentious, is inadvisable because it shifts the focus of therapy from the client's well-being to the dynamics of a power struggle.

Borderline clients will also often try to create conflict to get out of situations that are unfavorable to them. For example, a client may reframe a therapist's comment about inappropriate behavior as a personal criticism—"You don't like me"—thereby shifting the focus away from the behavior. Although borderline clients are not particularly adept at managing conflict or chaos, they understand that others are not either. This maladaptive coping mechanism allows them to maintain control over situations by shifting the attention where they want it. As described earlier, it is helpful to focus on the process rather than on the content of the conflict.

At other times, especially in group psychotherapy, clients will try to shift the focus onto themselves if they believe they are not the center of attention. Rather than directly asking for assistance, they may dominate conversations, behave inappropriately, or test limits to ensure that their needs are met. Again, pointing this out in a matter-of-fact, nonjudgmental way while it is happening will provide useful feedback and allow clients to ask for attention in more appropriate ways. Engaging in an argument will only escalate the situation and result in the client's becoming the center of attention.

Further, counselors working with borderline clients with HIV disease must contend not only with a serious psychiatric disorder but also with a serious medical illness. It is important for therapists to be familiar with the symptoms and course of both conditions. In particular, it is often necessary to distinguish between real medical problems and ones clients fabricate or report for secondary gain, for example, as attempts to get attention or to shift attention from such problematic behaviors as drinking or using drugs.

Team Management of Borderline Clients with HIV Disease

The medical, psychological, and social complexities of HIV disease usually necessitate the involvement of multiple providers and disciplines. This is particularly true at teaching hospitals where many people with HIV disease receive care. The team approach is a strength in the care of this population, but it can also be a liability in managing HIV-infected borderline clients who employ splitting and projective identification. In these settings, it may be most useful for therapists to serve as consultants to the treatment team rather than as counselors to clients.

The most important goal in providing care in institutions is to establish clear communication among treatment team members.[31] The first step is to assemble the team for a network meeting, or case conference, about the client. It is critical that all the primary providers are there, including the primary physician, nurse, and social worker. With especially difficult clients, assigning a primary contact person to the client will minimize opportunities for splitting. The network meeting also serves to defuse tension and gives the team an opportunity to vent frustrations.[32]

It is often necessary for mental health professionals to educate the treatment team about the features of borderline personality disorder and to help develop a treatment plan specifying treatment goals and client and staff responsibilities. In general, these plans structure as many aspects of team-client interactions as possible. For example, client responsibilities may include coming to appointments on time, taking medications regularly and as prescribed, monitoring and reporting physical changes, communicating complaints to appropriate parties, and asking for help directly when it is needed. If clients call repeatedly and inappropriately, the team should establish and enforce telephone limits. If clients begin trying to split staff, staff should directly acknowledge this behavior and encourage clients to speak directly with team members about their concerns. Staff responsibilities may include responding to clients' requests for help as soon as possible and seeing clients on time.

Team management of borderline clients must seek to balance the authentic medical, psychological, and practical needs of clients while setting reasonable limits for staff. As client needs change, the treatment plan should be appropriately modified. By providing clients with copies of their treatment plans, staff ensure that client needs are addressed; clarify responsibilities and commitments; and minimize opportunities for clients to act out to gain attention, split staff, or receive material gains. The following case example illustrates the value of appropriate team management.

Janine

Janine is a twenty-six-year-old White woman who found out she was HIV-infected two years ago when her six-month-old son Ronald became ill with AIDS. She and her boyfriend, Roger, also seropositive, have a long history of injection cocaine and crack abuse and were probably infected by sharing needles. They continue to use crack intermittently. In addition to Ronald, Janine has a seven-year-old daughter, Mary, who is uninfected. Ronald has been seriously ill with recurrent pneumonia and failure to thrive. Janine and Roger have been in relatively good health.

Janine was concerned about Ronald's health, and hospital staff initially viewed her interest as supportive. However, her behavior quickly became demanding and erratic. She alternately idealized then devalued different providers on the treatment team. She called several times a day to demand time, attention, money, and supplies, such as diapers and bus tickets, from administrative as well as clinical staff.

When her physician set limits on her interactions, she went outside the clinic to complain to hospital administrators and to other community institutions. Naturally, when she approached community groups claiming that her sick child was not receiving adequate care, they responded by confronting clinic staff.

Angry at Janine and concerned about Ronald, the team called in a psychiatrist, Susan Paterno, M.D., to consult about the case. Paterno organized a network meeting in which team members voiced frustrations and concerns. The team then assigned Janine and Ronald a primary nurse, physician, and social worker to manage the case. They arranged a schedule of visits to the clinic and informed Janine that she should contact her social worker no more than once a day, except in the case of medical emergency. They also developed a diaper distribution schedule to address Janine's concerns about this issue. The team distributed the plan to Janine and to all staff, including the frontline clerical staff and hospital administration.

At first, Janine tested how serious the staff were about enforcing the contract. For example, she approached the front desk clerk, Ellen, to ask for diapers when she knew she was not scheduled to get them for several days. Ellen, who was aware of the contract, politely excused herself and spoke with Janine's social worker, John, to ensure that the schedule had not been changed. Ellen and John then spoke to Janine to remind her about the contract, make sure there was no medical emergency, and reiterate the terms of the contract. When the staff repeatedly affirmed the contract, Janine settled in and followed it most of the time. Her satisfaction, Ronald's care, and the staff's frustration level were much improved.

Paterno held follow-up network meetings at regular intervals to support staff and help them enforce the plan. At one point, staff members became lax about the rules, and Janine returned to some of her old behaviors, but the team was able to resume the plan with good results. It is important to note that administrative staff—who dealt with Janine more than clinical staff—were critical players in the implementation of the plan.

∽✤⌇

Working with HIV-infected borderline clients is a difficult and challenging task even for the most experienced clinicians. This population provides unique challenges because of the complexities of their medical and psychiatric disorders. Providers must recognize and process the interpersonal and practical problems, the stigma of the disease, and the feelings of emptiness borderline clients face. Reasonable but firm boundaries and limits are crucial to avoid the chaos that borderline clients inject into therapeutic relationships.

Individual and group psychotherapy are generally helpful for borderline clients, and including mental health professionals in treatment teams can manage these clients in institutional settings. With borderline clients more than others, therapeutic goals must take into account physical limitations, clients' ability to work in therapy, and their desire for change.

Notes

1. Clarkin, J. F., and others. "Anti-Social Traits as Modifiers of Treatment Response in Borderline Inpatients." *Journal of Psychotherapy Practice and Research,* 1994, *3*(4), 307–319.
2. Perkins, D. O., Davidson, E. J., Leserman, J., and others. "Personality Disorders in Patients Infected with HIV: A Controlled Study with Implications for Clinical Care." *American Journal of Psychiatry,* 1993, *150,* 309–315.
3. Beck, A., and Freeman, A. *Cognitive Therapy of Personality Disorders.* New York: Guilford Press, 1990.
4. Widiger, T. A., and Weisman, M. M. "Epidemiology of Borderline Personality Disorder." *Hospital and Community Psychiatry,* 1991, *42*(10), 1015–1021.
5. Swartz, M., Blazer, D., George, L., and Winfield, I. "Estimating the Prevalence of Borderline Personality Disorder in the Community." *Journal of Personality Disorders,* 1990, *4*(3), 257–272.
6. Searight, H. R. "Borderline Personality Disorder: Diagnosis and Management in Primary Care." *Journal of Family Practice,* 1992, *34*(5), 605–612.
7. Widiger and Weisman, "Epidemiology of Borderline Personality Disorder."
8. Swartz, Blazer, George, and Winfield, "Estimating the Prevalence of Borderline Personality Disorder."
9. Perkins, Davidson, Leserman, and others, "Personality Disorders in Patients Infected with HIV."
10. American Psychiatric Association. *Diagnostic and Statistical Manual of Mental Disorders.* (4th ed.) Washington, D.C.: American Psychiatric Association, 1994.

11. Beck and Freeman, *Cognitive Therapy of Personality Disorders.*
12. Shapiro, D. *Neurotic Styles.* New York: Basic Books, 1965.
13. American Psychiatric Association, *DSM-IV.*
14. Searight, "Borderline Personality Disorder."
15. Maier, W., Lichtermann, D., Klingler, T., and Heun, R. "Prevalence of Personality Disorders in the Community." *Journal of Personality Disorders,* 1992, *6*(3), 187–196.
16. Kernberg, O. *Borderline Conditions and Pathological Narcissism.* Northvale, N.J.: Aronson, 1975.
17. Groves, J. E. "Patients with Borderline Personality Disorder." In N. H. Cassem (ed.), *The MGH Handbook of General Hospital Psychiatry.* (3rd ed.) St. Louis, Mo.: Mosby-Year Book, 1991.
18. Gunderson, J. G., and Singer, J. T. "Defining Borderline Patients." *American Journal of Psychiatry,* 1975, *132,* 1–10.
19. Eversole, T. "Psychotherapy and Counseling: Bending the Frame." In M. G. Winiarski (ed.), *HIV Mental Health for the 21st Century.* New York: New York University Press, 1997.
20. Kernberg, *Borderline Conditions.*
21. Groves, "Patients with Borderline Personality Disorder."
22. Gunderson and Singer, "Defining Borderline Patients."
23. Eversole, "Psychotherapy and Counseling."
24. Groves, "Patients with Borderline Personality Disorder."
25. Akiskal, H. S., Hirschfeld, R.M.A., and Yerevenian, B. "The Relationship of Personality to Affective Disorders." *Archives of General Psychiatry,* 1983, *40,* 801.
26. Searight, "Borderline Personality Disorder."
27. Kernberg, O. "The Treatment of Patients with Borderline Personality Organization." *International Journal of Psycho-Analysis,* 1968, *49*(4), 600–619.
28. Kernberg, O. "Technical Considerations in the Treatment of Borderline Personality Organization." *Journal of the American Psychoanalytic Association,* 1976, *24*(4), 295–329.
29. Beck and Freeman, *Cognitive Therapy of Personality Disorders.*
30. Eversole, "Psychotherapy and Counseling."
31. Kwasnik, D. C., Moynihan, R. T., and Royle, M. H. "HIV Mental Health Services Integrated with Medical Care." In M. G. Winiarski (ed.), *HIV Mental Health for the 21st Century.* New York: New York University Press, 1997.
32. Groves, "Patients with Borderline Personality Disorder."

Chapter Fourteen

The Diagnosis and Management of HIV-Related Organic Mental Disorders

Wilfred G. Van Gorp
James W. Dilley
Steve L. Buckingham

People with HIV disease can suffer from cognitive changes resulting from a variety of underlying conditions. In fact, clinicians have known for some time that the brain is more likely than not to be affected at some point in the course of the disease: autopsy studies have found that at least 90 percent of people who die with AIDS have some degree of central nervous system abnormality.[1]

HIV displays a predilection for certain portions of the brain, most notably those structures located below the level of the cortex. These areas, termed *subcortical structures*, are involved in mood, the regulation of affect, psychomotor speed, and fine-motor precision—and this helps explain the depressive symptoms and psychomotor speed and fine-motor slowing in illnesses that disrupt the subcortex.[2-8] Opportunistic infections can also directly affect the brain and cause physical or mental disability among some people with HIV disease. The most common of these infections include toxoplasmosis, cryptococcal meningitis, progressive multifocal leukoencephalopathy (PML), and lymphoma. In addition, delirium (which is associated with an underlying medical abnormality or toxicity) or toxic states brought on by substance abuse, can also cause cognitive changes among people with HIV infection.[9]

Not everyone with central nervous system (CNS) abnormalities experiences cognitive impairment, and among those who do, the degree of impairment is variable. Minor cognitive impairment typically includes mild memory loss or slowing during complex or timed tasks. Full-scale dementia comprises more severe problems with memory and other cognitive abilities that interfere with the ability to care for oneself or to fulfill work or social obligations. In addition, although emotional difficulties do occur among individuals who experience traumatic life situations, such as facing a potentially fatal illness, changes in mood and affect can themselves reflect central nervous system disease.

In general, cognitive dysfunction related to HIV infection can be diagnosed as "HIV-associated cognitive-motor complex."[10] Within this complex, clients with moderate to severe cognitive impairments are diagnosed with "HIV-associated dementia"; individuals with subtle to mild cognitive impairment are diagnosed with "HIV-associated minor cognitive-motor disorder impairment."

Some of the causes of cognitive impairment can be successfully treated, whereas others can only be managed. But in order to respond appropriately to the range of cognitive symptoms, mental health professionals who work with HIV-infected clients must be knowledgeable about the disorders that cause cognitive impairment and must feel comfortable managing them using both medications and psychotherapy. This chapter, following the case of Lisa, plots the course of HIV disease and its cognitive effects on a single client, offering insights into the assessment and treatment of HIV-related organic mental disorders.

Screening for Cognitive Impairment in HIV Disease

Because of the known association between HIV infection and cognitive impairment, the most important task for the mental health provider is to be alert to the potential signs and symptoms of impairment. These symptoms function as an "early warning system," and heeding them ensures that clients have the best chance of successful treatment. Among the symptoms that the provider should notice and monitor over time are slowing in thinking or psycho-motor speed and decreased spontaneity. Among the symptoms that can indicate acute illness are the onset of prolonged or severe headaches, seizures, and progressive muscle weakness evidenced as difficulty walking or abrupt changes in handwriting or other fine-motor skills. Should any of these symptoms develop or worsen, the provider should suspect neurological involvement and immediately refer their client to his or her physician for further evaluation.

In general, "slowed thinking" is a common complaint among many people with HIV disease, especially among those at later stages of the illness. For example, a person may initially report con-centration problems, forgetfulness, and difficulty balancing a checkbook. Depression or agitation, rather than an HIV-related central nervous system disorder, may be the cause for these com-plaints. More than one study of asymptomatic and symptomatic seropositive individuals has found that a subject's *self-report* of cog-nitive failures did not relate to the actual degree of his or her ob-jective neuropsychological functioning; instead, it related to mood state.[11,12,13] Those who were more depressed tended to complain of more cognitive failures than those who were less depressed, re-gardless of the objective level of their neuropsychological abilities.

Likewise, symptoms associated with substance abuse may over-lap with those associated with HIV-related neurologic disease. For instance, a client with a long-standing history of alcoholism may have clinically significant memory impairment, having difficulty es-pecially recalling information he or she has recently learned. Sub-stance-abusing clients may also have short-term memory loss (not being able to retain information over a period of five minutes or more) and difficulty completing multiple-step tasks. If a client is also infected with HIV, it is often difficult to tease apart these po-tential causes of cognitive impairment, particularly in those with more advanced stages of immunosuppression.

Brief tests of mental status, such as the Mini–Mental State Exam, have *not* been shown to be sensitive screening devices for cognitive impairment in individuals with HIV infection. Standard psycho-logical and neuropsychological tests administered and interpreted by a neuropsychologist are the most sensitive measures to detect subtle, HIV-related cognitive dysfunction. Comprehensive neu-ropsychological examinations may be necessary to uncover even more subtle, subclinical impairment and to assist in making a differential diagnosis among depression, chronic substance abuse, a history of learning disability, and HIV-related cognitive impairment.

Additional tools exist to enable clinicians to screen larger numbers of seropositive clients efficiently. Psychomotor slowing—a general slowness in thinking coupled with slowness in physical movement—and memory impairment are hallmark characteristics of mild to moderate levels of HIV-related cognitive impairment. Therefore, measures that assess these functions should most effectively detect the existence of HIV-related cognitive impairment. However, it is important to note that because psychomotor slowing occurs as a result of many conditions, detecting it gives little information about the actual cause of impairment. Among brief cognitive tests, the first two described here are particularly sensitive to psychomotor slowing and memory impairment:

- Trail Making Test A and B. Trail Making Test A consists of an array of the numerals 1 to 25 distributed on a page. Clients connect one number to the next, in order, as quickly as possible. Trail Making Test B includes both numerals and letters, and the client must sequentially alternate from a numeral to a letter, back and forth, as rapidly as possible (for example, 1-A, 2-B, 3-C).[14,15]
- Symbol Digit Substitution Test. In this test, the client is shown a series of numerals paired with symbols. Applying this "key," the client must write down as rapidly as possible the symbols associated with an array of numbers that are presented in a generally random order, within ninety seconds.[16,17]
- Other memory assessment tests. Memory assessment using a list-learning test such as the Rey Auditory Verbal Learning Test or the California Verbal Learning Test can also be useful. These tests consist of learning and then recalling a list of words presented over several trials, usually followed by a short- and longer-term delayed recall.

Testing using all of these measures must be conducted by individuals who are trained in the administration and interpretation of psychological tests and who understand psychological testing, normative databases, and brain-behavior relationships. Lisa's case offers an overview of screening and diagnosis of cognitive impairment including the application of this array of tests. (Note: Because Lisa represents a "teaching" vehicle to illustrate various aspects of HIV and its common effects on the brain, the case may appear somewhat contrived at times.)

Lisa: The Progression of Organic Mental Disorder

Lisa, a thirty-seven-year-old married woman, learned she was HIV-infected two years ago when she donated blood at her company-sponsored blood drive. To her dismay, her husband John also took the test and discovered that he too, although asymptomatic, was HIV-infected. After questioning, John acknowledged that he had occasionally engaged in sexual activities with men and had only recently discovered that one of his sexual partners had AIDS.

When she learned she was infected, Lisa's viral load was 60,000 copies per milliliter, and her CD4+ cell count was 180. (Although some disagreement exists about when antiretroviral therapy should begin, viral loads of greater than 5,000–10,000 are considered "high," and treatment is recommended. Also note that because Lisa's CD4+ count was below 200, she also qualified for a diagnosis of AIDS.) The fact that her immune system was already significantly compromised suggested that she had become infected several years ago. Her physician, Philip Garcia, M.D., recommended combination therapy, and she began treatment with zidovudine (ZDV, AZT); lamivudine (3TC), a drug similar in action to ZDV; and ritonavir (a protease inhibitor). Because her CD4+ cell count was below 200, Garcia also started her on Bactrim (an antibiotic) to prevent the development of *Pneumocystis carinii* pneumonia (PCP). During her initial appointment, Lisa also admitted to excessive alcohol use during her college years (three or four mixed drinks a day several times per week), but she said she had had no prior psychological or psychiatric treatment. She did describe a history of mental illness in her family, including an aunt with a bipolar disorder and a grandfather with Alzheimer's disease.

Lisa was upset when she learned she was infected with HIV and that John had been sleeping with men for years without her knowledge. Because of her distress, she began seeing a psychotherapist weekly. She expressed sadness, which was not severe and seemed to focus on her concerns about HIV infection and her anger about her husband's bisexuality. At Lisa's request, John joined Lisa and her therapist for several sessions to enable Lisa to confront John more easily about her sense of betrayal. Because her mood symptoms were not severe and she was able to continue working and to take care of herself and her family, Lisa was diagnosed with adjustment disorder with depressed mood and not with major depression. Lisa saw her psychotherapist for six months until she reported a significant improvement in her mood and believed that she had adjusted to her illness.

Lisa also saw Garcia regularly during this time. Unfortunately, because of a past history of chronic hepatitis, Lisa was unable to tolerate ritonavir or any of the protease inhibitors. Her viral load consequently remained high.

Depression and Delirium

Lisa remained psychologically stable for three months after terminating with her therapist. At that time, she gradually became depressed, lost ten pounds, and exhibited classic "neurovegetative" signs of depression: increased sleep—especially during the day—diminished appetite, decreased interest in sex, and failure to enjoy the activities she had found enjoyable.

In response, Lisa resumed outpatient therapy, this time with sessions twice a week. Because of the severity of her symptoms, her therapist referred her for psychiatric consultation. Her psychiatrist, Susan Lee, M.D., discovered that in addition to feelings of depression, Lisa was experiencing fatigue, night sweats, and nausea, which contributed to her weight loss. However, she also found that Lisa admitted to thinking about suicide—"Yeah, I think about it; it would solve a lot of problems and I wouldn't have to go through all this"—although she denied that she would ever do anything to harm herself. Susan also reported significant feelings of guilt and worthlessness. In response, Lee made a diagnosis of major depression. She prescribed the antidepressant sertraline (Zoloft) at the usual dose. (Had Lisa been able to tolerate a protease inhibitor, the dose would have been decreased because protease inhibitors strongly compete with the body's mechanism for metabolizing these antidepressants and cause the blood level to be effectively higher than in someone not taking a protease inhibitor. See Chapter Eleven for a more detailed discussion of this issue.) In addition, Lisa continued with ongoing psychotherapy.

Three weeks after resuming therapy, or about ten months after she was first diagnosed with HIV disease, Lisa's husband telephoned her psychotherapist to report that Lisa had awakened that morning feeling ill and confused. She was unable to say where she was and was easily distracted. She told her husband there were "lots of other people in the room, coming and going," even though no one else was present. John telephoned an ambulance, which took Lisa to her local emergency room.

At the hospital, the emergency room physician noted that Lisa's condition was stable and then phoned her psychiatrist and asked her to evaluate Lisa. Lee found that Lisa was confused and distracted and was experiencing both visual and auditory hallucinations and that her speech was tangential and rambling. Mental status testing demonstrated that Lisa had a severe attention deficit and impaired "digit span": she could immediately repeat only three digits forward and no digits in reverse (far below the normal seven digits forward—plus or minus two digits—and five in reverse). Lisa demonstrated other cognitive deficits as well, including difficulty with arithmetic calculations, memory, writing (agraphia), naming objects (anomia), and some word substitutions (paraphasia).

Lee gave Lisa a provisional diagnosis of delirium—an "acute confusional state" (as defined in the next section). In this case, subsequent laboratory and x-ray studies revealed an elevated white blood cell count, fever, and a previously undiagnosed pneumonia. Lisa was admitted to the hospital and treated with antibiotics, and her mental state gradually improved over the next seventy-two hours as her pneumonia subsided. At the time she was discharged, Lisa's mental status had returned to normal, and Lisa had resumed antidepressant treatment and weekly outpatient psychotherapy.

Delirium is probably the most common cause of abrupt change in the mental state of people with HIV disease, occurring especially among acutely physically ill hospitalized clients.[18] An abrupt onset, a striking deficit in attention, and the presence of hallucinations are characteristic of delirium. Because many of the ongoing medical conditions people with HIV disease face can lead to delirium and because delirium is associated with high rates of death, altered mental status requires immediate medical attention.

Delirium can be acute or chronic and may be caused by a number of medical abnormalities, such as toxicity related to medication; or metabolic disturbance, for example, an electrolyte imbalance related to dehydration, high fever, or undiagnosed infection. Other HIV-related causes might include toxoplasmosis (a parasitic brain infection), cryptococcal meningitis (a fungal infection of the covering of the brain), and neoplasm (a brain tumor), all of which in themselves can produce cognitive abnormalities.

Because delirium seriously affects attention, neuropsychological and mental status tests of attention and concentration will uncover the greatest impairment. In particular, delirium will degrade digit span and mental control. Because of their variable attention, individuals with delirium may experience a pattern of "spotty" neuropsychological deficits in other cognitive domains as attention waxes and wanes during the assessment. They may also suffer from agraphia and aphasia (a language abnormality affecting speaking and comprehension), rambling and tangential speech, and neuropsychiatric complications such as visual or auditory hallucinations and delusions.

Delirium is different from HIV-related minor cognitive-motor disorder or HIV-associated dementia in several ways. Delirium typically presents with an abrupt onset of confusion, dramatic attention difficulties, and a language impairment characterized by rambling, incoherent speech and writing. In contrast, HIV-associated dementia and HIV-associated minor cognitive-motor disorder usually appear more slowly over time and leave basic attention intact, affecting only the more complex attributes of divided and sustained attention.

After an acute delirious state resolves, neuropsychological testing can be useful in assessing whether and to what extent underlying cognitive impairment may be present. This follow-up analysis is important, because it is not uncommon for a delirium to be superimposed on an underlying dementing condition. In fact, because people with brain damage are at higher risk of developing delirium, it is likely that one of the reasons that delirium is common among people with HIV disease is that they frequently have underlying cognitive impairment caused by neurological damage.

Physiologic and biologic measures are also important tools necessary to diagnose the causes of delirium and to distinguish delirium from HIV-associated dementia. Neuroimaging (computerized tomography scans and magnetic resonance imaging scans) and an analysis of the cerebrospinal fluid are needed in order to rule out other neurologic infections. Blood analyses, including complete blood count (CBC) and vitamin B_{12} and folate levels; thyroid function tests; and a general blood chemistry panel, which tests electrolyte levels as well as kidney and liver function, are also important. Finally, an electroencephalogram (EEG) can aid in differential diagnosis by indicating an overall decrease in the brain's electrical activity—a classic sign of a dementing illness.

The Subtle Effects of HIV in the Brain

Six months after her episode of delirium (now sixteen months after her initial diagnosis of HIV), Lisa's depression had gradually lifted. Because her mood had improved significantly and because Lisa did not like the idea of taking medications, she insisted on stopping her antidepressant. Lee, her psychiatrist, discontinued her Zoloft, while Lisa continued weekly psychotherapy.

Three months later, Lisa's husband telephoned her psychotherapist to inquire whether Lisa had reported being in several minor automobile accidents over the previous two months. Lisa's psychotherapist reminded John that she was not at liberty to discuss the content of Lisa's therapy sessions. John acknowledged this position, saying that he only wanted her to know that these incidents had occurred and that, in general, Lisa did not seem to be herself: she had become emotionally "flat" and had difficulty maintaining her train of thought. John said that the reason he was calling now was that Lisa had telephoned him from a nearby shopping mall that morning and told him that she had lost her car.

Listening to John, Lisa's psychotherapist realized that she had noticed that Lisa had become increasingly withdrawn and had shown more pronounced psychomotor slowing over the past several months. Her therapist also remembered that Lisa had reported several memory lapses, which the therapist had ascribed to a mild clinical depression, and that during therapy, Lisa had appeared uninterested and emotionally flat. Further, she recalled that Lisa had seemed clumsy and weak when they last met. Her therapist referred Lisa to a neurologist, Kevin Sills, for evaluation of the memory lapses and clumsiness.

Sills examined Lisa and noted that although she exhibited all of these signs plus a slight increase in her reflexes (hyperreflexia), the examination detected no specific neurologic abnormalities. Sills ordered an MRI and a lumbar puncture, both of which were found to be normal. Lisa's responses to a general mental status screening exam were correct, but she was slow in her reactions and often appeared unsure of her answers. During the interview, Sills was struck by the discrepancy between Lisa's flat, slowed presentation and the lack of depressive or pessimistic content in her speech. In fact, despite her presentation, Lisa denied any pessimism and indicated that she expected to "maybe get better and fight off this thing until a cure is found."

Sills referred Lisa to a neuropsychologist for assistance in distinguishing between HIV-associated minor cognitive-motor disorder, HIV-associated dementia, or the effects of clinical depression. The neuropsychologist administered a comprehensive battery of neuropsychological tests, which detected lower than expected scores measuring psychomotor speed, set shifting (the ability to mentally shift from one task to another), and memory. (See Exhibit 14.1.)

Memory testing (the California Verbal Learning Test) revealed that Lisa's recall (the ability to remember recently learned new information) was more impaired than recognition (the ability to choose the correct answer from a list of answers). Because of this constellation of symptoms, Lisa's activities of daily

Exhibit 14.1. Neuropsychological Testing for HIV-Associated Cognitive-Motor Complex.

Intelligence

Wechsler Adult Intelligence Scale—Revised

Attention

WMS-R Attention/Concentration Index
Digit Span
Auditory Consonant Trigrams
CalCAP (computerized reaction time performance task)

Language

Boston Naming Test
Controlled Oral Word List Generation Test
Boston Diagnostic Aphasia Examination

Memory

Wechsler Memory Scale—Revised
California Verbal Learning Test
Recall of Rey Osterrieth Complex Figure

Visual/Spatial

Recall of Rey Osterrieth
WAIS-R Subtests: Block Design and Object Assembly

Executive Functioning

Wisconsin Card Sorting Test
Stroop Color Interference Test

Mood/Affect

Minnesota Multiphasic Personality Inventory-2 (MMPI-2)
Beck Depression Inventory

living—for example, balancing her checkbook and recalling a shopping list—were compromised. In contrast, Lisa's language and most visual-spatial functions were relatively intact. Lisa also scored within the normal range on the Beck Depression Inventory, with items that reflected her concerns about her physical appearance and weight loss resulting in a slightly elevated overall score. In the absence of significant findings of depression or other neurologic cause for her cognitive difficulties, and in light of the impact of these neuro-cognitive deficits on Lisa's ability to manage her activities of daily living, the neuropsychologist concluded that Lisa had HIV-associated dementia. The neuropsychologist suggested that Lisa come back in four to six months to con-firm the diagnosis based on retesting and to monitor Lisa's course.

Diagnosing HIV-Associated Dementia

HIV-associated dementia most closely resembles a subcortical de-mentia, which is distinguished from a cortical dementia such as Alzheimer's disease by several key neuropsychological features. Among the hallmark characteristics of a subcortical dementia are psychomotor slowing, memory disturbance, and difficulty with complex cognitive tasks that require shifting between two tasks or concepts. Unlike Alzheimer's disease, HIV-associated dementia is usually characterized by forgetfulness rather than a frank inability to learn new information.

For example, a person with an HIV-associated dementia may have difficulty recalling a list of words or medication instructions but will often be able to recognize the correct information from multiple choices—indicating that the individual has learned the material but has difficulty retrieving it. Lisa would frequently "for-get" agreements she had made with her husband, John, even after he made a concerted effort to repeat them when they were made. When Lisa failed to "remember" the agreement later, John would remind her, and she would be able to recall the discussion.

As noted earlier, because the range of impairment is broader than that encompassed by a diagnosis of HIV-associated dementia, HIV-associated minor cognitive-motor disorder describes more "mild" cases in which activities of daily living are not as seriously affected.[19] The essential difference between these two conditions is that in HIV-associated dementia, the client's symptoms are suf-ficiently severe to interfere significantly with social or occupational functioning. Lisa met this threshold and satisfied the four criteria for a diagnosis of HIV-associated dementia: she had a positive HIV antibody test result; she experienced disabling cognitive, motor, or behavioral symptoms that interfere with occupational or social functioning; her symptoms were confirmed by another person; and a medical work-up ruled out any other condition that might account for the impairment.

Of course, it is important to note that dementia itself may make the person with HIV disease an unreliable historian. For example, some clients will overinterpret their disabilities because of anxiety or depression; others may do so in order to qualify for medical disability payments or other social services. To relieve the clinician of having to rely solely on the subjective statements of the client, HIV-associated dementia must be diagnosed only if cognitive problems and their effects on a client's life can be confirmed by an "objective" means or a reliable informant. It is often a client's partner—in Lisa's case, John—who, because he or she has the benefit of witnessing a client's behavior often and under a variety of circumstances, first identifies cognitive problems. For example, John reported Lisa's impaired motor skills, memory loss, and general withdrawal and lack of social involvement.

Although the frequency of neurological abnormalities in people with AIDS is high, the expression of these abnormalities as symptoms of cognitive impairment is much lower; that is, most brain abnormalities do not lead to cognitive impairment. Two studies found an annual incidence of HIV-associated dementia to be approximately 7 percent in people with AIDS.[20,21] In addition, a study finding that HIV-associated dementia occurs more frequently in the very young and the very old suggests that these populations may be at increased risk for this condition;[22] another study, however, did not find increased frequency in the elderly.[23]

Although the literature is complex and sometimes contradictory, most researchers and clinicians agree that it is relatively uncommon for asymptomatic people with HIV disease to experience HIV-associated dementia. A comprehensive review of thirty-six cross-sectional and nine longitudinal studies stated, "If one accepts the heightened power of larger studies, then it must be concluded that there is insufficient evidence to support the argument for an increased prevalence of neuropsychological deficit in asymptomatic individuals."[24] Thus, although asymptomatic people with HIV disease can experience HIV-associated dementia, it is sufficiently uncommon that clinicians should thoroughly rule out all other potential causes for symptoms of cognitive impairment.

Although there is no cure for HIV-associated dementia or for HIV-associated minor cognitive-motor disorder, studies have found ways to curtail their development and manage them.[25,26,27] Among these approaches are the use of medications and environmental engineering, which are described in more detail at the end of this chapter. Furthermore, in light of HIV antiviral therapies, including combinations with protease inhibitors and new drugs, the incidence of HIV-associated cognitive decline may further decrease.

Differentiating HIV-Associated Dementia from Depression

Clinical depression, which can also produce symptoms of cognitive impairment, has been found in 6 to 15 percent of people with HIV disease at some stage of their illness.[28] These rates are consistent with findings that clients with a number of neurological disorders have elevated rates of depression even when compared to other medically ill clients. For instance, Parkinson's disease, Huntington's disease, and progressive supranuclear palsy—all of which can produce a subcortical dementia in some people—can lead to higher levels of depression when compared to other medically ill clients with comparable functional disabilities, such as severe rheumatoid arthritis.[29] These findings lead to the conclusion that mood disorders in people with subcortical disease, including HIV infection of the brain, may represent central nervous system changes rather than solely psychological reactions to illness or disability.

The symptoms of clinical depression may mimic those of HIV-associated dementia, and vice versa. Psychomotor slowing, fatigue, irritability, difficulty concentrating, weight loss, and insomnia may occur in either case. Whenever there is evidence of a subjective mood disturbance, marked by sad affect, crying, hopelessness, guilt, and self-loathing, clinicians should first treat the probable depression and then reevaluate clients for residual cognitive deficits that may represent a coexistent dementia.

Although this course of treating depression first is wise, there are several clinical features that may nonetheless help to differentiate clinical depression from HIV-associated dementia. First, clinicians should differentiate between a depressed and apathetic affect. Clients who are depressed may indeed be characterized as lethargic and indifferent, but they also communicate a sense of sadness or emotional pain. Apathetic clients usually do not emotionally reach out or communicate emotional distress. Clinicians or informal caregivers asked to evaluate a client should pay attention to the feeling they get when with the client. Being with depressed clients usually makes a person feel sadness or distress. Being with apathetic, dementing clients, in contrast, often leaves one feeling emotionally flat. This distinction may be a difficult one for informal caregivers who are emotionally attached to clients. Watching one's child or partner begin to change and become distant—whether because of sadness or apathy—is never easy and clouds the caregiver's judgment.

Second, consider a client's psychiatric history. People with a history of depression are much more likely to have a recurrence of major depression than those who do not, and this remains true even in the face of a life-threatening illness. In addition, clients with a family history of depression are at greater risk of being clinically depressed. Also, clients with dementia tend not to be motivated toward suicide—recall that they are more apathetic and less distraught than people who are depressed. Thus, clinicians should also consider the presence of suicidal thinking as a sign of depression.

Third, observe a client's functioning over time to verify clinical conclusions. If the cognitive impairment continues to predominate and progress, the diagnosis of HIV-associated dementia becomes more likely.

Fourth, keep in mind that dementia and depression can coexist. If the usual signs and symptoms of depression are evident, clinicians should refer clients to an HIV-knowledgeable psychiatrist for evaluation; these clients may benefit from a trial of antidepressant medications. Some researchers have also used psychostimulants for depressed people with HIV disease, and preliminary data suggest cognitive and affective improvement in people with early HIV-related cognitive impairment, without the addiction or drug seeking that may accompany psychostimulant use.

Finally, some medications—including steroids or anticancer drugs—may have depressive effects. Clinicians should consider their role when seeking to diagnose the cause of a depressive disorder.

HIV-Associated Psychosis and Mania

Two months after her diagnosis of HIV-associated dementia, Lisa became convinced that three strangers had moved into her house and would occasionally talk to her. John reported noticing her talking to "another person," even though no one else was in the room. When questioned, Lisa reported that she was talking to her new houseguests.

Psychosis can range from a single delusion ("someone is poisoning my food") or a group of related delusional ideas, to active auditory and visual hallucinations. Although HIV-related psychosis may be caused by a variety of conditions, it is usually connected to HIV-associated dementia; and although there have been some reports of psychosis occurring among the first symptoms of HIV-associated dementia, it is usually manifest as acute delirium in the late-middle or end stages of HIV-associated dementia.[30] Among the causes of psychosis in people with HIV disease are the following:

- An organic delusional disorder or organic hallucinosis
- Delirium, possibly caused by medication toxicity, drug withdrawal, or a metabolic disturbance
- A coexisting schizophrenia or a schizophrenia-like disorder
- Major depression with psychotic features

If psychosis accompanies a pessimistic, morbid outlook, this may suggest depression with psychotic features. A family history of psychosis may more strongly suggest a coexisting schizophrenic disorder. Finally, clinicians should review a client's medications and, if this is the first episode of psychosis, prescribe a general medical workup for the client to rule out medical causes of psychosis, including medication toxicity, metabolic imbalances, and central nervous system infections.

Symptoms of mania—including pressured speech, spending sprees, and sleeplessness—have been reported in clients with various neurologic disorders, including HIV disease, especially following injury to certain areas of the brain.[31] Mania may also occur in response to various pharmacologic agents—legal and illegal—and clinicians should be vigilant to the possibility of mania in response to withdrawal from these drugs. Finally, central nervous system disorders—including PML, toxoplasmosis, and tumor—can all produce mania, especially if they affect the frontal lobes or the frontal and subcortical connections.

Clients with cognitive impairment who also demonstrate psychotic or manic behavior can benefit greatly from psychopharmacological approaches in conjunction with supportive psychotherapy. Antipsychotic medications in low doses or with prophylaxis against side effects are particularly helpful for several reasons.[32,33] First, they decrease psychotic symptoms in those with organic mental disorders, including HIV-associated dementia, and cognitively impaired clients can tolerate dosages comparable to those used in the general population. Second, these agents can be used to control agitation. Finally, antipsychotics in modest dosages can be useful in clients with severe character disorders. The choice of antipsychotic agent should be dictated by the side-effect profile. Mid-range potency agents such as perphenazine (Trilafon) and thiothixene (Navane) rather than the high-potency haloperidol (Haldol) may be the first drugs of choice. Haloperidol has been associated with severe side effects in some people with AIDS.[34] Initial dosing may begin with 2 milligrams of Trilafon twice a day or 2–5 milligrams of Navane per day, with 0.5–1 milligram of benztropine (Cogentin) twice a day as prophylaxis against the development of extrapyramidal reactions (stiffness and muscular rigidity).[35] Upper levels of dosing are dependent on a client's tolerance, the severity of symptoms, and the emergence of side effects.

Treatment for HIV-Related Organic Brain Disorders

Cognitive and motor slowing makes it difficult for impaired clients to function in situations that require quick decisions and action. For example, working in a busy office where the individual must act quickly may frustrate the mildly impaired client and may promote a sense of failure. Further, unfamiliar environments may lead to increasing confusion.

Practical Recommendations

For clients like Lisa and others with HIV-related cognitive impairment, several practical recommendations can assist in the struggle to adapt to cognitive changes and the resulting limitations.[36] Many clients complain that it is the simplest of these limitations that create the most frustration. To respond to these difficulties, caretakers should consider the following approaches:

- Place a large calendar near the bedside or prominently in the living space to remain oriented to month, date, and year.
- Use notes, reminders, lists, and appointment books to cue recognition. Maintain a telephone log and a medication log.
- Use a tape recorder to dictate thoughts and questions.
- To respond to motor and gait disturbances, alter living arrangements as much as possible to avoid stairs.
- Limit the number of different caretakers and distractions.
- Avoid crowds or having more than one visitor at a time.
- Allow more time for conversations.
- Keep instructions as simple as possible and give one instruction at a time. Break large tasks into smaller ones, and keep a log for complex projects.
- Keep to a routine; for example, go to bed and get up at roughly the same time each day.
- If able to drive, plan routes in advance, allow plenty of time, and take a friend along. Don't drive in heavy traffic.

As is true for people with other subcortical disturbances, clients with HIV-associated dementia may lack the necessary initiative to begin an activity even if they are motivated to undertake it. Family members or loved ones may provide the crucial impetus for starting a desired activity.[37]

Friends, family members, and partners may be understandably frustrated by the physical and mental debilitation of their loved one. Many have little or no understanding of neurological functioning or of the diseases that affect cognition. Upon hearing the term *dementia,* many people imagine the most severe clinical characteristics, such as complete memory loss and a vegetative state. Helping clients and their loved ones to better understand neuropsychological functioning and the kind of changes associated with subcortical disease can reduce fears and worries about cognitive impairment.

Friends, family members, and partners may also feel a "need to blame" and may act on this impulse by attributing a client's forgetfulness to willful stubbornness or manipulation. Education of a client's caregivers is the best antidote to this type of misattribution. Families and caretakers must realize that cognitive impairment reflects actual brain damage rather than volitional behavior.

Psychotherapy may be an appropriate treatment approach for a client in the early stages of HIV-related cognitive impairment, when the therapist can help the client and his or her partners, family, and friends understand cognitive impairment and behavioral modifications that can manage it. For example, Lisa and John both found that Lisa's work with her therapist was helpful, especially as John began to take over more of the responsibility for running the household and having to manage their lives as well as Lisa's failing cognitive capacity.

Through this process of learning, therapy can assist clients in sorting out the activities they can continue and those they cannot, and in setting limits for activities that may create potential problems. Such planning may make the difference between success and failure in adapting to and coping with cognitive changes and may prevent further assaults on the self-esteem of clients already beset by limitations, frustrations, and feelings of failure on many fronts. Finally, therapy can offer clients emotional support to handle these assaults and the opportunity to express their frustrations about declining capacities.

Pharmacological Treatment

Pharmacological treatment of HIV-associated dementia is somewhat controversial and is focused on treatment either of the underlying HIV infection or of the symptoms associated with it. For example, research has shown that ZDV in high doses is sometimes helpful in improving cognition and that joint administration of ZDV and a protease inhibitor may also improve a client's functioning. In fact, had Lisa been able to tolerate a protease inhibitor, the development of HIV-associated dementia may have been avoided altogether.[38] Although protease inhibitors generally don't cross the blood-brain barrier in therapeutic amounts, the combination of a protease inhibitor plus ZDV or another similar drug seems to be effective in inhibiting progression of HIV-associated dementia and may even reverse it, presumably by reducing the viral load.[39] Another pharmacological approach is to treat the slowing nervous system with stimulants, although this strategy has been shown to have only short-term positive effects.[40]

∞

It is crucial for mental health providers caring for people with HIV disease to be aware of the effects of HIV infection on the organic aspects of mental health and cognitive capacity. Because of the complexity of the issues confronting clients and their providers, a team approach to handling HIV-related organic disorders facilitates the best care. The team should include the client, his or her physician, family members and caregivers, the client's psychotherapist, a neuropsychologist, and a psychiatrist. By ensuring a wide range of expertise, providers ensure coordinated care and accurate diagnosis and treatment. Cognitive impairment can be treated or at least managed, making a significant difference in the lives of people with HIV disease, but treating it demands vigilance: early detection, accurate diagnosis, sound clinical intervention, education, and flexibility.

Notes

1. Navia, B. A., Jordan, B. D., and Price, R. W. "The AIDS Dementia Complex. I. Clinical Features." *Annals of Neurology,* 1986, *19*(6), 517–524.

2. Nottet, H. S., and Gendelman, H. E. "Unraveling the Neuroimmune Mechanisms for the HIV-1-Associated Cognitive/Motor Complex." *Immunology Today,* 1995, *16*(9), 441–448.

3. McArthur, J. C., Selnes, O. A., Glass, J. D., and others. "HIV Dementia: Incidence and Risk Factors." *Research Publications Association for Research in Nervous and Mental Disease,* 1994, *72*, 251–272.

4. Heaton, R. K., Velin, R. A., and McCutchan, J. A. "Neuropsychological Impairment in HIV Infection." *Psychosomatic Medicine,* 1994, *56*(1), 8–17.

5. Starkstein, S. E., Robinson, R. G., and Berthier, M. L. "Differential Mood Changes Following Basal Ganglia vs. Thalamic Lesions." *Archives of Neurology,* 1988, *45*(7), 725–730.

6. Starkstein, S. E., Robinson, R. G., and Price, T. R. "Comparison of Cortical and Subcortical Lesions in the Production of Poststroke Mood Disorders." *Brain,* 1987, *110*(4), 1045–1052.

7. Filley, C. M., and Kelly, J. P. "Neurobehavioral Effects of Focal Subcortical Lesions." In J. Cummings (ed.), *Subcortical Dementia.* New York: Oxford University Press, 1990.

8. Heilman, K. M., and Satz, P. (eds.). *Neuropsychology of Human Emotion.* New York: Guilford Press, 1983.

9. Zeifert, P., Leary, M., and Boccellari, A. "Diagnosis of Cognitive Impairment." *FOCUS: A Guide to AIDS Research and Counseling,* 1996, *11*(3), 5–6.

10. Janssen, R. S., Cornblath, D. R., Epstein, L. G., and others. "Nomenclature and Research Case Definitions for Neurological Manifestations of Human Immunodeficiency Virus Type-1 (HIV-1) Infection: Report of a Working Group of the American Academy of Neurology AIDS Task Force." *Neurology,* 1991, *41*(6), 778–785.

11. Van Gorp, W. G., Satz, P., Hinkin, C. H., and others. "Metacognition in HIV-1 Seropositive Asymptomatic Individuals: Self-Ratings Versus Objective Neuropsychological Performance." *Journal of Clinical and Experimental Neuropsychology,* 1991, *13*(5), 812–819.

12. Moore, L. H., Van Gorp, W. G., Hinkin, C. H., and others. "Subjective Complaints Versus Actual Cognitive Performance in Predominantly Symptomatic HIV-Seropositive Individuals." *Journal of Neuropsychiatry and Clinical Neuroscience,* forthcoming.

13. Wilkins, J., Robertson, K., Snyder, C., and others. "Implications of Self-Reported Cognitive and Motor Dysfunction in HIV-Positive Patients." *American Journal of Psychiatry,* 1991, *148*(5), 641–643.

14. Lezak, M. D. *Neuropsychological Assessment.* (3rd ed.) New York: Oxford University Press, 1995.

15. Spreen, O., and Strauss, E. *A Compendium of Neuropsychological Tests: Administration, Norms, and Commentary.* (2nd ed.) New York: Oxford University Press, 1998.

16. Lezak, *Neuropsychological Assessment.*

17. Spreen and Strauss, *Compendium.*

18. Perry, S. W., and Markowitz, J. C. "Psychiatric Interventions for AIDS-Spectrum Disorders." *Hospital and Community Psychiatry,* 1986, *37*(10), 1001–1006.

19. Janssen, Cornblath, Epstein, and others, "Nomenclature."

20. Janssen, R. S., Nwanyanwu, O. C., Selik, R. M., and others. "Epidemiology of Human Immunodeficiency Virus Encephalopathy in the United States." *Neurology,* 1992, *42*(8), 1472–1476.

21. Portegies, P., Gans, J. D., and Lange, J. M. "Declining Incidence of AIDS Dementia Complex After Introduction of Zidovudine Treatment." *British Medical Journal,* 1989, *299*(6703), 819–821.

22. McArthur, J. C., Cohen, B. A., Selnes, O. A., and others. "Low Prevalence of Neurological and Neuropsychological Abnormalities in Otherwise Healthy HIV-1 Infected Individuals: Results from the Multicenter AIDS Cohort Study." *Annals of Neurology,* 1989, *26*(5), 601–611.

23. Van Gorp, W. G., Miller, E. N., Marcotte, T. D., and others. "The Relationship Between Age and Cognitive Impairment in HIV-1 Infection: Findings from the Multicenter AIDS Cohort Study and a Clinical Cohort." *Neurology,* 1994, *44*(5), 929–935.

24. Newman, S. P., Lunn, S., and Harrison, M. J. "Do Asymptomatic HIV-Seropositive Individuals Show Cognitive Deficit?" *AIDS,* 1995, *9*(11), 1211–1220.

25. Sidtis, J. J., Gatsonis, C., Price, R. W., and others. "Zidovudine Treatment of the AIDS Dementia Complex: Results of a Placebo-Controlled Trial." *Annals of Neurology,* 1993, *33*(4), 343–349.

26. Bell, J. E., Donaldson, Y. K., Lowrie, S., and others. "Influence of Risk Group and Zidovudine Therapy on the Development of HIV Encephalitis and Cognitive Impairment in AIDS Patients." *AIDS,* 1996, *10*(5), 493–499.

27. Portegies, P. "Review of Antiretroviral Therapy in the Prevention of HIV-Related AIDS Dementia Complex (ADC)." *Drugs,* 1995, *49*(Suppl. 1), 25–31, discussion pp. 38–40.

28. Markowitz, J. C., Rabkin, J. G., and Perry, S. W. "Treating Depression in HIV-Positive Patients." Editorial. *AIDS,* 1994, *8*(4), 403–412.

29. Dewhurst, K., Oliver, J. E., McKnight, A. L., and others. "Socio-Psychiatric Consequences of Huntington's Disease." *British Journal of Psychiatry,* 1970, *116*(532), 255–258.

30. Perry, S. W. "Organic Mental Disorders Caused by HIV: Update on Early Diagnosis and Treatment." *American Journal of Psychiatry,* 1990, *147*(6), 696–710.

31. Lyketsos, C. G., Hanson, A. L., Fishman, M., and others. "Manic Syndrome Early and Late in HIV." *American Journal of Psychiatry,* 1993, *150*(2), 326–327.

32. Breitbart, W., Marotta, R., Platt, M. M., and others. "A Double-Blind Trial of Haloperidol, Chlorpromazine, and Lorazepam in the Treatment of Delirium in Hospitalized Patients." *American Journal of Psychiatry,* 1996, *153*(2), 231–238.

33. Hriso, E., Kuhn, T., Masdeu, J. C., and others. "Extrapyramidal Symptoms Due to Dopamine-Blocking Agents in Clients with AIDS Encephalopathy." *American Journal of Psychiatry,* 1991, *148*(11), 1558–1561.
34. Zeifert, P., Leary, M., and Boccellari, A. *AIDS and the Impact of Cognitive Impairment: A Treatment Guide for Mental Health Providers.* UCSF AIDS Health Project Monograph Series, no. 1. San Francisco: UCSF AIDS Health Project, 1995.
35. Hriso, Kuhn, Masdeu, and others, "Extrapyramidal Symptoms."
36. Zeifert, Leary, and Boccellari, *AIDS and the Impact of Cognitive Impairment.*
37. Brown, G. R. "The Use of Methylphenidate for Cognitive Decline Associated with HIV Disease." *International Journal of Psychiatry in Medicine,* 1995, *25*(1), 21–37.
38. Skolnick, A. A. "Protease Inhibitors May Reverse AIDS Dementia." *Journal of the American Medical Association,* 1998, *279*(6), 419.
39. Ibid.
40. Buckingham, S. L., and Van Gorp, W. G. "AIDS-Dementia Complex: Implications for Practice." *Social Casework,* 1988, *69*(6), 371–375.

Chapter Fifteen

Addressing Substance Abuse in Clients with Psychiatric Disorders and HIV Disease

Joan E. Zweben

Substance use often functions as the "wild card" in AIDS care, influencing the diagnosis of HIV-related and psychiatric disorders as well as the efficacy of medical and therapeutic interventions. Any amount of substance use, even short of meeting criteria for addiction, can have an impact on HIV disease and psychiatric conditions. The combination of these three elements—substance abuse, psychiatric disorder, and HIV disease—presents mental health practitioners with the most complex clinical situation: working with "triply diagnosed" clients.

Although each component of the triad contributes its own complexities to the mix, it is alcohol and drug use that has the least predictable effect. Unfortunately, this is also the element clinicians are often the least equipped to handle.

From a mental health perspective, it is therefore important to understand the historical relationship between psychotherapy and substance abuse treatment. When traditional psychotherapeutic approaches were found ineffective to treat addiction, a number of

This chapter reflects ideas presented in *The Alcohol and Drug Wildcard: Substance Use and Psychiatric Problems in People with HIV,* by Joan E. Zweben, with Patt Denning (San Francisco: UCSF AIDS Health Project, 1998).

alternatives developed outside the mainstream of mental health care. Although these new approaches proved to be productive, the process resulted in the artificial separation of psychotherapy and substance abuse treatment. For a time, this separation obliged individuals to seek help for their alcohol problems from one system, their drug problems from another, and their mental health problems from a third. Although many of the barriers to integrated care have been removed, they have left a legacy: mental health and medical providers outside the alcohol and drug treatment system are often ill equipped to handle clients with multiple diagnoses. At the same time, the stigma attached to addicted clients has perpetuated their isolation and discouraged the development of integrated treatment.

This chapter first examines the relationships among the members of the treatment team who might treat a substance user with HIV disease and mental illness and then looks at how these relationships might facilitate effective assessment, diagnosis, and treatment of these intertwined disorders.

Basic Training and Addiction Treatment

Basic training for mental health providers typically has not required competence in addressing alcohol and drug use. Thus, the most seasoned therapists have been the least knowledgeable and skilled substance abuse providers. In most states, training and continuing education requirements have begun to address this situation, but until material on alcohol and drug use is integrated into the core curriculum of psychiatrists, psychologists, and social workers, professional training will not produce providers who are fully competent to handle these problems.

As epidemiological studies and clinical realities have moved alcohol and drug use into the foreground, medical and mental health practitioners have shifted from ignoring addiction to excluding substance abusers from care or requiring them to seek addiction treatment before receiving medical or psychiatric services. However, the addiction treatment system was, and remains, inadequately equipped to handle the influx of triply diagnosed clients that the system has experienced during the past several years. In addition, the treatment system is, by and large, designed for clients who understand from the outset that they need to do something about their alcohol and drug use. Those who do not yet embrace this goal but who are interested in other kinds of medical, psychological, or psychosocial help continue to fall between the cracks.

Finally, at times and in places where substance users have been able to access other forms of care, providers have been confused about how to prioritize treatment tasks. This has been one of the most confounding aspects of triple diagnosis. For example, if a co-existing psychiatric disorder has a strong influence on a client's alcohol or drug use patterns, should that disorder be addressed first? Will addressing it be enough to eliminate the client's problems? Can a psychiatric disorder be effectively treated if a client continues to drink or use drugs? Can a client achieve abstinence or even make progress toward abstinence if his or her psychiatric disorder is not confronted? How important is it to deal with psychodynamic factors in order to influence alcohol or drug use? These are the types of questions, addressed later in this chapter, that providers must face in seeking to treat HIV disease and mental health disorders in the context of substance use.

Addictive disorders are characterized by behaviors that are compulsive and under intermittent or unpredictable control, and persist in spite of adverse consequences.[1] Although triple diagnosis refers to people who meet these criteria as well as the criteria of a psychiatric disorder and HIV infection, clinicians should remember that alcohol and drug use can be a problem long before the person is considered to have an addictive disorder. People with severe mental illness, in particular, can be exquisitely sensitive to the substances they use; the effects of moderate use on less severe psychiatric disorders, immune function, and HIV progression are less clear.

Clinicians who are not addiction specialists lack the detailed knowledge of drug effects that might enable them to identify adverse consequences quickly, particularly if symptoms are relatively subtle. For example, alexithymia—the inability to identify or experience feelings—is present among people with a history of childhood trauma, but it is also common among marijuana smokers. The result is that once therapists arrive at a plausible psychodynamic explanation for a symptom or condition, they often do not consider other possible factors. In this way, the effects of substance use are underestimated.

The interplay of the three conditions that constitute triple diagnosis produces a separate entity, all the more challenging because the many interactions among the components are poorly understood. One condition, by itself, may not be severe; but when combined with symptoms of the other two, it may create a critical situation. For example, a person with HIV-associated cognitive impairment may be only slightly impaired in his or her daily life; but if substance use or a psychiatric disorder limits his or her ability to cope, this minor condition could have increasingly harmful effects.

Provider Subcultures and Systems Issues

At least three specialty systems—medical, mental health, and substance abuse treatment—are involved in the care of triply diagnosed clients. Each system has its own goals, its own language, and its own set of assumptions—assumptions that may remain unstated until conflict arises over how to address the needs of a particular client. Until recently, these disciplines have worked in relative isolation punctuated by misunderstanding. But collaboration, no matter how difficult, is essential in order to respond adequately to all aspects of the three disorders. It is a skill as complex as clinical intervention itself but, except among social workers, has received little emphasis in professional training. The result of this isolation has been confusion about what constitutes appropriate care for triply diagnosed clients. It is possible, however, to create a framework for clinical decision making that can guide collaboration and inform care, without artificially synthesizing theoretical approaches that are fundamentally different.

For example, medical staff in clinics and private practice are usually comfortable assuming a leadership role, making decisions, and taking action promptly. Under ever-increasing time pressure, however, they may be less inclined to initiate communications and share information and more likely to assign tasks to other members of the team. They may label a former addict as "drug-seeking"—because he or she is using more pain medication than was prescribed—without taking into account the increased tolerance created by the drug addiction. They may refuse adequate pain medication to a person known to abuse drugs; on the other hand, they may medicate anxious patients as a way of decreasing office or telephone time spent reassuring them.

Meanwhile, mental health providers often endorse a more holistic model and may be impatient with a physician's focus on a particular disease rather than on the general welfare of the client. When working collaboratively with medical staff, mental health providers can be invaluable because they typically spend more time with the client and can help address many of the issues—such as housing or insurance problems—that interfere with the client's adherence to medical treatment. The case management background of most social workers facilitates their ability to identify and address practical needs.

Finally, addiction treatment practitioners tend to be more comfortable making decisions and taking action than the average psychotherapist, in part because addiction treatment is usually highly structured, a feature that is objectionable to some psychotherapists. In addition, addiction specialists understand that someone who is drinking and using often has impaired judgment and may not be capable of making appropriate decisions. Both medical and mental health staff can become frustrated with the rigidity characteristic of some—but not all—aspects of the addiction treatment system. In the absence of effective communication, tensions among practitioners from these different disciplines can escalate quickly.

Addiction treatment is commonly characterized by structure, multiple behavioral expectations, and discrete treatment components. Psychotherapy, on the other hand, usually incorporates minimal structure, other than the schedule of regular sessions that are its primary component. Many therapists are uncomfortable with eliciting behavioral commitments. Most outpatient addiction treatment is abstinence oriented. Although total abstinence may be difficult to achieve, the goal itself does not usually vary, because abstinence is viewed as the foundation required before meaningful progress can be made on other issues. Psychotherapy, on the other hand, has a wider range of goals and less consistent priorities. Some psychotherapists may not even understand or endorse the need for abstinence as opposed to other forms of controlled use. For example, they may share the view that drinking is "normal" and hence controlled drinking a reasonable goal, even in clients who have repeatedly demonstrated they cannot moderate their use.[2] With the increasing acceptance of harm-reduction approaches, it is important to determine whether therapist endorsement of harm-reduction goals is based on a knowledgeable assessment of the client or on naïveté or discomfort with the goal of abstinence.

Whereas addiction treatment makes alcohol and drug use the primary focus, psychodynamic psychotherapy explores underlying psychological processes as a means of bringing about change. If ill timed, this focus on process can undermine sobriety by elevating anxiety before abstinence is firmly established. But in other circumstances, exploring dynamics can remove important obstacles to progress toward abstinence. Unlike addiction treatment, which often includes breath and urine testing when costs permit, psychotherapy rarely makes use of such testing, which many therapists consider invasive and abhorrent. Therapists and counselors in addiction treatment are active and directive; psychotherapists in private practice have a variety of styles, some of which are more compatible with addiction treatment than others. All of these differences pose challenges to practitioners working with HIV-infected patients with mental health disorders who also drink or use drugs.

Frustrations may also arise when addiction treatment providers have difficulty convincing mental health workers that a client's symptoms are typical of certain types of alcohol and drug use patterns rather than being related to "only" an emotional problem. On the other hand, mental health practitioners may object to what they see as a blanket labeling of a client as a drug addict when they believe the use is clearly initiated by emotional problems. Mental health workers may see a refusal to treat someone who is actively using as abandonment, whereas some addiction treatment practitioners see continuing to provide services as colluding in perpetuating the addiction. It is noteworthy that only physicians are bound by an oath to work with all patients, whether or not they are abusing drugs. Physicians thus have little understanding or patience for this conflict between mental health and substance abuse practitioners.

Cross-Training

Despite the aforementioned problems, there is reason to be optimistic about developing treatment protocols that marshal the varied expertise of several different professional "cultures."[3] This is particularly true when all providers can agree that services should be driven by the needs of clients.

The first step to ensuring client-driven services is making a commitment to comprehensive "cross-training." For example, successful cross-training in settings dealing with substance use and mental illness has consisted of training addiction specialists in some aspects of psychological assessment and in altering their tendency to use a confrontational approach when working with emotionally fragile clients. In turn, mental health workers learn about the nature of addiction, the stages of its progression, and the essential elements of successful recovery. Such cross-training is facilitated by regular case conferences and individual supervision.

To build a successful, cross-trained team, it is also important for all the members to clarify and agree on shared approaches to assessment, treatment planning based on client needs and available services, consultation, and protocols that allow flexibility to alter treatment plans or change providers. Among the tasks that should be addressed are

- Defining team leadership and how collaboration will be managed
- Agreeing on the parameters of a comprehensive assessment
- Prioritizing disorders and establishing a process for changing priorities
- Communicating among team members while respecting patient confidentiality
- Clarifying the shape of the client-provider interaction and the depth of the emotional relationship with the client
- Dealing with client crises and other issues related to the accessibility of each provider
- Understanding philosophical differences and filling gaps in knowledge across disciplines
- Discussing different perspectives on medication and psychoactive drugs
- Clarifying the complex insurance issues of multiply diagnosed clients

Any member of the team can take the initiative to define who will play what roles in these tasks and how the team agrees to function. The necessity of "passing the baton" as symptoms change or as HIV disease progresses should not be an occasion for professional turf wars. Mutual respect and an understanding of differences allow this "sharing" of the client, ultimately providing the client with the best of each of the professions.

Assessment and Diagnosis: Differentiating Substance Abuse from Other Disorders

The initial evaluation of any client should define his or her status in the context of safety, stabilization, and maintenance. Once safety and short-term stabilization have been achieved and any immediate crisis has passed, the clinician's first task is to assess the client's problems. Although problems in each area—substance use, psychiatric status, and medical condition—must be addressed, providers must prioritize treatment and define appropriate expectations for clients. A chronic amphetamine user, for instance, is unlikely to keep appointments for HIV-related care or to adhere to medication regimens. Unless a medical emergency requires hospitalization, he or she will probably be best served by first arranging for substance abuse treatment, which offers the best chance of improving the efficacy of all other interventions. This is true now more than ever, when successful treatment for HIV disease requires strict adherence to antiviral regimens. Alternately, a deeply depressed client may be unable to participate in the activities that promote sobriety, and a person with HIV-associated dementia may find himself or herself unable to maintain a previously well established sobriety. Because these conditions are highly fluid, clinicians must remain alert for improvement or deterioration on all three dimensions.

Another important consideration in assessment is that at the time of initial presentation there is usually no reliable way to distinguish between symptoms of alcohol and drug use and symptoms of psychiatric disorders. For example, the hallucinations described by a schizophrenic individual may be indistinguishable from those evoked by amphetamine intoxication, and depression seen among clients after a "speed run" can appear identical to the depression of someone who has never used amphetamines. A client's acknowledgment of alcohol or drug use, or a positive Breathalyzer test or toxicology screen, can support a clinician's hypothesis that symptoms will abate with abstinence, but these do not definitively settle the issue. The most practical approach to distinguishing

between addictive and other disorders is to establish an alcohol-
and drug-free window—verified by breath testing or urinalysis—
for a circumscribed period and to observe the client's symptoms
during this time. Knowing about the effects of the client's substances of choice and the temporal relationship between his or her
substance use and the appearance of psychiatric symptoms can further clarify the situation.

Differential Diagnosis

To establish a diagnosis in a client presenting for care, clinicians
must consider the relative contributions of medical conditions, psychiatric disorders, and substance abuse. For example, clinicians
need to understand how long after abstinence one can expect the
effects of substance use to disappear and how long it will take for
the body to restore equilibrium after a substance is eliminated
from the system. For example, after two or three days, a psychotic
condition resulting from stimulant intoxication will usually begin
to clear. However, among some long-term chronic methampheta-
mine users, psychotic symptoms may persist for months or years.
Attention and concentration in regular marijuana users may take
three to six months to improve noticeably. To further complicate
the process, each person's system adapts to abstinence at a different rate.

Interviewing a client about his or her history of drug and alcohol use can refine the differential diagnostic assessment. This
history should include the following factors (for each drug): age
at and circumstances of first use, date of last use, and typical patterns of use, including amounts, source of money to buy drugs, attitude of significant others toward use, and previous attempts to
treat addiction. During this process, it is important to remember
that mood has a strong influence on memory and thus can bias a
client's reporting. For example, clients crashing from stimulant use
will usually give a history consistent with depression; later, when
their mood has improved, a different perspective will emerge. In
addition, cognitive processes, including memory, can be affected
by both substance use and HIV-related cognitive impairment, and
information from others—family members, friends, and coworkers—can be a crucial supplement to a client's history. It is also crit-

ical to ask questions regarding the client's psychological function, especially covering depression and anxiety, and the stage of the client's HIV disease and current HIV treatments.

Once it is clear that a psychological disorder coexists with addiction, it is useful—though often difficult—to determine which disorder is primary and which is secondary. The primary disorder is the one that occurred first, and the interviewer must work to establish the temporal relationship among clinical symptoms and other factors. For example, the clinician might ask, "Can you tell me the first time you ever experienced significant depression? Were you also drinking at the time?" These distinctions are important, because although addictive disorders and psychiatric disorders must be addressed as independent, coexisting conditions, prognosis and treatment strategies follow the course of the primary disorder. For example, a person with a primary addictive disorder has a better long-term prognosis than a person with primary schizophrenia. Similarly, a person with a primary panic disorder who began drinking in order to reduce symptoms may well be happy to give up alcohol once the panic disorder is treated. Having said this, treatment must eventually address both primary and secondary disorders.

In undertaking assessment, consider the following questions:

- Do episodes of substance use occur after an upsurge of psychiatric symptoms?
- Do psychiatric symptoms tend to occur only after episodes of substance use?
- Does substance use continue in the absence of psychiatric symptoms?
- Do the symptoms of mental illness return when psychopharmacological treatment for these symptoms is discontinued?
- Does the client's history suggest the development of a particular mental health disorder that was delayed or obscured by substance use?

Diagnostic Cautions

Keep in mind several diagnostic cautions—in particular, the role of misdiagnosis in predicting treatment success and motivating providers. Making personality disorder diagnoses in the context of substance use is particularly difficult. For example, of those voluntarily entering treatment, only a small number of clients will meet criteria for antisocial personality disorder, despite the fact that many have anger management problems or engage in criminal behaviors such as drug dealing, prostitution, or stealing. Because the diagnosis of antisocial personality disorder has strong negative associations, it can lead to artificially low expectations for treatment success. Notably, when clinicians make rigorous efforts to establish the independence of antisocial behaviors from substance abuse–related behaviors, the rates of antisocial personality disorder among alcohol and drug users drop markedly.[4]

Newly abstinent clients may temporarily appear narcissistic or grandiose. Although these characteristics may serve positive motivational functions in treatment and recovery, they may also lead to misdiagnosis. Overlooking Post-Traumatic Stress Disorder can also lead to confusion. People with a history of severe trauma may appear unable to experience or express feelings. People who are unable to cope with their HIV diagnosis or who are suffering the effects of watching dozens of loved ones die appear similarly impaired. These factors can result in misdiagnoses that may discourage care providers from investing time and effort in a client.

Alternately, clinicians may overestimate the positive effects of substance use for clients with especially difficult lives. For example, high levels of substance use are well documented among people with severe mental illness. Taken as a whole, this group uses alcohol and drugs for the same reasons other populations do: to relieve discomfort, to socialize, and to celebrate. However, a look at the negative consequences of substance use in this population highlights the importance of alcohol or drug treatment.

At least two studies have found that substance abuse can temporarily reduce symptoms in subgroups of schizophrenic patients, who report feeling less dysphoric, less anxious, and more energetic while intoxicated.[5,6,7] In the short run, drugs that are abused do appear to modulate the effects of psychological distress and can mediate the side effects of prescribed medications. These improvements often fuel resistance among substance users to change their behavior. Continued or excessive use, however, almost always increases psychiatric symptoms, particularly among psychotic or cognitively impaired clients. People with chronic mental illness who regularly use alcohol and drugs show greater hostility, suicidality, and speech disorganization; have poorer medication compliance; and are less able to attend to regular daily activities such as eating regular meals, managing finances, and maintaining stable housing.[8,9] Even when a client offers a plausible explanation for self-medication, it is important to remember that drug use usually undermines long-term treatment progress.

Addiction Treatment: Setting Appropriate Goals

Most of the addiction treatment system in the United States focuses primarily on achieving abstinence. This position is derived from the disease model tenet that a person who has crossed the line to uncontrolled use cannot return to controlled use. This does not mean that a therapist should terminate a client who fails to achieve abstinence, rather that the therapist should validate every step of a client's progress toward abstinence—even if this includes controlled use—at the same time emphasizing to the client that abstinence offers the greatest benefits. The therapist seeks to avoid being controlling or punitive about drug use, without endorsing a goal of controlled use.

Furthermore, treatment stresses the goal of abstinence from all intoxicants, not just an individual's primary drug of choice. There are three major reasons for this recommendation. First, it addresses the tendency of an addict to substitute one drug for another. It is common for people who have successfully stopped using heroin or cocaine, for example, to turn instead to alcohol. Because problems with substitution may not occur immediately but can develop over a long period of time, the frequency of negative outcomes is often underestimated. For instance, a heroin user may remain free of heroin for ten years before appearing in an alcoholism inpatient unit for treatment, having been admitted for medical complications of drinking.

Second, many people relapse to their substance of choice following use of another substance. Most cocaine users readily acknowledge that if they have a glass or two of wine and someone offers them cocaine, the chance that they will refuse is small. What is less often appreciated is the frequency with which a glass of wine or a joint of marijuana taken today can influence relapse to the primary drug of choice six weeks from now.[10] Researchers postulate that there is a common craving center in the brain that stimulates the desire for the primary drug of abuse when any other intoxicant is used.

Third, the process of relapse also encompasses the state of mind—the longing to get high—that precedes the actual behavior. Hence, rationalizing the use of another intoxicant is a precursor to actual relapse behavior. "I just achieved something very significant; I deserve to celebrate," or "I'm stressed out with this bad news; I need to console myself," are examples of common justifications. Similar processes can undermine HIV risk-reduction behaviors. Rationalizing and longing for forbidden sexual practices may precede unsafe sexual behavior in a pattern quite similar to a drug relapse episode.[11]

Although the ultimate goal is abstinence, addiction treatment providers have increasingly accepted relapse potential as a common characteristic of addictive disorders. At the same time, they have recognized that many people reduce or eliminate alcohol and drug use without seeking specialized treatment. Those who seek such treatment represent a subgroup of substance abusers who, for a variety of reasons, face greater obstacles to abstinence.

Abstinence Versus Harm Reduction

For clients who cannot or will not achieve abstinence goals, other interventions may provide benefits. These alternatives are often grouped together under the rubric of "harm reduction." Harm-reduction education and intervention may be appropriate when clients will not accept abstinence goals even after they explore their resistance; when drug use is minimal or moderate, and significant adverse consequences are difficult to establish; or when cognitive impairment or other physical or mental deterioration makes abstinence goals unrealistic.

Harm reduction works through a process of identifying practices and beliefs that endanger individuals and communities and developing strategies that reduce these risks. Strategies encompass a wide range of programs and approaches, including HIV-related outreach and education; needle exchange; moderation or controlled use; and "wet" or "damp" housing—that is, housing for homeless people who are actively drinking and using or for a mix of active users and others trying to stop (see Chapter Six). Although they may not be labeled as such, elements of harm reduction are common in abstinence-oriented treatment. For example, trauma survivors may experience intolerable feelings when they stop using alcohol and drugs because they are flooded with emotions and memories. Securing an abstinence commitment from such clients may take time. In the interim, therapists may strive to help clients avoid situations that are most harmful—for instance, visiting certain neighborhoods that may trigger use, or driving while intoxicated.

Abstinence-oriented programs have been criticized for their failure to produce long-term continuous abstinence. Indeed, only 10 to 20 percent of those treated in such programs actually achieve relatively unbroken abstinence. But addiction treatment is complex. Even in abstinence-oriented programs, abstinence itself is only one criterion of success, and researchers and evaluators usually do not consider it the most important. The issue has become confounded because the drug and alcohol treatment programs themselves do consider abstinence to be the main indicator of their success—the result being that they fail to communicate to the public the considerable accomplishments they achieve that nonetheless fall short of abstinence.

In this light, it is useful to review the original federal outcome evaluation criteria for substance abuse treatment: reduction or elimination of alcohol and drug use, reduction in crime, increase in employment and self-support, improved family functioning, increased social support, and improved medical and psychosocial status. Measured by all these criteria, abstinence-based treatment, though imperfect, is remarkably effective.[12-15] Finally, a recent public policy paper, comparing substance abuse to hypertension, diabetes, and asthma, found that treatment outcomes were remarkably similar among all these chronic disorders. That is, there were similar rates of compliance with treatment among the conditions, even in the face of similarly serious consequences for noncompliance.[16] The data thus do not warrant the pessimistic attitude many hold toward abstinence-oriented treatment. Rather, it has been the failure to disseminate research findings that has resulted in the widespread view that abstinence-oriented treatment does not work.

Phases of Recovery

Once a client has committed to abstinence, even for a short time, the provider can begin to address other tasks of recovery. Although some elements unfold on their own or can be accomplished without professional help, there are many ways in which providers can accelerate and enhance the recovery process. What is most essential, regardless of theoretical orientation, is that the provider understand the tasks of recovery. These tasks can be summarized as follows:

- Becoming motivated to change
- Discontinuing alcohol and drug use
- Achieving and consolidating abstinence
- Changing life patterns (for example, in terms of employment, recreation, and interpersonal relationships) to support recovery
- Addressing the individual and interpersonal issues that emerge

It should be emphasized that although many seasoned therapists have been trained to believe that addiction must be addressed primarily through work on the "underlying" problems, there is little if any evidence from systematic studies to support this view. On the other hand, most addiction specialists hold the view that abstinence is the foundation of therapeutic progress and that work on coexisting issues must take into account a client's stage of recovery. At the far end of the continuum are some who maintain that no other issue should be tackled until abstinence is secure. This is impractical, especially in complex patients.

Many addiction specialists have adapted to the reality that for many clients, abstinence will never be achieved if care providers ignore coexisting problems such as low self-esteem or the desire to block out rather than experience painful feeling states. Regardless whether these coexisting problems are major psychiatric disorders or charged emotional issues, substance use is best viewed as an independent behavior or disorder requiring specific intervention, concurrent with or subsequent to working on other issues—a behavior that in fact quickly becomes functionally autonomous from these underlying problems and may be amenable to modification long before other issues can be resolved.

The goal is to achieve an appropriate balance in the provider's mind between the questions How can this client stop using? and Why is this client using? The task for providers is thus to pay attention to increased psychological insight in the service of abstinence-related behavior change—acknowledging that although insight and recognition often make change possible, they do not automatically produce it.

Treating Triple Diagnosis: The Challenge of Providing Comprehensive Care

The clinician treating clients with three disorders has a daunting task. He or she must prioritize treatment and integrate interventions to address all three disorders in a sequence that is appropriately timed. There is no simple formula for developing this plan.

Factors that affect the client's safety must be tackled first. These may include acute medical problems, abusive relationships, alcohol and other drug use, psychotic symptoms, or housing problems. The clinician must ask, Where is the best place to start if the goal is to keep my client safe and set the stage to permit my other efforts to bear fruit?

After clinicians have addressed any immediate crisis, they can consider other factors relevant to stabilizing the client. It is desirable to reduce disturbing psychiatric symptoms when possible, and it is important to motivate the patient to look at his or her alcohol and drug use and begin to make changes in behavior. Clinicians must also identify acute medical problems and develop a plan to address them. Important strategies for stabilizing the client also include assembling the elements in a support system: defining constructive participation of family and friends, connecting the patient to available benefits and services, and putting together a long-term plan to maximize improvement.

In the maintenance phase of care, it is important to monitor activities that sustain the gains achieved. These include all aspects of self-care. For example, when patients who have responded well to twelve-step programs begin to reduce their participation without discussing how they made their decisions, it may signal an impending relapse. Becoming careless about sleep, nutrition, or exercise can also destabilize a client. A client with bipolar disorder, HIV, and alcohol problems, for example, may be taught to recognize increasing sleeplessness as a warning sign that a manic episode is imminent. Warning signals are often best detected in mundane details the patient may not report unless specifically asked, so it is important that clinicians routinely review areas known to be sensitive indicators.

The greatest threat to effective treatment of triply diagnosed clients is the potential for fragmentation among the agencies, disciplines, and individual providers necessary for appropriate care. At one time or another, or simultaneously, the client may be involved with the social service, mental health, addiction treatment, and criminal justice systems. Each system has its own set of resources and expectations. As a result, implementing comprehensive treatment plans is time-consuming and frequently overwhelms clients with contradictory expectations and with the task of mastering the idiosyncratic demands of many systems. The potentially debilitating nature of HIV disease adds to this process the dimensions of fatigue and disability, making matters even more difficult.

Richard Ries discusses the strengths and limits of three models of care—sequential, parallel, and integrated—applied depending on the profile of a particular client.[17,18] This conceptual framework, described in more detail in the sections that follow, provides a good foundation on which practitioners may construct an appropriate treatment plan for triply diagnosed clients.

Sequential Treatment: Responding to a Severe Problem in One Area

In this model, clients are treated first by one system and then by another. For example, many clinicians believe that addiction treatment must precede other aspects of care and that clients must be abstinent in order for psychosocial interventions or psychiatric medication to be effective. At other times, psychiatric symptoms must become the focus, such as when a client makes a serious suicide attempt. In some cases, a client's alcohol or drug use so undermines the efficacy of other interventions that problems may need to be addressed concurrently in order to make progress. This undermining effect is the key issue in determining whether sequential treatment makes sense.

Sequential treatment may work well when a client has a severe problem in one area but only mild problems in other areas. For example, a schizophrenic client who uses drugs moderately and episodically may come to a psychiatric service because of a psychotic episode or seek medical services because of an exacerbation of HIV symptoms. If the alcohol and drug use is indeed not severe, addressing it can be postponed until the other crises are resolved. Although often an effective approach, rigid adherence to addressing problems sequentially may undermine substance abuse treatment efforts—for instance, leaving unexplored the client's psychological resistance to addressing the alcohol and drug use because the other issues are seen as "more central."

Another problem can arise when a client who has been stabilized on psychotropic medication enters an addiction treatment program that discourages the use of such medication. Although this situation is becoming less common as educational efforts change attitudes in the addiction treatment system, it nonetheless does occur in programs that remain isolated from recent staff training efforts.

Parallel Treatment: An Approach for Highly Functional Clients

Like sequential treatment, parallel treatment may work well when a client has a severe problem in one area and mild problems in others. In parallel treatment, clients are simultaneously involved in treatment undertaken by providers in different systems. In clients who are triply diagnosed, there is almost always an element of parallel treatment as the client receives medical care for his or her HIV disease at the same time he or she is receiving treatment for a mental health or substance abuse problem. Parallel treatment is usually initiated by the provider in the system in which the client first appears for help.

Notably, the application of parallel treatment often is dictated by the limitations of existing services in the community rather than by thoughtful decisions about optimal help. For example, a depressed client with HIV disease may first seek help from an individual therapist in the community, who then may identify an alcohol and drug problem. As the treatment unfolds, the client may take antidepressants, participate in psychotherapy, and attend classes on coping with depression, at the same time as he or she goes to twelve-step meetings, a recovery support group, and alcohol and drug refusal classes. Problems arise if this array of treatment is provided by clinicians who do not communicate with each other. Many psychotherapists, for example, emphasize the importance of the one-on-one relationship and do not initiate coordinating activities. While focusing on empowering the client, the therapist may miss the bigger picture of his or her client's multiple problems and limited resources. Clients in this situation must be highly functional to navigate treatment options and potential philosophical conflicts.

Integrated Treatment: The Alternative for Multiple Dysfunction

Integrated treatment combines mental health and addiction care, involving clinicians who have been cross-trained in both fields and applying unified case management. In many cases, integrated treatment has the greatest chance of success; certainly for clients with severe dysfunction in more than one area of diagnosis, this approach makes sense. For these clients, bouncing between two or three systems usually results in conflicting messages with inadequate opportunities for their resolution, and diminishes the chance of compliance with any treatment plan.

Integrated treatment places the burden of consistency and continuity of treatment on staff, not clients. In a setting designed for simultaneous treatment of both disorders, flexibility promotes the most effective resolution of conflict.

❧

Clients with HIV disease who also suffer from substance abuse and mental health disorders are the most challenging clients for providers and systems of care alike. They raise a host of complicated issues ranging from making a differential diagnosis to deciding on the goals of treatment.

Most recently, these clients have provoked a debate on the ethics of treating them with complex antiviral regimens. Some providers and policymakers have raised concerns about whether these clients can adhere to these regimens and about the consequences of nonadherence for individuals (resistance to the antiviral drugs in the combination) and for their future sexual and needle-sharing partners (the potential for infection with a drug-resistant virus). There is a growing consensus, however, that these clients deserve to be treated and that it is the responsibility of providers to establish structures that help these clients adhere, rather than to deny treatment based on the assumption that they cannot adhere.[19]

There have also been recent successes in creating environments where mental health, substance abuse, and medical treatments have been gathered together. Refinement and evaluation of these existing models will, we hope, bring clarity about which are the most effective. The HIV service community has an opportunity and an obligation to promote these kinds of arrangements for the well-being of their clients.

Notes

1. American Psychiatric Association. *Diagnostic and Statistical Manual of Mental Disorders.* (4th ed.) Washington, D.C.: American Psychiatric Association, 1994.
2. Brown, S. *Treating the Alcoholic: A Developmental Model of Recovery.* New York: Wiley, 1985.
3. Ries, R. *Assessment and Treatment of Patients with Coexisting Mental Illness and Alcohol and Other Drug Abuse.* Treatment Improvement Protocol (TIP) Series, no. 9, Center for Substance Abuse Treatment. Rockville, Md.: Substance Abuse and Mental Health Services Administration, 1994.
4. Gerstley, L. J., Alterman, A. I., McLellan, A. T., and others. "Antisocial Personality Disorder in Patients with Substance Abuse Disorders: A Problematic Diagnosis?" *American Journal of Psychiatry,* 1990, *147,* 173–178.
5. Dixon, L., Haas, G., Weiden, P., and others. "Acute Effects of Drug Abuse in Schizophrenic Patients: Clinical Observations and Patients' Self-Reports." *Schizophrenia Bulletin,* 1990, *16*(1), 69–79.
6. Dixon, L., Haas, G., Weiden, P., and others. "Drug Abuse in Schizophrenic Patients: Clinical Correlates and Reasons for Use." *American Journal of Psychiatry,* 1991, *148*(2), 224–230.
7. Serper, M., Alpert, M., Richardson, N. A., and others. "Clinical Effects of Recent Cocaine Use on Patients with Acute Schizophrenia." *American Journal of Psychiatry,* 1995, *152*(10), 1464–1469.
8. Drake, R. E., and Wallach, M. A. "Substance Abuse Among the Chronic Mentally Ill." *Hospital and Community Psychiatry,* 1989, *40*(10), 1041–1045.

9. Osher, F., and Kofoed, L. L. "Treatment of Patients with Psychiatric and Psychoactive Substance Use Disorders." *Hospital and Community Psychiatry,* 1989, *40*(10), 1025–1030.

10. Rawson, R. A., Obert, J. L., McCann, M. J., and others. "Neurobehavioral Treatment for Cocaine Dependency." *Journal of Psychoactive Drugs,* 1990, *22*(2), 159–172.

11. Gold, R. S., Skinner, M. J., and Ross, M. W. "Unprotected Anal Intercourse in HIV-Infected and Non-HIV Infected Gay Men." *Journal of Sex Research,* 1994, *31*(1), 59–77.

12. Gerstein, D. R., and Harwood, H. J. *Treating Drug Problems.* Vol. 1. Washington, D.C.: National Academy Press, 1990.

13. Hubbard, R. L., Marsden, M. E., Rachal, J. B., and others. *Drug Abuse Treatment: A National Study of Effectiveness.* Chapel Hill: University of North Carolina Press, 1989.

14. McLellan, A. T., Metzger, D. S., Alterman, A. I., and others. "Is Addiction Treatment Worth It? Public Health Expectations, Policy-Based Comparisons." In D. Lewis (ed.), *The Macy Conference on Medical Education.* New York: Macy Press, 1995.

15. McLellan, A. T., Woody, G. E., Metzger, D. S., and others. "Evaluating the Effectiveness of Addiction Treatments: Reasonable Expectations, Appropriate Comparisons." *Milbank Quarterly,* 1995, *74*(1), 51–85.

16. McLellan, A. T., Grisson, G. R., Zanis, D., and others. "Problem-Service 'Matching' in Addiction Treatment." *Archives of General Psychiatry,* 1997, *54*(8), 730–735.

17. Ries, *Assessment and Treatment.*

18. Ries, R. "Clinical Treatment Matching Models for Dually Diagnosed Patients." *Psychiatric Clinics of North America,* 1993, *16*(1), 167–175.

19. Barthwell, A. "Substance Use and the Puzzle of Adherence." *FOCUS: A Guide to AIDS Research and Counseling,* 1997, *12*(9), 1–4.

Part Four

Therapeutic Practice and Countertransference
Personal Challenges for Therapists

Therapists working in the midst of the epidemic have had to adjust to the myriad accommodations that AIDS work demands. HIV disease has required a flexibility of approach, therapeutic frame, attitude, role, and standards of care: from becoming fluent in virology and infectious disease treatment, to confronting ongoing disability and death, to applying appropriate self-disclosure, to responding to ever-challenging countertransference issues.

None of these concerns is new, and none may be in and of itself onerous. But of course, these issues are not "in and of themselves"; they are related, and together they can be overwhelming; over time, they can be exhausting. Seventeen years have taught that there is no obvious solution—only mitigation—to the effect of these demands. For many, the substantial rewards of working with HIV have balanced the burnout. But even though balancing may be as good a solution as can be expected, it may not be ideal.

As it becomes clearer that, despite treatment advances, HIV-related psychotherapy can become a lifelong career, therapists need to consider more consciously their approaches to therapeutic practice. No longer can they respond in extraordinary ways to what has become relentless.

This exploration must embrace a broad as well as a long view, taking into account all the accommodations an individual can conceive of over time, identifying those that seem achievable and sustainable, and then formulating ways of maintaining boundaries that protect—without calcifying—these commitments. Part Four, written by and for therapists practicing in the epidemic, provides a thoughtful discussion of these issues.

Chapter Sixteen

Present in the Balance of Time

The Therapist's Challenge

JD Benson
Jaklyn Brookman

Therapists who work with clients with HIV disease face profound challenges to their clinical skills and sense of hope. A unique circumstance in our time, the HIV epidemic has challenged therapists to serve clients in new ways and to integrate experiences that are sometimes very disturbing and often very stressful. It is through meeting these challenges, however, that many therapists have undergone transformative experiences and developed vital relationships that in some instances have provided rewards beyond what any of us might have anticipated.

In the first decade of the disease, many therapists responded to a crisis of health and community by entering into HIV-related work. With the identification of the virus, the door opened to research and to hope. Into the second decade of the epidemic, many therapists came to feel, as one therapist put it, "like an emotional punching bag," with so much devastation, illness, and death around them.[1] What was once motivated by a compelling sense of duty and a desire to jump into the fray gradually became complicated by a desire to escape what had become overwhelming.

By the time of the 1996 International Conference on AIDS in Vancouver, a revolution in HIV antiviral treatment once more shifted the experience of therapists working in the epidemic.

Although not a cure, the emergence of new drug protocols has provided new hope and the promise of the chronic, manageable disease that providers and clients have been talking about for years. After years of vacillating between the depths of despair and the heights of unmitigated optimism, many in the United States and other developed countries are currently experiencing renewed health.

For others, however, the new drug combinations have been ineffective. Check-ins at the beginning of HIV support-group sessions bear out this range of experience, revealing vast differences in clinical response to treatment and, as a result, emotional outlook. For clients on disability for whom treatment has been unsuccessful, seminars sponsored by AIDS services organizations on such issues as "Should you return to work?" are painfully out of reach. One therapist reports having gone to more funerals in 1997 than in many years, demonstrating to him that the epidemic is far from over and that for some, the promise of a long life remains elusive.

Identifying with the challenge, struggle, joy, despondency, and uncertainty of clients, therapists may progress through a delicate and parallel process as they struggle with the existential concerns and outcomes of this epidemic as it unfolds one client at a time. Therapists need to acknowledge and value the struggles and the resilience of individuals and communities while they continue to experience both the relentless quality of individual, interpersonal, and community destruction and the prospect of renewed health and rejuvenation.

This connection to the experience of the client is crucial to the empathic relationship therapy requires. The shadow side of this experience appears when the self-observing therapist loses sight of the separation between client and counselor, when lines that were parallel begin to cross. Whether evolution occurs in response to unattended grief and loss, survivor guilt, multiple loss, restimulation of past trauma, or a combination of these factors, the therapist may lose sight of appropriate boundaries and the distinctions between the client's and the therapist's experiences. The result is a blurring that can skew not only the therapist's experience but also the therapy itself.

In the second decade and for the foreseeable future, seasoned therapists working with HIV disease face challenges to clinical boundaries and the therapeutic frame, to their sense of meaning, and to conceptions of time. This chapter explores these issues and suggests ways therapists can approach them and continue their work. By addressing such concerns, this chapter attempts to provide validation for experienced therapists, to stimulate introspection and discussion—overcoming isolation where it may exist—and to encourage therapists to reach out for consultation and support as they continue to respond to a shifting and persistent epidemic.

Common Threads: A Review of the Literature

Articles and books addressing the psychosocial aspects of HIV disease now appear more frequently than they did earlier in the epidemic, but most focus exclusively on intrapsychic and interpersonal issues for clients, not for therapists. When therapists' experiences have been written about, several common themes have emerged, including responding to powerlessness, resolving anticipatory grief, maintaining clinical boundaries, and dealing with countertransference. The signal recommendation in the existing literature is for therapists to go beyond awareness of these issues, to avoid becoming inured to them as they arise, and to participate in ongoing case consultation.

Although therapists may be willing to comment on the rewards of HIV-related work, they often fail to discuss its profound personal toll.[2] Therapists generally define rewards in terms of personal and spiritual maturity, which can be conceived of as encompassing the following gifts: working with someone facing illness or death and confronting the paradox this poses; helping individuals evolve from despair to reengagement;[3] experiencing human resilience; and witnessing enormous courage and unanticipated revelation, which leads to the deepening of relationships with clients.

Facing Powerlessness

When therapists do acknowledge the shadow side of HIV-related therapy, it is expressed as feelings of helplessness and despair in response to the catastrophic nature of client needs.[4-9] An HIV-infected client's emotional life, which may become marked by increasing volatility, can also trigger an emotional response in therapists, and this can exacerbate feelings of inadequacy, ineffectiveness, and hopelessness.[10] Debilitating burnout results from the loss of professional distance, of appropriate levels of empathy, and of identification, and from the failure to see the bounds and limitations of therapy in light of a client's life-threatening illness.

Many therapists experience the hope-turned-fantasy that they can heal their clients or that the therapeutic relationship will contribute to physiological healing above and beyond its reasonable capacity to do so. But a client's declining health and physical presentation challenge the fantasy, leading the therapist to feel powerless and inadequate.[11] Although the new treatments are indeed resulting in increasing health for some, the difficulties of adhering to complex drug regimens and the uncertainty of treatment success and durability may amplify both hopes of revivification and sadness in response to treatment failure.

Facing a client's mortality and anticipating the ravages of disease can lend a sense of urgency to therapy and may contribute to the therapist's stress and pain.[12,13,14] A client's cognitive decline may affect the aspect of the therapeutic process by which clients gain insight and awareness. The therapist may fear being unskilled or ill equipped to work with a client who is cognitively impaired, a response that may reflect an objective assessment of clinical experience, a fear of dealing with this issue, or both. Further, fear may lead to the therapist's denial of this aspect of a client's reality, and, in an effort to avoid making the therapist uncomfortable, the client may deny failing cognitive abilities. In the face of real or anticipated decline in mental and physical functioning, therapist and client may also have different expectations of the goals of therapy. The therapist may want the client to resolve intrapsychic or family-of-origin conflicts, whereas the client may express a need to deal with day-to-day survival.[15]

Maintaining Therapeutic Objectivity

Clear expectations of therapy and the therapeutic relationship are paramount to successful care. Clarity is usually achieved by ensuring the stability of sessions, agreeing to concrete therapeutic goals, fostering a sense of support, and helping to define strategies for change. Although therapists are trained to balance emotional restraint and empathy, it is particularly challenging for them to maintain clear, albeit flexible, boundaries and therapeutic objectivity as the client's physical and emotional needs take on greater urgency.[16–20]

The loss of therapeutic objectivity may take forms ranging from overinvolvement to emotional distancing.[21] In one case of overinvolvement, a therapist insisted, "Giving clients my home number and letting them know they can call me any time of day or night is my way of letting them know I care, I'm here for them; they can trust me." The false equation of limitless availability and trustworthiness provided some secondary gain for the therapist. However, she also complained that she was always "bone tired" and that her life had "become HIV." To the uninitiated, she appeared a model of commitment; to close colleagues, she was martyring herself, to her own and her clients' detriment.

Emotional distancing may manifest as a flawed defense strategy that the therapist either brings to the work or calls on as a result of overinvolvement. "When one of my long-term clients called and said he couldn't make his appointment, that he was ill, I was relieved," observed one therapist. This therapist made no inquiry into his client's health nor any effort to reschedule the client or invite rescheduling. He never saw the client again. It was much later that the therapist examined the process and saw how anomalous it was. Allowing the ill client to "terminate by phone"—to spare the therapist uncomfortable feelings about the client's decline—was something he would never do with healthy clients. In both of these cases, failure to maintain therapeutic objectivity jeopardized the client's sense of safety, compromised the integrity of the therapy, and upset the therapist's emotional balance.

Confronting Countertransference Challenges

Diane Sadowy, a psychoanalyst describing her own conflicts treating a client with advanced HIV disease, speaks to this issue: "The transference that I had a magical cure and the countertransference that I was omnipotent initially defended me and [my client's] position of helplessness. I found that acknowledging our helplessness opened up possibilities of contact and other choices she might make for herself."[22] Sadowy's informed self-analysis enabled the therapy to progress with authenticity and integrity. Such struggles with intense countertransference can be life-shaking. Facing one's own mortality, life choices, helplessness, sexuality, and sexual problems, among other issues, provides enormous grist for the mill in the therapist's own growth.[23,24]

To support clinicians in their efforts to acknowledge and address these countertransference challenges, and to make use of the wealth of emotional and existential issues triggered by HIV-related work, therapists across disciplines and theoretical orientations emphasize the importance of consultation and collegial support. For therapists working in the arena of HIV disease, there is a tension between the compelling need for such support and the resistance to it, a tension arising from a sense of scarcity of time and resources.

The root causes of this resistance may include a "mentality of poverty"—for example, the belief that resources are too few and time too limited to allow for process groups for therapists—or personal inflexibility; that is, therapists may fear that they will be overwhelmed and incapacitated if they stop to reflect on personal ramifications of the work. Whether discussed in terms of the impairment or narcissism of the therapist[25] or in the language of codependency, resistance may lead some therapists to respond to the internal stresses of their work in isolation. These therapists assert that they have no need for support, that their needs do not compare to those of the people with whom they work and therefore do not need to be addressed. Coupled with a level of resentment or victimization, these therapists do not *permit* themselves to have needs. It is just such a psychological bind that underscores the necessity of including clinical consultation as a regular part of—not an optional adjunct to—the work of therapists in the field of HIV disease.

Acknowledging the Service Environment

The institutions in or with which therapists work have an important effect on therapists' response to HIV-related treatment challenges. To understand fully the nature of provider stress and to develop appropriate responses, therapists must examine the context in which they provide services.[26] In many cases, the phenomenon of burnout has been attributed more to these influences than to actual work with clients. Although some providers tend to resort to blaming the system in order to avoid looking at the difficult interpersonal and social issues related to working with clients with HIV disease, nevertheless the politics and bureaucracy of AIDS have indeed "chewed up and spit out" many providers. Program administrators at clinics and other institutions would do well to examine the work ethic at their sites and how the sites operate, to reward healthy limit setting and boundaries, and to nurture and support staff in their day-to-day work.

The Therapeutic Frame

The traditional therapeutic frame provides clear boundaries that protect both client and therapist, but it may fail to respond to clients living with what can become debilitating illness. Therapists are trained to work with clients in a room with a door—a therapy room, sacrosanct, neutral, where confidentiality is ensured. The therapy session starts on the hour or half hour and ends in fifty minutes. Therapists take great care in retrieving clients from their waiting chairs, guiding them to the therapy room, and closing the door before beginning. Therapists and clients agree on fees, and therapists adjust fees periodically. Clients pay for missed sessions or late cancellations. If a client wants to terminate the therapy prematurely, that is, at a time the therapist assesses as too soon, therapists will encourage discussion and suggest an appropriate number of sessions to address termination issues.

Redefining the Traditional Frame

As therapists have gained experience working with clients facing multiple bouts of debilitating illness, decreased mobility, or cognitive dysfunction, they have raised questions regarding expanding the parameters of the traditional therapeutic frame to fit the erratic picture of advanced HIV disease. To what extent should therapists intervene with other health care providers to facilitate care for clients? In what circumstances should they decrease or eliminate client fees? Should they conduct therapy in clients' homes or hospital rooms when clients are physically disabled? Committed to responding to the crisis of the epidemic, many therapists have made these adjustments without considering the long-term affects of extending themselves in these ways.

That therapists have begun to define personal limits reflects a maturity of involvement with clients with HIV disease. It is this honest reflection upon and permission to have personal limits that, in fact, supports both the authenticity and depth of the relationship.

The temporary or permanent failure of the therapeutic relationship to fit within the traditional frame may indicate the need for additional changes in order to further therapy. In fact, this process of change may actually facilitate the therapy: the adaptations themselves become grist for the therapeutic healing process. For example, advocacy—taking an active role on behalf of the client to initiate or enhance communications within the interdisciplinary care team—can serve therapy by modeling for the client ways of asserting his or her own needs and negotiating complicated and intimidating systems. One social worker put it this way: "Maybe it's my training, or why I sought the training I did, but I've always viewed my role as . . . helping clients to access both internal and external resources." Therapists without social work training, such as marriage and family therapists and psychologists, often find themselves facing these role-related conflicts, and by virtue of both their clinical training and their willingness to expand the frame of therapy, are equally successful in meeting the challenge.

Regardless of a therapist's training, the task of advocating for a client can seem daunting and outside the realm of therapy. The frustrations and the time-consuming nature of advocacy can cause anger and resentment toward the client as well as toward "the system." If the therapist begins unconsciously to blame the client for complicating factors such as insurance company bureaucracy, he or she may find ways, literally or figuratively, to let go of the therapy.

Whereas advocacy changes the content of the traditional therapeutic frame, home visits and free sessions alter its structure. The physical container for therapy is the therapy room. It is the place the therapist provides and, therefore, is an environment that he or she controls. The therapy room is perhaps one of the most fundamental aspects of therapy—on a par with the therapist's role as an attentive, caring other—and even in the most protracted therapeutic relationships, it provides a foundation for safety and trust.

In deciding whether to offer home or hospital visits, the therapist must acknowledge the declining health of the client and recognize that in order to continue the relationship, the frame must change to accommodate the client's health. The alternative is to interrupt or end the relationship, which may reinforce a client's feelings of abandonment and be detrimental to his or her sense of well-being. As we saw in the case in which a client's hospitalization enabled the therapist to terminate the relationship without seeing the client, logistical circumstances may seem to provide the therapist an easy escape hatch: by maintaining traditional structures, the therapist can avoid further involvement and pain, and retreat from the client's decline or dying process. This may be especially convenient if the therapist feels either closely connected to or alienated from the client.

By choosing to allow the therapeutic frame to change, the therapist can affirm the therapeutic relationship, address the client's fears of abandonment, and acknowledge the client's life force even in the face of his or her impending death. In accepting this course, the therapist must face being in a physical environment that, to some extent, is not in his or her control, that may make privacy or confidentiality difficult, and in which there may be interruptions to continuity and focus. Indeed, some of these conditions may already exist for therapists working in HIV outpatient settings; they require flexibility on the part of mental health providers and other staff to maximize privacy. Degree of flexibility and issues of privacy cannot always be anticipated, and therapists must evaluate on a case-by-case basis what will serve the integrity and content of therapy and what they feel they can and will do.

Likewise, therapists treating clients with HIV-related concerns must determine whether they are willing to participate in a relationship that requires responding to biological, psychological, social, and environmental factors in new ways. This legitimate and necessary question takes many therapists well beyond the boundaries of their previous professional training.

Experiencing Multiple Loss

Multiple loss has profound effects on therapists, particularly in areas with high incidences of HIV disease. Loss occurs when the therapist learns a client is HIV-infected, has an opportunistic infection, or is exhibiting symptoms such as memory loss or neuropathy that may affect the client's mobility or sense of security.

Because the pattern of HIV disease commonly includes ups and downs, therapist and client may have more than one opportunity to discuss these changes and losses. In some cases, they have the opportunity for closure nearer the end of the client's life.

Therapists may also experience loss when treatment fails, when a client engages in unsafe practices after having engaged in safer behaviors, or when the hope for survival gives way to visions of terminal decline. Even though the therapist may understand that both successful treatment and behavior change are difficult to achieve and sustain, lapses or setbacks in progress can contribute to a therapist's sense of hopelessness, grief, or feelings that undesired or feared consequences are inevitable. The therapist may collude with the client and fail to address feelings about such losses, particularly deteriorating health, in order to avoid the pain of such a discussion.

The therapist's expectations about the course of a client's disease may determine the therapist's feelings when decline does occur: sudden death will engender a loss different from long-term, incremental decline. The course of HIV disease may at one turn seem individual and unpredictable, whereas at another resemble past events that apparently prepare the therapist for what is about to unfold. Perhaps there are visual cues that anyone working with people living with HIV disease learns to see as signposts along the way. Even if there are not, when the uncertainty is too much for the therapist, he or she may reach for a fixed picture—even if it portrays an unpleasant reality—in order to rest the anxious heart.

It is impossible to talk about HIV-related loss without acknowledging suicide and suicidal ideation. Therapists must be open to the needs of clients to discuss their thoughts or plans, while considering the ethical issues inherent in "self-deliverance." Professional obligations do not fully relieve the conscientious provider from the ambiguity of these discussions. This ambiguity stems from distinctions between "rational" and "reactive" suicides, the traditional connection between depression and suicide, and the taboo associated, for some, with the religious "sin" of suicide.

Therapists often feel responsible for client suicides, and the fact that this feeling is vocational does not mitigate a sense of guilt. Second-guessing about interventions the therapist might have made to prevent a suicide may dominate the therapist's thinking.

The therapist may also feel reluctant to discuss his or her feelings with colleagues for fear of judgment and of comparisons with how other therapists have dealt with similar circumstances. This devaluation may, in turn, complicate the therapist's grieving process and interfere with more fully experiencing loss.

For the therapist working in the epidemic over time, the different levels of loss and the compression of losses may seem to offer little opportunity to grieve. For some, the sense that there is no room to stop, to allow oneself to feel the loss, reflects the relentless quality of the epidemic: there is always someone else waiting in the wings with therapeutic needs that require attention. This understanding does not preclude the possibility that the therapist may unconsciously avoid experiencing feelings about anticipated or past losses.

Therapists who have reflected on the ramifications of unattended loss and grief in their own lives report experiencing typical signs of burnout at one or more points over the years: inattentiveness, negative attitudes, argumentativeness, preoccupation with peripheral issues, sleep or eating disturbance, relationship problems, and depression. (See Chapter Seventeen for a larger discussion of this issue.) These therapists may project unattended feelings about one client onto another client, or fail to attend to client fears and concerns in an unconscious effort to ward off unwanted feelings.

There are, however, lessons that therapists seasoned with HIV-related experience have learned. Chief among these is the observation that in some measure we are all walking around with broken, or at least repeatedly wounded, hearts. Multiple loss and grief are rarely resolved, and resolution of grief and complete acceptance of a loss may be unrealistic and undesirable goals. Grief and loss must be attended to, acknowledged, experienced, and tolerated, but neither resolved and overcome nor pushed aside. Therapists can, in fact, bear both their own losses and, in a different relationship to the losses, those of their clients, colleagues, and communities. Perhaps it is therapists, when they avoid shouldering these emotions in isolation, who are by the nature of their training and attitude the most competent vessels for containing the emotions related to loss.

In this light, therapists may be better able than many other providers to tolerate and accept a lack of closure or a different kind of closure when a relationship ends with loss. Although death or illness may mean that a client did not resolve particular issues in the course of therapy, this loss can be balanced by a sense that what the client did address was, in a larger way, enough. The therapist's ability to appreciate incremental change will decrease the risk of burnout. With this perspective, the therapist has a better chance of experiencing more authentic closure with a client.

On the Matter of Time

In the context of therapy, time is measured in prosaic ways: by the fifty-minute hour, as the span of time over which a clinical plan is mapped, or in terms of the client's late arrival or missed sessions. For people living in the epidemic, however, time takes on a surreal elasticity: perhaps terrifyingly compressed if one is newly diagnosed, interminably slowed if one is a survivor watching one after another friend succumb. In this setting, time becomes a central theme of therapy.

Time represents hope, and whether conscious or unconscious, hope can motivate people to engage with life, the future representing an image of a fertile place where dreams and plans can blossom. For the client with HIV disease, time is framed by uncertainty. Questions of time arise at every transition: When will I get sick? How long will it be before I am unable to function as an independent adult? How much time before I die? For those for whom antiviral treatment holds hope of improved immune system function and overall health, the questions take a different shape: Should I return to work? Do I have time to pursue an education or new line of work? How long will treatment work? Can I get on with my life now?

The recurrent anxiety that accompanies these questions becomes the backdrop for the therapeutic relationship. The therapist can productively reflect and process this anxiety in order to enhance the client's coping skills. Conversely, the therapist, spurred on by his or her own anxiety for the client and ultimately for himself or herself, runs the risk of pushing the client, subtly or overtly, into a race against time in order to resolve intrapsychic material that has been problematic for much of the client's life. The danger of such an approach is that the therapy may proceed at the pace of the anxious therapist rather than at the psychological, cognitive, and emotional pace of the client. Such enmeshed boundaries will impair therapy and may lead to an increased sense of anxiety, helplessness, pain, and frustration for both the client and the therapist.

One therapist told a story of this enmeshment with a dying client: "I felt enormous grief, as if it were my own family that needed healing, when my client [became] disinterested in deepening the intimacy in his relationships with [his] mom and dad by telling them his true feelings." The therapist came to understand, as he witnessed this scenario so many times, that as people come to the very end of life, they may gradually let go of the people and things of this world in preparation for death.

Another therapist reported attending the memorial service of a group client. The client had only recently gotten together his résumé and was pursuing job interviews. Although the client had expressed hopes of getting on with his life, his work, and a new relationship, he had also expressed fears and doubts. "The treatments weren't working, that seemed true enough. But [the client] was pulled along by the current of optimism generated by the good response of other group members. I had felt the failure, the hopelessness, as did others in the group. But we all were pulling for him, almost like trying to will him onto the bandwagon. It just pulled out without him, and the helplessness we all felt was palpable."

Therapeutic goals must change with the changing needs and circumstances of any client. As a response to feeling emotionally overwhelmed—as if to stave off the feared decline of the client's health—therapist and client may collude in maintaining inappropriate goals that fail to reflect new circumstances and time constraints. It is the therapist, as well as others in a dying client's world, who must work at staying in sync with the client's measured journey. With the approach of death, time may be defined for the client by the form it takes around dying, a process that may become the primary focus. Others, including the therapist, may experience their own surrender to this new and fundamental human reality.

It is also important to acknowledge the changing expectations clients and therapists alike can develop in those instances in which clients' health is rebounding and clients are revisiting former goals regarding work, school, relationships, and family. In an epidemic in which many people have declined in health, lingered with long-term illness, and ultimately died, this shift can be disorienting. The shift calls for a redefinition, sometimes, of therapeutic goals and relationship.

This need for redefinition is most apparent in serodiscordant couples. As a partner supporting someone who is ill, facing illness and very possibly death, certain aspects of relationship sacrificed regain importance. One obvious issue is that of becoming a biological parent. When one has a sense that someday the partner will die, the noninfected individual may table hope of becoming a biological parent. However, because partners live without a current way to ensure that partners or offspring will not be infected, the noninfected partner faces the prospect of a life with someone with whom they may not wish to conceive.

The AIDS Warrior Syndrome

Like nurses on intensive care units, physicians on oncology wards, and soldiers engaged in trench warfare, psychotherapists working with HIV disease struggle to maintain balance and perspective. In the face of growing expectations, more and more therapists struggle to clarify a sense of personal and professional identity, purpose, and ability.

At its extreme, the "AIDS Warrior Syndrome" idealizes the role of the helper as ever willing and ever able to meet whatever client needs arise. It may be the product of overidentification, prolonged involvement, or an authentic empathic response. Some therapists will fail to acknowledge personal limits if to do so violates their sense of what the AIDS warrior should do. What distinguishes AIDS Warrior Syndrome from experiences of health care providers facing similar demands are those factors that distinguish HIV disease from other illnesses: the phenomenal increase in numbers of people affected, the fact that entire communities face devastation, and the social taboos and prejudices that lace the epidemic.

The almost heroic stature ascribed by society to people living with HIV disease is also ascribed to those who work with them. Although not all HIV providers are AIDS warriors in this sense, it is not uncommon to find those who cross that line. There is a romantic quality, an appearance of selflessness in some quarters, a bigger-than-life aspect to being one of these distinguished troops. Therapists are not immune to adopting this perspective, their training in self-observance and self-examination notwithstanding. The societal alienation that many of us face only adds to this response: some providers seek fulfillment from such compelling work because the richness of their lives is either absent or unrecognized, and the HIV community appears to be an ideal nest for emotional nurturing.

Over time, the AIDS warrior is unable to maintain perspective or boundaries and allows overidentification with the client or the HIV community to interfere with personal and professional wellness. When asked to identify what they were doing before AIDS work, these providers may struggle to recall. In day-to-day living, they may sacrifice serenity, personal relationships, and professional maturity to the cause.

Meaning for the Therapist

Is there any way to add balance to this sense of all or nothing, to get something out of AIDS work without sacrificing one's life to it? Many therapists look to their clients' struggles and triumphs for meaning and avoid unreasonable expectations for themselves. "Ninety percent of people with HIV disease who come into therapy, will die as they lived," a Berkeley therapist said. "Perhaps 10 percent come into therapy spurred on by this race with time and can do some incredible work very quickly." In some instances, a sense of limited time may quicken therapy, catapulting clients through difficult clinical issues in amazing ways. Many therapists say that such cases inspire and teach them and contribute to their professional and personal lives.

One of the more profound experiences therapists describe is witnessing the resilience of their clients. Inspired by a client's ability to grapple with painful clinical material—shame, mortality, parental rejection, internalized homophobia, failure to attain life goals, societal disdain, and disability—some therapists find the sustenance to continue the work. Although it is often the case that as a container for the material of the client, the therapist may experience feelings ranging from rage to hopelessness, these feelings may be less dominant than the sense of humility and wonder that comes from the experience of bearing witness.

The therapist who surrenders to the external reality of the disease, remaining connected to experience no matter what piece of reality presents itself from session to session, is likely to manage most successfully. The process becomes one of maturation for many therapists as they develop the ability to shift with what is happening and to resist devaluing their own experience of the therapy. Rather than an exercise in futility, therapy becomes a pathway through which both client and therapist can accept pain and frustration as parts of the treatment. As a result, some therapists experience a deepening intimacy and a greater capacity for intimacy.

HIV-related therapy confronts many therapists with their own life choices, and some examine these choices. What is really important to me? Is there balance in my life? What issues remain unexamined in my life? This reflection often leads to a more conscious focus on living, on life-affirming choices, and on conflicts regarding mortality, loss, and grief. To facilitate this process and provide a framework for it, some therapists use spiritual, religious, political, or social filters, or resources that combine several of these perspectives. In understanding the work of therapy in light of these new experiences, some therapists are arriving at new therapeutic models that posit a more holistic view of human experience, for example, a biopsychosocial-spiritual model.[27]

Therapists must bring the ability to set limits and manage an HIV-affected caseload to the process of therapy. Some therapists choose to diversify their client base, seeing clients other than those with HIV-related issues, and in this way maintain balance in clinical practice and enhance their emotional well-being and a sense of control over their lives. Working with clients with HIV disease thus becomes a more conscious choice.

❧

Perhaps the greatest personal rewards of this work are emotional growth and the spiritual journey, particularly for those therapists who remain open to the vulnerability clinical relationships evoke. With open hearts, therapists can use the experience of HIV-related therapy—combined with their own therapy and clinical consultation—as a means for personal healing.

For some, a healing occurs in a spiritual sense, as a resolution that takes them to a place more connected to the self yet also beyond the boundaries of body, roles, and projections. By accepting limitations, experiencing pain and release, obtaining collegial support, and seeking hope both through traditional sources (family, community, and spirituality) and in unacknowledged places (such as by working through the death of a client), therapists can transcend the difficulties of HIV-related work and, ultimately, discover truths about themselves.

Notes

1. The authors conducted more than twenty-five interviews with therapists working with clients living with HIV disease. All unattributed quotes from therapists are taken from these interviews as well as from discussions in consultation groups with other therapists.
2. Shernoff, M. "Eight Years of Working with People with HIV: The Impact upon the Therapist." In C. Silverstein (ed.), *Gays, Lesbians and Their Therapists*. New York: Norton, 1991.
3. Sleek, S. "AIDS Therapy: Patchwork of Pain, Hope." *APA Monitor,* June 1996.
4. Shernoff, "Eight Years."
5. Horsely, G. "Observations and Suggestions for Those Considering a Mental Health Internship with an HIV-Infected Population." *AIDS Patient Care,* 1993, *7,* 102–105.
6. Tunnell, G. "Complications in Group Psychotherapy with AIDS Patients." *International Journal of Group Psychotherapy,* 1991, *41*(4), 481–497.
7. Sadowy, D. "Is There a Role for the Psychotherapist with a Patient Dying of AIDS?" *Psychoanalytic Review,* 1991, *78*(2), 199–207.
8. McKusick, L. "The Impact of AIDS on Practitioner and Client." *American Psychologist,* 1988, *43*(11), 935–940.
9. Markowitz, J. C., Klerman, G. L., and Perry S. W. "Interpersonal Psychotherapy of Depressed HIV-Positive Outpatients." *Hospital and Community Psychiatry,* 1992, *43*(9), 885–890.
10. Tunnel, "Complications."
11. Schaffner, B. "Psychotherapy with HIV-Infected Patients." In S. M. Goldfinger M. (ed.), *Psychiatric Aspects of AIDS and HIV Infection.* New Directions for Mental Health Services, no. 48. San Francisco: Jossey-Bass, 1990.
12. See Note 1.
13. Shernoff, "Eight Years."
14. Sadowy, "Is There a Role."

15. Schaffner, "Psychotherapy with HIV-Infected Patients."
16. Shernoff, "Eight Years."
17. Sleek, "AIDS Therapy."
18. Schaffner, "Psychotherapy with HIV-Infected Patients."
19. Madover, S. "Psychotherapists' Response to Clinical Work with Persons with AIDS/AIDS-Related Conditions." Unpublished doctoral dissertation, California School of Professional Psychology, Alameda, Calif., 1989.
20. Winiarski, M. G. *AIDS-Related Psychotherapy*. New York: Pergamon Press, 1991.
21. McKusick, "The Impact of AIDS."
22. Sadowy, "Is There a Role," p. 206.
23. Shernoff, M. "AIDS: The Therapist's Journey." In M. Sussman (ed.), *A Perilous Calling: The Hazards of Psychotherapy*. New York: Wiley, 1995.
24. Barret, R. L. "Countertransference Issues in HIV-Related Psychotherapy." In M. G. Winiarski (ed.), *HIV Mental Health for the 21st Century*. New York: New York University Press, 1997.
25. Moore, J. W. *Healing Where It Hurts*. Nashville, Tenn.: Dimensions for Living, 1993.
26. Land, H. *AIDS: A Complete Guide to Psychosocial Intervention*. Milwaukee, Wis.: Family Service of America, 1992.
27. Winiarski, M. G. "Understanding HIV/AIDS: Using the Biopsychosocial/Spiritual Model." In M. G. Winiarski (ed.), *HIV Mental Health for the 21st Century*. New York: New York University Press, 1997.

Chapter Seventeen

Multiple Loss and the Grief of Therapists Working with HIV

Barbara E. Davis
David W. Cramer

Ned J., Richard K., Paul R., Kathy D., Vern H. . . . As Jan heard the names being read slowly over the microphone, above the hum of the people viewing the quilt, her heart began to beat more rapidly, her throat began to tighten, and she felt herself fight back an impulse to scream or run. When she had agreed to read the names of people she had known—mostly clients—who had died of AIDS, Jan had felt honored. But she had become preoccupied with making the list and wanting to leave no one out. It was very important to her that every person was named, was acknowledged for his or her life. She was surprised at the number of names—almost eighty. Could that be right? Now it was time to read those names aloud, and the feelings Jan had been suppressing for months were thundering to the surface.

Psychotherapists who work with HIV-infected clients are familiar with the emotional impact of the ceremonial reading of names at a presentation of the Names Project Quilt. Many of us carry our own quilts in our appointment books, and feel sadness, grief, and loss simply by glancing back through calendars from years past. Name after name, week after week, even year after year awakens remembrances of sessions with clients who shared their will to live and their struggles to cope with a devastating illness. Each memory raises emotions about how these therapeutic relationships affected and changed us and about the parts of our own grieving yet to be experienced.

Therapists who work with people with HIV disease customarily do not have the time to come to terms with the loss of one client before experiencing anxiety about the HIV status of the others. This experience of multiple loss is in the nature of working on the front lines of the epidemic; it defines the greatest challenge for therapists facing HIV-related bereavement and is among the complications of practicing psychotherapy with seropositive clients. Without proper care and attention, cumulative grief may quickly lead to burnout, frustration, and a reduced capacity to empathize with the suffering and struggles of our clients. This chapter looks at HIV-related grief from the therapist's perspective and focuses on the challenges of multiple loss to the therapist's ability to continue providing care. It also offers approaches for handling grief and minimizing the impact of multiple loss on care.

Jan

After seven years of working with HIV-infected clients, Jan has gained thirty pounds and has increasingly isolated herself. She still works with seropositive clients but tends to back off from taking new clients with HIV-related issues. She focuses instead on supervising other therapists working with HIV disease. Colleagues commend her for "doing this work," but they don't seem to want to hear what it is like. Her friends in the gay community refer to her as "the Death Lady"; in response, she tries to keep a superficially "up" attitude when around them.

Jake

This work has given Jake, a colleague of Jan's, an appreciation for "life in the moment" and a sense that he is privileged to share something very important with people with HIV disease. Because of the expertise he has developed by doing AIDS work since 1984, he is well respected in the community as an openly gay therapist. Losing friends and clients, however, has caused Jake to become numb; he is almost nonchalant when someone dies. He too has gained weight and is reticent to connect to new people—particularly clients with HIV. As a therapist in a close-knit community, the challenge of maintaining boundaries adds to his sense of isolation. This was highlighted when a client told Jake that Jake's own therapist was HIV-positive; because of the confidential nature of the interchange, Jake was unable to share this information and his feelings in the therapy group he attended, the very support he had set up for himself.

Robert

Robert experiences some of the same feelings that Jake does. After nine years of running a support group for people with HIV, Robert manages to find some comfort by viewing the deaths of clients as an end to their suffering, by maintaining a spiritual perspective on death, and by remembering positive experiences with these clients. As does Jake, Robert goes "numb" when a client dies, but he has found that later something will trigger a cathartic release for him.

Therapists working with people with HIV disease over the last few years have witnessed more pain and death than they could possibly have anticipated. The loss of clients has been compounded for many by the loss of friends, lovers, partners, colleagues, and even their own therapists or supervisors. The epidemic has gone on so long that to rest battle-weary psyches, many have stepped back to teach or supervise other therapists or have gone on to totally different work. Theirs is a "complicated grief" as they labor under conditions where a natural grieving and healing process is influenced by powerful factors including stigmatization, multiple and successive losses, and the anticipation of one's own death. Especially at a time when more people are doing well and fewer clients may be dying, therapists who have weathered multiple losses may finally experience the grief they may have had to put aside over the years.

Theoretical Perspectives on Grief and Loss

Elisabeth Kübler-Ross, William Worden, and Therese Rando each have proposed theories relating to the grieving process.[1,2,3] Kübler-Ross's stage model, a standard in the field, helps to delineate the emotional aspects that make up the grieving process. Her crucial contribution was to emphasize the importance of moving through the process of emotional work that comprises her five stages: denial and isolation, anger, bargaining, depression, and acceptance. Grieving involves resolving the emotional challenges encountered at each stage, although not necessarily in a linear order.

Worden defines four tasks that are necessary for a healthy outcome to the grieving process: accepting the reality of the loss; identifying and expressing feelings, particularly the pain of the loss; making an adequate adjustment to living without the deceased; and withdrawing emotional attachment from the deceased and reinvesting oneself through new or enriched activities and attachments.

Rando focuses on three possible reactions to grief: avoidance, an attempt to block or buffer the pain; confrontation, an attempt to deal with the cascade of emotions—anger, guilt, despair, loneliness, and shame—brought on by the loss; and reestablishment, an attempt to become reinvested in living and more future-oriented.

These theorists hold in common the idea that grieving is a healing process and that any impediment to the completion of this process can harm the individual. Each also attempts to delineate the necessary elements of a healthy grieving process. For just this reason, many have criticized stage models as being too restrictive,[4,5,6] suggesting that the wide variety of individualistic grieving patterns cannot be encapsulated into definitive, stepped, time-limited models. For example, Steven Schwartzberg argues that grief work may never be complete, never be finally resolved, particularly in cases where it is difficult to make sense out of a loss.[7]

Robert Woodfield and Linda Viney propose a framework for bereavement that is based on a personal-construct psychology model.[8] This framework does not assume a series of stages but is based instead on the psychological construct that people use to make sense of events and to anticipate the future. When a traumatic event, such as death, occurs, these constructs must change in order to accommodate the loss. New constructs may be either healthy and adaptive, or maladaptive. When our constructs fail to help us make sense of certain events, we may feel increased anxiety, depression, and anger. Multiple loss and cumulative grief can interfere with the process of accommodating to new constructs before facing yet another occurrence of loss. All of these theories suggest that HIV-related grief, particularly because of multiple loss, is unique, complicated, and often unresolved.

Whichever theory one ascribes to, grief is always an emotional reaction to a significant loss. As humans, we grow, develop, and thrive through our attachments to others.[9] Grief is an emotional response to a broken attachment. We grieve most deeply for those attachments that are most fundamental to our own sense of well-being and self-esteem. The more meaningful the attachment is to, for example, a lover, a pet, health, or ability, the more painful its loss will feel. Resolution, if any, depends in part on how well we are able to reattach emotionally and psychologically to other people, pets, and aspects of our lives.

Characteristics of Multiple Loss

Multiple loss is not a new issue for therapists working with cancer patients or in the hospice field.[10–16] Sheila Namir and Scott Sherman review the literature, noting the "intense reactions and painful feelings elicited by working with people who are dying." They suggest that such reactions result from the "need for therapists to confront their own separations and losses, fears of illness, death and dying, and unconscious fantasies related to rescuing others from death."[17]

HIV-specific studies describe several characteristics that make HIV-related grief and multiple loss particularly difficult for providers on the front lines of the epidemic. One study describes the effects of multiple loss on grief resolution.[18] Respondents, while exhibiting symptoms of the various stages of grieving, "jumped from one stage to another without establishing a pattern toward meaningful acceptance of one loss before experiencing another." For those living in a world that has been strongly affected by AIDS, grief and loss can become common, almost daily experiences. Grieving then may no longer be a process through which one is working toward resolution as much as a way of life that offers little respite.

With the loss of multiple clients, the grieving process for the therapist can also become complicated and ongoing. Martha Gabriel has written about bereavement among therapists who must constantly explore the fears and hopes of seropositive clients.[19] When loss and grief are constant, therapists are likely to have difficulty processing all the feelings, thoughts, transferences, and countertransference reactions that arise. Not only do therapists have to process their own losses, but because of the interpersonal nature of psychotherapy, many therapists also have to help contain and process the grieving of their clients, who themselves have experienced multiple losses.

Other commentators have described the traumatic stress indicators that multiple loss often produces in people.[20,21] These responses include guilt, a questioning of spiritual beliefs, increased stress on holidays and anniversary dates, demoralization, and sleep disturbance. Therapists are not immune to these responses and are likely to carry them both into and out of the therapy office. This can greatly affect their ability to maintain a therapeutic stance as they attempt to assist clients in survival and life enhancement. Several studies have found a strong correlation between the experience of multiple loss and the existence of posttraumatic stress symptomatology in gay men grieving HIV-related deaths.[22,23,24] These studies have also positively correlated adverse psychological reactions (such as demoralization) and suicidal ideation with the number of losses to AIDS.

Finally, HIV disease progression and its uncertainty may evoke an anticipation of grief among therapists. With each cough, sneeze, or new physical ailment, clients and therapists may experience "shadow grief"—a vague sense of anxiety and dread that points to an impending loss, whether real or fantasized. Sometimes the loss of a client's abilities, such as sight, mobility, or sexual desire or functioning also engender grief in the therapist.

Grief for therapists may be further complicated if they are stigmatized as a result of their treating people with HIV disease. In such cases, they may lose the support of peers and other people on whom they count for emotional sustenance. In general, society as a whole continues to treat people with HIV disease as modern-day lepers, and their pain and suffering, as well as the grief experienced by their survivors, are often shrouded in feelings of fear, shame, guilt, and even hatred. These feelings often extend to those who care for people with HIV disease, and if they become known as "AIDS experts," therapists may find themselves losing referrals or even friends at a time when they most need outside support to grieve. (Such was the experience of Jan, the therapist who became identified as "the Death Lady.")

Drawing from both the literature and anecdotal reports, several factors emerge that complicate grief and loss for therapists:

- Many therapists tend by nature to be comfortable only in caretaking roles and have difficulty actively seeking support for themselves.

- Because they must maintain professional boundaries, therapists may not able to participate fully in the grieving process with the friends and family of deceased clients, even though the therapeutic relationship may have been emotionally intimate.
- Because of the ongoing grief issues, it is more difficult for therapists to maintain boundaries. They may be more prone to acting out or discharging in inappropriate ways, for example, becoming lax about confidentiality, socializing with clients, or drinking too much.
- If blocked in their grief, therapists may avoid their own pain and may be unable to be present for the pain of their clients.

HIV disease itself adds to these difficult circumstances in the following ways:

- Because of the stigma connected with HIV disease, it is harder for therapists in some areas to find support in the psychotherapy community or in the general community.
- It is common for therapists to experience a sense of failure when clients are dying, particularly when—as with people with HIV disease—the clients are likely to be young.
- The nature of HIV-related multiple loss makes it difficult or impossible for therapists to complete the process necessary to resolve grief.
- Traditional boundaries may feel inappropriately constraining in the face of life-threatening illness, and this may become a source of conflict as therapists struggle to be available to clients in whatever way is needed, for example, by making hospital or home visits. Bertram Schaffner suggests that when confronting HIV-related issues, "the psychotherapist must be able to act in several different roles and to switch skillfully between them."[25]
- Therapists often deal with HIV-related illness and deaths in their personal lives, watching their friends, partners, and sometimes themselves succumb.

The Impact of Loss on Therapy and the Therapist

Therapists by the nature of their work are caregivers. But their ability to support and nurture their clients is directly tied to their own emotional well-being. If therapists do not acknowledge and resolve their own feelings of loss and grief, the therapeutic relationship is likely to suffer. Therapists working with seropositive clients may have a multitude of countertransference feelings to manage, including helplessness, survivor guilt, and fear of mortality, all of which are further complicated by the death of a client. Denial and countertransference arising from the unresolved grief may sabotage therapy, leading, for example, to the therapist's avoidance or incomplete processing of a client's current or past experiences of loss or of a client's feelings regarding deterioration and death. In addition, therapists who are not aware of their grieving are likely to avoid topics that are tangentially attached to loss, such as a client's diminishing physical prowess and health or the writing of wills and powers of attorney.

Therapists in denial of their own grieving process also risk misperceiving client issues as a reflection of unconscious or fantasy material, and this may result in the therapist's paying inadequate attention to the reality of a client's condition. For example, a client's cancellation may truly be more about the client's physical ability than about his or her unconscious anxiety about therapy material; conversely, not everything in the client's life is about their competing physical problems.

Failure to acknowledge, feel, and process grief will also affect therapeutic choices made about which issues to explore in sessions and how deeply and intimately the material will be processed. Anger about AIDS may be unintentionally displaced onto HIV-infected clients. Michael Shernoff has written about his personal experiences as a therapist struggling to handle the wide range of emotions and conflicts brought on by providing psychotherapy to clients with HIV disease.[26] Among these responses are anger, exhaustion, resentment, fear of mortality and disfigurement, a feeling of lack of closure from abrupt termination of therapy, and feelings of hopelessness and helplessness.

Shernoff discusses a specific incident: while dealing with progression of his own HIV disease and the hospitalization of his best friend and business partner, he broke connection with a long-time client who was dramatically deteriorating and nearing death. When, during a hospital visit, the client tried to discuss suicidal feelings, Shernoff "was annoyed with him and glibly replied, 'I can understand why you would feel that way,' and left." He used supervision to confront his countertransference issues and was able to go back to the client and explore the client's suicidal feelings in a more appropriate way. Shernoff explains that he was angry and sad that his client had AIDS. "I often felt relieved when he did not want to discuss his deterioration or dying because this provided me with a much desired reprieve from facing my own feelings about his illness and ultimate death. As his illness progressed, my anger at him increased. . . . By saying that I could understand his feeling the way he did, I implicitly suggested that he kill himself, thereby ending our work together and relieving me of facing my conflicting feelings."[27]

Unresolved grief can not only cause disruption in the client-therapist relationship but also foster frustration and burnout. Therapists in this situation may avoid processing and containing their clients' fears and anxieties and instead work unconsciously to ease their own pain. They may function as if their clients were constantly in crisis and provide more concrete practical and directive therapy in order to avoid deepening explorations of death and the afterlife. This tendency of therapists to numb their pain may lead to a collusion between therapist and client that keeps the relationship on a superficial level. In addition, "empathy fatigue" is likely to impair the therapist's ability to relate with compassion.

Awareness of grief and loss can also provide opportunities in therapy. The capacity to love and maintain intimacy with clients is directly connected to the capacity to grieve and feel despair for them. Avoiding one response will reduce the experience of the other. Facing fear and the pain of loss can profoundly enhance the ability to stay connected, both to the therapist's own emotions as well as to the client's, and this connection can enhance the therapist's self-esteem and sense of competence. Confronting the experience of death also provides an opportunity for change as one searches for meaning in the loss and attempts to adapt to tragedy.

Inevitably, providing psychotherapy to the seriously ill and dying places the therapist directly in the position of experiencing the multiple loss of important attachments. And, as therapists, each of us often has a strong desire to help ourselves and others heal and grow. There are events in this world, however, that produce senseless tragedies—terrorist acts, wars, famine, AIDS. The "growth" a person experiences in relation to these events is real and powerful but often forced, and most of us would chose to have our loved ones back, foregoing this opportunity to grow by coming to terms with loss.

These tragedies do remind us that there is much in life and, especially, death that we cannot control. Attempting to control the uncontrollable leads most likely to burnout and frustration. Although it may be important to advocate, raise money, push for better treatment, and take other actions to confront the epidemic, to some extent providers have to find ways to feel helpless in the face of the reality that all the attachments we make in the course of life will eventually be broken. Everything that is turned on is at some point turned off. Perhaps struggling to accept the inevitability of this fact will enable us to experience more fully the attachments we have today.

Coping Strategies

It is vitally important to develop methods of coping with the ongoing experience of illness and death for both the emotional survival of the therapist and the client-therapist relationship. Most therapists are in this field because of a desire to help others, but at some point along the way they have, in fact, realized personal growth; it is likely that therapists drawn to HIV-related therapy even have a desire, perhaps at an unconscious level, for the growth that is required to provide appropriate care. Such growth arises out of the vigilant exploration of countertransference issues, an openness to the therapist's process in relationship to clients' struggles, and the direct relationship with clients. It also often occurs in the development and improvement of the therapist's own coping skills. "It is in what we do to be more available to our clients that we can find our own healing."[28]

Coping in Professional Practice

Coping approaches can be divided into two categories, reflecting the overlap between the professional and personal lives of therapists. Strategies that relate directly to professional practice include having professional help in place, finding personal meaning in the work, being aware of personal and professional limits, and acknowledging grief.

Have Professional Help in Place

It is important that no therapist dealing with multiple loss tries to handle this alone. All the strategies in this section encourage the use of ongoing professional supervision and personal therapy.

Find Personal Meaning in the Work

What makes this work worthwhile? Working with people dealing with HIV disease helps many therapists to be more focused in the present, leads them to a fuller appreciation of life, and provides them with opportunities to explore issues relating to death. Therapists who work with clients with life-threatening illness often value the experience because it enhances their own awareness of the immediacy and preciousness of life and its fullness. Multiple loss forces many therapists to create a framework by which they can explore spiritual and existential questions regarding pain, suffering, and death. This framework might enable them to find meaning in the very thing that threatens their significance. Ernest Becker wrote, "What man really fears is not so much extinction, but extinction with insignificance. Man wants to know that his life has somehow counted, if not for himself, then at least in a larger scheme of things, that it has left a trace, a trace that has meaning."[29]

To reduce internal stressors, Richard Riordan and Sandra Saltzer recommend assuming responsibility for choosing to work with the dying and reviewing honestly the reasons for the choice. "Do the reasons include unresolved personal issues? Are the expectations of accomplishment realistic? For example, the desire to restore an individual's physical integrity may be unrealistic, but the goal of controlling pain and facilitating a better quality of life until death occurs may be realistic. To accomplish this, a personal philosophy of involvement must be developed which fosters empathic care while maintaining individuality."[30]

Sheila Namir emphasizes the personal meaning in her reply to the question "Which is really harder—to die or to witness death?": "I can't answer that, having experienced only the latter. But I can say that to witness is to participate, and to be forever changed by it."[31]

Be Aware of Personal and Professional Limits

Because of the life-and-death issues involved in this work it is easy for therapists to overextend themselves by, for example, offering to conduct sessions in the hospital, waiving fees, and attending funerals. But setting limits—perhaps by restricting the number of HIV-infected clients or defining a minimum sliding-scale fee—can raise concerns on the part of therapists that they are being selfish or not caring enough. For others, the illusion that they can do it all may be a way of defending against grief and powerlessness. It is necessary for each therapist to assess whether he or she falls into one of these categories. Being clear about limits can help therapists be more present with clients, extend their ability to do the work over time, and model for clients skills in taking care of themselves.

Acknowledge Grief

The memories of clients who have died will remain valuable after the therapist fully experiences the grief arising from their deaths. For many, acknowledging grief begins by honoring the deceased client. For some it helps to attend the client's funeral; for others, a more personal ceremony provides meaning, closure, and an opportunity to grieve. One therapist ceremonially burns clippings of her clients' obituaries and records their names in a book. Another releases a helium balloon with the deceased person's name attached. Other strategies include making AIDS quilt squares, inscribing the names of clients and friends who have died in a special book, or making charitable donations in memory of the client.

Many therapists report that the grieving process is easier when they are able to say good-bye to the client in person. Being able to tell the client that he or she has been important to the therapist, and in what way, brings closure to the relationship and eases the therapist's moving on. "It is important for people who work with AIDS to understand that experiencing grief and loss is not a failure of the therapeutic relationship, nor is it crossing over a professional boundary; rather it is a reflection of having had a genuine and real relationship with the person who is entering the final stages of his or her life."[32]

Telling stories about clients—even writing them down—can be an important part of processing loss. This can be done in a support group or in individual therapy. One counseling center for HIV-infected people offered a day-long retreat for staff members to tell stories and share in a ceremonial good-bye to clients. The desire to repeat stories about a person or people who have died as a way to process loss and to hold on to memories is an important, natural part of the grieving process. The need to repeat the story of a traumatic loss is exemplified by Chekhov's story "The Cabman." An old man driving a horse-drawn cab tries to tell each fare that his son has died. Although each of the passengers reacts differently, they all indicate disinterest. The story ends at the end of his work day when he unhitches his horse and says, "You know, my son died today."[33]

Therapists facilitating group therapy may acknowledge grief when a member dies, and a group ceremony may enhance this experience. The therapist plays an important role in helping the group deal with the loss, and by openly grieving, the therapist provides important modeling for group members. Be aware, however, that this sharing must be done in a way that does not lead members to take care of the therapist. One therapist brought in a consultant to colead the group after his cofacilitator had died. This enabled the therapist and the group to grieve together without losing track of client needs.

Coping in Personal Life

Strategies that relate directly to personal life include frequently examining feelings and beliefs about death, having some life away from HIV disease and outside of therapy, avoiding isolation, being aware of personal needs, being vigilant about "checking in" with yourself, finding ways to express and discharge feelings on a regular basis, and nurturing the physical self.

Frequently Examine Feelings and Beliefs About Death

The willingness to acknowledge their own mortality enables therapists to be more emotionally available to deal with issues of death raised by clients, whether or not they are terminally ill. This willingness also increases the ability to face each death more openly and will help in the resolution of each client's passing.

Death-related counseling may be especially difficult for therapists who have elevated levels of personal death anxiety, because clients' struggles with loss or death may trigger the counselors' fears of their own mortality.[34] One study found that beginning counselors responded to situations involving death with greater anxiety than they did to other situations, leading the researchers to conclude that an "exploration of one's own personal readiness to face death may be a prerequisite to helping the client struggling with life-and-death issues."[35]

Have Some Life Away from HIV Disease and Outside of Therapy

For many therapists working with HIV disease, it is difficult to escape the epidemic when the entire community seems to be dealing with the disease. AIDS may permeate every part of life: reading, thinking, dreaming. It is a challenge to avoid filling leisure time with political activities, fundraisers, and other HIV-related events. Don't do it; it is crucial to find social, physical, and other activities that relieve the sense that HIV disease is all there is.

When dealing with pain and loss of such enormous proportions, some people are not able to accept that they have done enough. A poignant example of this was seen toward the end of the film *Schindler's List* when Oscar Schindler, allowing himself to soften to the meaning of what he had done to save so many people, becomes overwhelmed by the sense that he had not done enough. Doing more may be a way to avoid feelings of helplessness and powerlessness in the face of devastation. Setting limits may mean that one has to admit a lack of control and to learn to experience and tolerate this feeling.

Likewise, if being a therapist is the primary focus of your life, it is too easy to fall into the trap of allowing or expecting clients to meet your intimacy needs. Dealing with life-and-death issues can be seductive to therapists who are more comfortable with the one-sided intimacy of therapy, in particular those who "need to be needed" and who thrive on intensity. The therapeutic relationship can take on an idealized magical quality, and therapists may use it as a reason to be less involved in the more mundane realities of relationships that have a greater potential for equal give and take. Such therapists must establish lives outside of therapy that include nurturing and supportive relationships. Reaching out to others and maintaining friendships may, however, require a great effort.

Avoid Isolation

Therapists, like clients, may isolate themselves for a variety of reasons, including HIV-related stigma and the difficulty of acknowledging the need for support. They may succumb to "the fallacy of uniqueness,"[36] which refers to the belief that one is alone and unusual in experiencing distressing feelings and thoughts.[37] Therapists may also isolate themselves because they judge feelings of attachment and caring for their clients as unprofessional, and they feel uncomfortable openly sharing their grief for the loss of the client. "These feelings of attachment, care, and concern must be acknowledged and validated."[38]

It is vital for therapists to face the issues that encourage their isolation and to learn to reach out for support. A number of authors stress the importance of support groups for health care providers dealing with multiple loss. In addition to providing a forum for mutual support and sharing, such groups can open the way for members to acknowledge grief.[39–42] Ultimately, it is the therapist's responsibility to create a support system by joining such support groups and seeking individual therapy or professional supervision. Support and consultation from others doing similar work permit therapists to share personal experiences and facilitate their identifying countertransference reactions.[43]

Be Aware of Personal Needs

It is important for a therapist to clearly understand personal needs and to be sufficiently aware of them to be able to contain the impulses that unmet needs might provoke. In the context of the disequilibrium that results from the loss of one client after another, clarity about these needs—for example, the needs for emotional and social support and for expressing grief—increases in importance. Without this clarity, therapists are more likely to put clients in situations in which they are indirectly meeting the needs of their therapists, which may inhibit clients from fully "being themselves."

To protect against this loss of professional boundaries, ensure that you are either meeting these needs or that your awareness of them protects your clients. For example, as members of the therapy group for people with HIV disease began to die, one therapist turned to members of the group for support and developed friendships that blurred boundaries and roles. In the process, the therapist lost track of group dynamics, the needs of some group members, and the awareness that group interactions were becoming more superficial. The therapist might have prevented this situation had she acknowledged her own bereavement, recognized her need for support, and acknowledged that however close she felt to her clients, she had to maintain her support system outside these therapeutic relationships.

Be Vigilant About "Checking In" with Yourself

By "checking in," therapists can stay in touch with their own needs and limits and ensure that they are not operating out of avoidance. Checking in can involve only a few minutes each day spent noticing breathing, feelings, and personal interactions. It is important to recognize the traumatic proportions of this epidemic and to be aware of the emotional impact on therapists who are supporting and sharing feelings of clients as these clients deteriorate and die. Supervision can also be a way of checking in. It is the responsibility of the therapist to seek out professional feedback when sensing he or she is "off" in dealing with a client or when suspecting that he or she may be operating in response to countertransference.

Find Ways to Express and Discharge Feelings on a Regular Basis

It is particularly important for therapists dealing with grief to focus on releasing strong feelings that may be difficult to express. This can be accomplished in individual therapy or among close friends. Some prefer to discharge strong feelings—cry or scream—alone, but having support may give the therapist the chance to receive comfort and the caring of another in the face of the deep pain. Having others around can provide a container that enhances a sense of safety and facilitates the letting go of the usual controls on self-expression. One therapist reported a very satisfying experience of discharging: she went to a scary movie with friends after the funeral of a long-time client. She was able to scream almost nonstop for two hours—joined by the entire audience.

Nurture the Physical Self

Emotional stress takes a toll on the body. Pay attention to needs for exercise, recreation, leisure, good nutrition, rest, and sleep. The effects of the other coping strategies will be greatly limited if therapists overlook this strategy.

⌘

There are no easy answers to questions about how to cope with multiple loss, an experience of such magnitude and with such an impact on our emotional, physical, intellectual, and spiritual well-being. One hopes that therapists, having experienced and integrated the darker side of life, will emerge empowered and with an enhanced capacity for hope, joy, intimacy, celebration, humor, affirmation of life, and compassion.

Dictionaries define *compassion* as "a feeling for another's suffering or misery coupled with an urgent desire to aid or to spare." It is derived from the Latin words *pati* and *cum*, together meaning "to suffer with," the ability to be with another in his or her pain. One can only be with another as much as one can be with one's self. After the death of his wife, C. S. Lewis wrote, "Why love, if losing hurts so much? I have no answers anymore, only the life I've lived. Twice in that life I've been given the choice, as a boy, and as a man. The boy chose safety. The man chooses suffering. The pain, now, is part of the happiness, then. That's the deal."[44]

Notes

1. Kübler-Ross, E. *On Death and Dying.* Old Tappan, N.J.: Macmillan, 1969.
2. Worden, J. W. *Grief Counseling and Grief Therapy: A Handbook for the Mental Health Practitioner.* New York: Springer, 1982.
3. Rando, T. A. *Grief, Dying and Death.* Champaign, Ill.: Research Press, 1984.
4. Leviton, D. "Education for Death." *Health Education,* 1977, *1,* 41–56.
5. Shneidman, E. *Voices of Death.* New York: HarperCollins, 1980.
6. Schwartzberg, S. S. "AIDS-Related Bereavement Among Gay Men: The Inadequacy of Current Theories of Grief." *Psychotherapy,* 1992, *29*(3), 422–429.
7. Ibid.
8. Woodfield, R., and Viney, L. L. "A Personal Construct Approach to Bereavement." *Omega: Journal of Death and Dying,* 1984–1985, *15*(1), 1–13.
9. Bowlby, J. *Attachment and Loss.* London: Hogarth Press, 1980.
10. Rando, *Grief, Dying and Death.*
11. Burton, A. "Death as a Countertransference." *Psychoanalysis and the Psychoanalytic Review,* 1962, *49*(4), 3–20.
12. Eissler, K. *The Psychiatrist and the Dying Patient.* New York: International University Press, 1955.
13. Kirchberg, T. M., and Neimeyer, R. A. "Reactions of Beginning Counselors to Situations Involving Death and Dying." *Death Studies,* 1991, *15*(6), 603–610.

14. Renneker, R. E. "Countertransference Reactions to Cancer." *Psychosomatic Medicine,* 1957, *19*(5), 409–418.

15. Riordan, R. J., and Saltzer, S. K. "Burnout Prevention Among Health Care Providers Working with the Terminally Ill: A Literature Review." *Omega: Journal of Death and Dying,* 1992, *25*(1), 17–24.

16. Weisman, A. D. "Understanding the Cancer Patient: The Syndrome of Caregivers' Plight." *Psychiatry,* 1981, *44*(2), 161–168.

17. Namir, S., and Sherman, S. "Coping with Countertransference." In C. Kain (ed.), *No Longer Immune: A Counselor's Guide to AIDS.* Alexandria, Va.: American Association for Counseling and Development, 1989, p. 264. Reprinted with permission. No further reproduction authorized without written permission of the American Counseling Association.

18. Biller, R., and Rice, S. "Experiencing Multiple Loss of Persons with AIDS: Grief and Bereavement Issues." *Health and Social Work,* 1990, *15*(4), 283–290.

19. Gabriel, M. A. "Group Therapists' Countertransference Reactions to Multiple Deaths from AIDS." *Clinical Social Work Journal,* 1991, *19*(3), 279–292.

20. Martin, J. L. "Psychological Consequences of AIDS-Related Bereavement Among Gay Men." *Journal of Consulting and Clinical Psychology,* 1988, *56*(6), 856–862.

21. Martin, J. L., Dean, L., Garcia, M., and others. "The Impact of AIDS on a Gay Community: Changes in Sexual Behavior, Substance Use, and Mental Health." *American Journal of Community Psychology,* 1989, *17*(3), 269–293.

22. Ibid.

23. Martin, "Psychological Consequences."

24. Viney, L., Henry, R., Walker, B., and Crooks, L. "The Psychosocial Impact of Multiple Deaths from AIDS." *Omega: Journal of Death and Dying,* 1991–1992, *24*(2), 151–163.

25. Schaffner, B. "The Crucial and Difficult Role of the Psychotherapist in the Treatment of the HIV-Positive Patient." *Journal of the American Academy of Psychoanalysis,* 1994, *22*(3), 506.

26. Shernoff, M. "Eight Years of Working with People with HIV: The Impact upon a Therapist." In C. Silverstein (ed.), *Gays, Lesbians and Their Therapists.* New York: Norton, 1991.

27. Ibid, pp. 230, 231.

28. Davis, B. E. "Vicarious Traumatization: Prevention and Care for the Psychotherapist." In B. J. Miller (ed.), *Shock and Trauma: A Bioenergetic Approach.* Pacific Northwest Bioenergetic Conference, 1993, p. 61.

29. Becker, E. *The Denial of Death.* New York: Free Press, 1973.

30. Riordan and Saltzer, "Burnout Prevention," p. 19.
31. Namir and Sherman, "Coping with Countertransference," p. 279. Reprinted with permission. No further reproduction authorized without written permission of the American Counseling Association.
32. Ibid., p. 274.
33. Feldman, A. "Bereavement Care." In B. R. Cassileth and P. A. Cassileth (eds.), *Clinical Care of the Terminal Cancer Patient.* Philadelphia: Lea & Febiger, 1982, p. 129.
34. Neimeyer, R. A., and Neimeyer, G. J. "Death Anxiety and Counseling Skill in the Suicide Interventionist." *Suicide and Life-Threatening Behavior,* 1984, *14*(2), 126–131.
35. Kirchberg and Neimeyer, "Reactions of Beginning Counselors."
36. Pines, A. M., Aronson, E., and Kafry, D. *Burnout: From Tedium to Personal Growth.* New York: Free Press, 1980.
37. Feldman, "Bereavement Care."
38. Namir and Sherman, "Coping with Countertransference," p. 269. Reprinted with permission. No further reproduction authorized without written permission of the American Counseling Association.
39. Riordan and Saltzer, "Burnout Prevention."
40. Korda, L. "Compassion, Conviction, Commitment: Creed for Quality Hospice Care, Core of Hospice Burnout." *American Journal of Hospice Care,* 1987, *4*(5), 39–44.
41. Lopez, D., and Getzel, G. S. "Strategies for Volunteers Caring for Persons with AIDS." *Social Casework,* Jan. 1987, pp. 47–53.
42. Ogle, A. J. "Sustaining the Spirit." In C. Kain (ed.), *No Longer Immune: A Counselor's Guide to AIDS.* Alexandria, Va.: American Association for Counseling and Development, 1989.
43. Namir and Sherman, "Coping with Countertransference." Reprinted with permission. No further reproduction authorized without written permission of the American Counseling Association.
44. Fleischer, L. *Shadowlands* (based on a screenplay by W. Nicholson). New York: Penguin Books, 1993, p. 263.

Chapter Eighteen

Making Difficult Decisions

Eric Glassgold
James W. Dilley

The practice of psychotherapy is a complex and uncertain under-taking.[1,2,3] Both therapist and client approach therapy unsure of the outcome and often even unclear about the factors that have led the client to seek professional help. Sometimes a general sense that "something is wrong" is the motivator—a broad feeling of discontent or a wish to be "happier." At other times, the client comes for very specific reasons: he or she has had a history of mood problems or relationship difficulties, is struggling to cope with a loss, or has recently been diagnosed with a life-threatening illness.

Therapists working with people with HIV will be faced with clients from all along this spectrum. There will, of course, also be clients whose stated reason for seeking therapy fades into the background as the truly salient issues come to the fore—a situation well known to any experienced therapist and not uncommon in HIV-related psychotherapy. Although it may be the "stress of living with HIV" that draws a client into therapy, it often turns out that the client actually copes very well with his or her illness and that it is, rather, coping with life that is the problem.

For some people, an HIV diagnosis is without question a call to action: a spur to view their lives in a new way; a wake-up call that their drug or alcohol use has been "way out of line"; an opportunity to question their choice of work, or their primary relationship—or lack of one. Some will clearly feel the press of time and want to understand the long-standing problems that have pursued them throughout their lives; some will want to explore the possibility of change.

For the therapist, the process of working with HIV disease is fascinating and rewarding: helping clients to face the initial task of coping with a life-threatening and stigmatized condition and then to examine their lives in the harsh light that HIV casts can be as exhilarating as it is challenging. This process also poses difficult questions for therapists, conundrums that are specific to working with seropositive clients, which often involve balancing legal and ethical concerns with clinical ones. Consider the following dilemmas:

- Working with a seropositive client who is having unsafe sex without informing his partner of his infection
- Managing a client who has become increasingly forgetful and slowed from HIV-associated cognitive impairment yet refuses to stop driving
- Counseling a client who refuses to take his doctor's advice about treatment because he or she "doesn't believe" in medication
- Responding to a physically failing client who wishes to end his or her life

It is precisely these kinds of difficult situations that make working with HIV compelling and at the same time daunting, even frightening. Where does the therapist's responsibility to the client end and his or her responsibility to the community begin? How can a therapist proceed beyond immobilization when a complex set of legal, ethical, and clinical questions converge and compete with each other? A therapist may find it easy to attend empathically to the underlying emotions when a client says, "There is no way I'm going through what I've seen my friends go through—I'm not going to have people I don't know putting me in diapers." But he or she may feel wholly unprepared to respond when the client asks the therapist to assist in his wish to end his life.

Such clinical demands are an integral part of the landscape of providing psychotherapy to people with HIV, and the advent of improved treatment will not eliminate these challenges. In fact, it may well raise new ones. This chapter examines two such therapeutic dilemmas and reviews the elements of clinical decision making that therapists may apply when facing extreme circumstances.

The Duty to Warn: The Case of David

David, a twenty-nine-year-old seropositive White gay man, was referred for psychotherapy by his physician, who had prescribed antianxiety medication to help David deal with debilitating anxiety. His psychotherapist, John Kramer, Ph.D., although not gay himself, has treated many gay and lesbian clients, including people with HIV disease.

When David came for his initial appointment, he presented as sad, angry, and mildly agitated. An actor and performance artist, David complained bitterly about not being selected for a role he felt he should have gotten. He stated that although he knew his HIV status had nothing to do with his not getting the job, he couldn't help but feel that "somehow it was related." David was ambitious, felt he deserved "to make it," and believed that he needed to work as much as he could, because eventually he would be seen by the "right people" who would "jump-start his career."

History

David was an only child. His parents were both professionals who had given him "everything but their time" while he was growing up. They wanted him to follow in their footsteps, but he never really liked school, so he just "coasted through," obtaining part-time work as an actor before he graduated from high school. His father died suddenly when David was in his last year of high school, leaving him feeling "surprisingly unaffected" and financially secure. After graduation, David moved to San Francisco, where he has lived alone since that time. He "came out" as a gay man shortly after the move. David has had a number of relationships, though none that felt deeply intimate to him, and he said he always found it easy to "find someone in the bars to go home with" whenever he wanted sex. He said he had no problems with drug or alcohol use.

David learned he was seropositive eight years ago, and despite some initial emotional upheaval and early physical problems, he has done well. He had taken zidovudine (ZDV, AZT) and didanosine (ddI) for the past five years without any problem. Recently, David's viral load skyrocketed, and his physician suggested it was time to begin a new antiviral regimen that included a protease inhibitor. David understood that any treatments he started now might be the ones he would be on for the rest of his life and that he would have to take them religiously to avoid viral resistance. He knew that the new treatment regimens were complicated and that if he declined treatment, he was likely to become ill more quickly. All of this prompted his anxiety.

Combination Therapy

Kramer agreed to see David weekly for several sessions to help him think through his decision regarding starting combination treatment. Eventually, David announced that he was glad he "had finally done it," going on to say that he had finally started a combination of four medications: ddI, stavudine (d4T), saquinavir, and ritonavir. David was clearly relieved, even elated.

David went on to say that he had met someone the previous weekend, someone he thought was going to be "important in my life," an older actor, Chris, who seemed to know many important theater people in the area. The two men had met at a weekend-long seminar on the future of innovative theater. David added that he was attracted to Chris and that they had gone out for dinner the previous week. During the meal, Chris raised the issue of AIDS and told David he was HIV-negative. David had worried he would scare Chris away if he disclosed his serostatus, so he changed the subject and said nothing.

David explained to Kramer that one reason he decided to take the plunge with the new medications was to get his viral load down as low as possible so that he could have sex without fear of infecting Chris. His doctor had told him that many people who undertook combination therapy had an "undetectable viral load" within a couple weeks, and, because the chance of infecting someone else was so small anyway, David reasoned that an undetectable viral load would make it close to impossible. He also said, "Besides, I only need him to make a few introductions for me," implying that he would be with Chris for only a short time and that his chance of infecting him would be small.

A Therapist's Fury and Uncertainty

While listening to this story, Kramer found himself becoming furious with David for putting someone else at risk. He also felt angry because he thought David might be putting Kramer into a situation where the therapist might have a duty to "warn" Chris.

Kramer saw David's disregard for the safety of his partner as an outgrowth of David's long-standing narcissism: David had learned early on from his busy, self-absorbed parents that he must "learn to take care of myself" and that "people are bound to disappoint you." The result was that David consistently used people to further his own wishes or satisfy his own needs.

Kramer commented to David that David's proposed actions might put Chris at risk of infection. David replied that Chris was a gay man who "knew the ropes"; if Chris wanted unsafe sex with David, Chris was responsible for making that decision and for whatever might happen as a result. Furthermore, David said, Chris had not insisted that David clarify his HIV status, so maybe Chris did not really want to know. David concluded by saying, "Anyway, none of this really matters because by the time I see Chris again, my viral load will be 'zip' and Chris will be safe."

Kramer was unsure about what to do next. He was afraid that if he insisted that David had a responsibility to disclose his serostatus to Chris, David would experience Kramer as behaving like his parents, putting his values ahead of David's without understanding David's needs. Disappointed, David would almost certainly leave therapy. On the other hand, Kramer felt that if he did nothing and David infected Chris, the therapist would feel responsible and would never be able to forgive himself. Kramer felt trapped between his professional obligations to David and his wish to protect others from infection. He also had to contend with his own anger about David's willingness to use Chris to further his career and to risk Chris's life in the process.

Ethical Responsibilities Versus Professional Obligations

What options exist for Kramer and David at this point in the therapy? Where is the line between Kramer's wish to continue to work with David and his concern about David's putting another person at risk of HIV infection?

One legal question arises immediately: Is this a Tarasoff "duty to warn" situation? Could Kramer be held liable in the future for not having "warned" Chris that David was seropositive? The answer is "probably not."[4] ("Probably" is in quotation marks because the law is, by its nature, arguable and evolving.) Three points are central to this question. First, the discussion about unsafe sex at this point is hypothetical and uncertain. In order to warn, there must be an imminent and specific danger to an identifiable or reasonably identifiable individual (or individuals). The danger is not imminent or specific: David is talking about something that "might" happen. He is not stating that he is "going" to have unsafe sex with Chris, only that if Chris wants unsafe sex, David will not be the one to say no. To "warn" Chris in this situation, Kramer would violate David's legal right to confidentiality about his serostatus and the professional standard that protects the therapist-client relationship.

Second, in this case, at least at this point, Chris is not a clearly identifiable person. Therapists do not have a duty to warn when the party to be warned is nonspecific or is a general class of individuals (for example, "all gay men" with whom David might have unsafe sex).

Third, does Kramer have an ethical obligation to tell David about the possibility that David could be found criminally liable if Chris were to become infected from having sex with David? In many states, an individual with a sexually transmitted disease—including HIV disease and sometimes specifically HIV disease—has a duty to tell a sexual partner that he or she has a sexually transmitted disease before engaging in activities that might transmit the disease. If David was unaware of this situation, he could be getting himself into legal as well as ethical difficulties. People with HIV in several states have been found guilty of criminal acts when they have infected others without telling these partners about the risk of infection. Finally, from a liability perspective, Kramer might also have a legal obligation to inform David that he could potentially be held criminally liable if Chris were to become infected, and as already noted, he almost certainly has an ethical obligation to do so.

Although Kramer understands all of this, he still feels unsure about what to do. He appreciates that even though he is probably not at risk legally, he still feels bad about the situation and worries that he is, in a sense, becoming an accomplice to a crime. Kramer also believes David when he says that if he and Chris were to have unsafe sex, it would be consensual. In this scenario, Chris does have a responsibility to protect himself. As a sexually active gay man, Chris is surely aware of AIDS and the risks associated with unprotected sex.

The Therapeutic Process

As a skilled psychotherapist, Kramer also believes that the therapeutic process can help resolve this situation—despite its complexities. Kramer reasons that David's plan to take protease inhibitors as a way of reducing his viral load is evidence that David does not really want to infect Chris and that David's biggest concern is that Chris will abandon him if he is honest about his HIV status. Kramer decides to take this tack with David and explore this possibility.

He also considers, reluctantly, what he would do if he were not eventually able to engage David successfully around this issue. He decides that because of their differences in opinion about this issue, he would simply no longer be able to work with David and would have to refer him to another therapist for ongoing care. By doing so, Kramer believes he would fulfill his obligation to himself by confronting the issue directly and doing all he could to work with David to resolve it; he would fulfill his legal and ethical obligation to his client by referring David to another therapist, thereby ensuring that David would not be abandoned.

In therapeutic terms, Kramer hypothesizes that David's placing his own wishes above Chris's safety was a reenactment of the times that David's parents had placed their needs above David's. He also wonders if David might well be bringing this situation into therapy as a way to test his therapist. Would Kramer confront him and help him reconsider his behavior, or would the counselor, like David's parents, be "too busy" to hear this veiled request for help? Having gone through this thought process, Kramer feels clearer about engaging David in further discussions about David's potential behavior, focusing on David's concerns about his career, his using of Chris, his fears of being abandoned by Chris, and what appears to be some sense of responsibility and a real desire to protect Chris.

Finally, the only way to ensure that clients and therapists understand the "rules" of therapy is for therapists to outline them at the beginning of working together. When this is done, the therapist can be more confident about interpreting a client's behavior. For example, had Kramer explained to David the therapist's responsibility to inform identifiable third parties of a client's physical threat, David may not have told Kramer about his plans for having unsafe sex with Chris. Alternately, knowing that David understands that Kramer would have to act under these circumstances enables Kramer to better interpret David's raising the issue, for example, as a way of asking Kramer to intervene. Another example of this dynamic is in the context of suicidal intent: if clients know that therapists are required to hospitalize people against their will if they express active suicidal intent, clients may choose not to relate these feelings to the therapist. If the client should raise these feelings, the therapist may more clearly interpret this disclosure as a request for help.

Some might argue that the adverse result of this approach is that clients will put limits on the information they might share in therapy. Although this may be true, the degree to which clients express themselves is always up to them. If both therapist and client have clearly articulated the rules and the expected outcomes of these rules, both will be in a much better position to understand the meaning of the client's disclosures. The result is that clients may be more willing to share because they will better comprehend the breadth of confidentiality protections by recognizing their limits.

❧

Responding to Suicide: The Case of Steve

Steve was a thirty-six-year-old seropositive man of racially mixed descent—Native American and African American. He identified as bisexual and in recent years had been romantically involved only with gay men. He started therapy with Joan Callen, L.C.S.W., to talk about his HIV status and romantic relationships. Callen had practiced psychotherapy for nineteen years. She had two children, one adopted; her husband died of cancer about two years earlier, and she herself had been in therapy recently, initially to deal with sadness and depression related to her husband's death.

Steve was frustrated by the pattern of his romantic relationships: he usually broke off these involvements after nine to twelve months, often fearing that he could not take care of himself or get taken care of in the relationship. At such times, he would very pragmatically seek other sources of fulfillment—intellectual, cultural, sexual. He seemed so able to cope that even as the relationship dissolved, it was a source of some pride that he could take care of himself so well.

Steve talked frequently and in no uncertain terms about his "selfishness," a word he used to refer to this capacity to know when to say no to someone else's needs and when to focus on his own. Steve's mother relied on him—as the oldest of four children—to handle his younger siblings, disregarding her eldest son's own needs. As a result, Steve learned to escape from the house to meet those needs. As Callen and Steve worked together and explored his problems with romantic attachments, Callen began to suspect that Steve's calm, self-sufficient style might be guarding him from pain. Evidence of this submerged pain would surface from time to time, often in asides and in comments Steve would make about the success of his friends' relationships. When asked to explore these issues, Steve would most often divert the question. Eventually, Steve admitted that this way of coping, though comforting, sometimes left him feeling helpless and depressed.

Callen knew from the start that she liked Steve tremendously, but she was not initially aware how much she admired his coping skills, his self-assertion, and his insistence on maintaining an active sexual life while living with HIV. As time passed, Callen grew to understand that this admiration—even envy—contributed to an idealization of Steve's abilities, a positive countertransference that obscured from Callen Steve's fear that she would not be there if he needed her. When he learned that Callen had taken a leave after the death of her husband, Steve took this news to mean that he could not get the care he needed from her and that instead he must be careful about his therapist's feelings, a dynamic that recalled his family relationships.

Antiviral Treatment

Two years into therapy, Steve became symptomatic, and during the subsequent eight months, his illness progressed quickly. Steve had begun triple combination therapy: zidovudine (ZDV, AZT), didanosine (ddI), and indinavir (Crixivan), a protease inhibitor that caused chronic nausea and fatigue. As time went on, Steve became resistant to the effects of his regimen, his viral load shot through the roof, and he began to get sick: he lost weight, eventually developed pneumonia, and was hospitalized several times. For a few months, Steve regularly attended therapy, but this took a tremendous effort. He stopped his antivirals, feeling they had clearly outrun their efficacy. During his last visit to the hospital, Steve's primary care physician started him on an antidepressant, and he became more awake, active, and tolerant of frustration.

Callen and Steve agreed to bend the therapeutic frame, allowing for missed sessions and for hospital and home visits. Except during Steve's hospitalizations and Callen's vacations, they had met two times a week for three and a half years. When Steve left the hospital, he resumed regularly scheduled therapy again. But, strangely, when he did, Callen began to notice in herself a sense of fatigue that was particularly intense just prior to the beginning of Steve's session. On a few occasions, she even dozed—with great pleasure—for a few minutes at a time. She also found herself daydreaming, sometimes wishing she could delay Steve's session for just a few minutes more.

Callen came to recognize her feelings of fatigue before sessions with Steve as an important clue into Steve's unconscious life. She realized that Steve's recent sessions had been substantially different: he was less present and involved. She further realized that what was happening in the therapy was a repetition of an old pattern: as he had as a child, Steve absented himself from—that is, ended—romantic relationships rather than risk the pain of feeling a loss of affection. The forays into various intellectual, cultural, or sexual pursuits seemed to obscure his fears that yet another relationship would fail to attend to his needs. And Callen noted that Steve's withdrawal, though subtle, had resulted in her feelings of boredom and exhaustion in anticipation of his sessions.

Callen pointed out to Steve the parallels between his emotional distancing, her fatigue, and his problems in moving his romantic relationships toward a lasting intimacy. During these discussions, Steve had the opportunity to observe these parallels and experience Callen as being able to handle his deepest fears of abandonment without tuning out, falling asleep, or dismissing these fears. Despite her feelings of uncertainty and even pain, Callen believed that this disclosure about her feelings was appropriate and important and that it deepened the focus on her client.

Dependency and Escape

It was after the fourth or fifth session before which Callen felt so exhausted that Steve raised the issue of assisted dying—almost as an aside. He told her that a close friend had researched the issue and that his friend's physician had prescribed barbiturates for self-deliverance. Steve joked that the physician had been extremely clear that his friend must not use more than a certain dose, lest it prove lethal, and that if he were to overdose, the only real risk would be if something incidentally happened to suffocate him.

Steve continued to joke, first about his friend's plan to use Glad brand freezer bags to self-deliver, then about Steve's own black humor in joking about an issue as serious as dying. Noting his own seeming nonchalance, Steve described the oddity of the discussion he had had with his friend. In particular, Steve wondered that his tone was "so casual, as if he were talking about making a plan for a weekend getaway." Callen made a mental note that Steve was bringing up the idea of a pleasurable trip, an escape, something she saw as akin to her pre-session escape into sleep.

Steve had spoken frequently of being able to cope with adversity. But he had a harder time considering or assessing his feelings about depending on others for help. In the past, he had minimized his feelings both about being taken care of and about not having anyone to attend to his needs. When Steve casually joked about self-deliverance, Callen returned to the issue of dependency, asking him if envisioning a "getaway" relieved his discomfort about being dependent on other people. She also wondered if he felt that he could depend on her.

In later sessions, Steve and Callen talked about the possibility that Steve managed painful, conflicted feelings by taking short and pleasure-filled "escapes" instead of taking deeper journeys to explore what might be troubling him. Could he talk about death only as a brief vacation? Callen asked Steve if he felt he could demand more from her. Or was he careful not to demand too much? At this point, Steve mentioned his hesitation about talking about these issues, considering her husband's death. (Callen had taken a month off at the time her husband died.) Steve expressed his fear that Callen would not welcome him back for further treatment if he honestly expressed his need to talk about dying, let alone his wish to make plans for his own death.

Self-Deliverance and Letting Go

Callen continued to work regularly and consistently with Steve, who had rebounded physically, for the subsequent six months. Steve began to date another man, who was also seropositive, although he was clear that their relationship was "nothing serious." As she and Steve began to talk about coming to the end of their work together, Steve also began to complain of ongoing fatigue and shortness of breath as well as having worsening night sweats and nausea. He was diagnosed with KS of the lungs, and he continued to become more and more ill; he had trouble eating, sleeping, and breathing, and found it difficult to concentrate and stay awake during sessions at his home.

Callen felt an intense sadness and helplessness. She had always related to Steve by talking. Now he could hardly speak, and his silences appeared to be full of suffering. She felt unsure about how to come to terms with Steve's physical deterioration. Although Steve's home care staff deferentially dropped what they were doing when she visited, it seemed to Callen that she was the only person in the room who did not have a job to do.

Perhaps most frustrating to Callen was that Steve had done so much work to free up his life, and now he was losing it all. Callen began to learn how to sit with her frustrations and spend time just visiting the client she knew so well. Nonetheless, she found herself full of anger and sadness, and preoccupied with rushes of memory of her work with Steve.

About a month into Steve's decline, Callen received a note from Steve's boyfriend inviting her to a farewell gathering in Steve's honor. Although no mention was made of Steve's planning to end his life, she intuited that the invitation was an indirect way to announce his self-deliverance. She wanted to attend Steve's gathering, as she had always found that memorials enabled her to deal with and mark the death of a client—but she also felt conflicted: this was not an ordinary memorial.

Among her other feelings, Callen wondered if she would be held responsible if Steve's death were considered a suicide. But all the evidence suggested that Steve was neither depressed nor mentally incompetent. Steve had seen a psychiatrist periodically and had responded well to antidepressants, and neither Callen nor the psychiatrist currently saw him as depressed. Despite his physical deterioration, he appeared lucid and capable of making his own decisions. Steve's psychiatrist confirmed Callen's impressions.

Steve and Callen had never actually talked about the possibility of his choosing to end his own life; indeed, he had only mentioned it once, when talking about his friend. Steve had commented then that he would consider doing the same thing if and when he got really sick. Back then, more than two years ago, "getting really sick" had appeared very distant, almost hypothetical.

Callen decided to go to the ceremony but to ask no questions about Steve's plans for self-deliverance. She felt guilty about this decision. On one hand, her training had taught her that she should examine any internal conflict she had to see if it might tell her something about her client's experience. On the other hand, she had seen Steve in bed at home, barely able to talk. She believed her therapeutic relationship with Steve had come to an end. Attending the ceremony offered her the chance to acknowledge this.

The Right to Die

Many therapists speak of the conflicts they experience when working with end-stage clients who actively contemplate ending their lives. Concerns range from fears about potential legal repercussions should a clinically depressed client commit suicide, to conflicts with spiritual, religious, and ethical beliefs. They also complain about a "shroud of silence" that leads supervisors and colleagues to avoid discussing the issue, leaving therapists on the front lines without support or peer consultation to help guide their actions. In a survey of volunteer therapists at the UCSF AIDS Health Project, 72 percent of the sixty-four licensed mental health professionals who participated in the project's Volunteer Therapist Program stated that they confronted this issue in their work.[5]

The professional organizations that certify and license mental health professionals have actively participated in public debate over what has been variously called suicide, self-deliverance, and the right to die. In 1994, the National Association of Social Workers approved standards that allowed social workers to attend but not participate in assisted suicides and active voluntary euthanasia.[6] Other professional organizations, such as the National Association of Marriage and Family Counselors and the American Psychological Association, have not yet taken a position on the issue but have encouraged discussion within the framework of their organizations' conferences, publications, and journals. The codes of ethics of all professional associations emphasize that it is a professional's duty "to comply with the law" as well as "to confront ethical issues in research and clinical practice" and "to avoid doing harm where it is foreseeable and unavoidable."[7]

These standards are hardly black and white. For example, the American Psychiatric Association (APA) code of medical ethics notes that a psychiatrist "shall respect the law and also recognize a responsibility to seek changes in those [parts of the law] which are contrary to the best interest of the patient." The code goes on to admit that a clinician might act in ways that are at once ethical and illegal. Nonetheless, in a separate position paper on physician-assisted suicide, the APA Ethics Committee explicitly states that it is "unethical" for a physician to advance death for any reason, under any circumstance.[8] In 1991, Timothy Quill, a New York physician who knowingly prescribed sufficient medication for his terminally ill patient (whom he had treated for many years) to use to end her life, published a discussion in which he described the position of a physician who acts outside the letter of the law but in an ethical and competent fashion.[9] Quill's patient had repeatedly requested assistance in dying, and a psychological assessment by an outside consultant found no signs of clinical depression. A court heard a case against Quill and took no action against him, and he received no other form of punishment.[10]

Perceptions of Suicide

Concurrent with the rise of professional medical authority, political and social constraints of the nineteenth and early twentieth centuries led to the "medicalizing" of suicide in order to maintain state control over individuals and to ensure social order.[11,12] Psychiatrists had the authority to manage and control suicide by sequestering mentally ill patients in psychiatric hospitals. Until recently, the psychiatric literature has classified suicidal ideas or behavior almost exclusively as manifestations of mental illness.[13,14] However, past research in the psychiatric literature made use of unreliable methodologies to establish this connection. Biases in the research included the reconstruction of clients' motives from psychiatric autopsies: studies relied on the selective examination of clients who had long-standing histories of psychiatric illness or whose death certificates bore "suicide" as the cause of death. Such methods effectively excluded patients whose deaths seemed unremarkable—as is likely for those who were assisted in self-deliverance by compassionate physicians.

Recent research on psychiatric assessment suggests that in terminally ill populations with problems that mimic symptoms of depression, major depression is overdiagnosed and minor depression is underdiagnosed. The reason may be that diagnostic criteria are too roughly hewn to differentiate affective, cognitive, and vegetative symptoms of depression from nonpsychiatric symptoms of physical illness and grief.[15] Consequently, clinicians may dismiss a person's expressed wishes to end his or her life as being the result of a treatable depression.

Surveys of gay men with advanced HIV disease suggest that it is far from a small minority who might wish to actively end their lives. For example, in an Australian sample of 105 White, well-educated gay men, 94 percent said that an individual with a life-threatening illness should have the option of euthanasia.[16] In the Netherlands, voluntary, active euthanasia and physician-assisted suicide are legal and account for 2.1 percent of all deaths. Research suggests that under these circumstances, the decision to end life takes place when there is a very high likelihood of death occurring in the immediate future, usually within less than one month.[17]

The effort to attribute the desire for self-deliverance to depression is perhaps the result of anxieties about letting death run its course. One therapist, a former hospice worker, described the struggle with control that many of her patients experienced as they began hospice-level care. Hospice care involves more intensive pain control and attendance from nurses and thereby takes away much autonomy from patients. Dealing with a newfound dependency on hospice staff is often a major challenge and transition, although not necessarily a negative one. In the eyes of this therapist, hospice care offered the chance to let go gradually, as one was increasingly "held" by hospice workers through the process. For many, this gradual release of control was a "natural" stage in the process of dying, constituting, in developmental terms, almost the reverse of the child's movement toward separation and individuation.[18]

The Laws of Self-Deliverance

In spite of change in professional codes of ethics and a broadening view of what constitutes suicide, therapists should realize that any involvement with a client's death may result in criminal or professional disciplinary proceedings or in malpractice suits. According to current standards of care, a clinician has a duty to prevent suicide, and any breach of that duty constitutes malpractice. Even if the death occurs after a clinician's treatment has terminated, the family or friends of a client who self-delivers may later charge abandonment if they believe the death was avoidable.

What can therapists do to respect their clients wishes, maintain ethical standards of care, and prevent legal action? Most protective actions are consistent with good clinical care and require careful documentation of the treatment plan and progress. It is important to establish a client's competence to make informed decisions, his or her wishes to end life, and the absence of clinically significant depressive episodes. Other, more labor-intensive steps may be necessary, especially when a client's clinical presentation defies easy categorization—for example, when a fully competent, terminally ill patient also exhibits depressive symptoms.

New laws in New York and Oregon, and those in the Netherlands and parts of Australia, where assisted suicide is now or soon to become legal, offer clinicians some guidelines. For example, in all of these cases, a clinician who hears about or witnesses a client's request to die with assistance must document the following: first, that the client is terminally ill or has a "hopeless," progressive, and incurable condition causing unrelenting suffering; second, that he or she experiences intractable symptoms despite optimal supportive care; third, that the client has a documentable physical cause for his or her suffering; fourth, that his or her request is voluntary, informed, and repeated; and fifth, that the clinician involved has a long-term relationship with the client.[19,20]

Considering that most therapists do not prescribe medications of any kind, such guidelines—drafted with physician assistance in mind—might be too stringent. They do offer some useful models for the psychiatrist who wants to assist, however. In such cases, it would be wise to seek outside consultation with another psychiatrist or another mental health professional and to evaluate a client's competence to give informed consent. Documentation should include evidence of a client's seeking medical consultation regarding appropriate treatment of pain and other forms of non-lethal, palliative care, including hospice care; of the client's physician having considered all available treatment options; of the reasons for declining alternative treatments such as medication or hospitalization; and of repeated mental status exams that are free of significant depressive ideation.[21]

⁂

Adjusting to HIV disease is complex not only because it is, as is often said, a stigmatized, life-threatening, and confusing illness but also because it potentially raises or amplifies a host of dilemmas for clients. For both client and therapist, such dilemmas may be new and without precedence. And for therapists, many of these challenges bump up against fundamental principles of law, ethics, and philosophies of life. As with most of life's greatest riddles, there are no easy answers to these conundrums and sometimes no answers at all.

This situation is frustrating and sometimes frightening. Therapists may find some guidelines in the law and in professional codes of ethics, in their own moral and philosophical perspectives, and in their hearts. But despite these uncertainties, the epidemic has shown that therapy can be effective for many and even transcendent for some. It is this knowledge that must guide our actions and nurture our efforts to deal with issues of life and death.

Notes

1. Roth, S. *Psychotherapy: The Art of Wooing Nature.* Northvale, N.J.: Aronson, 1987.
2. Ogden, T. *The Primitive Edge of Experience.* Northvale, N.J.: Aronson, 1989.
3. Bruch, H. *Learning Psychotherapy: Rationale and Ground Rules.* Cambridge: Harvard University Press, 1971.
4. Wood, G. J., Marks, R., and Dilley, J. W. *AIDS Law for Mental Health Professionals.* San Francisco: UCSF AIDS Health Project, 1992.
5. Glassgold, E., and Dilley, J. W. "Survey of Attitudes Toward Rational Suicide: A Survey of Volunteer Therapists at the UCSF AIDS Health Project." Unpublished manuscript, 1994.
6. National Association of Social Workers. "Client Self-Determination in End-of-Life Decisions." In *Social Workers Speak.* (3rd ed.) Washington, D.C.: NASW Press, 1994.
7. American Psychological Association. *Ethical Principles of Psychologists and Code of Conduct.* Washington, D.C.: American Psychological Association, 1992.

8. Council on Ethics and Judicial Affairs, American Medical Association, "Physician-Assisted Suicide," *Ethics*, 1995, *11*(2).

9. Quill, T. E. "Death and Dignity: A Case of Individualized Decision-Making." *New England Journal of Medicine*, 1991, *324*(10), 691–694.

10. Lo, B. *Resolving Ethical Dilemmas: A Guide for Clinicians.* Baltimore: Williams & Wilkins, 1995.

11. Werth, J. L., Jr. *Rational Suicide: Implications for Mental Health Professionals.* Washington, D.C.: Taylor & Francis, 1996.

12. Foucault, M. "Right over Death and Power over Life." *The History of Sexuality.* Vol. 1. New York: Vintage Books, 1980.

13. Conwell, Y., and Caine, E. D. "Rational Suicide and the Right to Die: Reality and Myth." *New England Journal of Medicine*, 1991, *325*(15), 1100–1103.

14. Breitbart, W. "Suicide in Cancer Patients." *Oncology*, 1987, *1*(2), 49–55.

15. Chochinov, H. M., Wilson, K. G., Enns, M., and Lander, S. "Prevalence of Depression in the Terminally Ill: Effects of Diagnostic Criteria and Symptom Threshold Judgments." *American Journal of Psychiatry*, 1992, *51*(4), 537–540.

16. Tindall, B., Forde, S., Carr, A., and others. "Attitudes to Euthanasia and Assisted Suicide in a Group of Homosexual Men with Advanced HIV Disease." Letter. *Journal of Acquired Immune Deficiency Syndromes*, 1993, *6*(9), 1069–1070.

17. Bindels, P. J., Krol, A., Van Ameijden, E., and others. "Euthanasia and Physician-Assisted Suicide in Homosexual Men with AIDS." *Lancet*, 1996, *347*(9000), 499–504.

18. Personal communication with S. Holland, May 10, 1996.

19. Quill, T. E., Cassel, C. K., and Meier, D. E. "Care of the Hopelessly Ill: Proposed Clinical Criteria for Physician-Assisted Suicide." *New England Journal of Medicine*, 1992, *327*(19), 1380–1384.

20. Hemlock Society Boston. "A Model State Act to Authorize and Regulate Physician-Assisted Suicide." *Euthanasia World Directory* [http://www.efn.org/~ergo/mdlact.shtml].

21. Werth, *Rational Suicide.*

Epilogue
The Psychotherapist and HIV Disease
James W. Dilley

Over the course of the AIDS epidemic, psychotherapists have become recognized as important members of the multidisciplinary team created to care for people living with the disease. They have done their work with great enthusiasm, care, and compassion. Yet, similar to other aspects of the epidemic, the role of the psychotherapist has evolved over time, and, as we have come to expect, change is once again upon us. Recent advances in the medical treatment of HIV disease have been remarkably effective, and although the "cure" is still elusive, current treatment success has significantly changed the landscape of psychosocial care.

The Role of the Psychotherapist

In the early days of the epidemic, psychotherapists were confronted primarily with clients who were acutely ill, young, gay men who were frightened and confused by the specter of an unknown and virulent illness. These young men—often estranged from their families and living alone as they adjusted to life in the "Big City" after migrating from homophobic small towns—found themselves having to confront life-and-death situations with whatever emotional support they could muster. Many found solace in the consulting rooms of therapists as it became clear that HIV would, at least early on, be fought as much with psychosocial support and therapy as with medication.

Together, therapists and their clients sought to understand the implications of a "damaged immune system" and the development of exotic illnesses such as Kaposi's sarcoma lesions or *Pneumocystis carinii* pneumonia. Therapists, along with their clients, had to become versed in medical jargon and concepts that were well beyond the scope of their training. They also had to deal with the confusion related to HIV transmission—at times even fearing that their clients might in some mysterious way spread HIV or some other strange "opportunistic disease" to both the therapist and other clients. As did others in the epicenters of the epidemic, therapists had to manage their own fears in order to help their clients adjust.

Empathic Containment

Before 1985, when the HIV antibody test was licensed, the survival of people with AIDS was measured in months. The role of the therapist was to function largely as an "empathic container." He or she created a "holding environment" in which clients could share their pain and openly discuss their fears. There was usually little time for much else. Therapists offered a safe haven: a port in a storm populated by doctors, social workers, friends, and sometimes families, all well-meaning and important people, but all with an agenda that they imposed, consciously or unconsciously, on the person with HIV. There were papers to be filled out, decisions to be made, medications to take, and appointments to be kept. Through it all, there was a palpable sense of fear, anxiety, and uncertainty, and a desire to make sense of a catastrophic and unexpected event.

Exercising personal restraint and remaining client-centered, the therapist became a willing partner, providing an opportunity for the client to "think out loud," to sort out his or her feelings about a whirlwind of events. The therapist was there to "be" with the client and accept his or her anger, fear, and despair: a human acknowledgment that there are events in life that can only be experienced and understood but cannot be "fixed" or changed. The therapist didn't "give advice" or try to solve clients' problems, but rather sought to assure clients that they were not alone and to help clients find a way to understand what had befallen them. By the late 1980s, having witnessed the devastation and confusion of the epidemic, many therapists took on a more activist role in their clients' care.[1,2] This activism manifested itself, in some cases, as therapists taking on a role similar to that of case managers: advocating on behalf of their clients with physicians, social service systems, and substance abuse or other service providers.

Therapists also spent a good deal of time helping their clients cope with grief and mourning. Because HIV disease—particularly among gay men and injection drug users—is a disease of communities, it was not uncommon for both seropositive and seronegative community members to have lost many friends, family members, and partners to the disease. For seropositive individuals who cared for lovers and friends as they died, the inevitable and heartbreaking question was, Who will be there for me? For seronegative people, the question, no less grave, was, How can I go on with so many of the people who were important to me now dead? In the early days of HIV, therapists were also confronted with clients whose first knowledge of their infection was a serious disease, and managing the psychological trauma of an acute illness became a common task. Soon thereafter, as it became clear that HIV disease can cause progressive neurological damage, therapists had to be concerned about whether their clients would develop such problems and how these clients would manage if they did.

With the introduction of the HIV antibody test, therapists began to see a new class of individual in their offices: the person "living with HIV." These were people who appeared to be well but who carried with them a miniature time bomb set in some mysterious way to go off at some unknowable time. The therapist frequently played the role of supporter, always holding in the back of his or her mind the questions, How will you live today, given that tomorrow is so uncertain? What can we accomplish together now that will help you live more fully each day? How much time do we have, and what therapeutic goals are achievable within this period?

The reality of living with "the virus" yet feeling well, combined with an uncertain future, became and continues today to be a major psychological theme. Over the years, therapists have had to manage enthusiasm about potential "breakthroughs" in treatment—always heralded with insufficient data as people clamored for hope and information—followed by a predictable "crash" as evidence showed that the breakthrough was not all we had hoped it would be. Yet, in the late 1980s, zidovudine (ZDV, AZT) and other antiviral drugs plus advances in treating and preventing opportunistic infections were effective in extending life, and client and therapist alike found that as acute illness faded somewhat, other life issues came into focus. During this period, therapists worked to maintain realistic attitudes toward HIV infection, encouraging clients to seek and maintain medical treatment and to reinvest in life.

A New Era in AIDS Care

Today, advances in treatment have led to steadily declining death rates in the United States and other industrialized nations. In San Francisco, the number of people actually living with AIDS increased 50 percent between 1991 and 1996.[3] Although the experience of narrowly escaping death is by no means universal, it is a frequent event; and although it is unclear how long effective treatment might last, the data suggest that many people continue to do well two and three years after beginning combination treatment.

Despite these dramatic improvements, therapists face an old challenge: helping clients manage the psychological impact of being "pulled from the lion's jaws" all the while knowing that the lion is ready to pounce again. And for the therapist, statistical probabilities do not describe the situation of the client sitting across the room. Uncertainty remains.

The New Pharmacopoeia

At the 1996 International Conference on AIDS, held in Vancouver, researchers presented some of the first public data on the effectiveness of highly active antiretroviral treatment (HAART) or what has become known as combination therapy. Combination therapy usually includes three to five drugs, often two nucleoside analog reverse transcriptase inhibitors, plus either a protease inhibitor or a non-nucleoside analog reverse transcriptase inhibitor (NNRTI). Among the current nucleoside analogs are ZDV, didanosine (ddI), zalcitabine (ddC), stavudine (d4T), and lamivudine (3TC). Current protease inhibitors include ritonavir, indinavir, saquinavir, and nelfinavir. Current NNRTIs are nevirapine and delavirdine. There are more medications in the pipeline, and if you are reading this book a year after its publication, you are probably familiar with whole new families of antiviral drugs. The fruits of many years of labor have ripened, and researchers, clinicians, and people with HIV alike acknowledge that a new era in AIDS care is upon us.

After initial successes with combination treatment, the lay press and even researchers talked about the "eradication" of infection. If combination therapy could reduce viral load (a measure of the amount of virus present in the blood) to very low levels,[4] and if this extended life,[5] maybe it would be possible to eradicate HIV infection if treatment "hit hard and hit early." In those moments, it was easy to imagine the evolution of AIDS into a chronic, manageable illness.

Several recently published long-term studies, however, have now shown that despite the suppression of viral replication for up to ninety-six weeks, virus that was taken from patients with viral loads that were beneath detectable levels and allowed to grow in the laboratory are fully capable of replicating.[6,7,8] This is partly the result of viral particles resting in "reservoir sites" (for example, the brain and lymph nodes) that are relatively protected from the effects of antiviral drugs circulating in the blood, and partly the result of the apparent capacity of the virus to remain latent. It is important to note that the good news about these recent studies is that the HIV found in these reservoir sites had not developed resistance to the individual medications used in the combination therapy. This suggests that if treatment is initially successful, continued therapy should keep active HIV in check.

The bottom line is that the antiviral combinations currently available have been shown to be powerful and effective over time. But there is no evidence that they can eliminate HIV infection, so treatment must continue, presumably for life.

Treatment Adherence

To further complicate treatment, it has become clear that strict adherence to antiviral combinations is crucial to their success. The blood level of antiviral drugs that is needed to stop replication is fairly high, and if it is not maintained through regular dosing, the virus can multiply. In addition, if doses are skipped or missed for whatever reason, the virus not only will begin to multiply again but also can develop resistance to the drugs in the combination. Once resistance develops, the drugs in the combination become ineffective, and HIV infection can reestablish itself and lead to progressive destruction of the immune system.

To make matters worse, most HIV strains that become resistant to one type of protease inhibitor become "cross-resistant" to other protease inhibitors; resistance to one drug in this medication family often confers resistance to others in the family, thereby greatly reducing the number of other drug combinations that may work.[9,10,11] The effect of resistance is already apparent in the field: small studies have found that as many as 50 percent of patients see their viral loads rebound as early as six months after beginning treatment.[12]

One of the biggest reasons for the failure of antiviral drugs is the difficulty of sticking regularly to complex treatment regimens. Combination therapy is difficult: it usually requires multiple pills, and each drug has its own time schedule with its own requirements (for example, some are taken with meals, others on an empty stomach) and its own side effects, some of which may be so intolerable for a given individual as to make treatment with that drug impossible.

Making Decisions About Treatment

The risk of resistance has led many clinicians to believe that people with HIV have very few chances to decide what treatment plan to undertake. This approach is different from the approach mental health providers might take with psychiatric disorders—depression, for example. A client might decide to start an antidepressant with the intention of stopping if side effects are too uncomfortable or if the drug is felt to be ineffective. But presenting an antiviral drug to HIV gives the virus a chance to "figure out" how to become resistant to it, the result being that, for many, the decision to start treatment is actually a decision to continue treatment.

In the context of all this information, it is crucial for therapists to appreciate the difficulty and the momentous nature of HIV treatment decisions.[13,14] The media have made it seem that antiviral treatment is the obvious choice, but there is a daunting number of physiological and psychological factors that affect a person's decision making regarding HIV treatment.

⚮

In a sense, these changes in the landscape of HIV care mean that therapists will reembrace the role they had taken earlier in the epidemic: that of creating a "holding environment" and offering clients an opportunity to "work through" their feelings. In the early days, this process was focused on adjusting to an early death. Now, for people for whom antiviral treatment is working, it is focused on adjusting to living with difficult treatment regimens; for those for whom treatments are not working, it is focused on the possibility of more effective treatments in the future and on managing disappointment and disintegrating health.

As people with HIV disease live and maintain physical health for longer periods, they will spend more time worrying about living, as opposed to dying. Providing support and helping clients find meaning in catastrophe will continue to be part of the psychotherapist's task, but therapists will also be asked, more and more, to help clients sustain. That is, therapists will help clients sustain themselves by refocusing on life and life problems and sustain treatment by maintaining a schedule of doctor's appointments and taking a handful of pills several times a day.

For more than fifteen years, psychotherapists have played a central role in AIDS treatment, performing their work with commitment and sensitivity. As members of the multidisciplinary team that has grown out of the need to provide comprehensive treatment for people living with HIV, they have earned the respect and gratitude of clients and coworkers alike. In an epidemic that encompasses so much of life, the therapist's role will always be to help clients and clinicians make sense of their life experiences. The hope of the moment is that although the past may remain on some level inexplicable, the future holds the promise of clarity, survival, and rejuvenation. Psychotherapists will continue to play an important role in this future.

Notes

1. Winiarski, M. G. (ed.). *HIV Mental Health for the 21st Century.* New York: New York University Press, 1997.
2. Cadwell, S. A., Burnham, R. A., and Forstein, M. (eds.). *Therapists on the Front Line: Psychotherapy with Gay Men in the Age of AIDS.* Washington, D.C.: American Psychiatric Press, 1994.

3. Division of Seroepidemiology, San Francisco Department of Public Health. *1997 Consensus Report on HIV Prevalence and Incidence in San Francisco.* San Francisco: San Francisco Department of Public Health, 1997.

4. Coffin, J. M. "HIV Viral Dynamics." *AIDS,* 1996, *10*(Suppl. 3), S75–S84.

5. Mellors, J. W., Rinaldo, C.R.J., Gupta, P., and others. "Prognosis in HIV-1 Infection Predicted by the Quantity of Virus in Plasma." *Science,* 1996, *272*(5265), 1167–1170.

6. Wong, J. K., Hezareh, M., Gunthard, H. F., and others. "Recovery of Replication-Competent HIV Despite Prolonged Suppression of Plasma Viremia." *Science,* 1997, *278*(5341), 1291–1295.

7. Finzi, D., Hemankova, M., Pierson, T., and others. "Identification of a Reservoir for HIV-1 in Patients on Highly Active Antiretroviral Therapy." *Science,* 1997, *278*(5341), 1295–1300.

8. Chun, T. W., Stuyver, L., Mizell, S. B., and others. "Presence of an Inducible HIV-1 Latent Reservoir During Highly Active Antiretroviral Therapy." *Proceedings of the National Academy of Sciences of the United States of America,* 1997, *94*(24), 13193–13197.

9. Deeks, S. G., Smith, M., Holodniy, M., and others. "HIV-1 Protease Inhibitors: A Review for Clinicians." *Journal of the American Medical Association,* 1997, *277*(2), 145–153.

10. Roland, M. "Antiviral Adherence Dilemmas." *FOCUS: A Guide to AIDS Research and Counseling,* 1998, *13*(3), 1–4.

11. Deeks, S. G. "New Principles of HIV-Related Medical Care." *FOCUS: A Guide to AIDS Research and Counseling,* 1997, *12*(5), 5–7.

12. Fatkenheuer, G., Theisen, A., Rockstroh, J., and others. "Virologic Treatment Failure of Protease Inhibitor Therapy in an Unselected Cohort of HIV-Infected Patients." *AIDS,* 1997, *11*(14), F113–F116.

13. Deeks, "New Principles."

14. Fischhoff, B., and Downs, J. S. "Decision-Making Theory and HIV Disease." *FOCUS: A Guide to AIDS Research and Counseling,* 1997, *12*(5), 1–4.

Name Index

Subject Index

transmission of, 4–6; control and change in, 202–203; and hope for future, 198–200; and mood, 227–248; new era in care for, 392–395; past and future in, 203–204; psychological circumstance of, 140–142; psychosocial issues of, 173–174, 176–177; spectrum of experience with, 198, 199–200; stressors with, 174–175, 192; and survival issues, 204–208; and therapist's role, 389–396; and uncertainty, 200–204

Holocaust, 205–206

Home Access, tests from, 31, 44

Home/hospital visits, by therapists, 342–343

Home testing, and test counseling, 30–32

Hopelessness, and behavior change, 64

I

Identity, psychological development of, 76–77, 94

Indinavir, 380, 392

Individual psychotherapy approach, 184–187

Inferiority, brief psychotherapy for, 190–191

Information: lack of, and behavior change, 59–60, 65; in substance use outreach, 130–131

Injection drug users, behavior change among, 36–37, 40

Innocent victim concepts, 4

International Conference on AIDS of 1996, 335, 392

Interpersonal conflict, brief psychotherapy for, 189–190

Interpersonal psychotherapy: for adjustment, 142–143, 145, 147–151; for depression, 238

Interventions: for behavior change, 64–69; for bereavement, 259–

267; for borderline personality disorder, 277–283; for organic mental disorders, 305–308; for substance use, 127–130

Intimacy, psychological development of, 77–78

Isolation: and psychological development, 77–78; for therapists, 366–367

J

Johnson and Johnson, and home tests, 31

Judgments, unconscious, 212–213

Justice: immanent, 81; orientation toward, 86–87

K

Klonopin, 244

Knowledge utilization, in prevention, 95–96

L

Lamivudine (3TC), 294, 392

Lamotrigine, 240

Latinos. See Hispanic Americans

Laws: and suicide, 385–387; and values, 84–86

LEARN model, and culture, 114–115

Linkage, in case management, 123

Lithium carbonate, 240, 244

Lorazepam, 233, 244

Loss, multiple: and bereavement, 250, 253, 262–264; characteristics of, 357–359; conclusions on, 368–369; impact of, 359–362; theories on, 355–359; and therapeutic opportunities, 361–362; for therapists, 343–346, 353–371

Luvox, 237

M

Mania: characteristics of, 304–305; organic, 239–240

127–130; treatment goals for, 323–327

Suicidality: and anxiety and depression, 229, 232, 233, 239; and borderline clients, 280; and ethical decision making, 373, 378–383; and impact of grief, 360–361; and organic mental disorders, 295; and therapist role, 344–345

Suicide: and laws, 385–387; perceptions of, 384–385

Survival issues, 204–208

Symbol Digit Substitution Test, 293

T

Tarasoff duty to warn, 376

Tardive dyskinesia, 240

Teams: for borderline personality disorder, 285–287; for organic mental disorders, 308

Tegretol, 240

Temazepam, 233, 244

Test counseling: aspects of, 25–49; and behavior change, 34–40; functions of, 25–26; and home testing, 30–32; literature review on, 40–41; paradigm for, 26–32; process of, 26; programmatic weaknesses of, 41–42; recommendations on, 42–44; and viral load testing, 32

Testing: demographics of, 28, 30; motivation for, 33–34, 41

Therapeutic frame, redefining, 341–343, 380

Therapeutic goals, and time issues, 347–348

Therapeutic relationship: and borderline personality disorder, 280–283, 284; clarity in, 338–339; and duty to warn, 377–378; literature review on, 177–179; stereotyping confronted in, 216–223

Therapists: and addiction treatment, 316, 317–319; advocacy by, 342, 391; AIDS warrior syndrome for,

348–349; aspects of practice for, 333–388; background on, 335–337; boundaries for, 336–337, 347; challenges for, 335–337; "checking in" by, 368; conclusion on, 350–351, 395; coping strategies for, 362–368; empathic containment by, 390–392; ethical decision making by, 372–388; grief for, 345, 353–371; isolation for, 366–367; limits for, 363–364; literature review on, 337–341; loss for, 343–346, 353–371; needs of, 367–368; nurturing, 368; objectivity of, 338–339; personal life strategies for, 365–368; powerlessness of, 337–338; process groups for, 340, 364–365, 368; rewards for, 337, 349–351; and right to die, 383–387; roles of, 344–345, 389–392; service environment for, 340–341; stance of, 141–142; therapeutic frame for, 341–343, 380; time issues for, 346–348. *See also* Countertransference; Transference

Thinking, concrete and abstract forms of, 78–83, 91

Thiothixene, 305

Time-limited psychotherapy: for adjustment, 144–145, 148–149, 164–170; approach of, 188–191; client-centered, 12; for grief, 264. *See also* Brief psychotherapy

Touch, need for, 89–90

Trail Making Test A and B, 293

Transference: and borderline clients, 280; in client-centered counseling, 21–22; in psychotherapy, 178, 182; in self psychology, 155, 156, 157; in time-limited psychotherapy, 168

Transformation: HIV as agent of, 139–172; and psychotherapy, 137–224

Trazodone, 233, 237, 238